THE GROWTH OF
BOER OPPOSITION TO KRUGER
1890–1895

THE GROWTH OF
BOER OPPOSITION
TO KRUGER
1890–1895

C. T. Gordon

CAPE TOWN
OXFORD UNIVERSITY PRESS
London   New York   Toronto
1970

Oxford University Press, Ely House, London W. 1

GLASGOW NEW YORK TORONTO MELBOURNE WELLINGTON
CAPE TOWN SALISBURY IBADAN NAIROBI DAR ES SALAAM LUSAKA ADDIS ABABA
BOMBAY CALCUTTA MADRAS KARACHI LAHORE DACCA
KUALA LUMPUR SINGAPORE HONG KONG TOKYO

Oxford University Press, Thibault House Cape, Town

🔹 PRINTED IN SOUTH AFRICA BY
THE RUSTICA PRESS, PTY., LTD., WYNBERG, CAPE

Contents

Acknowledgements

THE author wishes to thank particularly the staffs of the State Library and the Government Archives in Pretoria for their considerable assistance in his research and for permission to make use of material in their custody.

Grateful acknowledgements are made also to the following for permission to publish copyright material in this book:

Chapman & Hall Ltd., London: *The Kaleidoscopic Transvaal* by Carl Jeppe.

The Clarendon Press, Oxford: *A History of South Africa, Social and Economic* by C. W. de Kiewiet.

James Nisbet & Co., London: *Vengeance as a Policy in Afrikanderland; a plea for a new departure* by Francis Dormer.

Random House Inc., New York: *A Short History of the United States* by A. Nevins and H. S. Commager (Modern Library).

J. L. van Schaik Ltd., Pretoria: *Paul Kruger, die Volksman* by J. P. la Grange Lombaard.

A. P. Watt & Son, London, and the Estate of J. P. Fitzpatrick: *The Transvaal from within* by J. P. Fitzpatrick, published by William Heinemann Ltd.

Preface

THE main aim of this investigation has been to attempt to trace the emergence of an active opposition among the burghers of the South African Republic towards the policies pursued by the Kruger government, in the six years immediately preceding the Jameson Raid, and to show what the main grounds for the growth of opposition to the régime were.

In the course of this opposition there emerged a self-styled Progressive party, under the nominal leadership of Kruger's chief rival, Commandant-General P. J. Joubert. In the presidential elections of 1893 Joubert came within an ace of defeating Kruger. Indeed, in the eyes of his followers, he did virtually do so; they regarded the election as illegal and demanded, in vain, a new election. In this study an attempt is made to assess the question of the legality or illegality of the 1893 presidential election, to establish the nature of Joubert's leadership of the Progressive party, and to estimate the degree of Joubert's 'progressiveness'.

But the main subject of this investigation has been to trace the emergence (under the pressure of sweeping changes in the nature and composition of their State) among a highly conservative and self-willed people, of a group of 'Progressive' politicians; to examine, in some detail, the issues around which that Progressive group coalesced; to show the steadily increasing importance of the Progressives in the political life of the Transvaal; and to estimate, to some extent, what might have happened if the Transvaal had been allowed to go its own way, without Imperial intervention.

I have tried to give a reasonably detailed picture of the issues and personalities involved, and have quoted fairly extensively from reports of public speeches and debates, as well as from newspaper articles and letters, in an attempt to recreate something of the political life of this period and give the reader a little of the 'feel' of the times.

In the writing of this book, which deals so largely with the movement of popular opinion, and on the subject of which so little other detailed primary material exists (besides passing references of a general character in occasional books of memoirs) I have of necessity used as the major sources of my information the fertile mass of material provided by the Dutch-language newspapers of the Republic, the *Volksstem* and *Land en Volk* (largely pro-Kruger and bitterly anti-Kruger respectively), as well as the English editions of the *Press* and *Weekly Press* (published also in Dutch), which were in close touch with governmental policy, and generally—though by no means invariably—supported it loyally; and, secondly, the official *Notulen* of the proceedings of the First and Second Volksraads.

Intensely politically conscious, and alive to every rumour of policy, personalities or politics, the opposed newspapers provide an invaluable day-to-day commentary on the political life of the Transvaal in this period, and I have been pleasantly surprised at the vivid and well-informed picture of the life of the past which emerges from the reading of their voluminous pages. The more responsible of them, particularly the *Volksstem*, took very seriously indeed their duty of keeping the reading public thoroughly well informed of what was going on in the country. Volksraad debates, departmental reports, important public speeches, financial information, important court cases, political meetings, teachers' congresses, and a host of other matters major and minor, were given detailed, often verbatim, coverage of the type on which the more staid nineteenth-century newspapers prided themselves.[1] V. F. Engelenburg, who succeeded Jan F. Celliers as editor of the *Volksstem* in 1889 and retained this position throughout the period under discussion, insisted throughout on his right to complete independence,[2] and his undoubtedly pro-government newspaper often vigorously attacked the government when it felt it to be failing in its duties. The *Press*, referred to by the *Volksstem* (1 March 1892) as 'the generally recognized organ of the government', asserted equally boldly its duty to 'support the Government where we think it is right, and criticize it as strongly when it is necessary in the interests of the State' (22 February 1893); and, though generally supporting Kruger's government, it gave a

---

[1] This is more particularly true of the *Volksstem*, *Press* and *Weekly Press*; less so of *Land en Volk*.

[2] *Volksstem*, 8 Aug. 1893 (leading article celebrating the *Volksstem*'s 20th birthday).

good deal of coverage to Progressive ideas and actions, often strongly supported Progressive attacks on official corruption, educational policy, railway policy, and the policy of concessions and monopolies, and frequently pleaded for a more liberal policy towards uitlanders. *Land en Volk*, under its editor Eugène Marais, was violently anti-Kruger and pro-Joubert, and regarded the Progressive party as the only true 'Afrikaner' party in the Republic, and itself as the Republic's only genuinely 'patriotic' newspaper. Its criticism of the government was unceasing and often unmeasured.

Between these three very different newspapers (which, incidentally, were very quick to attack one another on any suspected error of fact or comment) it is possible to build up a reasonably balanced view of the political state of affairs in the South African Republic, and by using the *Notulen*, the Joubert Papers, the Leyds Papers, and other unofficial primary and secondary sources to check them, to come (I hope) reasonably close to the actual truth. They are, in any case, the only available source of information on political developments at this period. Contemporary politicians used the newspapers as the source of much of their information. One of the most frequent phrases in General Joubert's letters to his family and friends is—'the newspapers tell all the news', and the worst he ever had to say of them was that 'they [the papers] tell you all the news, sometimes a little bit mixed up or inaccurate but still the news' (soms wel is waar een wynig verwart of verdraait maar tog al nieuws).[3] The debates of the First Volksraad[4] show that most politicians agreed that the newspapers gave a fairly accurate report of their proceedings, and that the official *Notulen* were too short. And if by any chance the newspapers erred (for acoustics in the Volksraad Chamber were by no means perfect)[5] Volksraad members lost little time in writing to demand a correction of faulty reporting.

It will be seen from the footnotes to this study that I have generally cited the newspaper reports of debates first and followed them by reference to the relevant articles of the official *Notulen*. There are two main reasons for this. One is that the newspapers are the only source which, throughout the period under review, regularly indicate which way members voted in the Volksraads; and the other is that

[3] Joubert Papers, Uitgaande Stukke, II A/1–A/3, 1997 (Archives, vol. 17), letter of 18 Apr. 1893 to his son, J. S. Joubert.
[4] *Notulen*, Eerste Volksraad, 1894, art. 83.
[5] *Volksstem*, 21 May 1892.

there is good reason to believe that the newspaper accounts are generally closer to the actual words of the speaker than the highly condensed versions in official Dutch to which the Volksraad *Notulen* reduced their speeches.

To take each of these two points separately. Although it was frequently the custom during this period for members to request that their names be noted in the *Notulen* as voting for or against a particular measure, names do not otherwise appear to have been regularly recorded. Indeed, there were strong objections on the part of the majority of Volksraad members to having their votes personally set down in the *Notulen*. A Progressive motion to have 'yes' and 'no' votes officially recorded was defeated, on 24 June 1893, by 14 votes to 9.[6] The *Press* (5 September 1894) declared that 'for obvious reasons both Raads object strongly to entries on the minutes of which way members voted'; and the *Volksstem* (9 March 1895) condemned the Progressive 'desire to change the procedure of the Volksraads . . . by including votes for and against in the "Notulen" '. The newspapers are thus often the only source of information about the side on which a particular member voted. Quite often, too, they are the only source from which one can determine on which side a member spoke. The *Notulen* frequently contents itself with reports such as 'a short discussion then took place' or 'after a number of further remarks the discussion was closed', whereas the newspapers usually tend to go into very much more detail.

Secondly, although the *Notulen* possessed the virtue of being read out daily in the two Volksraads to enable members to check their accuracy (though Schalk Burger complained that members did not, in fact, listen, and had constantly to be called to order by the Chairman)[7] they were a very much abbreviated record of proceedings. It took between 30 and 45 minutes[8] to read the record of some five hours of Volksraad discussions; and even Carl Jeppe, one of the most zealous of the Progressives, was forced to admit that 'though he would gladly see every word recorded, this was, he knew, impossible; one could not demand so much'. In the circumstances there is some reason to believe that the newspaper version of the debate may reflect the members' actual words more accurately. A

[6] *Volksstem*, 27 June 1893.

[7] *Notulen*, Eerste Volksraad, 1894, art. 83.

[8] Van Hoek, K. *Kruger Days* (Volksraad sessions generally lasted from 9 to 12 and 2 to 4).

number of comparisons may illustrate this point.

The *Volksstem*'s version (6 September 1893) of President Kruger's remarks in favour of granting locations to small groups of loyal natives describes the President as calling for

'the allocation of sufficient locations to natives, so that the tribes should not be oppressed. . . . Was it fair or Christian to drive them from the land' (was het billijk of Christelijk om hen te verdrijven van het veld).

The official version in the *Notulen*[9] gives his words as:

'H.E. the State President explained that, even though a native tribe was small, we must give it a location if it was loyal. We could not, after all, alienate such a loyal native tribe from us.'

The first version, somehow, sounds closer to Kruger's usual style of oratory than the second.

Similarly the *Volksstem* version (24 June 1893) of Taljaard's remark in the Second Volksraad, 'Mr. Celliers claimed to speak for all South Africa—but what have I to do with South Africa?' (maar wat heb ik met Zuid Afrika te doen?), sounds more like Taljaard than the official version, which reads:

'People spoke here of the interests of South Africa. He had nothing to do with that. He stood for this Republic.'[10]

So, too, does *Land en Volk*'s report of C. B. Otto's[11] speech in 1895 on the 1895 uitlander petition for extension of the franchise, 'Who were these thirty-five thousand people? People who had come to enrich themselves. He feared no threats from these people. If they wanted to fight, let them come—and the sooner the better! (Cries of "Order"!)', in comparison with the version given in the *Notulen*,[12] 'and now they try to frighten us with thirty-five thousand signatures, but that would not work; it would inspire us to a greater manliness, and if it could not be otherwise, let us fight it out. Once before we had, with God's help, gained the victory.'

Similarly J. P. L. Lombaard's[13] remark, on a petition for equal

[9] *Notulen*, Eerste Volksraad, 1893, art. 1320.
[10] *Notulen*, Tweede Volksraad, 1893, arts. 399–400.
[11] See p. 157.
[12] *Notulen*, Eerste Volksraad, 1895, art. 919.
[13] See below, p. 11.

rights for Catholics and Jews, as reported in the *Volksstem* of 4 August 1891 that 'their forefathers had suffered much under the Roman Catholics. It was time the Raad took measures to ensure that the Roman Catholics and Jews did not bother it again', has a certain tang of reality about it that the more official version,[14] 'The attention of the memorialists should be drawn to the fact that freedom of belief existed. He was opposed to granting equal rights to these sects, because they had a totally different faith from that of Protestants . . .', does not possess.

It will be noted, however, that though these very typical parallel passages from the newspapers and the *Notulen* differ in flavour, they do not differ materially on points of fact.

All quotations or pieces of information drawn from the newspapers are backed by references to the corresponding articles of the *Notulen*, or where the *Notulen* differ in any major point (which is rarely the case) or omit a point made by the newspapers (which happens more frequently) this is stated in the footnotes. Conversely, on the rare occasions when the *Notulen* appear to be fuller on a particular point than the newspapers, the footnotes give the reference to the relevant articles of the *Notulen* first, and quote the newspaper reports of the debate afterwards.

References in the footnotes to published sources are given in full the first time they are quoted, and more briefly thereafter; but the full titles will be found in the bibliography at the end of this book.

Where a remark in the original Dutch possesses a flavour that is not wholly translatable into English, or contains an element of untranslatable ambiguity, it has been quoted in Dutch, accompanied by a reasonably close translation into English.

Some brief remarks on the background and prejudices of the *Volksstem*, *Land en Volk* and the *Press* would not be out of place.

The *Volksstem* was founded in August 1873 by Jan F. Celliers, who remained its editor until 1888. It was then, besides the *Staatscourant*, the only newspaper in Pretoria. In that year Celliers sold his printing business, including the *Volksstem*, to the government.[15] The government sold the *Volksstem* to a Hollander named Jonker, but he died shortly afterwards, upon which it was taken over by another Hollander, Hogerzeil,[16] and thereafter turned into

---

[14] *Notulen*, Eerste Volksraad, 1891, art. 1204.

[15] *Volksstem*, 8 Aug. 1893.

[16] Van Winter, P. J. *Onder Kruger's Hollanders*, vol. i, p. 238 ff.

a public company. From 1889 its editor was a Hollander, F. V. Engelenburg. That the government subsidized certain newspapers in return for their political support is beyond doubt;[17] but the *Volksstem*, though agreeing that it received preference in government advertisements over all other Dutch-language newspapers, insisted (5 October 1895) that this did not in any way affect its policy. Certainly, as this study repeatedly indicates, it did not hesitate to criticize—sometimes very strongly indeed—any aspect of official policy of which it disapproved.

By and large, however, the *Volksstem* can be regarded as a strong supporter of Kruger and his government, and of the conservative attitude which that government enshrined. Its attitude towards the uitlander population was not a liberal one.[18] It dourly defended Kruger's preference for Hollander officials, and was the unremitting advocate of the Netherlands Railway Company's interests against the attacks of the Progressive party and other critics. It defended (though not without reservations) Kruger's policy on the vexed question of the dynamite monopoly; and it made such excuses as could be made for his increasingly unpopular concessions policy. On the education and language issue it was strongly conservative and bitterly opposed any significant concession to the desires of the uitlander population. Both before and after the 1893 election it regarded Kruger 'with all his faults' as the only possible president of the Republic.

But, with all these biases duly taken into account, the *Volksstem* is an invaluable mine of information on the political life of the South African Republic. Its coverage of all important matters was extensive and responsible. It often gave four columns of fine print to the report of a Volksraad debate to which *Land en Volk*, for example, was only able to afford a quarter of a column. It generally separated fact from comment, and though its leading articles reveal the *Volksstem*'s prejudices clearly enough, it gave full and fair presentation of the Progressive as well as the Conservative point of view, whether in the shape of manifestoes, important public speeches, Volksraad debates or 'Open Letters'. It appeared twice weekly between the beginning of 1890 and May 1891, three times weekly

[17] See pp. 87–9.
[18] See *Volksstem* leaders of 5 Dec. 1893 and 17 Aug. 1895 in particular. (The latter invited uitlanders to 'pack their bags and go home if they cannot live without the franchise'.)

between May 1891 and June 1894, and twice weekly again between June 1894 and the end of 1895. Without the *Volksstem* our knowledge of the political life of this period would be very much the poorer.

Land en Volk (a weekly newspaper) first appeared in October 1887.[19] From July 1891 it was taken over by one Roos and Eugène Marais, who continued its previous policy of attacking the Kruger government, and announced, on 7 July 1891, that the paper's policy would be to support the 'Afrikaner cause', and without indulging in personalities 'to strip the veil from all corruption and injustice and bring them to the judgement of the people'. Fitzpatrick refers to it as 'the leading Dutch paper',[20] but the truth of this is doubtful. It claimed to be completely independent and to be in the sole ownership of Marais and Roos.[21] Marais agreed that he and Roos also worked privately as reporters for the pro-Kruger *Press* and the Johannesburg *Star* respectively, but denied (and quite justifiably to judge from the columns of *Land en Volk*)[22] that this in any way affected the politics of their newspaper. By September 1893 Eugène Marais appears to have been the sole editor and owner of the newspaper.[23] Van Winter (vol. I, p. 238) refers to *Land en Volk* as 'the organ of Piet Joubert, which sets itself against everything that the policies of Kruger achieve'. It was cordially detested by the *Volksstem*, with which it conducted a running vendetta, and by Kruger, who declared that the newspaper's 'only aim was to sow disunity among the Transvaalers'.[24] Certainly there were few facets of the Kruger régime that the newspaper did not attack. Its 'spirited editor' (the term is Fitzpatrick's)—while fighting off the attacks of 'that newly arrived Hollander, Engelenburg [editor of the *Volksstem*] . . . the hireling of the Hollander clique'[25] and 'the lying Jew, Weinthal[26] [editor of the *Press*] . . . a miserable hireling of the Government'[27]—still had ample energy over for attacks on Kruger, whom the paper condemned, *inter alia*, for such alleged faults as his autocracy and evil temper,[28] his toleration of corruption,[29] his

---

[19] *Land en Volk*, 11 Oct. 1894.
[20] Fitzpatrick, *The Transvaal from within*, p. 72.
[21] *Land en Volk*, 12 Apr. 1892.
[22] See below pp. xvi–xvii.
[23] Declaration in *Land en Volk* of 21 Sept. 1893.
[24] *Land en Volk*, 14 Apr. 1891.
[25] *Land en Volk*, 12 Apr. 1892.
[26] *Land en Volk*, 6 July 1893.   [27] *Land en Volk*, 12 Jan. 1893.
[28] *Land en Volk*, 12 Apr. 1891.   [29] *Land en Volk*, 19 Jan. 1892.

servitude to Dr. Leyds,[30] his love of Catholics, Jews and Hollanders,[31] his touchiness and melodramatic behaviour,[32] his 'unctuous manner',[33] his 'bloodsucking family',[34] and even his 'loyal help and support for Rhodes'.[35]

Land en Volk was far less responsible than either the *Volksstem* or the *Press*. It is loud, tasteless and brash. It used the words 'Jew' and 'Hollander' as a hate-inspiring incantation. Its attitude towards Indians and natives was even more virulent than that towards Hollanders and Jews.[36] Nevertheless it was the recognized organ of the Joubert party, and the resolute supporter of that party throughout the period under review. With its eager nose for anything that was 'rotten in the state of Denmark' it played a significant part in bringing various aspects of corruption and maladministration to the light of day. It is an important source of information on Progressive party affairs; and it provides a valuable insight into the nature of the motives of those who rallied behind General Joubert as the leader of the 'Afrikaner cause'.

The *Press* (which seems to have appeared, on the average, about twice a week, and which included a Dutch version, *De Pers*, and the *Weekly Press*) started its existence towards the end of 1889.[37] Its owner was A. H. Nellmapius, the well-known speculator and concessionaire, and one who was generally believed to be a close confidant of President Kruger's.[38] After his death in July 1893 it was taken over by the mining magnate J. B. Robinson,[39] also, throughout this period, a close friend of the President.[40] Its chief editor from mid-1891 till mid-1897 was Leo Weinthal, South African born, of German–Jewish origins, and a devout believer in the theory that 'one must look at all things from the Africander point of view' and that 'all things could be settled by the South Africans themselves, without interference from outside'.[41] Both the con-

---

[30] *Land en Volk*, 22 Mar. 1892.

[31] *Land en Volk*, 17 May 1892, 13 Oct. 1892.

[32] *Land en Volk*, 7 June 1892.   [33] *Land en Volk*, 20 Apr. 1893.

[34] *Land en Volk*, 27 Sept. 1894.   [35] *Land en Volk*, 26 Dec. 1892.

[36] See, for example, *Land en Volk*, 24 Mar. 1891 and 12 Jan. 1893.

[37] *Weekly Press*, 22 May 1897, p. 5.

[38] See *Press*, 31 July 1893, for full details of his life, career and influence. Also *Weekly Press* of 22 May 1897 and Leyds's letter of 18 Nov. 1886 to Schmüll (Joubert Papers, Inkomende Stukke, I A/18–26, Archives, vol. 10).

[39] Van Winter, ii, p. 11. *Volksstem*, 22 Nov. 1893. *Press*, 7 Sept. 1894.

[40] Fitzpatrick, pp. 226, 245.   [41] *Weekly Press*, 22 May 1897.

temporaries of the *Press* regarded it as the mouthpiece of the government. The *Volksstem* (1 March 1892) referred to the *Press* as 'the generally recognized organ of the government' and complained bitterly (22 July 1893) of government favouritism towards it in the allocation of official advertisements. *Land en Volk* (9 January 1893) referred to the *Press* as 'the Jewish organ of His Excellency the State President and Mr. Eloff' (Kruger's son-in-law); and one B. Gluckstein, an earlier editor dismissed in 1891 by Nellmapius, declared that its policies and indeed many of its newsitems were personally inspired by Kruger, Leyds and Nellmapius.[42]

Certainly the *Press* followed a fairly consistently pro-Government line, particularly up to the 1893 election; but it never ceased to attack what it called, in a leader on 4 May 1891, 'an attitude of persistent and incoherent nepotism and narrow conservatism, which conserves nothing but a tattered semblance of power, and must cease in the presence of the eternal verities', or to criticize the government when it felt so inclined. Its attitude to education and to the extension of the franchise was a liberal one. It was forthright in its criticisms of official maladministration. After Kruger had been safely re-elected in 1893[43] it turned strongly against the government-sponsored Netherlands Railway Company; and it gave full coverage and frequent encouragement to Progressive views.

These are hardly the actions of a paid lackey. The general tone of the *Press*, conceding its preference for Kruger over Joubert, was fair, tolerant and reasonably balanced. Its predictions and analyses in the political field often showed a shrewd common sense. It was, for example, the first newspaper to suggest (on 22 August 1893) that Ewald Esselen might succeed Dr. Krause as State Attorney, a suggestion which the *Volksstem*, seven months later, on 31 March 1894 (and quite wrongly as it turned out), dismissed with contempt. On the whole, with the provisos I have mentioned, it may be taken as a fairly reliable source of information. It is certainly less biased than *Land en Volk*, and perhaps even less so than the *Volksstem*. The *Weekly Press*, in particular, is a most useful source of information, for it gave a very full coverage to all main debates, political meetings, official reports, important court cases and other matters

[42] *Land en Volk*, 12 Jan. 1893 (letter from B. Gluckstein—'The "Press"; what is it? by a founder').
[43] See *Press*, 22 Feb. 1893 for an explanation of why it intended to criticize the government more freely now that the elections were over.

from which much material to illustrate the political life of the Republic may be gleaned.

For the rest the main (though not the only) primary sources upon which I have depended have been, in order of importance, the papers of General Joubert (referred to here as the 'Joubert Papers') and the Leyds Papers (both of them in manuscript or in typewritten form); and, in published works, Carl Jeppe's *The Kaleidoscopic Transvaal*, J. R. Fitzpatrick's *The Transvaal from within*, F. J. Dormer's *Vengeance as a policy in Afrikanerland*, Dr. W. J. Leyds's *Onze Eerste Jaren in Zuid Afrika*, and such portions of the official British 'Blue Books' and S.A.R. 'Green Books' as seemed likely to contain relevant information.

The 'Joubert Papers' (Joubert Versameling) in the Transvaal Archives are a voluminous collection of semi-official and private papers, mostly in manuscript, in Joubert's own hand, but sometimes typewritten. At times they are almost indecipherable, for Joubert, though a frequent and facile correspondent, was not a particularly legible one. They also include many volumes of letters written to Joubert, as well as odd copies of important official letters, contracts and proclamations. Although unindexed, so that it is necessary to read through many pages of often irrelevant material, they are sorted into volumes of roughly related subject-matter, each of which has been arranged and numbered in chronological order; and they are divided, basically, into letters received and letters dispatched (Inkomende Stukke and Uitgaande Stukke). They include Joubert's private letters to and from his family and friends, as well as a vast mass of correspondence on the innumerable financial matters with which Joubert was concerned.[44] Between them they throw an important light on Joubert's own personality, on the feelings of the burghers towards him, on his relations with Kruger and other members of the government of which the Commandant-General was himself a member, and some light on the political life of the times.

The 'Leyds Papers' (Leyds Archief) are a similar semi-official and private collection. Their contribution towards greater understanding of the subject of this book is indirect rather than direct. They give us some information about press affairs[45] and about the subjects discussed by the secret sessions of the Volksraad. They contain a vast mass of correspondence, press-cuttings, copies of contracts and

44 See pp. 246–8.
45 See pp. 87–9.

legal reports on the dynamite question and on railway policy. But there is little in them that throws any direct light on the personalities and background of the political life of this period.

Jeppe's *The Kaleidoscopic Transvaal*, though published in 1906 and therefore having the advantage of hindsight, and though erring on the side of generosity towards the South African Republic (e.g. in such statements as that on page 77, that 'it can safely be asserted that the Transvaal Republic spent more per capita on education than any other country in the world' and its complacent description on pages 36–44 of the Republic's native policy), has, nevertheless, the advantage of being written by a basically fair-minded and honest man who spent most of this period in the thick of the political struggle. His descriptions of personalities and politics are shrewd and balanced, and, though one of his main aims is to defend the policies and actions of the Progressive party (of which he was himself a distinguished member), his treatment of Kruger and the Conservative party is fair and objective, as are his remarks on such controversial questions as the nature and extent of bribery and corruption in official circles. He tends to overestimate the rigidity of Kruger (p. 160) and he is occasionally guilty of inaccuracies (such as his repetition of the untrue story that the President 'opened the new synagogue in Pretoria in the name of the Saviour', p. 161); but on the whole his book may be regarded as a useful and well-informed commentary on this period.

Fitzpatrick's *The Transvaal from within* is avowedly an 'attempt to present the case for the Uitlander' (preface, p. xxv) and to defend the thesis that the South African Republic deliberately prepared for and carried out an aggressive war against Britain in the pursuit of its aim of dominating South Africa. It is therefore clearly a work of propaganda, as the author himself admits. 'The reader', he writes on p. xxvi of the preface, 'is not invited to believe that the case is presented in such a form as it might have been presented by an impartial historian. It is the Transvaal *from within*, by one who feels all the injustice and indignity of the position. [Nevertheless] . . . an earnest attempt has been made to state the facts fairly.' In spite of the strongly partisan spirit of the book, it is well documented; and Fitzpatrick had the advantage of being from 1892 in the midst of the events he describes. Making due allowance for his strongly anti-Boer bias, his inaccuracies and omissions, the book (as long as its statements are checked by comparison with more reliable sources) provides useful corroborative evidence on the actors and events of this period.

F. J. Dormer's *Vengeance as a policy in Afrikanerland*, published in 1901, consists of a series of essays or articles written between 1895 and 1899. Dormer was an ex-editor of the *Cape Argus* and the Johannesburg *Star*, from the latter of which newspapers he resigned early in 1895 'as the most emphatic means that were open to me of marking my dissent from the policy of intervening in the affairs of the Transvaal on which Mr. Rhodes had already made up his mind to embark' (pp. 19–20). He had lived in the Transvaal from 1881 to 1895 (p. 150). He believed in the Republic's right to complete independence, regarded Rhodes as the 'fons et origo of 1895 [and the man] who engineered and made inevitable the collision that occurred in 1899' (preface, p. xxxi), and considered that Britain's policy towards South Africa had been 'a long succession of almost incredible blunders' (preface, p. xxiv); but he was, in spite of this, no admirer of Kruger's government (p. 193). Nevertheless he is extremely fair in his assessment of its good and bad points, contemptuous of unjustified criticism of it, and his summing up of Kruger shows remarkable insight. 'Mr. Kruger as a domestic tyrant', he writes (preface, pp. xxi–xxii), 'was not much to be dreaded; he was at all times perilously near the end of his tether. But Mr. Kruger as the champion of Republican independence and Afrikander nationality was, in the circumstances, scarcely less formidable than a first-class European power.' Dormer worked for understanding between the two white races and believed in the rightness of 'Africa for the Afrikanders—not in the sense of exclusiveness, but in the sense that local questions must be locally settled'. He declared himself to be 'in complete accord with Progressive Afrikanderdom'.[46] His knowledge of many of the leading personalities, and his belligerently neutral stand between the extreme Boer and British viewpoints make his opinions on Transvaal affairs and his judgement of personalities and parties of particular interest.

Dr. W. J. Leyds's *Onze Eerste Jaren in Zuid Afrika* is a collection of private letters to friends and family in Holland by Leyds and his wife. Written between 1884 and 1889, they were never meant for publication; but in his old age Leyds thought they might as well see the light of day. In consequence they are extremely frankly written, and throw an interesting light on personalities and events. It is a

[46] Joubert Papers, Inkomende Stukke, I A/18–26 (Archives, vol. 10), no. 1368, letter of 9 Dec. 1898 to Reitz.

great pity that they stop in 1890. Nevertheless they supply useful background information for the period with which we are dealing.

These are the primary sources which I have found most useful. Others, from which items of additional information have been gleaned, will be found listed in the bibliography at the end of this book.

The secondary sources which have been used are too numerous to comment on individually. The main fount of material has been the primary sources, and more particularly the newspapers, the *Notulen* of the First and Second Volksraads, and the Joubert Papers. Secondary sources have been used largely as corroborative evidence, or to fill in the gaps. This method of approach has its dangers (and I am more than conscious of the many weaknesses of this book), but it is not, I hope, entirely without its usefulness.

Although most of this book was written before the publication of Professor J. S. Marais's *The Fall of Kruger's Republic*, I cannot end this introduction without a tribute to that meticulous work of scholarship, which has been an invaluable lighthouse to me in finding my way across the intricate and largely uncharted seas of this difficult but fascinating period. The publication of Professor Marais's book did not entail any major changes in my arguments, but where any changes have been made, or where *The Fall of Kruger's Republic* has been used in corroboration of points made, this is (gratefully) acknowledged in the footnotes.

I should like, finally, to record my thanks to the late Professor J. S. Marais of the University of the Witwatersrand for his advice and encouragement; to Professor K. Kirkwood of St. Antony's College, Oxford University, without whose encouragement this book would probably never have been published, and to my wife for her devoted help in the laborious task of repeated proof-readings.

1

Introduction

The Nature of Transvaal Conservatism

I

WHAT was the nature of the dour conservatism of the country Boers, much of the essence of which Kruger shared, against which, nevertheless, he frequently struggled in the interests of his country, and which no politician—no matter how much he might dislike and condemn it—could afford to disregard?

In the first place the Boer (and few white inhabitants of the Transvaal in the 1890s, whether Progressive[1] or Conservative, Afrikaner or Englishman, would differ fundamentally with him on this point) prided himself on the 'whiteness' of the S.A. Republic's civilization, and on the complete exclusion from all say in affairs of church or State of any coloured person.[2] Natives 'were frankly viewed primarily as a source of labour'.[3] As the *Weekly Press* of Pretoria (a strong defender of governmental policy on this, as on most matters) phrased it, the proposed hut-tax law of 1895

'is especially aimed at the huge locations, where natives in hundreds, if not in thousands, loll about at their ease, whilst the Europeans who are endeavouring to develop and civilise the country are handicapped in their efforts through scarcity of native labour'.

The newspaper (12 October 1895) viewed with favour any scheme which would compel the able-bodied male native to leave his kraal and labour for at least nine months in the year. This view was cordially shared by the mining interests,[4] who made constant representations to the government on the inadequate facilities for the apprehension of runaway labourers; and who felt that a wage of 50s. to 60s. per month to the native labourer was 'far in excess of the exigencies of his existence' and ought to be reduced to a sum

[1] See chapters VI to VIII.
[2] Grondwet of the S.A. Republic, art. 9.
[3] Walker, *History of South Africa*, p. 351.
[4] See Minutes of interview between Chamber of Mines and Minister of Mines, 19 Feb. 1890 (*Volksstem*, 3 Mar. 1890).

which would make it impossible for him to save more than £5 a year, 'which is quite enough for his requirements, and will prevent natives from becoming rich in a short space of time'.[5]

The Transvaal Boer, however, nourished strong feelings of hostility towards the native. His state had been built up only after a long series of native wars, and these continued well into the 1890s. The determination to maintain complete and unquestioned white domination (with which, incidentally, few uitlanders would have disagreed),[6] was shown in a hundred and one ways. Objections were raised in the Volksraad in 1890 to even considering memorials from coloured people together with those from Europeans as 'it looked too much like equality'.[7] The rights of self-government and domination over coloured races were regarded as corollaries, as a leader of 7 October 1893 in the *Volksstem*, welcoming self-government in Natal, shows. The editor solemnly thanks God that the days are now over when Natal could be regarded only as 'een soort broeinest van naturellen-gespuis' (a sort of breeding-ground for native rubbish), and assures Sir John Robinson of the support of all true Afrikaners in any endeavours 'om op politieke gebied de absolute alleenheerschers te zijn' (to retain exclusive control in the political sphere). The same paper, in reporting with approval the imposition of a sentence of four months' hard labour and twenty lashes on a native who had used threatening language and gestures to a white woman, stressed the vital importance of dealing firmly with 'Kaffirs guilty of impudence' and of 'keeping Kaffirs off the pavements in Johannesburg' (a town which it regarded as much too lax in these matters).[8] A member of the First Volksraad, C. J. Tosen, complained bitterly that 'people' (menschen) had to do all the work while natives lolled around in idleness.[9] Schalk Burger, regarded as one of the more progressive opponents of the Kruger régime, objected strongly to a presidential

[5] G. Albu, in evidence to the Industrial Commission, on 19/4/1897 (*Weekly Press*, 24 Apr. 1897).

[6] See Marais, *The Fall of Kruger's Republic*, pp. 182, 265; Fitzpatrick, *The Transvaal from within*, p. 329.

[7] O. J. Coetzee, member for Lydenburg, 22 July 1890 (*Volksstem*, 31 July 1890. *Notulen*, Eerste Volksraad, 1890, art. 1130).

[8] *Volksstem*, 17 Feb. 1894. (It added, 'Johannesburg is still a part of the South African Republic, in which the Sons of Ham can learn to keep their place'.)

[9] *Volksstem*, 22 May 1895 (*Notulen*, Eerste Volksraad, 1895, art. 152). See also Leyds, *Onze Eerste Jaren in Zuid Afrika* (letter of Mrs. Leyds, No. 18 of 17 Jan. 1886).

proposal to allow civil marriages between natives (in spite of the President's assurance that such marriages would be performed by native commissioners and not by landdrosts) as 'practically amounting to equality of blacks and whites in the eyes of the civil law'.[10] Much horror was expressed at the shocking state of affairs in Cape Town, where 'Her Majesty's white soldiers can be seen arm in arm with coloured women'[11] and in which 'official circles accepted kaffirs as guests at official receptions without the least protest'.[12] Among other reasons for rejoicing at the departure from South Africa of Sir Henry Loch, the High Commissioner, the *Volksstem* (10 March 1894) mentions that 'a Governor who tolerates a Kaffir as his guest at receptions insults all white people'. A typical letter to the *Volksstem* of 3 April 1894, ridiculing the agitation in Johannesburg because some of 'their beloved kaffirs have got a good hiding for using the white men's stoeps and pavements', proclaims: 'Isn't the street good enough for kaffirs? If we allow them on our stoeps we will soon have to allow them in our churches!'

The difficulties of trying to persuade the members of the legislature to make even the smallest concession to a more liberal point of view are clearly illustrated by the arguments put forward in the First Volksraad debate of 11 to 12 August 1897, when the President and Executive Council, 'considering that the desirability has appeared afresh of freeing those natives who have attained a higher degree of civilisation' from the prescriptions of some of the more restrictive laws, recommended freeing from the pass laws 'all native and coloured missionaries, and native or coloured schoolmasters, as well as such natives who have attained to a higher degree of civilisation, and exercise a trade, business or calling'.[13] General P. Cronjé, who had succeeded Joubert as the Superintendent of Native Affairs in September 1896, when the offices of Commandant-General and Native Affairs had at last been split, argued 'that a very large section of the natives had come to a high level of civilisation, and were undeniably ahead of their fellow creatures in the country kraals'. President Kruger urged members to realize that 'civilised natives and raw heathens could not be placed on the same tray. . . . It was

[10] *Press*, 5 June 1895 (*Notulen*, Eerste Volksraad, 1895, art. 244).
[11] *Volksstem*, 10 Feb. 1894.   [12] *Volksstem*, 31 Jan. 1894.
[13] This, and all extracts quoted on this matter, come from the First Volksraad debate of 11 and 12 Aug. 1897, as reported in the *Weekly Press* of 14 Aug. 1897 (*Notulen*, Eerste Volksraad, 1897, arts. 832–6).

unchristian to hold civilisation from their subjects. . . . Civilisation was everything. Let them do everything in their power to enhance it.' B. Vorster, the member for Zoutpansberg, declared that 'this law would, despite all present opposition, be passed eventually. Time would bring it about.'

On the other hand, J. du P. de Beer, the member for the Waterberg, often regarded as a 'progressive',[14] argued that 'a kaffir was a kaffir whether he was educated or not. . . . The Pass Law was the only remaining statute that kept the kaffir in his proper position. Natives were fast becoming proud and overbearing. They could not be ruled without an occasional twenty-five lashes, but by the draft resolution they were to be let at large with the liberties of whites.' He then delivered a homily on the virtues of humility (for natives, at any rate) and the sinfulness of pride, concluding that 'he could show from the Bible that God withstood the proud, and was merciful to the humble'. A. A. J. Dieperink, the Progressive member for Johannesburg, considered that 'not a single native should be allowed to move about the country without passes'. R. K. Loveday, the Progressive member for Barberton, 'could not see where the line of demarcation between advanced kaffirs and others should be drawn. A native on a bicycle or in a new suit was advanced! (Laughter) The law should apply to them all.' Louis Botha, Progressive member for Vryheid, opposed the idea of distinctions. 'Cape boys and cabdrivers would fall under this law. They were proud, vain, ignorant, impertinent and obstinate. . . . The [Volksraad] would do well to keep bastards in their right place. By giving them the little finger, they would eventually grasp the whole hand.'

The government got its way, but only after a good deal of this sort of thing, most of the Progressive members voting against exemption from the Pass Laws for educated natives.[15] The general attitude of most of the Boer population towards Indians and coloured people was much the same. The opposition paper *Land en Volk* (24 March 1891), approving the very proper punishment of 'coolies' for daring to protest against being transported to a location outside the town, was indignant that 'die ellendige vuilgoed' (these miserable bits of rubbish) were considering a protest to the British Government. D. P. Taljaard, member for Standerton, and a strong Conservative, vehemently attacked people who employed 'these stinking

[14] See *Volksstem*, 27 May 1895; *Land en Volk*, 27 Sept. 1894.
[15] See *Weekly Press*, 14 Aug. 1897 for record of individual votes (p. 22).

coolies' as clerks or servants.[16] In the Volksraad debate of 5 August 1892, although a few members felt some pity for these 'schepsels' (creatures) and considered that 'all living creatures had a right to exist', it was decided by 16 votes to 6 to 'remove from the towns all coolies who had entered commerce since 1889'.[17] C. Jeppe, Progressive member for Johannesburg, in the First Volksraad on 11 July 1894, demanded that 'coolies be forced to live in locations, [for] his constituents were not prepared any longer to live side by side with Asiatics'.[18] Some time later he and R. K. Loveday joined in declaring that the Transvaal had 'not been cleared to be colonised by coolies and coloureds'.[19] Cape Coloured people received summary treatment at the hands of the police.[20] In a Second Volksraad debate of 20 May 1896 strong exception was taken to the fact that coloured people were allowed to deposit money in the Post Office Savings Bank, one member declaring that it was a violation of the Constitution that the State should pay interest to such people.[21] The punishment of a coloured man guilty of intercourse with a consenting white woman was laid down as hard labour for up to six years and up to sixty lashes.[22]

In the light of these feelings it is not surprising that a fair degree of cruelty, even by the standards of those times, was experienced by the 'lesser breeds without the law'. Twenty-five lashes with the 'cat', references to which occur every few days in press reports, were regarded as what Lord Charles Somerset would have described as 'mild domestic punishment'. We have seen that J. du P. De Beer 'considered an occasional 25 lashes' to be essential for all natives. The flogging of natives for walking on the pavements was defended by the Acting Commandant of Police in Johannesburg, and his attitude was upheld by the Pretoria *Press* (14 March 1894). In April 1893 one Louis Freeman of Suikerboschfontein (in the Lydenburg district) wrote to the *Volksstem* (the letter appeared on 9 May 1893) to complain of the action of the local landdrost, who had sentenced a 'coolie' to eight days, and twenty-five lashes, for a 'nietige over-

---

[16] *Volksstem*, 19 May 1890.

[17] Not done, owing to intervention by the British Government.

[18] *Volksstem*, 14 July 1894 (*Notulen*, Eerste Volksraad, 1894, art. 784).

[19] See also Correspondence between British Government and S.A.R. on the Indian question in Leyds Papers, section 90, part III, and Blue Books C. 7911 and C. 7946 re British Indians in the S.A.R.

[20] Milner to Leyds, 10 Mar. 1899, and S.A.R. reply of 22 Mar. 1899 (Leyds Papers, section 89, part II).

[21] *Weekly Press*, 23 May 1896.   [22] *Weekly Press*, 20 Feb. 1897.

treding' (a very minor offence) and had made every difficulty when a doctor had wished to attend to him. In April 1894 Justice E. J. P. Jorissen expressed himself forcibly about the action of a rural veld-kornet who without hearing any evidence had had one Abdol Kasiem Rachman, described as 'een jong beschaafd Maleijer' (a young well-mannered Malay) and his companion, a Hottentot called Alexander, stripped and given ten lashes with the 'cat' by his son and nephew. This had been done in spite of their willingness to pay the 10s. fine for 'trespass', and in spite of the fact that they were already bleeding from a severe beating given them by the owner of a farm which they had entered to ask, quite politely, if certain lost donkeys of theirs had strayed on to it.[23]

Illegal assaults, when reported, were dealt with by the courts. Jorissen, in this last case, awarded judgement with costs to the plaintiff.[24] A certain Mr. Blaine, Compound Manager of the New Rietfontein Gold Mining Company, who had had a number of natives 'virtually tortured', was fined £5 or one month, and three of the company's native constables who had carried out his instructions were sentenced to six months and twenty-five strokes of the 'cat'.[25] The system of 'apprenticing' prisoners to farmers after native wars was still continued. The *Volksstem* (on 17 February 1890), while denying that there was anything remotely approaching slavery in the system, admitted the 'taking under the protection of the farmers of refugee and deserted women and children, who are looked after better than they would be in their own homes. . . . The children do very little, act as shepherds etc., and are paid a cow or its equivalent value per year. The same thing was done in the Colony after the Gaika-Galeka war of 1878.' The Joubert Papers include a number of requests for 'little kaffirs' of which the following, a letter to the Commandant-General's wife, is typical:

'Please ask the General to let me have a little Malaboch kaffir, as of course there are some whose father and mother have been killed. I don't mind if it is a boy or a girl. I want one about 7 years old, or any one that the General will give me.'[26]

---

[23] *Volksstem*, 17 Apr. 1894.

[24] There is no record of any action having been taken against the veld-kornet, who was, indeed, represented by lawyers at Government cost (ibid.).

[25] *Volksstem*, 13 Dec. 1893.

[26] Joubert Papers, Inkomende Stukke (B) Privaat, 1543–1704 (Archives, vol. 12), letter no. 1967 from E. Schweifer, Pretoria, 6 Aug. 1894. See also Inkomende

The fear of natives of being 'caught' by the Kaffir police was occasionally referred to in the Volksraad.[27] President Kruger exhorted burghers to report such illegal capture, as 'this kind of thing would get the country a bad name'. The Commandant-General, also (until 1896) Superintendent of Native Affairs, declared that, in any case, experience had shown the system of forcible apprenticeship to be useless, as these natives 'took the first opportunity to escape'.[28]

There was in the old Transvaal Boer a strong suspicion of all novelty, and this characteristic the more conservative members of the legislature faithfully reflected. The character sketch of P. G. Roos, member of the First Volksraad for Pretoria, published in the *Volksstem* (1 September 1894), gives us a very typical picture of the qualities shared by many of his fellow-legislators.

'A man of the old stamp, strongly conservative and against all "nieuwigheden". He regards all changes in the law as contraband, and to be strongly resisted as threatening the State's independence. . . . For the rest Mr. Roos is strongly for economy and not easily convinced of *any* need for expenditure. . . . And if he works too hard at the brake of our wagon of state, it often wants to go too fast, and it is good that there should be some who resist novelties until their goodness is proved, and remind members of the old customs and of their goodness. We hope he will keep his seat for a long time.'

In general this doughty conservatism showed itself in a fierce determination to keep the control of the country and of its morals and education in the hands of the old population;[29] but often it revealed itself in a suspicious dislike of everything new or unfamiliar which made it, to more progressive eyes, at once pathetic and ridiculous.

Thus P. C. Greyling (member for Heidelberg) was expressing a quite commonly-held view when he declared[30] that 'he did not see any necessity for railways. The country was prosperous enough

Stukke 105–226 (Archives, vol. 2), letter no. 220 of 5 Jan. 1899 from H. S. Bosman asking for Magato children.
[27] See First Volksraad debate of 31 Aug. 1893 (*Volksstem*, 2 Sept. 1893; *Notulen*, Eerste Volksraad, 1893, arts. 1254–5).
[28] *Weekly Press*, 3 Aug. 1895, p. 11.
[29] See pp. 139–83, 188–91.
[30] *Volksstem*, 30 Aug. 1893 (First Raad debate of 29 Aug. 1893. No reference in *Notulen*).

without them'; and so was A. A. Stoop (member for Wakkerstroom) in opining[31] that 'trams were not necessary, and would easily hit and kill people in the dark' (a view not entirely negated by our more modern experience). O. J. Coetzee (member for Lydenburg) showed a somewhat more progressive conservatism when he said[32] (no doubt with the interests of fodder-growers in mind) that 'the public was solidly against a steam tramway, but not against a horse-drawn one'. Kruger himself successfully opposed the erection of postal pillar-boxes in Pretoria on the grounds that city-dwellers ought not to have conveniences which were denied to the rural population.[33] The President's attempt, in a more enlightened mood, to persuade the legislators to accept the necessity of registering births, marriages and deaths among the European population was decisively rejected by 17 votes to 7, A. D. W. Wolmarans (member for Pretoria, and Chairman of the First Volksraad) declaring that the burghers of Pretoria were 'distinctly opposed to it' and other legislators seeming to regard it as an attack on religious principles.[34] J. du P. De Beer (member for Waterberg) protested against an attempt to found a museum on the grounds that 'every schoolboy had seen a scorpion, a chameleon, and such other nonsense', was particularly upset at the fact that £100 of public money was being spent on the purchase of foreign papers for the official files, and summed up his whole feeling at the trend of events in the words, 'Shame! Yes, I say, shame! . . . No, Mr. Chairman, the longer the Raad sits the more I see that there is too much to disgust me!'[35] Even parks were looked upon with disfavour, and in spite of a gallant attempt by General Joubert to assert that they were 'not so much for pleasure as for providing trees, seed and other useful things for the whole country', the majority of Volksraad members, led by Messrs. Taljaard, Greyling and Stoop, called upon the authorities 'rather to divide up any available ground into erven and give it to needy burghers', and rejected the government's suggestion by 22 votes to 11.[36]

[31] *Volksstem*, 7 July 1890 (debate of 4 July 1890); *Notulen*, Eerste Volksraad, 1890, art. 590.

[32] Ibid. (debate of 3 July 1890). No reference in *Notulen*.

[33] *Volksstem*, 12 Sept. 1894 (debate of 7 Sept. 1894); *Notulen*, Eerste Volksraad, 1894, art. 1616.

[34] *Press*, 18 May 1893 (*Notulen*, Eerste Volksraad, 1893, art. 119).

[35] *Weekly Press*, 12 Mar. 1898, p. 11 (*Notulen*, Eerste Volksraad, 1898, arts. 231, 262).

[36] *Volksstem*, 22 May 1890 (*Notulen*, Eerste Volksraad, 1890, art. 155).

Foreigners were regarded with the same suspicion as foreign ideas. Though open hostility to the English (understandable enough in view of the Transvaal's chequered history) was rarely expressed, the English language, spoken by the vast majority of the great uitlander population of Johannesburg,[37] was subject to frequent and bitter attack. A. D. W. Wolmarans spoke strongly of the danger of children being 'poisoned by English ideas'.[38] J. P. L. Lombaard (Standerton) declared that if it was alleged that English should be learnt because it was the language of commerce 'they should also force our children to learn the "Koelie-taal" '.[39] J. M. Malan (Rustenburg) called for 'the banning of English from our Christian schools'.[40] And even President Kruger, moderate though he was in most things, opposed attempts to increase the amount of English taught in State schools, ending with the words: 'Every attempt to expand education in English will help towards the destruction of the "landstaal".'[41]

Feeling against the Hollanders, although undoubtedly exaggerated for political purposes,[42] was also strong in certain circles. Both Joubert and Schalk Burger found it a useful weapon against Kruger in the election campaign of 1898. As early as 1886 Dr. Leyds wrote of the Commandant-General as 'hating the Hollanders with an inborn hatred';[43] the *Star* in August 1892 described Joubert as one who 'doesn't like the English, but likes the Hollanders even less'; and Joubert himself, in a private letter to C. B. Otto, wrote of his determination to keep the Republic independent not only of England 'but also of the foreign unhealthy influences which are undermining our national existence and character'.[44] Schalk Burger's election manifesto of 1898 asks: 'Why are our offices filled with foreigners? Hollanders and Germans who draw high salaries, while our own

---

[37] See census figures given in *Weekly Press*, 31 Oct. 1896.

[38] *Volksstem*, 8 Sept. 1894 (*Notulen*, Eerste Volksraad, 1894, art. 1615).

[39] *Volksstem*, 12 Sept. 1894 (*Notulen*, Eerste Volksraad, 1894, art. 1616).

[40] *Volksstem*, 12 Sept. 1894; *Land en Volk*, 20 Sept. 1894 (*Notulen*, Eerste Volksraad, 1894, art. 1616).

[41] *Volksstem*, 10 Aug. 1895 (*Notulen*, Eerste Volksraad, 1895, art. 866).

[42] J. P. la Grange Lombaard, *Paul Kruger die Volksman*, p. 162. See also pp. 126–39, below.

[43] Leyds's notorious letter to Schmüll, of 18 Nov. 1886 (published in *Land en Volk*, 1 June 1893).

[44] Joubert Papers, Uitgaande Stukke, II A/1—A/3, 1997, p. 318, dated 24 Aug. 1892.

sons are treated as outcasts [worden als bastaards behandeld] unless they belong to the clique.' And one of the strongest arguments in *Land en Volk's* unceasing tirade against the President and his régime was the fact that Kruger was, allegedly, 'surrounded by a commando of Hollanders and foreign Jews' most of whom were 'dronkaards en modernen' (drunkards and modernists) so that the whole country was 'filthy with Hollanders'.[45]

This dislike of foreigners did not exclude Afrikaners from the British colonies of Natal and the Cape, or even from the Republican Orange Free State. In a First Volksraad debate of 26 June 1895, F. G. Wolmarans (ex-Chairman of the First Volksraad) opined that 'those reared in Natal and the Cape Colony were to be distrusted as much as men of other nations. . . . A man might be an Africander in name, and by birth, but not in heart and soul';[46] and the Chairman of the Volksraad (Schalk Burger) declared that 'the word Africander should be interpreted as Transvaaler. Everyone from beyond the borders of the Republic must be viewed as a stranger, no matter if he came from the Free State, the Colony, England or Holland, etc.'[47] There were, indeed, many in the Transvaal who would have cordially agreed with old Mr. Taljaard[48] who answered a claim by J. F. Celliers (Second Volksraad member for Johannesburg) to speak for all South Africa with the scornful words, 'Maar wat heb ik met Zuid-Afrika te doen?'[49] (But what have I to do with South Africa?)

Catholics and Jews, though allowed to carry on their daily occupations in peace, came in for their share of the general distrust of all that was outlandish. The Memorials Commission of the Volksraad, placing before the Raad 'memorials' from Johannesburg and the Barberton goldfields requesting equal rights with other burghers for Catholics and Jews, opined that such memorials 'showed great ingratitude by Roman Catholics and Jews in asking for more privileges than they already had. There was no State Church and there

[45] *Land en Volk*, 5 May 1891.

[46] *Weekly Press*, 29 June 1895, p. 14 (*Notulen*, Eerste Volksraad, 1895, arts. 497–8).

[47] *Weekly Press*, 29 June 1895, p. 14 (*Notulen*, Eerste Volksraad, 1895, arts. 497–8).

[48] First Raad member for Mooi River, and later Standerton, for 22 years, and at this time Second Raad member for Standerton. Described as 'the Nestor of our Parliament' (*Volksstem*, 27 June 1891).

[49] *Volksstem*, 24 June 1893 (*Notulen*, Tweede Volksraad, 1893, arts. 399–400).

was complete freedom of religious belief.' J. P. L. Lombaard (Standerton) said their forefathers had suffered much under the Roman Catholics. It was time the Raad 'took measures to ensure that the Roman Catholics and Jews did not trouble it again'. J. P. Meyer (Witwatersrand Goldfields) said that 'as a descendant of the Huguenots he would never agree to such a request'. A motion rejecting the request as being in conflict with the Constitution was adopted by 18 votes to 3, the dissentients (Messrs. A. D. W. Wol-marans, P. G. Roos and Malan) voting as they did because they had desired a far more strongly-worded rejection.[50] Two years later a similar memorial signed by the Rev. James Gray and others praying for the removal of the political disabilities of Roman Catholics and Jews was rejected just as decisively, Carl Jeppe (the member for Johannesburg) being the only dissentient. In the course of this debate Schalk Burger declared that the spread of Romanism must be countered and said that his district regretted that the law was not more stringent. In support of this, memorials from burghers of Lydenburg were read which alleged that 'much ungodliness was practised in secret in the Roman Catholic Church', enjoined the people of the country to remember 'the martyrdom of their ancestors in the dark days of medieval history', and requested the Raad 'to make a law to persecute the Catholic Church, and proclaim that within eighteen months the Roman Catholic Church shall sell all their fixed property'. The Chairman of the Raad, A. D. W. Wol-marans, while reluctantly rejecting this, 'for the law must be obeyed', declared, nevertheless, that 'there must be a growing terror in each Christian's heart'.[51]

Although, because of the threat presented by the uitlanders, the burghers of the S.A. Republic realized the essential need of educa-tion for their children if the State was to survive,[52] education did not entirely escape the rather lukewarm regard usually awarded it among pioneer communities. Speaking at a debate on education in the 1892 session of the Volksraad, the Chairman, A. D. W. Wolmarans, said that:

[50] *Volksstem*, 4 Aug. 1891 (*Notulen*, Eerste Volksraad, 1891, art. 1204).

[51] *Press*, 16 June 1893 (*Notulen*, Eerste Volksraad, 1893, art. 342. Note 'Pro-testant's', not 'Christian's' in *Notulen*).

[52] Note also that the final oral examination of pupils of the Staats-gymnasium was attended on occasion by the members of both Volksraads! See also J. Ploeger, *Onderwys en Onderwysbeleid in die S.A.R. 1881-1900*.

'his experience had taught him that if a girl spoke half a dozen words of English correctly she despised her nationality. Their morality would be ruined by giving their daughters higher education. An Afrikaner girl did not require arithmetic and book-keeping. These sciences might be necessary for English girls, who sometimes served in shops; but they would ruin the morality of their race by teaching their girls these things.'[53]

J. du P. de Beer (Waterberg), who favoured education for women, warned, however, that 'females were a haughty race, and if they became very educated they were still more haughty'.[54] At a political meeting later that year, addressed by Chief Justice Kotzé, O. J. Coetzee (ex-member for Lydenburg of the First Volksraad) declared that 'as for education, they had had an educated President [i.e. President T. F. Burgers]; he himself had voted for him. And what was the result? He had handed the keys of the State to Shepstone and the English!'[55] Could the connexion between moral weakness and 'higher education' be more convincingly proved? Not that any very great demands were made on teachers in this connexion. Dr. Mansvelt, Superintendent of Education from 1891, admitted that 'it was not necessary for district teachers to pass any examination',[56] though Volksraad members had complained some years earlier that 'many teachers could not spell words like Pretoria, Potchefstroom, or the months of the year, and could not do on paper sums which any respectable farmer could do mentally'.[57] Legislators grumbled that they now had to pay £8 for a teacher, though previously farmers had paid them £2 to £3 a month 'and they had answered well enough'.[58] But the educational fraternity were not entirely without their defenders. A. D. W. Wolmarans, objecting to the dismissal of a teacher in his constituency, agreed that 'he would acknowledge that this old gentleman was not one of the most enthusiastic teachers, but he was one of those old men who were always satisfied to accept any salary which the burghers could afford

[53] *Press*, 30 May 1892.

[54] *Press*, 30 May 1892 (*Notulen*, Eerste Volksraad, 1892, art. 300).

[55] Meeting at Lydenburg, 1 Oct. 1892 (*Volksstem*, 19 Oct. 1892).

[56] *Weekly Press*, 12 June 1897, p. 17 (*Notulen*, Eerste Volksraad, 1897, art. 283).

[57] *Press*, 7 May 1892 (*Notulen*, Eerste Volksraad, 1892, art. 45).

[58] *Weekly Press*, 12 June 1897 (*Notulen*, Eerste Volksraad, 1897, art. 283). Note that a white mine labourer was paid between £18 and £30 a month (*Weekly Press*, 14 Sept. 1897. Report of Industrial Commission).

to pay'.[59]

The deep religious piety of the Transvaal Boers is too well known to need much illustration. The President himself frequently delivered 'powerful and closely reasoned sermons' which displayed 'an immense knowledge of scripture',[60] declared fervently that an education not based upon religion was utterly abhorrent to him,[61] and on one famous occasion turned down an invitation to be the patron of a ball with the remark that 'balls were services of Baal, and God had commanded Moses of old to exterminate all services of Baal'.[62] Commandant-General Joubert, another typically patriarchal figure, is described as quoting texts from the Bible 'on every possible occasion',[63] and his letters to his family and friends reveal a deep piety. To one of his sons, for example, he wrote: 'Never forget prayer. It is the Jacob's ladder by which one may climb towards God our father and our Lord Jesus.'[64] The chief complaint against the newcomers was their 'godlessness'. The secular education policy with which E. J. P. Jorissen had been associated in President Burgers's time 'was as shocking to many of the burghers as that of De Mist and Janssens had been to their grandfathers'[65] and memorials from the burghers criticized, as late as 1894, Jorissen's 'lack of belief'.[66] A shrewd thrust was delivered at Chief Justice Kotzé's election chances when O. J. Coetzee (ex-member for Lydenburg) accused him of having asked him sixteen years before 'whether he was the kind of fool who believed in a God'.[67] There was a strong belief that all plagues and other tribulations (whether locusts, uitlanders or President Kruger's régime, according to the taste of the complainant) were a direct punishment from the hand of God. Du Toit, a First Volksraad member, ascribed the rinderpest to the coming of the uitlanders, 'for in former years, before these people and the gold-fields were known, there were no plagues'.[68] On the other hand, at

[59] *Weekly Press*, 30 July 1898, p. 11 (*Notulen*, Eerste Volksraad, 1898, art. 870).

[60] C. Jeppe, *The Kaleidoscopic Transvaal*, pp. 160–1.

[61] *Volksstem*, 13 Jan. 1890 (speech at Lydenburg on 28 Dec. 1889).

[62] *Volksstem*, 23 May 1891 (the letter is quoted in full in Fitzpatrick, *The Transvaal from within*, p. 304).

[63] H. W. Struben, *Recollections*, p. 189.

[64] Joubert Papers, Uitgaande Stukke, II A/4—B/3 (Archives, vol. 23), no. 2309.

[65] Walker, *History of South Africa*, p. 362.

[66] *Volksstem*, 7 Apr. 1894.

[67] *Volksstem*, 19 Oct. 1892.

[68] *Weekly Press*, 21 Nov. 1896 (*Notulen*, Eerste Volksraad, 1896, art. 1987).

Schalk Burger's election meeting at Heidelberg (reported in the *Weekly Press* of 11 December 1897) an old burgher of 75, Mr. Maré, said that he was deaf and could not hear what was going on at the meeting but that if Mr. Burger was standing against President Kruger he would vote for him, for 'they had voted for President Kruger and what was the result? Five years of plagues, troubles and misery throughout the land!' Much concern was expressed in the First Volksraad at the impiety of an attempt to make rain by firing into the clouds, which 'was a defiance of God and would most likely bring down a visitation from the Almighty'.[69] Much opposition, similarly, was offered to a government suggestion that it might take action against locusts.[70] A. A. Stoop (Wakkerstroom) declared that locusts were a punishment from the hand of God and that nothing would help against them. P. G. Roos (Pretoria) considered action by the government would be defiance of the hand of God, and would have no truck with it. He considered that the best measure against locusts was repentance for one's sins. J. van der Merwe (Lydenburg), somewhat less logically, considered locusts to be 'a plague from on high, which every burgher must work against, but not the government'. The frivolous statements of Jan Meyer (Witwatersrand Goldfields) that 'everything was from the hand of God, and that he had heard that certain birds in Europe ate up locusts' and that 'with God's blessing even plagues could be conquered', the demand of J. J. Spies (Utrecht) to know 'how one could call anything a plague until one had tried to conquer it', and the question of Lukas Meyer (Vryheid) as to 'why nobody had objected to the extermination of lions, leopards, wolves and jackals, which would otherwise still be with us', were tellingly answered by J. P. L. Labuschagne (Utrecht) who stated that 'everybody knew that locusts were a punishment from the hand of God. They had been away from our country for a long time, and there were reasons for their return. If members read their Bibles they would know this (Groote sensatie).' Finally, after much debate, the government gained (by 12 votes to 11) permission to correspond on the question with neighbouring countries; but only on condition that it also arranged a day of prayer with neighbouring states to intercede for the lifting of God's punishment.

An important obstacle to the development of the State's mines and industries was a dour and determined Sabbatarianism. In the First

[69] Fitzpatrick, *The Transvaal from within*, p. 311.
[70] *Volksstem*, 23 July, 1892 (*Notulen*, Eerste Volksraad, 1892, art. 887).

Volksraad debate of 9 July 1896[71] a number of members wanted all mines completely closed on Sundays, Paul Maré (Zoutpansberg), for example, insisting that 'to allow batteries to crush on Sundays was a disgrace to a Christian people and an insult to the Supreme Being'. In a further debate in November of the same year A. D. W. Wolmarans (Pretoria), Schalk Burger (member of the Executive Council) and D. Joubert (Carolina) considered 'that it was the sacred duty of the Raad to take steps against the prevalent desecration of the Sabbath, and to appease the wrath of God, whose hand lay heavily on the people'. A considerable number of members wanted all railway traffic to cease on Sundays. A. D. W. Wolmarans stated that 'the trains must be stopped as well. There was no room for half measures. The penalty should be imprisonment and not fines.' The Chairman, F. G. Wolmarans, rejecting Lukas Meyer's opinion that 'other, and perhaps more grievous, sins were committed than the automatic crushing of quartz', and brushing away the objections of the mining and industrial interests, declared that the burghers' memorials (against Sunday work) were well founded 'and were the result of the operations of 35,000 godless people who had come into the State, and who had no regard for God's law. . . . These people had no conscience with regard to religious or godly things, and their opinion could therefore not be of much weight.' Finally a compromise motion was accepted by the House exempting from the Sunday Law pumping, crushing by automatic machinery, and other work the stoppage of which would necessitate the closing down of a mine, provided there was no interference with neighbouring churches, and provided that not more than 5 per cent of employees were involved. This passed by the narrow majority of 14 votes to 10.[72]

As is often the case with puritanism, however, this abundant moral indignation did not always extend to financial, commercial and administrative irregularities.[73] The question of the extent of corruption in the South African Republic will be gone into in more detail later,[74] but it would be a fair summing up at this stage to say that the financial morality of governing circles and of the admini-

---

[71] *Weekly Press*, 11 July 1896 (*Notulen*, Eerste Volksraad, 1896, arts. 870–2).

[72] *Weekly Press*, 14 Nov. 1896, p. 22 (*Notulen*, Eerste Volksraad, 1896, art. 2001).

[73] Walker, *History of South Africa*, p. 434.

[74] See chapter III, section V.

stration bore closer affinities to that of contemporary America (or eighteenth-century England) than to that of Victorian Britain. Indeed, as Jeppe points out in a very fair survey of the whole question, it would have been strange had it been otherwise considering how officials of modest means were placed in contact 'with people who had grown rich reyond the dreams of avarice in a few years, and to whom the favour of the man in authority might make a difference of many thousands'.[75] That there was considerable laxity there can be no doubt.[76] The Auditor-General laid before the Volksraad evidence of deficits in the accounts of magazine masters in Ermelo, Middelburg and Zoutpansberg. In Pretoria, government property to the value of £1,600 was missing.[77] The Postmaster-General reported £877 short in the Johannesburg Telegraph Office.[78] The Commandant-General, demanding that magazine masters be required to lay down a sum of money as surety, declared at various times that many magazine masters had betrayed their trust,[79] that some of the 13,000 Martini-Henry rifles distributed to the burghers had found their way into native hands,[80] that there was a substantial deficiency in the funds of the Native Commissioner's Office in the Zoutpansberg,[81] that there were some 150,000 cartridges short in the Pretoria Central Magazine,[82] and that a deficiency of 'about £11,000' had been discovered after the death of one, Van der Merwe, Native Commissioner of Rhenosterpoort.[83] (This was later found to be £11,646 and the failure to detect the embezzlement was explained by the Auditor-General on the ground that Van der Merwe 'had neglected to send in his monthly statements').[84] A further allegation made against native commissioners in general was by G. Albu, of the Chamber of Mines, who, speaking presumably from considerable experience, declared that, whether the government was aware of it or not, native commissioners always demanded 10s. or £1 per head for natives collected and forwarded to Johannesburg. He asked the government to take measures 'to see that its servants in the native

[75] Jeppe, pp. 144–6.   [76] See Marais, pp. 18–22.   [77] *Volksstem*, 11 Aug. 1894.
[78] *Land en Volk*, 7 July 1891 (*Notulen*, Tweede Volksraad, 1891, art. 689).
[79] *Weekly Press*, 24 Aug. 1895 (*Notulen*, Eerste Volksraad, 1895, art. 939).
[80] *Weekly Press*, 31 Aug. 1895 (*Notulen*, Eerste Volksraad, 1895, art. 1003).
[81] *Weekly Press*, 31 Aug. 1895, p. 11 (*Notulen*, Eerste Volksraad, 1895, art. 991).
[82] *Weekly Press*, 27 June 1896, p. 7 (*Notulen*, Eerste Volksraad 1896, art. 619).
[83] *Weekly Press*, 27 June 1896, p. 19 (*Notulen*, Eerste Volksraad, 1896, art. 660).
[84] *Weekly Press*, 29 Aug. 1896, p. 20 (*Notulen*, Eerste Volksraad, 1896, art. 1273).

districts are sufficiently honest.'[85] Long-current rumours about the Prisons' service in Pretoria finally broke in the revelation that all the warders in the Pretoria gaol were involved in systematic robbery of government goods, that a kaffir-beer brewery was flourishing among the native prisoners, and that white prisoners, for payment received, could get virtually anything that they wanted.[86] The report of the Inspector of Offices in 1897 showed defalcations on the part of officials during the years 1884 to 1896 amounting to £18,590, only a few hundreds of which were ever recovered.[87]

There were constant allegations of the bribery of officials.[88] The pro-government *Volksstem* (24 May 1893) admitted that the frequent criticism in overseas papers of the honesty of officials of the Republic was 'painful to read, particularly when one knows that the allegations are not totally imaginary'. The pro-government *Press* of Pretoria attacked in a leader of 23 March 1894 the 'widespread corruption in the Civil Service', declaring that petty officials expected little bribes for little favours, and that senior officials cared more about their own enrichment than that of the State; and *Land en Volk*, the government's virulent opponent, made frequent detailed and general allegations of widespread bribery and corruption.[89]

Members of the Volksraad were not immune from temptation or from tempting others. A letter to Commandant-General P. J. Joubert by J. van Soelen of Pietersburg alleges that Barend Vorster junior (member for Zoutpansberg of the Second Volksraad) had presented Dominus Coetzee of that district with a 'spider' (a light two-wheeled vehicle drawn by one horse) as an inducement to support his appointment as Native Commissioner to Magato, and declares, 'I visited the Dominus immediately, and found that this was the case'.[90] Vorster, at a public meeting in Pietersburg, admitted that he and eleven other members of the Volksraad had received 'spiders' as presents from his fellow-directors of the proposed Selati Railway Company, but denied that his vote had been influenced by this present and

[85] Evidence to Industrial Commission on 19 Apr. 1897 (*Weekly Press*, 24 Apr. 1897, p. 18); *Notulen*, Eerste Volksraad, 1897, art. 811.

[86] *Volksstem*, 28 Mar. 1894.

[87] Z.A.R. Green Book No. 19 of 1897. See also Z.A.R. Green Book No. 14 of 1898.

[88] Fitzpatrick, *The Transvaal from within*, appendix C and appendix I.

[89] See, for example, *Land en Volk*, 5 May 1891, 12 May 1891 and 26 Jan. 1893.

[90] Joubert Papers, Inkomende Stukke, 105–226 (Archives, vol. 2), no. 154a of 5 Nov. 1894.

added that those who wrote letters to the papers complaining of this 'could for his part, fly to the moon!'[91] Schalk Burger and J. van der Merwe (First Volksraad members for Lydenburg) admitted to having received a hundred £1 shares from Vorster, 'as a token of friendship'[92] and A. D. W. Wolmarans (Pretoria) agreed that he had received 'a present' from Vorster;[93] but like numbers of other legislators who openly admitted having accepted 'spiders and other presents' from the same source, all denied that this had in any way influenced their votes. Carl Jeppe defends this behaviour, on the grounds that 'this was, however, at an early stage of development, and the offending members, most of whom probably did not realize what they did when they accepted the gifts (after they had voted) had an exceedingly bad time of it both in and out of the House'.[94] This defence is, perhaps, more charitable than accurate, for the Selati Railway Company was to stand, for many years yet, in very great need of the goodwill of the Volksraad.[95]

The President himself was from time to time accused of enriching himself and his relatives at the expense of the State. *Land en Volk* (23 June 1891) thundered at his attempts to get the railway line from Pretoria to Delagoa Bay to go over the farms of his relatives and friends (Eloff and Nellmapius) and declared that 'the friends of the President are becoming rich while the burghers sweat'. There was much criticism of the way in which the concession to bring water to Johannesburg from the Vaal had been granted by the Executive Council, via the President's son-in-law, F. C. Eloff,[96] who was alleged to have made £20,000 on the deal.[97] And even Jeppe, who inclines towards the charitable side (in 1906 when he wrote his book, at any rate, if not ten years earlier, when he was one of the fiercest critics of the government), opines that Kruger was 'by no means averse to seeing his friends and relations enrich themselves by con-

[91] *Volksstem*, 23 Mar. 1891. See also *Volksstem*, 26 Mar. 1891, for admission by Mr. J. J. Spies (Utrecht) of acceptance from Vorster of a shotgun and a salted riding-horse.

[92] *Volksstem*, 26 Mar. 1891 and 6 Apr. 1891.

[93] *Volksstem*, 27 Apr. 1891. (It was a golden repeater watch worth £75. See *Land en Volk*, 5 Dec. 1895, for details.)

[94] Jeppe, p. 145.   [95] See pp. 79–85.

[96] Second Volksraad, 29 June 1893; *Volksstem*, 1 July 1893 (*Notulen*, Tweede Volksraad, 1892, art. 469).

[97] *Land en Volk*, 16 Jan. 1893, 26 Jan. 1893, 2 Feb. 1893, 14 Dec. 1893; Fitzpatrick, p. 69.

cessions and similar means', though he points out that the President himself 'did not share in the spoils. His financial prosperity is easily explicable in other ways.'[98]

The attitude of the legislators and burghers towards this somewhat lax state of affairs was a tolerant one. With so much money being made out of the country by foreigners it was not felt to be wrong that some pickings, at any rate, should come the way of the 'Zonen des lands'. In spite of a considerable press agitation little objection appeared to exist to the acceptance of 'presents' by legislators. At the meetings addressed by Schalk Burger and J. van der Merwe in which they admitted these allegations and 'left it to their constituents to judge',[99] votes of full confidence were passed without a question being asked.[1] And the *Volksstem* (18 July 1891) grudgingly admitted that there was no very strong public feeling on the matter.

Major offenders, it is true, were charged and often sentenced to short periods of imprisonment,[2] but minor offenders were usually dismissed and sometimes reappointed to other posts in the government service.[3] Speculation by officials was defended on more than one occasion in the Volksraad. In spite of the fact that Law 19 of 1892 forbade speculation by officials, I. J. Meijer (Middelburg) felt that 'officials could not be blamed for speculating if they saw a chance of profit in it'. The President declared that although officials should not speculate 'in matters concerning their work, it was unfair to say that an official could not fairly act in his own interests otherwise'.[4] N. S. Malherbe (Potchefstroom, and later Chairman of the Second Volksraad) said 'it pained him to hear His Excellency repeatedly defending the right of officials to speculate. . . . One must choose between being a speculator and an official', but his motion asking for an investigation by the government into malpractices by officials was defeated by 15 votes to 8.[5] As late as 1896 Lukas Meyer (Vryheid) was declaring that in spite of repeated discoveries of shortages of cash and equipment 'it was shameful that no Magazine Master had as yet been prosecuted and punished for any deficiency'.[6]

[98] Jeppe, p. 168.
[99] S. W. Burger at Weltevreden (Komati); *Volksstem*, 26 Mar. 1891.
[1] *Volksstem*, 26 Mar. 1891 and 6 Apr. 1891.
[2] Z.A.R. Green Book No. 19 of 1897.
[3] See the case of Ribbink, *Land en Volk*, 7 July 1891.
[4] *Volksstem*, 5 Aug. 1893 (*Notulen*, Tweede Volksraad, 1893, art. 728).
[5] *Volksstem*, 8 Aug. 1893 (*Notulen*, Tweede Volksraad, 1893, art. 733).
[6] *Weekly Press*, 9 May 1896, p. 11.

Most of the legislators seemed to share the feelings of P. J. Schutte (Potchefstroom), who, in discussing the admitted disappearance of 150,000 cartridges from the Pretoria Magazine, declared that 'he could not believe that the Magazine Master, who was a trusty old burgher, had been guilty of wilful fraud. It was probably a mistake in the books.'[7]

In short, while it is not necessary to take as literal truth Commandant-General P. J. Joubert's allegation that 'if the French people lived here and we could have an impartial investigation into all financial matters, we should find the same things here as the present Panama scandal in France is now revealing',[8] it is nevertheless clear that a considerable degree of laxity in matters of financial morality among legislators and State officials was tolerated.

II

Here then are some of the beliefs, prejudices and preconceptions in the teeth of which a modern state had to be created. We have seen that President Kruger to some extent shared these preconceptions. His colour prejudices were the same as those of most burghers. He was capable of making pronouncements such as that 'every adult kaffir ought to pay hut tax whether he had a hut or not. He ought to have a hut!'[9] He shared the burghers' dislike of Indians and spoke in favour of a motion to remove from the towns all 'coolies' who had entered commerce since 1889; they could become farm labourers.[10] He, with every other member of the Volksraad, agreed that there was no question of franchise rights on any terms for coloured people.[11] Nor, as we have seen, can his attitude towards education be regarded as particularly progressive. The standards he set were low. 'Certificated teachers', he declared, 'were not needed for country schools. If they were religious and could write a little it would do; but if they failed in these two branches of education they were incompetent.'[12] This was hardly in tune with the crying need of the times. Further we

[7] *Weekly Press*, 27 June 1896 (*Notulen*, Eerste Volksraad, 1896, art. 620).

[8] Joubert Papers, Uitgaande Stukke, II A/1–A/3 (Archives, vol. 17), no. 361, letter of 20 Feb. 1893 to Veld-kornet of Potchefstroom.

[9] *Volksstem*, 9 Aug. 1892 (*Notulen*, Eerste Volksraad, 1892, arts. 1078–9).

[10] *Volksstem*, 9 Aug. 1892.

[11] *Volksstem*, 6 June 1894 (*Notulen*, Eerste Volksraad, 1894, art. 287).

[12] *Press*, 7 May 1892 (*Notulen*, Eerste Volksraad, 1892, art. 45). See also Manfred Nathan's criticism of his neglect of elementary education. (*Paul Kruger, His Life and Times*, p. 253).

have noted that he was prepared to tolerate, and frequently to defend, somewhat lax standards on the part of his officials.

There is, however, a credit side, which in the light of his own limited education and narrow background[13] shows a flexibility of mind and an ability to adapt himself to changing circumstances which do not entirely bear out the picture of a granite Cromwellian patriarch entirely unmoved by the fierce blasts of what modern times would call the 'winds of change' assailing his state. This is the essence of the admiring picture given of him by Jeppe who, after talking of 'his marvellous intellect, coupled as it was with an indomitable will power', describes his failure as 'due to the defects of his type. Virile and unbending in the highest degree, Kruger refused to accommodate himself to circumstances; and, disdaining to stoop, he was crushed by the irresistible storms he encountered.'[14]

In one thing, certainly, Kruger was entirely inflexible, and that was in his determination to preserve the Afrikaner and republican character of the State,[15] and in his opposition to all that threatened to weaken or undermine this he was indeed 'unbending in the highest degree'. Preservation of the independence of the State he regarded as a sacred duty, neglect of which would bring down upon him the curse of God.[16]

In most other matters, however, the President used his influence on the side of moderation and of concession to the reasonable demands of the uitlanders and the needs of progress. The President could not go too far ahead of his burghers,[17] and the conservatism and prejudice against the newcomers of the mass of the burghers, and of the legislators, were considerable. The Pretoria *Press*, a constant if critical supporter of Kruger, was not exaggerating by very much when it stated (15 February 1892) that the President was 'the only person who could reconcile the old and new populations' and referred to his vital role in 'converting the burghers from their bitter old-time prejudices'. A clear instance of this was the introduction in 1891 of the Second Volksraad, which met with some opposition from the burghers,[18] and which, though in no way satis-

[13] Walker, *History of S. Africa*, p. 262; *C.H.B.E.*, vol. viii, pp. 500–1; Nathan, *Paul Kruger*, pp. 9–17.

[14] Jeppe, pp. 159–60. See also Fitzpatrick, pp. 1–2.

[15] See pp. 139–83.

[16] See quotation on p. 176.   [17] But see pp. 171–5.

[18] *Volksstem*, 28 Apr. 1890, 19 June 1890, 23 June 1890 (*Notulen*, Eerste Volksraad, 1890, arts. 366–9, 381–446).

fying uitlander demands, did at least give the newcomers some slight voice in the affairs of the State. His doughty opponent, J. F. Celliers (member for Johannesburg of the Second Volksraad), declared in a speech to the Pretoria Literary and Debating Society that 'the measure to create a second Chamber met from the very outset with strong opposition in the Volksraad, and it was ultimately passed through the sheer force of the President's personality'.[19] (Celliers had been one of the opponents of the idea when a member of the First Volksraad in 1890.[20]) In proposing the Second Volksraad as 'a middle way' the President stated that although there was a danger of the loss of their independence if thousands of strangers got the franchise, since the number of newcomers already exceeded the number of original burghers, 'there was also the injustice of granting them no rights' and a danger of disturbances. 'Many of the newcomers, moreover,' he pointed out, 'meant well by the country and were prepared to throw in their lot with it, and it would be wrong to reject them.'[21] In the same debate (which occurred shortly after the notorious flag incident in Johannesburg, in the course of which the President and the flag of the Republic had been insulted[22]) the President, in answer to protests against giving any rights at all to people who insulted the flag of the Republic, declared that many had wished to defend him at that time, including Englishmen, and that 'there were as many loyal people in Johannesburg as elsewhere in the Republic'. In an equally bitter debate in 1894 on a memorial asking for the removal of members who had fought on the side of the English in 1881 (this was directed at Jeppe and Loveday) the President called upon members to forgive and forget. The franchise had been given to those persons by law. What they had done before was therefore irrelevant. 'If they did evil *now*, let complaints be made.'[23] And in his opening speech to the First Raad in May 1898 he went out of his way to praise those who had become naturalized burghers and even those 'who preferred to remain strangers in the country. The government welcomed them and allowed them to make as much money as they could, and would even help them in the accumulation of riches, and when they had made their fortunes and

[19] *Press*, 29 Mar. 1892.

[20] *Volksstem*, 19 June 1890 (*Notulen*, Eerste Volksraad, 1890, art. 381).

[21] *Volksstem*, 19 June 1890 (*Notulen*, Eerste Volksraad, 1890, art. 395).

[22] *Volksstem*, 6 Mar. 1890, 10 Mar. 1890.

[23] *Volksstem*, 1 Sept. 1894 (*Notulen*, Eerste Volksraad, 1894, art. 1546).

left the country the government regretted to lose friends, but should they want to come back at any time they would be welcomed.'[24] On the other hand, of course, there must be weighed against this the President's adamant determination to keep the control of the State in the hands of the old burghers,[25] and his resistance to any attempts by the Second Raad to increase its power. From the beginning he stressed the First Raad's absolute power of veto upon any decision of the subordinate body;[26] and he adamantly opposed Esselen's request for a sum of money to be placed at the disposal of the Second Raad on the grounds that 'the finances of the country were a matter for the First Raad alone' (alleen thuis zijn bij den Eersten Volksraad), that all decisions of the Second Raad had to be approved by the First, and that if the First Raad approved an action projected by the Second Raad it would itself allocate the necessary funds.[27]

Nevertheless, on balance, it is fair to say that Kruger did stand for a policy of reconciliation between the old and the new inhabitants of the country, and a very cursory acquaintance with the bitter feelings of some of the real diehard Anglophobes[28] will show how comparatively moderate the President was.

On most other matters the President was well in advance of the sentiments of the more conservative legislators, and not always successfully so. In a speech at Christiana he attempted, without much result (*Volksstem*, 20 March 1890), to persuade the burghers of the need for a Department of Agriculture; and a few months later he spoke strongly for it in the Volksraad, but was defeated by 22 votes to 10.[29] We have noted his failure to persuade the Volksraad of the necessity to register births, marriages and deaths. (The vote was 17 to 7 against the proposal.) He was a little more successful in convincing the Volksraad of the need to allow the marriage by civil law of natives, the proposal being carried by the narrow majority of

[24] *Weekly Press*, 14 May 1898 (*Notulen*, Eerste Volksraad, 1898, art. 9).

[25] See the report of his discussion with Justice De Villiers (*Weekly Press*, 19 Feb. 1898, p. 9); below, pp. 151–2.

[26] *Volksstem*, 4 June 1891 (*Notulen*, Eerste Volksraad, 1891, art. 245).

[27] *Volksstem*, 23 July 1891 (*Notulen*, Tweede Volksraad, 1891, art. 886).

[28] See, for example, the sentiments expressed by J. P. L. Lombaard, A. D. W. Wolmarans, C. J. Tosen and J. de Beer (First Volksraad, 4/5 June 1894), P. G. Roos, P. Schutte and J. de Clercq (First Volksraad, 30 Aug. 1894), J. H. de la Rey, P. de la Rey and C. B. Otto (First Volksraad, 14 Aug. 1895).

[29] *Volksstem*, 12 May 1890 (*Notulen*, Eerste Volksraad, 1890, art. 42).

12 votes to 10,[30] and in securing the exemption of civilized natives from the necessity of carrying pass badges.[31] He supported the successful motion of the two progressive members of the Second Raad, E. P. A. Meintjies (Pretoria) and E. Esselen, to abolish public executions;[32] and even went so far as to defend science, at Krugersdorp, as long as it 'did not endeavour to ignore and overthrow religion'.[33] He expressed, and showed, a remarkable degree of tolerance, for a man of his narrowly Calvinist views, of Roman Catholics and Jews. He answered objections to the principle of educational subsidies for Catholic children by stating bluntly that as long as Catholics obeyed the law they were entitled to equal treatment,[34] and, although bowing to popular feeling in the matter of head officials, defended the right of 'deserving' Catholics to hold junior posts in the government service.[35] His friendship with a number of Jews was the (unavailing) subject of constant bitter attack in *Land en Volk*. He gave money generously to Jewish (and Anglican) charities,[36] and declared in a speech at the opening of the Johannesburg synagogue, 'I call those my people who obey the laws of our land. . . . The Jews are God's old people. . . . I respect the Jewish and other faiths without distinction' (*Volksstem*, 17 September 1892). By August 1899, though no doubt under pressure, he proposed to the Raad the abolition of the religious tests which debarred Catholics and Jews from membership of the Volksraad and appointment as state officials, and expressed his desire to have the words 'all who believe in the revelation of God through His word in the Bible' put in the place of the word 'Protestants' in the relevant laws.[37]

On the even more touchy colour question, although he was, as has been indicated, no 'liberal', he was at any rate consistently more progressive than a good many of the legislators. At a public meeting near Pretoria (*Volksstem*, 6 January 1890) he refused to agree with a questioner who opined that natives ought to have fewer legal rights than white men. A little later, in the Volksraad, answering objections

[30] *Weekly Press*, 13 June 1896 (*Notulen*, Eerste Volksraad, 1896, art. 529).

[31] *Weekly Press*, 14 Aug. 1897 (*Notulen*, Eerste Volksraad, 1897, arts. 832–6).

[32] *Volksstem*, 22 June 1892 (*Notulen*, Tweede Volksraad, 1892, art. 490).

[33] *Press*, 7 Dec. 1892.

[34] *Volksstem*, 16 Jan. 1890 (speech at Carolina).

[35] *Volksstem*; 25 July 1894 (*Notulen*, Eerste Volksraad, 1894, art. 929).

[36] *Volksstem*, 27 Mar. 1895; Nathan, p. 276; *Volksstem*, 14 Nov. 1893.

[37] *Weekly Press*, 19 Aug. 1899 (letter of President Kruger to the Volksraad). See Marais, p. 203, note 1.

to the consideration by the Raad of memorials from coloured people, 'because it looked too much like equality', the President declared that the Raad should make no distinction in such matters between the various races in this country. 'Let distinctions exist in the social sphere—the greater the better—but as far as law and justice were concerned, the highest body in the country must always be open to receive and consider requests and complaints, no matter from whom, even from the lowest'[38] (laagstgezonkenen). He opposed, but unsuccessfully, the rather mean proposal by Tosen (Piet Retief) to reduce the annual salary of the native constable of Amsterdam from £26 to £13 10s.[39] In 1893 he called for 'the allocation of sufficient locations to natives, so that the tribes should not be oppressed', and opposed suggestions that no locations be given to small groups of natives, declaring that such small groups were often the most faithful to the government 'and was it fair or Christian to drive them from the land'.[40] In 1895, after the Malaboch campaign, he proposed, against considerable opposition (including that of A. D. W. Wolmarans, who accused the President of 'wanting equality for kaffirs'), to distribute a sum of £10,000 among loyal native supporters in the recent war.[41]

Of course from time to time President Kruger's prejudices did peep out, as, for example, in his opposition to postal pillar-boxes for Pretoria, and in his advice to the First Raad (accepted by 19 votes to 7) not to approve of a Second Raad motion allowing the purchase of diamond drills for prospecting purposes 'for already there was enough gold discovered in the State'.[42]

That the President was not the obdurate and intransigent foe of progress that he was sometimes represented to be, has, I think, been sufficiently indicated. Kruger, personally, did not regard himself as the foe of progress. In his closing speech to the special session of the Volksraad in March 1898, he declared that the Republic's enemies said, ' "Paul Kruger does not go ahead. He is too slow, and there is

[38] *Volksstem*, 31 July 1890 (*Notulen*, Eerste Volksraad, 1890, art. 1130, refers only to 'some discussion').

[39] *Volksstem*, 17 July 1890 (*Notulen*, Eerste Volksraad, 1890, art. 829, does not record Kruger as having spoken).

[40] *Volksstem*, 6 Sept. 1893 (*Notulen*, Eerste Volksraad, 1893, art. 1320).

[41] *Land en Volk*, 20 June 1895 (*Notulen*, Eerste Volksraad, 1895, art. 331). (Misprinted in *Notulen* as 231.)

[42] *Weekly Press*, 5 Oct. 1895 (report of First Raad debate of 27 Sept. 1895. Not mentioned in *Notulen*).

no progress in this country." But, gentlemen, that is not so. What they really do believe in their hearts, and what they hate, is that we are going too fast for them. They don't like the rapidity of our progress.'[43]

This was not without a certain inner truth, in the sense that the Transvaal's wealth and economic strength were expanding with impressive speed. Imports, for example, had increased from £367,544 in 1883 to £5,371,701 in 1893. By that date, too, nearly 5 million ounces of gold had been produced, worth £17½ million.[44] The production of gold had risen from 208,122 ounces in 1883 to 729,268 ounces in 1891, 2,024,163 ounces in 1894 and 3,034,678 ounces in 1897.[45] The revenue to the State from the mines was £972,311 in 1894. In that year the mines spent £6,153,410, of which £3,479,623 went in wages. The value of buildings in Johannesburg alone was placed at £4,254,441.[46] The revenue of the Republic, which in 1885–6 had amounted only to £177,877, had increased by 1896 to £3,912,095.[47] Money was plentiful, the cities provided a flourishing market for the farmers, and land values increased. Officials were now paid salaries that would have shocked their predecessors of fifteen years before. The President received a salary of £8,000 per annum and a £300 rent (or coffee) allowance,[48] though the salary was reduced, at his own request, to £7,000 in 1893.[49] Non-official members of the Executive Council were paid £1,350 annually. The State Secretary's salary was £1,500.[50] The Chief Justice received £1,850 to £2,000,[51] the State Attorney £1,350, and civil service clerks from £130 to £550.[52] (This was at a time when house rents in the cities varied from about £4 to £8 a month[53] and a suit could be bought for

[43] *Weekly Press*, 19 Mar. 1898, p. 5 (*Notulen*, Eerste Volksraad, 1898, art. 351.)

[44] *Volksstem*, 5 May 1894.

[45] *Weekly Press*, 16 Apr. 1898.

[46] Report of Minister of Mines for 1894. *Weekly Press*, 22 June 1895, p. 4.

[47] *C.H.B.E.*, vol. viii, p. 543.

[48] *Volksstem*, 10 July 1890 (*Notulen*, Eerste Volksraad, 1890, arts. 604, 609); Nathan, p. 276.

[49] *Volksstem*, 6 Sept. 1893 (*Notulen*, Eerste Volksraad, 1893, art. 1307).

[50] Ibid. (*Notulen*, 1893, arts. 1310, 1313.)

[51] *Notulen*, Eerste Volksraad, 1893, art. 597, 'Begrooting', ch. XV.

[52] *Volksstem*, 11 Aug. 1894 (*Notulen*, Eerste Volksraad, 1894, arts. 1205, 1215, 1228).

[53] Joubert Papers, Letter Book 2318A, p. 87 (Archives, vol. 24), for rents charged by Joubert to various tenants.

35s.,[54] to give some standards of comparison.)

In this sense, certainly, the 'progress' of the Republic was beyond dispute. The Gold Law, too, was 'liberal, far more so than that of Rhodes's Chartered Company', and its Pass Laws, Illicit Liquor and Gold Thefts Law, 'though poorly administered . . . had at least been passed in the interests of the new industry'.[55] Indeed there is much to be said for J. H. Hofmeyr's view in his chapter of the *Cambridge History of the British Empire* that, 'taken unawares as it was by a set of new problems for which it was entirely unequipped, the Republican Government met the situation, at least during the first few years, with what was in the circumstances surprising success. The legislation necessitated by the birth of the new industry was well conceived; towards the town of Johannesburg the Government acted with a great deal of liberality, and in the choice of many of its chief officials on the Witwatersrand it was very fortunate.'[56]

But whether after those first few years the progress permitted by the government was at all adequate to the growing needs of the times was a very much more arguable question. Certainly there were an increasing number of Transvaal burghers who did not think so; and as the years went by and uitlander discontent mounted, so more and more burghers and legislators began to regard President Kruger's régime with an ever more critical eye. Hostility to the government among the burghers mounted with surprising rapidity. It is to the growth of this movement of opposition to Kruger and his régime among his own people, and to the policies and motives of the leaders of that opposition, that we must now turn.

[54] *Weekly Press*, 15 Aug. 1897 (evidence of Mr. Robert Barrow, miner, to the Industrial Commission), p. 6.
[55] Walker, *History of S. Africa*, p. 434.
[56] *C.H.B.E.*, vol. viii, p. 543.

2

The Issues around which Opposition Crystallized

In essence the opposition to Kruger's government, among the burghers (and they largely echoed uitlander sentiment in this, if indeed they were not largely impelled by it), coalesced around some half-dozen basic issues, each of which in its turn ramified into a number of subordinate issues, and all of which were to a considerable degree interdependent. Acting upon one another, stepping into the breach to do duty for one another in the assault upon the government, one issue receding as another took the foreground, sometimes gaining and sometimes losing adherents, these issues, between them, formed a nucleus around which a considerable body of opposition formed itself, an opposition which in the elections of 1893 very nearly ejected Kruger from his Presidency, and which, but for the violent events of 1895 and subsequent years, might well have achieved a reformed South African Republic, much more progressive in its policy, taking a co-operative and leading place among the states of South Africa.[1] Basically, these issues (arranged neither in order of merit nor chronologically, for they all operated throughout the five-year period under consideration in this book) were (I) the financial policy of the Republic, (II) the policy of concessions and monopolies in general, (III) the dynamite monopoly in particular,

---

[1] (a) Mr. Merriman, speaking at Dordrecht on 3 Aug. 1898 declared that, in his opinion, Rhodes had pushed the Raid on because he feared just such a Republic. 'The Raid', he declared, 'had rehabilitated the Transvaal Government' (*Weekly Press*, 6 Aug. 1898).

(b) General Joubert, writing to the editor of the *Zuid Afrikaan* on 1 Oct. 1899, declared that it was neither the franchise nor uitlander grievances that had caused the war, but fear of an Afrikaner-dominated South Africa, led by the Transvaal. ('Het is niet de stemrecht, het is niet Uitlander-grieven, neen, het is de Afrikaner Bond in de Kaap Kolonie, haar schuld alleen. U heeft Cecil Rhodes, Jameson's baas, uitgehaald uit het premierschap, en nu de Bond zal over het hoofd van Chamberlain's Empire groeien, en daarom en daarvoor, zullen nu eerst de Transvaal en O.V.S. en de Afrikaner Bond uit de map van Zuid Afrika moeten gewascht worden' (Joubert Papers, K.G., part I, 1 Oct. 1899).

(IV) railway policy, (V) the alleged inefficiency and corruption of the administration, (VI) educational policy, (VII) the policy of appointing Hollanders to important posts in the civil service, and (VIII) the all-important question of the admission to or exclusion from the franchise of the uitlander population.

It would perhaps be wisest if we were to consider as briefly as possible the nature of each of these issues, and estimate to what extent each acted as a precipitating factor in the growth of opposition to the régime. After that, it will be easier to trace the growth of that opposition between 1890 and 1895, to try to estimate to what extent a 'Progressive Party' in any real sense of either of those words had arisen by 1895, to determine what the relationship of Commandant-General P. J. Joubert with that party was and to what extent he may be considered 'progressive' in his principles, and to outline who the members of the party were and what the part was that each played in opposing the policies of the President. These questions will form the main body of the remainder of this study.

I. FINANCIAL POLICY

The financial situation of the Republic during 1890 and 1891 was admitted by friends and enemies alike to be far from rosy.[2] The financial disasters of 1889 (when, after much expenditure of capital, a number of companies had collapsed and mining shares had fallen into disrepute[3]) were still making their effects felt.[4] The report of the Finance Committee presented to the Volksraad on 4 July 1890[5] criticized the government for its large payments by way of loans to the Netherlands Railway Company. By 1891 the total income of the State had sunk from £526,202 in 1890 to £333,472, a decrease of some £192,730, and import duties from £159,542 in 1890 to £97,323 in 1891.[6]

The call for economy in administration, and for greater efficiency, rose in intensity even among the government's supporters. The *Volksstem*, in a series of leading articles during January 1892, criticized the Volksraad's lack of any real control over expenditure by

[2] See *Land en Volk*, 6 Jan. 1891, 1 Mar. 1892; *Volksstem*, 7 July 1890, 14 July 1890, 8 Dec. 1891, 24 Dec. 1891.

[3] De Kiewiet, *History of South Africa, Economic and Social*, p. 130.

[4] *Land en Volk*, 6 Jan. 1891.

[5] *Notulen*, Eerste Volksraad, 1890, arts. 567–8.

[6] *Volksstem*, 14 July 1891.

the Executive, and poured scorn upon the remarkable vagueness of the estimates. It rejected, however, any suggestion for the appointment of a proper Finance Minister, responsible to the Volksraad and not to the Executive, as out of tune with the Transvaal's system of government, and pressed instead for detailed estimates of expenditure.

Meanwhile the government's opponents were not letting the opportunity slide. In October 1890 Ewald Esselen, who had recently resigned as a judge of the High Court in order to more openly oppose the government,[7] made a vigorous attack at Potchefstroom on the whole financial policy of the State, and demanded a commission of inquiry into the financial administration of the last ten years. There was no country in the world, he declared (*Volksstem*, 30 October 1891), where the people were so ignorant and careless of what happened to the national finance. His accusations, and demands, were echoed by Lukas Meyer, that greatly respected patriot of 'New Republic' fame, who had just offered himself to the electors of Vryheid as a candidate for the First Volksraad.[8] R. K. Loveday, the strongly anti-government member for Barberton of the First Volksraad, violently attacked the wastefulness of State expenditure, before an enthusiastic audience.[9]

Towards the end of 1891 the public were informed, by proclamation in the *Staatscourant*, that, from 1 December, tolls of 30s. would have to be paid on all main roads by ox-wagons carrying loads of up to 6,000 lb. There was immediate opposition on the ground that it would send up the already high cost of living.[10] Nor was the haphazard system by which it was applied particularly popular, for the right to levy these tolls at the stipulated points was put up to public auction, the successful applicant paying the amount of his tender to the government and taking his chance of making a profit or loss.[11] In June 1892, in response to public pressure, the newly elected Second Volksraad requested the abolition of tolls, and the First Raad, rejecting a Presidential plea, decided by 11 votes to 10 to yield to the public clamour, and abolished all tolls.[12]

---

[7] *Volksstem*, 14 Aug. 1890, 28 Aug. 1890.

[8] *Volksstem*, 26 Nov. 1891; *Land en Volk*, 24 Nov. 1891.

[9] *Volksstem*, 31 Dec. 1891; *Land en Volk*, 15 Dec. 1891.

[10] *Land en Volk*, 15 Dec. 1891; *Press*, 28 Apr. 1892.

[11] *Press*, 28 Apr. 1892.

[12] *Volksstem*, 29 June 1892 (*Notulen*, Eerste Volksraad, 1892, arts. 598–626).

A simultaneous agitation had been going on, as is the case at all times of financial stringency, for a reduction in officials' salaries. In July 1890, by 25 votes to 11,[13] the Volksraad refused the President's request to raise the salary of the Secretary of the Volksraad from £500 to £550, and also rejected his suggestion to raise that of the non-official member and secretary of the Executive Council, W. E. Bok,[14] from £1,000 to £1,200.[15] The urge for economy was further satisfied by the reduction of the annual salary of the native constable at Amsterdam (near Piet Retief) from £26 to £13 10s.[16] The 1892 session saw a number of memorials calling for the reduction of the President's salary from £8,000 to £5,000 or even £4,000 per annum, and for a 10 per cent reduction in all official salaries. The latter suggestion was rejected by 13 votes to 8; but it is interesting to notice that the minority included the hard core of what was later to become the Progressive party. The attack then shifted to the President's salary. L. Meyer (Vryheid) said that it had been doubled in 1888 to £4,000 and doubled again in 1889 to £8,000 and was 'an unheard of salary for a Republic such as this'. His Excellency, who declined all invitations to leave the Chamber, protested that 'The Raad had decided not to reduce salaries, and is it fair now to reduce only mine'. However, the Raad decided by 17 votes to 5 to make no reduction.[17] Nearly all those who spoke for reduction (J. J. Spies— Utrecht, P. G. Maré—Zoutpansberg, C. Birkenstock—Vryheid, L. Meyer—Vryheid, R. K. Loveday—Barberton, and Schalk Burger— Lydenburg) became, later, recognized members of the Progressive party. (The Presidential salary was, in fact, later reduced to £7,000 p.a. by the President's own motion, because of continual public complaint against it,[18] although by that time, as we shall see, the financial situation had improved beyond all recognition.)

A closely related financial issue around which opposition crystallized was the question of import duties. These duties, whether protective or revenue-producing, had been, and were to become increasingly, a serious bone of contention between the mining

[13] The Volksraad consisted of 36 members at this time. It was reduced to 24 after the 1890 session. (See *Volksstem*, 4 Aug. 1890.)

[14] See p. 133–4, and Leyds: *Onze Eerste Jaren in Zuid Afrika*, for an explanation of the general dislike of Bok.

[15] *Volksstem*, 10 July 1890 (*Notulen*, Eerste Volksraad, 1890, art. 611).

[16] *Volksstem*, 17 July 1890 (*Notulen*, Eerste Volksraad, 1890, art. 829).

[17] *Volksstem*, 2 July 1892 (*Notulen*, Eerste Volksraad, 1892, art. 595).

[18] *Volksstem*, 6 Sept. 1893 (*Notulen*, Eerste Volksraad, 1893, art. 1307).

industry and the government. In March 1890 during the crisis of confidence referred to at the beginning of this section, a deputation from the Chamber of Mines, led by Hermann Eckstein, had pressed the Minister of Mines, C. J. Joubert, for a reduction of the import duties on foodstuffs, mining machinery and other items. It was, perhaps, in response to this that Kruger, shortly afterwards, announced the temporary suspension of import duties on certain foodstuffs.[19] By the middle of 1892, however, returning prosperity led to the raising of the *ad valorem* duty on general goods from 5 to $7\frac{1}{2}$ per cent, and to the raising of tariffs on a number of specified articles (ranging from 3*d.* a pound on dynamite, 5*s.* per 1,000 rounds of ammunition, 2*s.* 6*d.* per 100 lb. of tea, to £4 10*s.* per 100 lb. of bacon, 3*s.* per gallon on beer, 6*s.* to 10*s.* per gallon on other alcoholic drinks and 100 per cent on printed matter).[20] The latter duties were designed to protect Transvaal products. This led to an immediate storm of protest not only in the Cape and in England,[21] but inside the Transvaal itself. By late October 1892 the *Volksstem*, which had welcomed the raised tariffs and poured scorn on Cape and British opposition, was admitting that this move had had the opposite effect upon the farming population to what had been intended, and that the Volksraad would have to lower tariffs. President Kruger, on his electioneering rounds in the platteland, encountered consistent dissatisfaction over the cost of imported products, and, though declaring that the sole aim of the increase had been to please the farmers and protect local produce, was forced to promise the removal of these unpopular duties.[22] At the opening session of the First Raad in May 1893, consequently, the President recommended the lowering of import duties on certain articles not produced in any quantity in the Republic.[23]

A year later memorials to the First Raad from Johannesburg were still complaining of the high duties on bread (which cost three times what it cost in Europe, Australia or America) and other foodstuffs. A petition from the Johannesburg Chamber of Commerce asked for the reduction of the *ad valorem* duty on general goods from $7\frac{1}{2}$ to 5 per cent and complained particularly of the heavy duty of 100 per

[19] *Volksstem*, 8 May 1890 (*Notulen*, Eerste Volksraad, 1890, art. 10).
[20] *Volksstem*, 16 Aug. 1892 (*Notulen*, Eerste Volksraad, 1892, art. 1150).
[21] *Volksstem*, 3 Sept. 1892.
[22] *Volksstem*, 5 Nov. 1892.
[23] *Volksstem*, 2 May 1893 (*Notulen*, Eerste Volksraad, 1893, art. 14).

cent on printed matter.[24] But the Raad, by 16 votes to 8, supported the President in refusing reductions. Six members specifically desired their contrary votes to be recorded (C. Jeppe—Johannesburg, L. Meyer—Vryheid, L. de Jager—Ermelo, G. de Jager—Wakkerstroom, R. K. Loveday—Barberton, and J. J. Spies—Utrecht).[25] It is clear that opposition to the régime was hardening around this, as around other issues, and even the pro-government *Volksstem*, in a leader of 16 June 1894, condemned the government's policy and demonstrated from the import figures that many of the duties protected no one and benefited no one. The pro-government *Press*, though declaring that the Transvaal duties could be favourably compared with those levied by the Cape Colony,[26] admitted that of the £1,987,800 received by the State from all sources in the eleven months ending on 30 November 1894, customs duties headed the list with the handsome total of £811,000. The government did eventually bow to the popular clamour and reduce special duties on foodstuffs considerably; but not before it had earned considerable unpopularity—not only with the uitlanders, but with the burghers themselves, for, as Jeppe points out,[27] these 'extremely unpopular duties . . . often carried only by the strenuous efforts of the President, were as hotly opposed in Pretoria as in Johannesburg'.

While all this was going on, another aspect of financial policy, the government's decision to found a State-sponsored bank, the 'Nationale Bank der Zuid Afrikaansche Republiek Beperkt' with a capital of £4 million, was also arousing some opposition. By the terms of its concession the National Bank was to have the preferential right to carry out all the Republic's financial dealings overseas, was to advance money to the government at 6 per cent and was to establish a mint, at its own cost, in Pretoria, ownership of which was to be ceded to the government upon completion, although it was to be hired to the bank for twenty-five years. Control was to be vested in a board of not more than eleven members, of whom the majority had to reside in the Republic.[28] After considerable argument in the Raad a concession on these terms was granted by 17 votes to 10, a number of usually pro-government members (including those two old con-

---

[24] *Volksstem*, 9 June 1894.   [25] *Volksstem*, 9 June 1894.

[26] It should be remembered, of course, that the inhabitants of the S.A.R. had to pay *both* duties. (See P. J. Joubert's speech in London; *Volksstem*, 15 Sept. 1890.)

[27] Jeppe, p. 142.   [28] *Volksstem*, 7 Aug. 1890.

servative stalwarts, D. P. Taljaard, the 'Nestor of the Raad', and
J. P. L. Lombaard, both of Standerton) joining the more usual
opponents of the government.[29]

It was not long before objections began to be voiced. The *Volksstem* (11 May 1890) considered that a concession for fifty years was
too generous, and that the bank should pay interest on the considerable sums of State money that it would hold, though in general
welcoming the new bank as a steadying influence. It considered
6 per cent a very high rate for the State to pay;[30] and opined that a
3 per cent minting rate compared more than generously with
$\frac{1}{3}$ in Holland and no charge at all in England. *Land en Volk* (20
January 1891) inveighed against the National Bank as 'not the
cornerstone but the gravestone of the country'. The Republic survived, however, and although sporadic criticisms continued, the bank
prospered and became generally accepted.[31] Nevertheless its foundation and continuance remained a source of grievance in anti-
government circles, and as late as 1897 Schalk Burger used it in his
attack on the government, asking, 'What advantage have we had
from the so-called National Bank, and who are its shareholders?'[32]

A further issue on which the legislators were sharply divided was
the matter of the State loan of one to three million pounds which
President Kruger sought permission to raise in 1891. This amount
was required chiefly for the Netherlands Railway Company's
Delagoa Bay line, although allegedly also for public works.[33] The
failure of European capitalists to support the loan at $4\frac{1}{2}$ per cent
brought further sharp criticism of the government.[34] The President
was therefore forced to approach the First Raad again, this time to
raise the same sum at 5 per cent via Rothschilds of London.[35] There
was much reference to public opposition against loading the country
with debt, but an earnest plea by Dr. Leyds finally secured the necessary permission from the Raad, by 15 votes to 7. However, those who
voted against the motion consisted largely of members whose names
were becoming increasingly familiar as habitual opponents of the
government (L. Meyer—Utrecht, R. K. Loveday—Barberton, P.
Maré—Zoutpansberg, Schalk Burger—Lydenburg, J. de Clercq—

[29] *Volksstem*, 14 Aug. 1890.
[30] *Volksstem*, 14 Aug. 1890.   [31] *Volksstem*, 15 July 1893.
[32] Joubert Papers: Inkomende Stukke, I A/10–17 (Archives, vol. 7), no. 726.
[33] *Volksstem*, 1 Aug. 1891; *Land en Volk*, 30 June 1892.
[34] *Press*, 15 Feb. 1892; *Volksstem*, 29 Oct. 1891; *Land en Volk*, 1 Mar. 1892.
[35] *Land en Volk*, 30 June 1892 (*Notulen*, Eerste Volksraad, 1892, arts. 572–3).

Middelburg, C. Birkenstock—Vryheid, and E. C. Hamman—Lichtenburg).[36] The amount eventually raised was £2,500,000 at 5 per cent. There was a phenomenal response in London,[37] and the loan was oversubscribed by three times.[38] Nevertheless the President's opponents were able to use the country's increased indebtedness as a weapon against him.[39] General Joubert, for example, lost no opportunity of referring gloomily to the financial load upon the country,[40] although at the original debate he had stated[41] that, while generally opposed to loans on principle, he regarded this one as desirable in view of the great need for it.[42]

To sum up, these various aspects of general financial policy enable us to detect the beginnings of what was later to become a steady and organized opposition to Kruger's régime. But none of the aspects here considered was to remain a fruitful field for continued opposition, because of the rapid rise to prosperity of the State's finances. Already by July of 1892 there was much less talk than there had been in 1890 and 1891 of the need for economy and retrenchment. By June of that year the Auditor-General was able to report a surplus of nearly £300,000.[43] By May of 1893 the surplus was over £450,000;[44] and by August of 1894 it was over £1,000,000.[45] The attack had now to shift its ground, and a much more vulnerable sector of governmental policy came, particularly between 1892 and 1894, under increasingly strong fire.

II. CONCESSIONS AND MONOPOLIES

The main aim, in what follows, is not so much to outline the concessions policy as such (though that will have to be done to some

[36] *Volksstem*, 29 June 1892.

[37] See General N. J. Smit's description of the scene outside Rothschild's in London (*Press*, 3 Aug. 1892).

[38] *Press*, 6 July 1892.

[39] See *Land en Volk*, 7 July 1892, 1 Sept. 1892; and *Volksstem*'s attack on Joubert's allegations, *Volksstem*, 29 Oct. 1892.

[40] See Joubert's speech at Middelburg (*Land en Volk*, 17 Nov. 1892).

[41] Joubert had spoken because so many members of the Raad had asked if the Executive Council had been united on the matter (*Notulen*, Eerste Volksraad, 1891, art. 1194).

[42] *Volksstem*, 1 Aug. 1891 (*Notulen*, Eerste Volksraad, 1891, art. 1194).

[43] *Volksstem*, 2 July 1892; *Press*, 1 July 1892 (*Notulen*, Eerste Volksraad, 1892, art. 587).

[44] *Volksstem*, 2 May 1893; *Press*, 2 May 1893.

[45] *Volksstem*, 11 Aug. 1894; *Press*, 21 Jan. 1895.

extent) as to show how it operated as an issue around which a formidable opposition to the President coagulated, both in the Volksraad and in the country. The dynamite monopoly, possibly the most important item of contention, will be outlined at the end of this section.

The case for concessions, that is the handing out by the State to private individuals or private groups of the exclusive right to manufacture certain articles (such as liquor, or soap or cyanide) subject to certain guarantees, and in return for a substantial payment, was clearly stated by President Kruger in 1883 and on subsequent occasions.

'As far as internal policy is concerned, the first essential is the development of the resources of the country, so that our imports are reduced and our exports increased; or to speak more clearly, so that we export goods and import money, and not (as happens too frequently now) import products, to pay for which money flows out of the country. . . . Why should our products, such as wool, etc. be processed in foreign countries and expensively re-purchased by us. Already, under the government's protection, factories are being erected to manufacture our own gunpowder and ammunition, our sugar and strong drink, from the products of the country; a concession has been granted for a wool factory and others have been requested for the preparation of leather. I shall always, in so far as it does not interfere with the freedom of trade, advance the cause of factories. . . . I support the principle of concessions [in mining] as productive, among other things, of the following advantages. . . .

'1. That by the competition of companies proper machinery is imported, and our mines are run in the best way, with less costs and more profit.

'2. That through them [concessions] the Republic is assured of a steady and substantial income, and

'3. Because by this means the mining population is brought under the better control of responsible persons.'[46]

In the Second Raad debate of 23 June 1891 the President declared that, while not favouring *all* concessions, good concessions which resulted in the erection of useful factories should be encouraged and supported. The factory at Eerste Fabrieken, 'unfortunately a liquor factory', had, even in bad times, bought 20,000 muids of grain from

[46] Le Grange Lombaard, *Paul Kruger die Volksman*, pp. 147–8.

the burghers.[47] In an impassioned defence of the principle of concessions, a year later (*Volksstem*, 21 June 1892), he stressed the
further point that industrialists would not take the risk involved in
setting up factories unless they were given protection and a guarantee, for a period of some years at any rate, of freedom from competition. The burghers had opposed the granting of a concession for
a sugar factory and for a wool factory ten years ago, and the result
was that they still had neither in the Republic. The country must be
independent of supplies from outside, he emphasized, and that was
why it had to have factories.

'Even if factories were slightly harmful to the State, he would still
say—Give the factories protection for a period—because only
through the erection of factories could the State become self-
supporting.'

The direct and indirect advantages of concessions, Kruger went
on, totalled far more than the import duties one would otherwise
levy on such articles if they had to be imported. Finally, even if
concessions were asked for only to be sold again, what was the harm
in this? When, for example, an old burgher was given a concession
and he sold it, he still profited from it. They got money for it, and
that money stayed in the country. And if those who bought the concessions allowed them to lapse, they reverted to the State. He repeated
that one could not expect anyone to lay out £40,000 to £50,000
without the safeguard of a monopoly for at least an initial
period.

The main objections to the policy of concessions and monopolies
are powerfully outlined by Jeppe:

'Ostensibly, perhaps honestly, granted in the first instance to foster
local industries, they soon became mere gambling counters, or
gratuities to those who were in the good graces of the Government.
In few cases only were these monopolies to manufacture any and all
articles a fertile imagination could suggest brought to the stage of
actual production. In most cases they were sold by the concessionaires for a few thousand pounds to a syndicate who hoped to (and
occasionally did) make large sums out of them by floating a company for the purpose of exploiting them. . . . All these concessions
(whether exploited or not) were accompanied by heavy protective

---

[47] *Volksstem*, 25 June 1891 (*Notulen*, Tweede Volksraad, 1891, art. 564).

duties,[48] raising prices greatly. They were extremely unpopular, and often carried only by the strenuous efforts of the President. They were as hotly opposed in Pretoria as in Johannesburg.'[49]

Here is the essence of the argument against the rather illogical defence by the President and his supporters of the concession and monopoly policy. There were few, even among the most bitter opponents of the President, who were totally against all concessions. *Land en Volk* itself, which missed no opportunity of attacking the régime on this issue,[50] agreed (24 November 1891) that 'concessions in themselves were not always bad, and were sometimes necessary', and in the earlier Volksraad debates, before the very word 'concessions' had acquired an almost magical value as an anti-governmental incantation, only two members, R. K. Loveday and P. Maré, were resolute enough to request that their names be recorded as against *all* concessions, a view that was rejected by 20 votes to 2; and Schalk Burger pointed out,[51] quite correctly, that in all countries *some* matters were arranged by means of concessions.

What was objected to was the way in which the policy was carried out, and the unhealthy spirit of speculation which it fostered. No one denied that concessions and monopolies had helped the State's struggling finances in the early 1880s; but what opponents of the policy did declare was that the trading in concession rights for factories that were never erected and for manufactures that were never produced harmed the reputation of the State and did nothing whatsoever (except in a few rare cases) to foster local industries or to increase the Transvaal's independence of outside sources of production. As Chief Justice Kotzé pointed out in his election address at Lydenburg (*Volksstem*, 29 November 1892), there was a big difference between protecting local industries by tariffs and other devices, and speculative trade in concession rights. Far from encouraging local initiative and enterprise among the burghers, the way in which the policy was administered undermined these qualities. By granting to private persons, he pointed out, a Pretoria water-concession, electric light concession and market concession, for instance,

---

[48] These were, of course, not imposed until a concession or factory became operative.

[49] Jeppe, *Kaleidoscopic Transvaal*, pp. 141–2.

[50] See *Land en Volk*, 14 Apr. 1891, 15 Dec. 1892, 16 Jan. 1893, 9 Feb. 1893, 14 Dec. 1893, 12 Apr. 1894, etc.

[51] *Volksstem*, 7 May 1892 (*Notulen*, Eerste Volksraad, 1892, arts. 24–5).

valuable sources of income to a future Pretoria municipality had been taken away, and the formation of such a municipality (much desired in more progressive circles[52]) had been made very difficult, if not quite impossible, for the city could look only to the general finances for support.

That the complaints of the purely speculative value of many concessions were well founded can be clearly seen from the report of the Concessions Committee of the First Raad in July 1890[53] which deplored strongly the fact that:

'many persons requested concessions not for the purpose of developing that branch of industry and then enjoying the benefits of it, but merely to convert the concession into a company, to sell their shares, and not to bother themselves any further with the matter.'

Six years later the Report of the Inspector of Concessions[54] includes a long list of concessions, many of them of some antiquity, which had lapsed, or in which nothing had been done to carry out the terms stipulated, or in which there were 'irregularities', and which should therefore be cancelled. (These included both the sugar concession and the wool concession referred to by the President in a speech reported in the *Volksstem* of 21 June 1892, as well as concessions for the manufacture of string, paper, oil and grease, soap, and the Pretoria market concession referred to by Chief Justice Kotzé.)

The concession for the supply of water to Johannesburg, granted to Messrs. F. C. Eloff and C. Schürmann, is a typical instance of the kind of goings-on to which opponents of the government took such strong exception. *Land en Volk* in a series of allegations,[55] none of which was ever denied in pro-government papers, and none of which, as far as can be ascertained, ever formed the subject of a libel action, presented a most unpleasant picture. The main points of its allegations were that F. C. (Frikkie) Eloff, the President's private secretary and son-in-law, had gained £20,000 by using his influence

[52] *Weekly Press*, 23 Nov. 1895, pp. 5, 12. (It must be pointed out that most of these particular concessions seem to have actually worked. See Marais, pp. 23–24.)

[53] *Volksstem*, 3 July 1890 (*Notulen*, Eerste Volksraad, 1890, art. 513, para. 17).

[54] Z.A.R. Green Book No. 19 of 1897, section XV, Industrial Concessions.

[55] For full details see J. F. Celliers's letter in *Land en Volk*, 16 Jan. 1893, and *Volksstem*, 11 Jan. 1893. Also *Land en Volk*, 29 Dec. 1892, 2 Jan. 1893, 19 Jan. 1893, 26 Jan. 1893 and 2 Feb. 1893.

to obtain a concession to supply Johannesburg with water from the Vaal River; that this concession had been granted to Eloff by the Executive Council on 27 November 1889 and permission to go ahead with it sought from the Volksraad only on 14 June 1890; that the necessary deposit had not been paid and that the concession had legally lapsed; that, in spite of this, when Messrs. Woolf Joel and Co., acting for Barnato Bros., had become interested in acquiring the concession, it had been illegally revived on the pretence that it had not really lapsed because the concessionaire, Eloff (owing to the error of an official), had not been given the one month's statutory notice of its having expired; and that the President, though fully aware of the fact that his son-in-law would receive 'the full bribe of £20,000' (*Land en Volk*, 26 January 1893) for his efforts in this direction, had used his influence in the Executive Council to secure the extension of a concession which had clearly expired. Though nothing eventually came of this concession[56] and though it faded away in the general defeat of the concessions policy, it presents the classic symptoms of everything that the opponents of concessions objected to. It was 'arranged' by a member of a favoured coterie;[57] it granted monopolistic rights to the concessionaire;[58] it was a pure speculation, out of which Eloff had made considerable profits 'without so much as digging a spadeful of earth' (*Land en Volk*, 29 December 1892); it had been negotiated through the Executive Council without proper consultation with the Volksraad;[59] it had abandoned the interests of citizens of the Republic to a handful of private speculators.[60]

In the violent debates, initiated by J. F. Celliers (Johannesburg), which took place in the Second Raad on 29 June and 3 July 1893,[61] there was no denial by the President or any other speaker on the government side of any of these allegations, and the Chairman insisted that the Raad confine itself to the question of the legality or

[56] *Land en Volk*, 14 Dec. 1893, refers to it as having fallen through, and to the President as having turned against it.

[57] See Nathan, *Paul Kruger*, pp. 226–7, on the composition of the so-called ' "Third Volksraad" with whom seekers of favours negotiated for concessions, grants of land, and appointments to office'.

[58] See *Land en Volk*, 9 Feb. 1893, for full terms of the concession.

[59] *Land en Volk*, 2 Jan. 1893.

[60] J. F. Celliers in *Land en Volk*, 16 Jan. 1893.

[61] *Volksstem*, 1 July 1893 (*Notulen*, Tweede Volksraad, 1893, art. 469), and *Volksstem*, 4 July 1893 (*Notulen*, Tweede Volksraad, 1893, art. 481).

otherwise of the government's action in granting, and later extending, the concession. On this comparatively narrow issue the Second Raad supported the government's action by 17 votes to 6, almost all the Progressive members (E. P. A. Meintjies—Pretoria, J. W. Joubert— Pretoria, B. G. Brecher—Vryheid, D. F. Petersen—Heidelberg, J. F. Celliers—Johannesburg, and W. J. Jooste—Potchefstroom) voting in the minority.[62]

Nevertheless the years between 1890 and 1894 saw a steady rise in the feeling of the burghers against concessions and monopolies, a feeling which President Kruger, for all his influence and power over his fellow-countrymen, was unable to oppose, and to which eventually he had, at least partially, to yield. Around this issue, so fundamentally opposed by the uitlanders and an increasing number of burghers,[63] much of the 'Progressive' opposition coalesced.

In 1890 President Kruger was still able to afford an attitude of confident rectitude on the question. When Paul Maré (Zoutpansberg) went so far as to describe concessions as the country's 'financial cancer', the President, supported by the majority of the legislators, firmly demanded the withdrawal of such 'a direct insult to the government', and Maré was forced to modify his statement into a milder declaration 'that in his opinion a monopoly worked in a manner detrimental to the financial interests of the country'.[64] A few days later Kruger told the Raad bluntly that in the matter of concessions it 'must trust the government, or else choose another government which it can trust. . . . He would never dream of concluding any major concession without the concurrence of the Raad, but the line must be drawn somewhere. He could not ask for tenders every time a pane of glass was broken in this building.'[65] But the President's idea of a minor concession was certainly somewhat catholic, for on the previous day he had included among such concessions, road repairs, bridges, the Johannesburg water concession,[66] the Pretoria tramway concession, and the central abattoir concession, declaring that such matters required speed, 'and the Raad must trust the government, otherwise there was no need for a govern-

---

[62] *Volksstem*, 1 July 1893 (*Notulen*, Tweede Volksraad, 1893, art. 479).

[63] Jeppe, *Kaleidoscopic Transvaal*, p. 142; Chamberlain to Milner, 10/5/1899 (Leyds Papers 89).

[64] *Volksstem*, 3 July 1890 (*Notulen*, Eerste Volksraad, 1890, art. 539).

[65] *Volksstem*, 7 July 1890 (*Notulen*, Eerste Volksraad, 1890, art. 590).

[66] So 'minor' that F. C. Eloff allegedly received £20,000 for negotiating it (see above, pp. 39–40).

ment'.[67] (It would have been interesting, perhaps, if he had made it clear what the need for a Raad was under such circumstances!) There was little opposition in the face of the President's outraged innocence, and the matter was not even brought to a vote.[68]

By 1891 the opposition had taken a little heart. *Land en Volk*, in May, set the ball rolling with an outspoken attack upon the whole policy by 'Afrikanus Junior',[69] who declared, in the first of a long series of virulent attacks:

'Do you think that we are all blind donkeys, Mr. President? Believe me that what I honestly tell you here is the opinion of the majority of the people, even though most of them are frightened to express it in your presence. Today we feel the same dissatisfaction as we felt under the British flag. Think of that, Mr. President. The free people of the South African Republic regard you in the same light as they would regard the British Government! I do not say that your motives have been bad ones—only God can know that—but I do say that your actions (in surrounding yourself with speculating Jews and Hollanders and granting them concessions) have given every reason for suspicion. . . .

'Stand upright again, President. Chase the Jews and Hollanders away from you. . . . Forbid the granting of concessions, and show the world by doing so that you have no personal interest in them.'[70]

By this time the attack had been taken up in the newly elected Second Volksraad. Speakers in the debates on concession applications which took place in late June and July 1891 stressed the undesirability of monopolies, pointed out that the Natal sugar industry did very well without them, insisted that if concessions were to be granted at all the conditions must be made as rigid as possible, and pressed instead for protective duties. The chief opponents of concessions in the Second Raad were E. Esselen, E. P. A. Meintjies, B. G. Brecher, F. Watkins, J. F. Celliers, J. W. Joubert and D. F. Petersen, with the occasional support of N. S. Malherbe.[71] At the

[67] *Volksstem*, 7 July 1890 (*Notulen*, Eerste Volksraad, 1890, art. 589, does not record this remark).

[68] *Notulen*, Eerste Volksraad, 1890, art. 590.

[69] For some evidence on the identity of 'Afrikanus Junior' see p. 196, footnote 32 below.

[70] *Land en Volk*, 5 May 1891 (open letter of Afrikanus Junior to President Kruger).

[71] See Second Raad debates of 23 June 1891, 27 June 1891, 29 June 1891.

end of the year the *Volksstem*, in a leader (24 November 1891) referred to the rise of a spirit of opposition among the burghers against concessions.

By the middle of 1892 the agitation against concessions had grown. In the Second Raad powerful opposition to the whole system was apparent. After considerable argument a concession to manufacture sugar was passed by 12 votes to 11.[72] A request for the grant of a concession to manufacture cyanide, against which the Chamber of Mines had petitioned, was rejected by 11 votes to 10 (3 members being absent).[73] Two applications for concessions to extract vegetable oil were rejected by 16 votes to 7 and 14 votes to 9. An application for an ore-smelting concession was turned down by 16 votes to 3. The hard core of opposition on this issue was, once again, Messrs. Esselen, Meintjies, Brecher, Watkins, Celliers, J. W. Joubert and Petersen, with the occasional support (depending on which concession was under discussion) of I. J. Meijer, De Jager, Van Niekerk and Steenkamp.[74]

Towards the end of the 1892 session the First Raad received numbers of memorials from all parts of the country complaining of the injurious effect of concessions on the economy, of favouritism in grants, and of the abuse by the Executive Council of the 'Volmacht' granted to it by this Volksraad, to grant concessions which were subsequently not brought before the Raad.[75] Government supporters noted with some uneasiness that these memorials had been signed by large numbers of old burghers, but tended to discount them as due to ignorance and acceptance of rumours. The Chairman of the First Raad, F. G. H. Wolmarans, declared magnanimously, much to the annoyance of the anti-government members, that 'he did not blame the memorialists; they were the victims of rumour-mongers', and the President contemptuously rejected the protests as 'of little value'.[76]

Nevertheless at the end of the session the First Raad took the unprecedented step of refusing to grant the usual complete legislative powers to the Executive during the adjournment, by 10 votes to 9,[77]

---

[72] *Volksstem*, 25 June 1892 (*Notulen*, Tweede Volksraad, 1892, art. 531).

[73] *Volksstem*, 29 June 1892 (*Notulen*, Tweede Volksraad, 1892, art. 577).

[74] *Volksstem*, 25 June 1892, 29 June 1892, 2 July 1892; *Land en Volk*, 30 June 1892. The First Raad, though it had power to override the Second, appears to have been wary of using this power in minor matters.

[75] *Volksstem*, 13 Aug. 1892 (*Notulen*, Eerste Volksraad, 1892, art. 1100).

[76] *Volksstem*, 13 Aug. 1892 (*Notulen*, Eerste Volksraad, 1892, art. 1100).

[77] *Notulen*, Eerste Volksraad, 1892, art. 1333.

though members denied that this betokened any lack of confidence in the government.[78] During the crucial election campaign of 1892–3, as press reports of public meetings throughout the country show, President Kruger found his concessions policy the subject of frequent hostile question and comment. In his opening address to the 1893 Volksraad the President's tone on the matter of concessions had become markedly cautious,[79] although he still defended them in principle. His plea to the Second Raad in June 1893 in favour of granting a cyanide concession was far less confident. He was, he said,

'against concessions, but if something could be made here that would compete with an imported article a monopoly could work well. If we had to buy everything in the cheapest market, everything would have to come from overseas, and when would the country become independent. He therefore favoured granting the applicants the right to erect a factory.'[80]

But, in spite of this plea, the Raad rejected the application by 17 votes to 3. On 14 June, the request of E. P. A. Meintjies (Pretoria) that all concessions, with dates, should be laid before the House, was answered (rather literally) when three officials entered carrying numbers of large books and the President declared with some satisfaction that there was much more to come. J. F. Celliers (Johannesburg) was provoked to wrath by this jocularity, and declared that the Raad 'had asked for a list of the concessions, and not a pack of books which it would take six months to go through. It must not be thought that the Raad could be frightened in this way.'[81] On the 14th the Second Raad decided by 18 votes to 3 to appoint a three-member committee to go into the documents on concessions laid before them.[82] A month later, in spite of an eloquent plea on its behalf by the President, the Second Raad declined, by 12 votes to 10, to grant the Grobler jam concession.[83]

[78] *Land en Volk*, 1 Sept. 1892; *Volksstem*, 31 Aug. 1892 (*Notulen*, Eerste Volksraad, 1892, art. 1336).

[79] *Volksstem*, 2 May 1893 (*Notulen*, Eerste Volksraad, 1893, art. 14).

[80] *Volksstem*, 3 June 1893 (*Notulen*, Eerste Volksraad, 1893, art. 238).

[81] *Volksstem*, 14 June 1893; *Land en Volk*, 22 June 1893 (*Notulen*, Tweede Volksraad, 1893, art. 317).

[82] *Volksstem*, 17 June 1893 (*Notulen*, Tweede Volksraad, 1893, art. 319).

[83] *Volksstem*, 19 June 1893; *Press*, 18 July 1893 (*Notulen*, Tweede Volksraad, 1893, art. 612).

The final blows came when on 20 August 1894 the Second Volksraad decided by 14 votes to 9 to reject all concessions unconditionally.[84] The President used all his influence, nevertheless, to attempt to persuade the First Raad to grant a concession for the making of jam to Messrs. Grobler and Gillingham. (*Land en Volk*, on 10 and 17 May 1894, alleged that large-scale bribery had been used by Gillingham—a leading member of the notorious so-called 'Third Volksraad'—in an attempt to get this concession through; and that 'a son of President Kruger and other blood-relations of the President' were vitally interested in securing the passage of this concession.) In acting thus the President demonstrated the truth of *Land en Volk*'s sarcastic prophecy in an article of 23 August 1894 congratulating the Second Raad on its total rejection of all concessions.

'What will become of the country! What is the use of being friendly to the government if it can't get you even the tiniest little concession? One thing we must say—the President has courage! In spite of all the outcry he defended the Jam Concession to the last. It is said that Gillingham is going to have another try to get it through the First Volksraad.'

But the attempt which that newspaper correctly prophesied was unavailing, and the First Raad, like the Second, refused to grant the concession, by 12 votes to 10.[85] *Land en Volk*, the foremost crusader against the government and all its works, raised a loud cry of jubilation, and under the headline 'Concessies Dood!' (13 September 1894) thanked 'in the name of the people' the twelve members who had voted against the concession (L. Meyer, P. Maré, R. K. Loveday, C. Jeppe, G. de Jager, L. de Jager, C. Birkenstock, J. H. de la Rey, J. du P. de Beer, J. de Clercq, J. P. Labuschagne and P. Schutte).

By the following year even such a devout supporter of the government and of concessions as the Pretoria *Press* was constrained (10 May 1895) to admit that the days of the concession policy were apparently numbered, and on 18 July 1895 the First Raad pronounced itself, by 17 votes to 3, as against concessions and monopolies in principle; and a committee was appointed to go into the question of the payment of bonuses as a better incentive to industrial

[84] *Land en Volk*, 30 Aug. 1894; *Volksstem*, 22 Aug. 1894 (*Notulen*, Tweede Volksraad, 1894, art. 974).
[85] *Land en Volk*, 13 Sept. 1894; *Volksstem*, 15 Sept. 1894; *Press*, 13 Sept. 1894 (*Notulen*, Eerste Volksraad, 1894, art. 1656).

development.[86] The Industrial Commission (set up by the Volksraad to 'institute a thorough and searching inquiry into the alleged grievances of the Mining Industry') endorsed this decision. Though paying lip-service to their expediency in the past, they declared that 'Your Commission entirely disapprove of the Concessions through which the industrial prosperity of the country is hampered'.[87] Not that the system of concessions died an immediate death. As late as 1899 Chamberlain complained to Lord Milner that from the *Staatscourant* it appeared that within the last three years concessions had been granted by the government for the manufacture of matches, paper, chocolates, wool, starch, mineral waters, soap and oils.[88] But this was after the Jameson Raid. As a political issue, that is, as a focus of Boer opposition to the government, the concessions issue barely raised its head after 1895.

Nevertheless, the issue had played its part in bringing together, particularly in the Second Volksraad, a strong nucleus of opposition to President Kruger's policies; and there is little doubt, to judge from press reports of the electoral meetings in 1892–3, that it played a significant part in the unprecedented opposition to the régime which the 1893 elections demonstrated.

III. THE DYNAMITE MONOPOLY

The contentious dynamite concession has been examined in a detailed thesis,[89] and it will not be necessary to do more than recapitulate its essential points. Once again, therefore, the emphasis will be on the importance of this issue in arousing general discontent among the burghers and legislators, rather than on the details of the dynamite question itself.

In December 1887, a concession granting the exclusive right to manufacture dynamite, gunpowder, explosives, and ammunition had been granted to Edouard Lippert, a German, for a term of sixteen years. He was permitted to import all raw materials and machinery free of duty; but not dynamite itself. The necessary factory was to be erected within a year, and once its output was able to meet the

---

[86] *Weekly Press*, 20 July 1895, p. 19.

[87] Report of the Industrial Commission, given verbatim in *Weekly Press*, 14 Aug. 1897, p. 5 ff. Also in *Notulen*, Eerste Volksraad, 1897, pp. 496–503.

[88] Chamberlain to Milner, 10 May 1899 (Leyds Papers, 89).

[89] D. A. Etheredge, The Early History of the Chamber of Mines (University of the Witwatersrand, 1949).

entire demand of the Republic, no further import of dynamite would
be allowed. The Raad approved in July 1888. Meanwhile, the 'Zuid
Afrikaansche Maatschappij voor Ontplofbare Stoffen Beperkt' (The
South African Explosives Company Ltd.) was registered in London
and the concession offered to two firms of the great Anglo-German
(Nobel) Trust. They refused, because of the inadequate maximum
price (£7 10*s.* per 50 lb. case); upon which Lippert offered it to the
rival French or Latin Trust, of which the leading firm was the
Société Centrale de Dynamite. The headquarters of this French-
financed explosives company were transferred to Pretoria, with
L. G. Vorstman as Managing Director and E. Lippert as Head
Agent, but the real headquarters were in Paris, as the shareholders
were largely French. In January 1889 the company began production, but meanwhile the Anglo-German Trust had taken advantage
of the fact that dynamite could still come in on permit to stock up
the Republic for two years. There were at first many complaints of
the inferior quality and danger of the local product, but government
investigation tended to discount this, and the government, in due
course, cancelled all import permits for dynamite except those upon
which orders had already been placed. Complaints about the quality
continued throughout 1890, and were again refuted by a government
commission of inquiry. In April 1891, as it was clear by this time that
the explosives company was importing dynamite instead of manufacturing it,[90] the Chamber of Mines petitioned the Raad to allow
free import of dynamite. The President, answering the complaints of
R. K. Loveday (Barberton) and J. P. Meyer (Witwatersrand Goldfields) that dynamite was being imported from abroad and that no
local materials whatsoever entered into its composition, stoutly
defended the concessionaires and declared that the dynamite was
being made locally. The Raad supported the President by 14 votes
to 9, but called on the company to adhere to the terms of the concession and also to pay the usual duties on any actual dynamite
imported.[91] (A Cape scientist had declared that the so-called 'guhr
imprégné' and 'cellulose imprégné', which the company described as
the raw materials from which dynamite was made, were neither more

[90] Joubert Papers, Inkomende Stukke, I A/10–17 (Archives, vol. 7), no. 772.
Historical Survey in letter of 7 Nov. 1892 from French Consul at Pretoria to his
government.
[91] *Volksstem*, 30 July 1891 and 1 Aug. 1891 (*Notulen*, Eerste Volksraad, 1891,
arts. 1183–4).

nor less than dynamite itself.) The company, it appears, did not protest against this, as the President had assured it privately that any tax it would have to pay would be subtracted from the annual amount payable to the government.[92]

By this time the British Government had entered the lists, declaring that the import of what was, in fact, French dynamite, free of duty by the company (while dynamite made by English manufacturers was excluded), constituted a contravention of article 14 of the London Convention of 1884.[93] Inside the Transvaal protests were already being made, in the mining areas at any rate. Answering questions at Barberton, General Joubert found it necessary, in a typically equivocal speech,[94] to prepare a number of possible lines of retreat or attack.

'I must make it clear that I was not against the grant of the concession. It was represented to the government as if the whole dynamite trade of the world was in the hands of one company,[95] and that it was highly desirable for the Transvaal to be independent of this monopoly, particularly as dynamite could be manufactured from materials found in this country. It was on this basis that the concession had been granted, and if this was not all true the government had been humbugged. I cannot say personally what the position is. . . . I am not prepared to say now that the concession must be cancelled. The matter demands further investigation.'[96]

On 4 April 1892 the government appointed a commission under the State Mining Engineer, Klimke, to investigate, and the tests which it conducted confirmed that the 7,500 cases imported by the explosives company in the s.s. *Highfield* were nothing other than dynamite. Needless to say the explosives company had made every effort to evade these tests.[97] *Land en Volk's* description of what allegedly happened is worth quoting.

'Rarely has such a scene taken place in a free Republic as occurred during the eleven o'clock adjournment of the Volksraad last Saturday

[92] French Consul, Pretoria, to his government, 7 Nov. 1892; Joubert Papers, Inkomende Stukke, I A/10–17 (Archives, vol. 7), no. 772.

[93] See also State Attorney (J. C. Smuts's) Report to the Volksraad, 8 Mar. 1899 (*Weekly Press*, 11 Mar. 1899, p. 2).

[94] See chapter IX.   [95] Obviously the Anglo-German (Nobel) Trust.

[96] *Volksstem*, 16 Feb. 1892.

[97] Etheredge, p. 56. (See also Leyds Papers, 627; GR 42/94.)

morning. The experts Col. Magendie and Prof. Hahn both found, acting on the suspicions of the Cape Government, that what Lippert was importing was nothing else than dynamite, and customs duties had to be paid accordingly by Mr. Lippert. Yet the stuff was allowed into the Transvaal in flagrant violation of the terms of the concession. On the motion of Jan Meyer a Committee of the Volksraad was then set up. The whole Volksraad then decided to go and test the material and see if it was explosive. Between 10.30 and 11 the President got hold of Jan Meyer, and quite audible to the Press Gallery—indeed in the street—shouted at him that it was grossly unfair to make such a test. He and everyone else knew well enough that it was explosive. The only question was, was it dynamite? Jan Meyer was weak enough to give way, and the tests thus took place only in the presence of the State Mining Engineer, the Minister of Mines, the Manager of the Dynamite Factory and the scientific experts. The stuff that Mr. Lippert alleged was not dynamite exploded with terrific force, throwing great masses of rock into the air.'[98]

There was an acrimonious debate in the Raad when the result of the tests was made known, R. K. Loveday demanding that the company be criminally prosecuted for flagrant smuggling,[99] and others insisting that the concession be cancelled. President Kruger, however, pleaded for a compromise. To cancel the contract, he declared, would be an act against the government not against the company. 'It would destroy the credit of the State completely and bring rejoicing to our enemies.'[1] The majority of the Raad agreed and by 18 votes to 5 decided to put the question to arbitration as provided for in article 16 of the concession. Those voting against the motion were R. K. Loveday, L. Meyer, P. Maré, L. de Jager and J. J. Spies.[2] The nature of the opposing points of view at this stage of the crisis is clearly shown in the reaction of the pro-government *Volksstem* (16 July 1892) and the anti-government *Land en Volk* (21 July 1892). The former opined that:

'The granting of an exclusive concession to manufacture explosives was a pity, and should not have happened; but the only thing to do now is to ensure that the existing concession is run to the greatest

[98] *Land en Volk*, 7 July 1892. See *Volksstem*, 16 July 1892, for report of Volksraad Committee (First Volksraad, 14 July 1892).

[99] *Volksstem*, 16 July 1892 (*Notulen*, Eerste Volksraad, 1892, art. 783).

[1] *Land en Volk*, 21 July 1892 (*Notulen*, Eerste Volksraad, 1892, art. 783).

[2] *Land en Volk*, 21 July 1892; *Volksstem*, 16 July 1892.

benefit of the country and of the dynamite users. Even if Lippert's Company could be proved guilty of flagrant violation of the concession conditions, it does not mean that we must allow Nobels to return to this country from England with drums beating and flags flying!'

The latter, under the headline 'Gigantic Fraud', declared:

'We cannot credit the President's behaviour. We understand his reluctance to expose the rottenness of his concession-politics, but to suggest to the Volksraad that the State buy the factory and appoint the fraudulent company as officials is too much! We expect but little of the Volksraad; but will the People allow this? . . . Lippert is having coffee with the President every morning.'

On 22 August 1892 the government decided to cancel the dynamite concession, and the First Raad by 15 votes to 6 agreed to leave it to the government to make whatever arrangements seemed best to them. Those voting in the minority were, once again, R. K. Loveday, L. Meyer, and L. de Jager, and they were joined on this occasion by Jan Meyer (Witwatersrand Goldfields) J. de Clercq (Middelburg) and Schalk Burger (Lydenburg). Meanwhile, despite the protests of the French Consul, English, German and French firms were to be allowed to import 15,000 cases of dynamite each. The explosive company was only temporarily successful in stopping this by means of a court interdict, and the High Court upheld the legality of the government's action.[3] This was the position by October 1892, by which stage election fever was already gripping the country.

That the dynamite issue played its part in the near-defeat of President Kruger in the 1893 elections is indicated by the tone of numbers of letters and manifestoes in support of General Joubert's candidature,[4] by Joubert's own (rather half-hearted) attacks on the policy in the course of his election tour,[5] and by the necessity under which Kruger frequently found himself of defending the dynamite concession during his meetings with the burghers.[6] Nevertheless, at this stage, it was a matter which affected Johannesburg and the uitlander population far more than it did the average rural burgher, and

[3] *Volksstem*, 15 Oct. 1892.

[4] Joubert Papers, Inkomende Stukke, I A/10–17 (Archives, vol. 6), nos. 639, 652, 656. See also *Land en Volk*, 1 Sept. 1892.

[5] *Land en Volk*, 27 Oct. 1892, 17 Nov. 1892, 24 Nov. 1892.

[6] See, for example, *Volksstem*, 22 Oct. 1892, 1 Nov. 1892, 5 Nov. 1892.

the *Volksstem* (2 November 1892) was probably quite right in declaring that it 'had been most skilfully inflated into a major national issue by the government's opponents'. *Land en Volk* (12 October 1893) asserted that the cancellation of the concession at the end of August 1892 was largely dictated by election considerations, and that in June 1892 the French Consul was given a verbal promise by the President that the government would reappoint the existing concessionaires as their agents under a new concession. Though British and German protests played a considerable part,[7] this is certainly partly true. The French Consul confirms this in the letter to his government of 7 November 1892, though he pressed in vain for the promise to be made in writing.[8]

Fresh opposition to the government, however, boiled up in the course of 1893 when the new arrangements proposed by the government were laid before the Raad. These provided for the government to take over the dynamite monopoly itself and empowered it to appoint such agents and transfer to them such powers as it might see fit.[9] This was accepted in principle in the First Raad debate of 12 August 1893, but only by a majority of 13 votes to 10. Those who voted against the government were[10] R. K. Loveday (Barberton), P. Maré (Zoutpansberg), L. Meyer (Vryheid), L. de Jager (Ermelo), C. Jeppe (the new member for Johannesburg), J. J. Spies (Utrecht), G. J. W. de Jager (the new member for Wakkerstroom), Schalk Burger (Lydenburg), J. du P. de Beer (Waterberg) and C. B. Otto (Marico).

The pro-government *Volksstem*, on 15 August 1893, hailed this defeat of the 'Progressive' opposition with joy, declaring that this opposition

'was nothing more nor less than a pro-Nobel agitation. The result of yielding to it would be that within a short time a sum of at least half a million pounds per annum would be leaving the South African Republic for England. ...

'Moreover [the Volksraad's decision] will show Downing Street that its Swaziland actions will not go unpunished. The exclusion of foreign, in other words of English, dynamite from the South African

[7] Marais, p. 29.

[8] Joubert Papers, Inkomende Stukke, I A/10–17 (Archives, vol. 7), no. 772 of 7 Nov. 1892.

[9] The full terms are published in *Volksstem*, 2 Sept. 1892.

[10] *Volksstem*, 15 Aug. 1893.

Republic will be a good lesson to those gentry on the other side of the sphere. . . .

'Very probably the existing Explosives Company will be given the opportunity to establish the dynamite industry on a solid basis in spite of the mistakes committed by it (for which, incidentally, our government is not entirely blameless . . .).

'Whatever some uitlander elements may feel the national party will support this arrangement with all its power.'

In view of the merger with the Nobel Trust which took place early in 1894 and the continued opposition of the 'Progressives' thereafter,[11] the first allegation can be discounted; and in 1897 and 1898 alone under the new arrangements so warmly welcomed by the *Volksstem*, profits of nearly £600,000 went overseas[12] without a word of protest by that paper. However, the rest of the extract reflects faithfully enough the views of the 'national party'.

But, in spite of the last sentence, with its very typical suggestion that resistance to governmental policy was unpatriotic, there was strong opposition from many more sources than merely the 'uitlander elements'. The regulations proposed for the new monopoly were argued article by article in the First Volksraad. The suggested import duty of 9*d.* per lb. on imported dynamite was opposed by Jeppe and other 'Progressives', but carried by 13 votes to 10 (Loveday, Maré, L. Meyer, L. de Jager, Jeppe, Spies, G. de Jager, De Beer, as usual, voting in the minority, and being joined, on this issue, by Birkenstock and Labuschagne).[13] Article 4, allowing the government to transfer its powers in the new monopoly to other persons, was passed by 13 votes to 8 (Loveday, L. Meyer, G. de Jager, L. de Jager, Jeppe and P. Maré desired their names to be recorded in the minority), article 6, laying down a maximum price for dynamite of £5 per case, by 15 votes to 7, and article 11, providing for payment to the government by such agents as it might transfer its rights to of 5*s.* per case of dynamite sold and 20 per cent of 'surplus' profits, by 12 votes to 10.[14] There was, clearly, substantial opposition, in which General Joubert joined.

On 25 October 1893, as the *Volksstem* had prophesied, the govern-

[11] *Volksstem*, 15 Sept. 1894.

[12] Etheredge, p. 70; *Weekly Press*, 14 Aug. 1897, pp. 4–6.

[13] *Volksstem*, 2 Sept. 1893.

[14] *Volksstem*, 5 Sept. 1893 (*Notulen*, Eerste Volksraad, 1893, arts. 1275–8, 1290–1).

ment signed a contract with L. G. Vorstman of the old South African Explosives Company by which the company became the government's agents for the manufacture and sale of dynamite for a period of fifteen years.[15] The maximum price for Dynamite No. 1 was laid down as £4 15*s*. a case. The government undertook, until such time as the factory was completed, to import all materials required for the manufacture of dynamite and explosives, and to place these freely at the disposal of the agent. The agent undertook to erect the necessary factories within a maximum period of two and a half years.

The opposition press was not slow in voicing its indignation. *Land en Volk*, on 2 November 1893, declared:

'Readers will see in our columns that the Kruger Government has had the inordinate impudence ['verregaande brutaliteit'] to give the Dynamite Agency to Messrs. Lippert & Vorstman. Those whom the Gods wish to destroy, it seems, they first make mad! This is the man whom the people hoped would take warning by the last election! So the agency goes to the French Company which the President and Leyds *themselves* admitted in the Raad had committed a great fraud upon the Transvaal. There is no more shame in these people. J. M. A. Wolmarans, Member of the Executive Council was a shareholder and Commissioner in this Company[16] and was highly praised in its report for the way he defended it (against the South African Republic!) and yet this patriot took a leading part in the discussions affecting it, in the Executive Council, and gave his voice for the re-award of the monopoly to the Company. Our birthright is being sold to pedlars, Jews and Hollanders. Believe no one any more who talks of our "independence"!—our independence!'

In a leading article at the end of November, headed 'Unrest among the People', it declared that the discontent with government policy among the burghers was much greater than was generally admitted, linked this with the 'scandalous handling of the Dynamite question', and warned that 'as for our own people, they are at last truly awakening, and the day of reckoning comes ever nearer'. The *Volksstem* admitted the existence of discontent, though decrying it as artificially aroused.[17] Nevertheless the President felt strong enough to

[15] A manuscript copy (or original) of this contract may be found in Leyds Papers, 627, no. 158 (marked G663/1893). (See also *Volksstem*, 31 Oct. 1893.)

[16] For further information on Wolmarans's role see Etheredge, p. 45, and Scoble and Abercrombie, *The Rise and Fall of Krugerism*, p. 94.

[17] *Volksstem*, 18 Oct. 1893 and 22 Nov. 1893.

turn down, courteously but firmly, the protest against the new arrangements made to him by a joint deputation of members of the First and Second Raads. It was led by J. F. Celliers (Second Raad member for the Witwatersrand) and included from the First Raad, Jeppe, Loveday and Paul Maré, and from the Second Raad, Petersen, Vorster and Meintjies.[18] All except Vorster were recognized members of the 'Opposition'.

Meanwhile, behind the scenes, negotiations were being pushed forward by the Anglo-German Nobel Trust[19] as a result of which on 24 May 1894 the 'Zuid Afrikaansche Fabriek voor Ontplofbare Stoffen Beperkt' was registered as the government's sole agent for the import, export and sale of all explosives.[20] Of the nominal capital of £450,000 Nobels held 225,000 and the French Ring 224,500 one pound shares, which included 25,000 shares given to Lippert. In addition, Lippert was to receive a royalty of 8s. (after three years 6s.) per case of dynamite and Messrs. Lewis and Marks a similar royalty of 2s. per case.[21] The French company received from the government of the Republic 182,500 shares as indemnification for the cancellation of the original contract by the government, and Dr. Gobert, a German lawyer, 22,500 shares 'for services rendered'.[22] In a review of the tangled history of the concession, the later State Attorney, J. C. Smuts, wrote in 1899:

'It is clear that the government was well acquainted with all these terms, whereto it expressly or practically agreed. . . . It appears to me as if the government was eager to avoid or remove diplomatic difficulties, and determined to indemnify the old French Company in spite of its cancellation of the concession.'[23]

The less charitable critics of the government tended to suspect that the second of the reasons advanced by Smuts bulked larger than the first. The arrangements, as soon as they became known, were strongly attacked in the Volksraad. Jeppe, in a powerful speech, in which he hammered home the exact details of the new arrangements,

[18] *Volksstem*, 18 Oct. 1893 and 21 Oct. 1893.

[19] Leyds Papers, 627, GR 15/94, GR 30/94, GR 42/94, GR 62/94 and GR 249/94.

[20] Etheredge, p. 65 (the actual contract, in the original, is to be found in Leyds Papers, 627–R 2635/94, no. 186).

[21] Leyds Papers, 627, R 2635/94.   [22] *Weekly Press*, 11 Mar. 1899.

[23] *Weekly Press*, 11 Mar. 1899. Report of State Attorney to First Volksraad, 8 Mar. 1899.

pointed out that far from their having secured a State monopoly, virtually every share was in the hands of one foreign company or another.[24] In what way, he asked, did these new arrangements bring the Republic any nearer to the 'independence of foreign factories' so frequently insisted upon by the President as the essential purpose of his dynamite policy? That the feelings of the Volksraad had been aroused was clearly demonstrated in this debate when a request from the new explosives company, to extend beyond two and a half years the time by which the factory must be in production, was rejected by 18 votes to 4, in spite of a presidential speech in defence of the company. Instead, the Raad instructed the government to see that the terms of the contract were strictly carried out.[25]

1895 saw a lull in the dynamite controversy, and it is beyond the terms of reference of this book to trace the further development of this issue beyond the end of that year. It is interesting to note, however, that the report of the Industrial Commission set up by the Volksraad in 1897 declared, among other things, that, by that year still (*a*) the cost of dynamite was 40*s*. to 45*s*. a case higher than it need be, (*b*) nearly all the profits went overseas, and (*c*) 'none of the raw material used is found in this country, or in such small quantities as to make it valueless'.

'Your Commission . . . are forced to the conclusion that the factory has not attained the object for which it was established, and that there is no reasonable prospect of its doing so.'

It recommended, further, 'that the case be placed in the hands of the legal advisers of the State, with a view to ascertain whether the contract can be cancelled'.[26]

It seems therefore that President Kruger's sincere desire to ensure the self-sufficiency of the Republic in the matter of dynamite, had led him into an uncritical acceptance of the views of Leyds, Lippert and others,[27] and there is no doubt that his reiterated statements on the

[24] Details of the shares held by each German, British and French company are given in Jeppe's speech (*Volksstem*, 22 Sept. 1894; *Land en Volk*, 20 Sept. 1894; *Notulen*, Eerste Volksraad, 1894, art. 1708).

[25] *Press*, 15 Sept. 1894 (*Notulen*, Eerste Volksraad, 1894, art. 1711).

[26] *Weekly Press*, 14 Aug. 1897, p. 5–7 (verbatim report of the Industrial Commission 6 Aug. 1897. Also printed in *Notulen*, Eerste Volksraad, 1897, pp. 496–503).

[27] See Etheredge's statement (p. 72) that the company spent between 1897 and 1899 some £39,000 in Pretoria to influence Leyds, Wolmarans, Klimke and others.

essential points at issue, viz. that the explosives company was not importing dynamite but manufacturing it,[28] and that the Republic's 'independence' of overseas resources was being achieved,[29] were not, as has been shown, in line with the true facts. Nor can what the *Press*, a friendly critic, charitably describes (on 30 September 1893) as the government's 'tender feeling for the Transvaal Explosives Company' be considered to have been in the best financial interests of the Republic. There can be little doubt that the President was sincere in his statement to a public meeting in Pretoria that 'the Dynamite Factory is the cornerstone of our independence, and those who cannot see it are blind'.[30] He repeated it at Lydenburg later that year: 'As to dynamite, burghers, I won't give up my factory, for it's our cornerstone.'[31]

In this, Kruger, though sincere, was premature. For it was not till 1898 that the company was able to satisfy the requirements of the mines.[32]

The President's stubborn defence of his position, and the tangled big business intrigues behind the scenes, of which inspired whispers regularly reached the press, played their part, as we have seen, in arousing a determined opposition in the Volksraad and among the burghers. The deepened division between the parties and among the burghers which 1894–5 brought, and the increasing importance of the Progressive opposition,[33] coincided with the furious debates on dynamite policy and were undoubtedly influenced to some extent by antagonism to that policy and its consequences. The one defence that can be made of the President's policy, and it was an important one from the Republic's point of view, was that the factory 'if it did not actually make dynamite ... could at least make cartridges.'[34] But this could have been achieved far more simply, and without the enormous

[28] *Press*, 13 Aug. 1894 (Krugersdorp speech), and *Notulen*, Eerste Volksraad, 1891, art. 1181.

[29] *Volksstem*, 21 June 1892, 18 Oct. 1893, 13 Feb. 1894; *Weekly Press*, 1 Jan. 1897, p. 8, 10 Nov. 1897, p. 10; *Notulen*, Eerste Volksraad, 1891, art. 1181; 1892, arts. 783, 1225; 1893, art. 1069; 1897, arts. 41, 1644.

[30] *Weekly Press*, 1 Jan. 1897, p. 8.

[31] *Weekly Press*, 11 Dec. 1897, p. 7. (He referred, of course, to ammunition. See Marais, p. 32.)

[32] Marais, pp. 30–1.

[33] See chapter VIII.

[34] Walker, *History of S. Africa*, p. 470. But even then (*a*) most of the Republic's ammunition still had to be bought abroad and (*b*) the company imported all its cartridge-cases (Marais, p. 32).

and irritating cost to the mining industry that the dynamite monopoly entailed. The best condemnation of the dynamite policy was undoubtedly that given by Schalk Burger's Industrial Commission of 1897, 'in terms which the Uitlanders could hardly have bettered'.[35] And De Kiewiet is making a virtue out of no particular necessity (as far as dynamite policy, at any rate, is concerned) when he says:

'Modern criticism looks more favourably upon Kruger's mining policy. The system of monopolies and concessions enabled the Transvaal Government to tap the industry at various points, and through the vital dynamite monopoly to keep a tight rein upon it as well. In spite of the bitter complaints of the mining companies the results of the heavy charges placed upon the industry were not always harmful. To maintain their profits the companies were compelled to mine more efficiently and to eliminate waste more resolutely. To the burden which Kruger placed upon the mines were due in large measure, therefore, the feats of engineering and business administration which are an astounding chapter in their history.'[36]

This passage contains some half-truths. For it was not the Transvaal Government which 'tapped the industry', so much as foreign shareholders, Lippert, and Lewis and Marks. It is true that the Transvaal Government received 5s. per case and 20 per cent of the 'surplus' profits; but this was small compared to the profit of 40s. to 45s. per case which the company made. The essence of the complaint of Kruger's own burghers in the Volksraad, and in the Industrial Commission, was not only against the heavy burden placed upon the mines by the dynamite monopoly[37] but also against the fact that inordinate profits went into the pockets of foreign investors; that it was in fact not so much a State monopoly as a foreign monopoly aided and protected by the State; that, for a long time, it neither produced dynamite nor rendered the Transvaal independent of foreign supplies; and that, in the words with which Carl Jeppe ended his eloquent attack upon the whole policy in September 1894, 'for the rest, the government would import guhr imprégné (i.e. virtual dynamite) out of State funds, for the benefit of overseas shareholders'.[38]

[35] *C.H.B.E.*, vol. viii, p. 579.
[36] De Kiewiet, (*a*) p. 135.
[37] Over £600,000 a year (C. 9317). See also Nathan, pp. 192–3.
[38] *Volksstem*, 15 Sept. 1890 (*Notulen*, Eerste Volksraad, 1890, art. 1710).

3

The Issues around which Opposition Crystallized
(continued)

IV. RAILWAY POLICY

OPPOSITION to the concession granted to the Netherlands Railway Company (Nederlandsch Zuid Afrikaansche Spoorweg Maatschappij) in 1884,[1] and to a very much lesser extent to that granted to the Selati Railway Company in 1891,[2] formed a regular item of controversy between the government and its opponents in the years under review. We shall deal with each concession separately.

In August 1884 the Volksraad, with some trepidation, but persuaded thereto by President Kruger,[3] granted to the Netherlands-German company (in spite of its German share of the capital, in essence a Dutch concern),[4] Messrs. Maarschalk of Amsterdam, a concession to build the Transvaal portion of the railway to Delagoa Bay. But it was not until 1887 that the company was successfully floated, and not till the end of that year that the survey of the line from Pretoria to the Portuguese border was successfully completed. In 1883, on the other side of the border, a concession had been granted to Colonel Edward McMurdo, an American, to build a line from Delagoa Bay to the Transvaal border. But by 1888 the line was making painfully slow progress, and in the following year the Portuguese Government took over the railway itself and carried it through to the Transvaal border. Meanwhile the Netherlands company, stoutly supported by the Transvaal Government in any difficulties that it encountered,[5] was pushing ahead with the construction of the Transvaal section of the line, and by February 1890 was 8 miles from Komatipoort. By the end of September 1891 a regular service was operating between Lourenço Marques and

---

[1] *C.H.B.E.*, vol. viii, p. 521; Van Winter, vol. I, pp. 60, 267 ff.

[2] *Land en Volk*, 14 July 1891 (*Notulen*, Eerste Volksraad, 1891, arts. 875–86, 890–7); Nathan, p. 193, gives the date as 1894, and Fitzpatrick, p. 56, as 1890, but both are incorrect. See also Van Winter, vol. II, p. 117.

[3] Nathan, pp. 190–1.

[4] Marais, p. 34.

[5] *Volksstem*, 13 Jan. 1890, 9 May 1891, 1 Aug. 1891.

Hectorspruit. In June 1892 the line was operating as far as Nelspruit, a distance of 74 miles from the border; and by 10 October 1894 the *Press* was proclaiming exultantly that 'Cape Town might well weep', for the greatest day in President Kruger's life would dawn in three weeks' time, when, with a golden bolt, he would ceremonially complete the construction of the Delagoa Bay line and bring Pretoria within 21 hours of the coast. The ceremony duly took place at Brugspruit (beyond Bronkhorstspruit) in November, and on 1 January 1895 the Transvaal's own line to the coast was open to traffic— exactly two years after the first train had entered Pretoria on the Cape–Orange Free State line,[6] and some ten months before the completion of the Durban–Johannesburg line. The official opening of the Delagoa Bay line took place at Pretoria on 8 July 1895.

These are the bare facts of the achievement of the President's great dream; but every step in its achievement was marked by stormy opposition. Much of this opposition was no doubt fostered by the powerful external political and economic interests whose workings make this period one of the most tangled and fascinating episodes in South African history,[7] and into which it is not the business of this study to enter; but many Transvaal patriots, sometimes for similar and sometimes for different reasons from those which motivated the endless outside pressures upon the Transvaal, opposed strongly many facets of Kruger's railway policy. Chief, but by no means alone, among these was Commandant-General P. J. Joubert; and of his patriotism, at any rate, there can be no doubt.

General Joubert's objections were laid out fully in a twenty-four page pamphlet, or 'open letter' to the Netherlands Railway Company, published on 21 April 1890.[8] He asked, first, why, so many years after the concession had been granted, the line to Pretoria was still not in existence; why shareholders in the company continued to draw 6 per cent on their capital although, in the absence of a line, no possible profit could be made; and, why, after three years of surveying, the company had still not been able to arrive at an estimate of the probable cost per mile. He objected strongly to the fact that the Transvaal stood security for the capital, and had been paying a high rate of interest on it since 1887; to the considerable

---

[6] Walker, p. 439; J. H. Hofmeyr, *Life of Jan Hendrik Hofmeyr*, p. 425.

[7] See J. van der Poel, *Railway & Customs Policies in South Africa, 1885–1910*, and Van Winter.

[8] *Volksstem*, 22 May 1890; Van Winter, i, p. 246.

powers vested in the company, so that no plans or regulations or decisions on personnel need be submitted to the government's approval; to the preferential rights granted to the company by which it was empowered to lay down rates for all lines in the Republic, not only its own—a monopoly power which, he declared, could not but make conditions difficult for any other lines, and could not but be against the interests of the State; and to the extortionate conditions to which the State was subject should it choose to exercise its right to expropriate the company before the due expiry date of the concession in 1915.[9] Finally, in an appendix, he noted with disapproval the small number of shares held by the State itself.[10]

Here is the basic theme-song of the opposition to the Netherlands Railway Company, which, with further developments and overtones, was to swell louder and louder during the ensuing years, and never to die down completely until the death of the Republic itself.

General Joubert had, before publishing this letter, complained in similar terms to Van den Wall Bake, a director of the company in Amsterdam, and on 10 March 1890 the *Volksstem* had printed a point-by-point answer to Joubert's allegations. Starting with a declaration that it was of the most vital importance that the concession should not be in the hands of unscrupulous promoters but 'in the hands of those to whom the welfare of the South African Republic meant much', Van den Wall Bake declared that the financial conditions had been well known to the Transvaal Government and fully approved of by them. 'The raising of the loan was naturally not done by the bankers for nothing.' The company had every interest in the speediest possible completion of the line, but the natural obstacles were considerable. The cost per mile could not be estimated because labour and material costs varied from year to year, but every extra penny that the company spent diminished its own profits, so that its interests and those of the Transvaal went hand in hand on this point. As for the high interest rates, they were as sorry about it as Joubert, but the credit of the Republic had not been high then; the position was different now and the Republic was only paying 4 per cent on money raised more recently. He did not deny the allegations about tariffs, and agreed that high tariffs could hold up the whole development of the Republic, 'but the Netherlands Rail-

---

[9] See Fitzpatrick, p. 54, for an analysis of this point.

[10] The Republic eventually acquired some 5,606 shares out of a total of 14,000 (Van Winter, ii, p. 142).

way Company has given no cause for fear that any abuse will occur of the trust placed in it'. He agreed also that the right to control other steam transport in the Republic 'certainly does limit the government's rights. But for the Netherlands company it has the great value that others will not pluck the ripe fruit which they as pioneers have brought into existence with great effort.' If it were found possible to achieve this assurance by any other means, the company would not be found unwilling, if requested to do so by the government, to limit its preferential rights. He ended, after a sidelong hit at General Joubert's unfamiliarity with business and concession matters,[11] by appealing to the general's patriotism. The Republic had shown clearly what pre-eminent political importance it attached to the Delagoa Bay line; it should therefore be supported with might and main, even if it was to the detriment of other routes, and opponents of the Netherlands company should banish their suspicions and let the company's deeds speak for it.

In essence, therefore, Van den Wall Bake's reply does not deny Joubert's main points, and excuses rather than refutes them. This is particularly the case on the question of the company's preferential right to control rates—a right fraught with the most vital political consequences, for railway and customs rates were at the very heart of the Transvaal's relations with other states. Van den Wall Bake's basic slogan is 'Trust the Company; its interests and those of the Transvaal are identical'.

The *Volksstem*, on 19 May 1890, joined in this call to rally behind the company, urging the public to 'use its common sense and neither regard the Company as a blood-sucking monster, nor as an angelic philanthropic agency'.

'Why oppose yourself', it asked, 'to what cannot now be altered? The concession has its faults, but it has its good points too. It may be true that the Netherlands company has advantageous terms, and that in European countries well supplied with railways small profits are made. But the Natal Railway, for instance, is a veritable gold mine and where Natal gives the example, why should the South African Republic not follow?'

This last point is possibly an indirect hit at General Joubert, who at that time, with General N. J. Smit, B. Vorster, F. C. Eloff, Schalk Burger and others, was attempting to secure from the government a

[11] A totally unjustified insinuation (see below, pp. 246–8).

concession to continue the rapidly-approaching Natal line from Charlestown to Johannesburg.[12]

However, the fact that growing criticism of the Netherlands company was worrying both the company and the government was admitted by the *Volksstem* to be the reason for certain modifications in the allegedly 'unalterable' concession terms which the company, in June 1890, declared itself prepared to accept. These included (*a*) willingness to allow the Volksraad to decide on the direction which lines should take, (*b*) the granting by the company to the State of the right to build such sidelines as it considered necessary, (*c*) the acceptance of time limits in the construction of lines, and the payment of fines for delays, (*d*) the surrender of the company's right to lay down tariffs itself, and the acceptance of maximum prices based upon O.F.S. and Cape tariffs, and (*e*) acceptance of the right of the government to decide interest rates on shares and loans, such rates not to exceed 4 per cent. These were substantial modifications. They were accepted, after some debate, by the Volksraad on 25 June 1890 and the concession was altered accordingly.[13] The voting was 30 to 8 in favour, those voting against being Messrs. O. J. Coetzee (Lydenburg), P. G. Maré (Utrecht), J. C. van Zyl (Heidelberg), J. de Clercq (Middelburg), J. J. Spies (Utrecht), J. du P. de Beer (Waterberg), Paul Maré (Zoutpansberg) and L. de Jager (Ermelo). Of these gentlemen only the last four can by any stretch of the imagination be regarded as potential future 'Progressives',[14] though De Clercq from time to time seemed tempted towards the opposition side, and may perhaps best be described as a pro-government member of independent views.[15] Nevertheless on this issue we see, even before the debates on finance, the general policy of concessions and the dynamite monopoly, the beginnings of a small but steady opposition, and one that felt itself openly supported, on this matter at any rate, by the declared views of Commandant-General Joubert.

By the next year opposition to the Netherlands company had

[12] Joubert Papers, Inkomende Stukke, I A/10–17 (Archives, vol. 7), no. 776 (Barend Vorster to Joubert, 17 June 1890), 777 (N. J. Smit to Joubert, 18 Oct. 1890), 779 (W. Y. Campbell to Joubert, 9 Mar. 1891), 780 (J. A. Kieser to Joubert, 22 July 1892). See also *Volksstem*, 1 Feb. 1893 (admission by Joubert of having applied for this concession).

[13] *Volksstem*, 26 June 1890 (*Notulen*, Eerste Volksraad, 1890, arts. 470–503) See also Van Winter, i, pp. 282–7.

[14] See below, p. 245.

[15] See character-sketch in *Volksstem*, 1 Sept. 1894.

swelled very considerably. It had become necessary for the company to borrow more money at higher rates of interest, and it claimed that 4 per cent was too low. The President supported its plea forcefully, and, after an excited debate, a motion giving the government the right to act as it saw fit in the matter was passed in the First Raad by the narrow majority of 13 votes to 11.[16] Those who voted against the government were R. K. Loveday, Paul Maré, L. de Jager, J. J. Spies, C. Birkenstock, J. du P. de Beer, Jan Meyer (Witwatersrand) and Schalk Burger, and they were joined on this matter by such normally pro-government members as J. van der Merwe (Lydenburg) and A. A. Stoop (Wakkerstroom), and even by J. M. Malan (Rustenburg), whom the *Volksstem* (1 September 1894) accurately describes as 'a veteran . . . who clings to the old principles on which the Republic is founded, an enthusiastic supporter of President Kruger and his Government . . . a bulwark of our independence . . . a pillar of the Raad'.

The views of the President's opponents were well summed up in a strong, and very typical, article in *Land en Volk* of 12 May 1891 which declared:

'Surely no government in the world has ever passed a resolution comparable to that of the Volksraad last Friday in the matter of the interest on the loan capital of the Netherlands Railway Company. . . . As the unfortunate company has borrowed over a million pounds and European capitalists do not wish to give it any more, they now want to offer higher rates of interest than 4 per cent. The company therefore comes to the government and asks its permission to break its contract, in its own favour, in that the State must make the interest just as high as the company needs to obtain fresh loans. The President has used all his influence to get this proposal through, assuring members that if they do not vote for it they will be strangling our independence. As if our independence depends upon a Dutch company! . . . Dr. Leyds alleges that the difficulty in getting money is because the credit of the South African Republic is bad. Just the opposite. Our only contact with the financial world is the company, and *its* reputation has dragged our credit into the dust. The financial state of Natal is far worse than ours, and yet it has no difficulty in borrowing money at $3\frac{1}{2}\%$.'

[16] *Volksstem*, 9 May 1891; *Press*, 7 May 1891; *Land en Volk*, 12 May 1891 (*Notulen*, Eerste Volksraad, 1891, art. 32).

The *Press* (7 May 1891) was constrained to admit that 'the majority of only two votes may be liable to offensive construction for party purposes', but comforted itself by asserting that the victory, narrow though it was, 'showed that President Kruger had lost none of his power in the Volksraad', and pointed out that the Executive Council had for some time been seriously considering the desirability of increasing the rate allowed for borrowing, and that the company's plea that money was not obtainable at 4 per cent was not in itself a command upon the Volksraad.

The truth was that the government was committed, for political reasons, to seeing the Delagoa Bay line completed—at all costs—and from the Transvaal's point of view quite justifiably so. Few members of the Volksraad would have opposed, in principle, the building of such a line, though Joubert, it is true, had talked in 1889 of blocking the Delagoa Bay project and admitting the Natal line instead.[17] What Volksraad members, and public opinion, objected to was not the idea of a line to Delagoa Bay (to which, apart from other considerations, the short-sighted customs policy of the coastal colonies, before the discovery of gold on the Witwatersrand, had virtually encouraged her to turn), but a line under the control of a foreign company, and built by virtue of a concession which many of them felt to be unnecessarily generous in its terms. Nevertheless, it must be noted that the motion put before the Volksraad by J. du P. de Beer and H. P. Beukes (Marico) to declare the concession lapsed, and for the State itself to raise a loan and build the railway was overwhelmingly rejected, by 21 votes to 3.[18] It was clearly better control of the Netherlands company, rather than the abolition of its concession, that the majority of members desired at this stage.

In July 1891 the government approached the Volksraad for permission to raise a loan of between one and three million pounds, chiefly for the Delagoa Bay line. On this occasion the President was supported by General Joubert and by such normally anti-government members as L. de Jager and J. J. Spies. R. K. Loveday was the main speaker against the loan, and he used the opportunity to inveigh against the alleged Hollander control of the State. Nevertheless the permission to raise the loan was passed by acclamation.[19] The subsequent failure of the loan in Europe, at $4\frac{1}{2}$ per cent, led to a sharp

---

[17] Walker, p. 409; Van Winter, ii, p. 132; Van Oordt, p. 499.

[18] *Volksstem*, 9 May 1891 (*Notulen*, Eerste Volksraad, 1891, art. 31).

[19] *Volksstem*, 1 Aug. 1891 (*Notulen*, Eerste Volksraad, 1891, arts. 1195–6).

criticism of the government, as we have seen in our discussion of financial policy.

It was the failure of this loan that led to the agreement between the Netherlands Railway Company and the Cape Government, by which the Cape Government was to lend the company sufficient money to enable it to raise the necessary loan from Rothschild's to finish the Delagoa Bay line. In return the Cape was allowed to carry its line over the Vaal River to Pretoria,[20] and had the right to fix the rates from Cape Town to Johannesburg until December 1894, or until the Delagoa Bay line was completed. Local traffic inside the Republic would be under Netherlands Railway Company control, but any traffic coming from or going further south than Kroonstad would be under the control of the Cape Government. This was a heavy price to pay, but the need to get the Delagoa Bay line completed was paramount. The *Volksstem* tried to disguise the extent of the injury to the government's prestige by saying:

'Our government, it is well known, is in no mood to take financial help from the Cape. Thus this private agreement between the Netherlands Company and the Cape Government. It gives the Cape Government no more and no less rights than any other holder of shares in the Netherlands Company. . . . Once the Delagoa Bay line is completed, and in spite of the unfavourable circumstances at the moment we have no doubt it will be, the Netherlands Company will have the complete right to set its own terms.'[21]

But President Kruger, on his annual tour of the country districts at the beginning of the next year, found himself nearly everywhere constrained to answer hostile questions[22] about the Netherlands Railway Company, the new loan, and their inevitable concomitant—the Hollander control of the country. Some of this hostility he probably owed to the consistent anti-Hollander campaign of *Land en Volk*,[23] which, on 26 January 1892, in a characteristic article on this theme declared:

[20] The line was to be built by the Netherlands company (see Van Winter, ii, pp. 127–9, 135, 137–9, 151; Marais, p. 36).

[21] *Volksstem*, 10 Dec. 1891.

[22] See reports of meetings at Ermelo, Bethal, Amsterdam, Piet Retief, Wakkerstroom, Lydenburg, etc. (*Volksstem*, 26 Feb. 1892, 9 Mar. 1892, 16 Mar. 1892, 23 Mar. 1892; *Land en Volk*, 22 Mar. 1892).

[23] See below, pp. 128–30, and Van Winter, i, p. 238.

'President Kruger had a wonderful chance to make the Transvaal a strong Afrikaner state. . . . Instead he has devoted his utmost powers to building up and supporting a Hollander party. To it we owe our present financial disasters, and every other mistake that has been made.'

A public meeting at Bosfontein (Lydenburg district) unanimously adopted a motion, calling for close control of the Netherlands company and doubting whether Dr. Leyds could act simultaneously as an efficient State Secretary and Commissioner for the Netherlands Railway.[24] At Barberton[25] and again at Pietersburg,[26] General P. J. Joubert attacked the government's railway policy, declaring that 'his general opinions about that policy had been clearly set out in his pamphlets and in the newspapers, and they were still unchanged. He was sorry to say that the terms and conditions of the Netherlands Railway Company's concession had never been discussed in his presence in the Executive Council.'[27] At Potchefstroom, similarly, Ewald Esselen, later chairman of Joubert's election committee, attacked the government on this issue.[28] There was considerable criticism of the Netherlands company in the Volksraad debate on the State loan, and President Kruger found it expedient to emphasize that the raising of the loan would give the government greater control over the company.[29] There was frequent reference in this debate to the unrest among the public on the issue, and *Land en Volk* on 7 July 1892 underlined this feeling in a leader which declared:

'We now owe England £2 million.[30] Debt is never anything to rejoice about, particularly when it is a debt to your enemy. Now the President will have the money to hand over to his beloved Netherlands company. Talk of expropriation is highly optimistic. The Hollanders will fight to the last, just as they are fighting for the scandalous dynamite concession. The President has taken the Hollanders and the Jews under his special protection, and he completely domi-

[24] *Volksstem*, 9 Mar. 1892.

[25] *Press*, 8 Feb. 1892; *Volksstem*, 9 Feb. 1892 and 16 Feb. 1892.

[26] *Volksstem*, 29 Mar. 1892.

[27] This was a favourite gambit of Joubert's (see below, pp. 257, 270) though in this case it happened to be true (see Van Winter, i, p. 254).

[28] *Press*, 24 Mar. 1892; *Volksstem*, 23 Mar. 1892.

[29] *Land en Volk*, 30 June 1892; *Volksstem*, 29 June 1892 (*Notulen*, Eerste Volksraad, 1892, art. 573). For those voting against see pp. 34–5, above.

[30] Actually £2,500,000 (see above, p. 35).

nates the First Volksraad. He will not give way. In any case, even if the Netherlands Railway Company were prepared to be expropriated, with what would we buy them out? The line is only one-third complete to Nelspruit, and that has already cost almost £2 million.[31] With what will we complete the line from Nelspruit to Pretoria? We are chained to the company with strong chains. . . . "Land en Volk" has always said that the Netherlands Railway Company was the South African Republic's most dangerous enemy. Events have proved this true. It has sold our line to Rhodes and the Cape Government, and since their line will reach Pretoria first the whole purpose of the Delagoa Bay railway is negated;[32] and, secondly, it has put us in bondage to England. Are these not the acts of an enemy? Why has great-hearted Holland not helped us?"[33]

Ridiculous as the basic allegation of this passage is (i.e. that the President was, either via the company or in any other way, prepared to 'sell out' to Rhodes and the Cape Government) its tone reflects accurately enough the general nature of opposition criticism of the Netherlands company.

The Report of the Volksraad Railway Commissioners (Chairman Jan P. Meyer with Lukas Meyer, J. P. L. Lombaard and J. van der Merwe) set up on 19 July to inquire into the company's progress,[34] served to pour some cold water upon these energetically-fanned flames. It predicted that, in spite of the loss of a virtual year through lack of funds, the Delagoa Bay line would be completed by the end of 1894. The members of the Commission were 'satisfied that the company was using the minimum of staff and exercising every economy', and that it was 'making every effort to recruit as much of its personnel as possible from the burghers of the country'. It gave full details of expenditure to date, and estimated that the cost of construction, taking the whole line from the Portuguese border to the Vaal River, would work out at £11,250 a mile. It concluded that, although the rumours of wastefulness were not usually entirely base-

---

[31] Actually £1¾ million (see Report of Volksraad Railway Commission, *Volksstem*, 17 Aug. 1892).

[32] This was hardly proved by subsequent events.

[33] This is sarcastically meant. One of Kruger's chief debating points was that Holland had been the Republic's only friend in its days of poverty (see, for example, Kruger's speech at Wakkerstroom, *Volksstem*, 22 Mar. 1892, also Nathan, p. 273).

[34] *Volksstem*, 17 Aug. 1892 (*Notulen*, Eerste Volksraad, 1892, art. 1193).

less, they were generally wildly exaggerated generalizations drawn from minor instances.

Nevertheless, there was strong criticism of the Report in the debates of 17 and 19 August.[35] Loveday declared that no proper investigation had been made, and that such investigation as there had been had consisted of accepting the answers given by Dr. Leyds and Netherlands company officials to the allegations made in various memorials. He called for a proper committee of inquiry. Dr. Leyds, in his capacity as Acting Railway Commissioner,[36] although admitting some of Loveday's more minor charges (such as over-spending on cement, and the purchase of a considerable quantity of unnecessary dynamite—later resold at a slight profit) had little difficulty in bringing the Raad round to the official point of view, and the Railway Commissioners' Report was adopted by 18 votes to 3[37] (Loveday, Paul Maré and Lukas Meyer—himself a member of the Commission—voting in the minority). Schalk Burger, L. de Jager and J. P. L. Labuschagne were absent,[38] and the first two members would almost certainly have voted with the minority had they been there.[39]

During the election campaign of 1892–3 the Netherlands Railway issue played its part with other grievances in arousing opposition to the President. General Joubert declared in his election addresses that 'half the money spent on the Delagoa Bay line had been wasted'[40] (a rather sweeping allegation which would have been difficult to prove), and asserted that the terms of the concession had never been dealt with by the Executive Council, but arranged at a private meeting,[41] and only later put before the Volksraad for approval.

'He himself had never seen the concession, though he had been told it was advantageous to the State. They were merely told that the Hollanders would build the line for them "as cheaply as possible". Another company had offered to build the line at £8,000 a mile, but

[35] *Volksstem*, 17 Aug. 1892, 20 Aug. 1892, 23 Aug. 1892; *Land en Volk*, 25 Aug. 1892 (*Notulen*, Eerste Volksraad, 1892, arts. 1195–1244).

[36] *Volksstem*, 4 June 1892; Fitzpatrick, p. 57. He had resigned some months earlier (*Volksstem*, 4 June 1892).

[37] *Notulen*, Eerste Volksraad, 1891, arts. 1243–4.

[38] Ibid., art. 1238.

[39] *Land en Volk*, 12 May 1891.

[40] *Land en Volk*, 3 Nov. 1892 (speech at Marthinus Wessel Stroom). See also Election Manifesto (*Land en Volk*, 1 Sept. 1892).

[41] This was true (see Van Winter, i, p. 254).

this had not been accepted as it had been said that the Netherlands company would do it for £4,000. He had asked why this was not in the concession, and had been told that the members of the company were honest men. Yes, grey with honesty! (Laughter). He had not been prepared to identify himself with such vague conditions. He had been treated as if he were mad [als een gek beschouwd] because of this and because he had asserted that "business was business" [dat bezigheid, bezigheid was] and sent away next morning on government service. On his return he had found that everything had been settled, that the Volksraad had given permission to the Executive Council to act. He had immediately had a pamphlet printed, in which he had declared his grievances. The result was that the country was now in great debt.'[42]

But Joubert suggested no alternative policy, apart from his consistent advocacy of the Natal line.[43]

Chief Justice Kotzé, the third candidate for the Presidency in the 1893 election, also attacked the whole railway policy of the government.[44]

President Kruger, as in his tour of the constituencies early in the year, found his railway policy the subject of much hostile criticism.[45] His speech at Krugersdorp on 6 December 1892 gives a characteristic defence of his railway policy, and is clearly intended as an answer to Joubert's allegations. The *Press* of 7 December 1892 reports it as follows:

'He wished to disabuse the burghers of the absurd impression that prevailed among the farmers[46] that debts contracted by the State heaped contumely upon it in the eyes of other nations. He explained the necessity of borrowing money in furtherance of public works, and repeated over and over again with eloquent emphasis that these railway systems and schemes were regulated in such a way that the Companies bore the full brunt of any possible losses, and that the

[42] *Land en Volk*, 17 Nov. 1892 (speech at Middelburg, 1 Nov. 1892). See also Bronkhorstspruit speech, *Volksstem*, 15 Nov. 1892.

[43] *Land en Volk*, 3 Nov. 1892; above, pp. 61–2; *Volksstem*, 11 Jan. 1893; *Press*, 17 Nov. 1892.

[44] *Volksstem*, 19 Oct. 1892.

[45] *Volksstem*, 22 Oct. 1892, 1 Nov. 1892, 5 Nov. 1892; *Land en Volk*, 1 Sept. 1892, 13 Oct. 1892, 17 Nov. 1892.

[46] This is an interesting admission of the widespread public discontent on this issue.

State and burghers were fully indemnified.[47] The State took over the Company's railways as soon as they were run on profitable lines. Then, and not before, did the State participate in the profit-sharing or loss-bearing. Whatever happened, his line would reach Pretoria and Johannesburg first.[48]

'One of the advantages of railways was—well, he was an old man; but not too old to build iron ships (Applause).'

The Presidential opening speech to the 1893 Volksraad session began with a confident survey of railway prospects.[49] He formally announced the successful conclusion of a State loan of £2½ million at 5 per cent, and the connexion, during the recess, of Pretoria and Johannesburg to the Cape Railway system. The Delagoa Bay line was pushing ahead in spite of the ravages of fever on the workmen. A definite survey of the proposed Selati line had started, steps were being taken to connect Barberton to the eastern (i.e. Delagoa Bay) railway system, and a survey of the line from Charlestown to Johannesburg had been ordered.

That supporters of the government had been more than mildly shaken by the extent of the disquiet among the burghers on the railway issue is suggested, perhaps, by the hostile attitude which the pro-government *Press*, hitherto largely non-committal on the matter, began to assume once President Kruger was safely back in office.[50] On 18 May 1893 it launched a violent attack on the running of the Pretoria–Johannesburg line. The fares were exorbitant, the 30-odd miles took between four and seven hours to cover. There were too many accidents. 'Monumental chaos' reigned, and the public were being driven back to the ox-wagon. On the 24th it called for a commission of inquiry into the Netherlands Railway Company, alleging, among other things, that fortunes were being made in Amsterdam by suppliers of material, and that the company's administration was characterized by extortionate charges, insolence, inefficiency, and a complete lack of sympathy for the public. In a long and detailed analysis of the company's finances a short time later it stressed that the State's liability in interest payments now totalled £347,300 per

[47] This was certainly not true of the Selati Concession (see *Weekly Press*, 23 Oct. 1897; Fitzpatrick, pp. 56–8; below, pp. 79–85).

[48] That is, before the Natal line.

[49] *Volksstem*, 2 May 1893; *Land en Volk*, 4 May 1893; *Press*, 2 May 1893 (*Notulen*, Eerste Volksraad, 1893, art. 14, paragraphs 6 to 11).

[50] See Preface, p. xviii, footnote 43.

year (£250,482 on the Rothschild loan and payment of interest on share capital and debentures and £96,818 on redemption payments— for by the terms offered the whole of the loans and debentures had to be redeemed within 55 years).[51] On 23 June, in a leader headed 'Away with this intolerable incubus!' it declared that 'the prosperity of the State is being messed and muddled away by insolent autocratic nincompoops who have no more idea of railway management than so many raw Mashonas'. Mr. Loveday, or *Land en Volk*, could hardly have done better.

In August, in an interview with the *Press*, the General Manager of the Netherlands Railway Company, G. Middelberg, denied most of these allegations, and took much of the sting out of them by announcing that, at the request of the government, the company had taken over the whole of the State (or Rothschild) loan of £2,500,000, and was itself now responsible for all obligations, sinking fund, and the repayment of capital when the loan expired.[52]

The First Raad debate which occurred in the same month, on the allied question of whether or not to allow the extension of the Natal line from Charlestown to Johannesburg, demonstrated the mounting division in that body over railway policy. The fact that the Cape Town–Pretoria line had been operating since the beginning of the year had taken the heart out of the old single-minded opposition to all railways except the Delagoa Bay one. Even the *Volksstem*, on 11 August 1893, had given qualified support to the Natal line, and with Joubert and his followers powerfully supporting it, the main target of the government's striving had dwindled to a determination to keep the Natal line from completion until the Delagoa Bay line had reached Pretoria. A somewhat confused debate[53] revealed the divided minds of many members on the matter. Some, like J. Malan and P. G. Roos, 'Conservatives of the old stamp',[54] totally opposed the Natal line and 'did not wish to be the murderers of the Delagoa Bay line'. Others, like A. D. W. Wolmarans, admitted that many of their constituents were in favour of the Natal line, but said that they themselves distrusted it. President Kruger 'while he would not say

[51] *Press*, 3 June 1893. (These payments were, of course, charged to the company's account, and would only fall upon the State if the company defaulted. See below, p. 74, footnote 66.)

[52] *Press*, 31 Aug. 1893.

[53] *Notulen*, Eerste Volksraad, 1893, arts. 1193–5 (*Volksstem*, 26 Aug. 1893; *Land en Volk*, 25 Aug. 1893).

[54] *Volksstem*, 1 Sept. 1894.

that the Natal line must not be built until the Delagoa Bay line had been completed', pleaded rather ambiguously for delay until 'various difficulties in the way had been cleared up'.[55] The 'Progressives', on the other hand, were wholeheartedly for the Natal line. The voting after the debate demonstrated the divisions on this issue clearly. A Conservative motion, submitted by Wolmarans and Roos, to postpone consideration of the matter, was defeated by 16 votes to 6;[56] a slightly more enthusiastic one, by Schutte and Prinsloo, to reject the Natal line until the Delagoa Bay line had been completed, was defeated by 14 votes to 8. A 'Progressive' motion, by L. Meyer and C. Jeppe, to approve the Volksrust–Johannesburg line and to encourage the government to remove any political difficulties in the way as speedily as possible, to appoint a commission of five members to report in consultation with the government, and, finally, not to open the line until the Delagoa Bay line had been completed, was narrowly defeated by 12 votes to 11. (Those voting in the minority were R. K. Loveday, L. Meyer, Paul Maré, L. de Jager, G. de Jager, C. Jeppe, Schalk Burger, J. du P. de Beer, C. Birkenstock, C. B. Otto and E. C. Hamman.) Finally, after further debate, a compromise resolution put forward by Schalk Burger and J. C. Fourie (the two members for Lydenburg) was adopted by 17 votes to 6.[57] It approved the building of the line, and the putting of the construction of the line out to tender, but it left it to the government 'to remove any difficulties in the way with all possible speed'. Upon receipt of the news flags were flown in Durban and joyous crowds besieged the newspaper offices;[58] but, as if to underline the somewhat ambivalent nature of the Volksraad resolution, the *Volksstem* leader of 30 August 1893 declared that:

'Though there has been much criticism in the Bloemfontein papers of the Volksraad decision, and the South African Republic has been accused of breaking treaties etc. we must point out that there is no question of the breaking of the Potchefstroom Convention[59] until

[55] Probably a reference to negotiations over Swaziland, in which the Natal Railway was a bargaining counter, and also to O.F.S. and Portuguese objections.

[56] *Notulen*, Eerste Volksraad, 1893, art. 1193.

[57] *Notulen*, Eerste Volksraad, 1893, arts. 1194–5, gives only Loveday, P. Maré, J. du P. de Beer and Lukas Meyer as specifically asking for their names to be recorded in the minority.

[58] *Press*, 25 Aug. 1893.

[59] The Transvaal–O.F.S. agreement of March 1889 which 'tied the Orange Free State to Kruger's chariot-wheels' (*C.H.B.E.*, viii, p. 525).

an actual beginning has been made with the line. There is many a slip 'twixt the cup and the lip!'

Nevertheless the Volksraad decision was an important step in the direction of completion of the Natal line, and in some sense a surrender to 'Progressive' pressure, and the *Press* was able, quite fairly, to say on 30 August, in summing up the 1893 session, that:

'Although referred to by some as more retrogressive than ever, its policy has been most progressive with reference to railways. The Charlestown line will open up the Wakkerstroom, Ermelo and Standerton districts. The Vryheid line, sanctioned on 28th August by 18 votes to 5, is a natural corollary. The Pietersburg line will at once be put in hand. With these and the Delagoa Bay, Selati and Barberton lines all under way the Volksraad may well rest content for some time to come.'

The 1893 Volksraad session, however, did not end on this note of general all-round congratulations. The Report of the Volksraad Railway Commission (consisting, significantly enough, of Schalk Burger, as Chairman, aided by Lukas Meyer and R. K. Loveday), which was presented on 6 September,[60] contained considerable criticism of the Netherlands Railway Company. It took strong objection to the company's statements that its financial difficulties were due to decreased confidence in the Republic; it declared itself shocked at the director's inability, in spite of the Raad's frequently expressed desire, to tell them what the line to Nelspruit had cost, and itself estimated the cost to have been £23,959 per mile; it disapproved of the fact that no final estimate of the cost of the southern line had yet been given, and considered the tentative estimate of £11,628 per mile to be excessive over such relatively easy terrain; and it recommended that the Government Railway Commissioner (J. S. Smit, who had succeeded Dr. Leyds in this position in October 1892) make more use of the powers of investigation and control given him by article 11 of the concession. Fortunately for the company, the Volksraad decided that the Railway Report was too important to discuss cursorily, and full consideration of it was postponed to the following session.[61]

---

[60] *Volksstem*, 9 Sept. 1893; Van Winter, ii, p. 187; *Notulen*, Eerste Volksraad, 1893, art. 1329.

[61] *Volksstem*, 9 Sept. 1893 (*Notulen*, Eerste Volksraad, 1893, art. 1332).

In February 1894, Loveday, from the first the foremost critic of the Netherlands company,[62] returned to the attack, accusing the government of having involved the State in almost £7½ million of debts.[63] He was angrily answered by A. D. W. Wolmarans,[64] who declared that it was unjust to include in the State's liabilities the entire capital of the Netherlands company, of which only the interest was guaranteed by the government, accused him of having been false to the State in 1877 by petitioning for British annexation, and declared that it 'was a painful thing that such a traitor should sit in the highest council of the land'. In reply[65] Loveday stood by his allegations and published a detailed statement of the total debts of the Republic, chiefly the result of railway loans, which amounted to over £7 million, and involved the State in yearly interest payments of £347,253.[66] With the further railway expansion projected, this debt would rise to over £10 million. Every penny of the Netherlands company's capital had been underwritten by the State, which thus made itself financially responsible for the whole amount. (This, of course, is substantially correct.) Without such underwriting the Netherlands company would never have been able to obtain funds from overseas investors. He still maintained that the company was a clique of speculators, and a very lucky clique. (So shrewd a propagandist as Loveday should have realized that the second half of this last statement, in business circles, generally wipes away any reproach which the first half may conceivably contain.) Finally, he declared that he was as good an Afrikaner as Wolmarans, but 'one of those Afrikaners who wishes to expose and crush fearlessly the cursed corruption and immorality which . . . was undermining the foundations of the Republic', and not one of those who 'looks upon the Republic as a milch-cow maintained at the cost of the burghers of the South African Republic for their especial benefit'.

This, needless to say, drew a virulent three-column reply from Wolmarans,[67] in which he declared that he had never denied the underwriting of the loans by the State, but stressed that this would

---

[62] Fitzpatrick, p. 51.

[63] *Land en Volk*, 25 Feb. 1894.

[64] *Volksstem*, 13 Mar. 1894.

[65] *Volksstem*, 14 Apr. 1894 (letter dated 31 Mar. 1894).

[66] It is true that the State did not actually pay the interest. This had been taken over by the company and debited to the State's account, until such time as the State took over the railway (see *Press*, 20 Mar. 1894).

[67] *Volksstem*, 1 May 1894.

never be of any practical importance unless the Netherlands Railway Company collapsed.[68] He 'answered' the indelicate aspersions in the latter part of Loveday's letter by asserting that 'a lamb which grows up among goats does not turn into a goat, and goes back to its own kind as soon as it gets the opportunity'.

With the stage thus dramatically set by the somewhat uninhibited polemics of the foremost opponent and the foremost supporter of the Netherlands company, the coming 1894 session seemed to promise pleasing excitement. Nor was it long in coming. On 16 May 1894 the member for Barberton was the object of an excited attack by Wolmarans, the chief point of which was an unfortunate phrase in Loveday's letter to *Land en Volk* in which he had described certain members of the Raad as 'stupid enough or crooked enough [dom genoeg of schelm genoeg] to tell their constituents that there was no national debt.'[69] On the 18th a motion was passed by 16 votes to 7 asking Loveday to withdraw his allegations in *Land en Volk* of 25 February, 'which insulted the whole Raad'. If he declined to do so, the matter would be put in the hands of the State Attorney. (Those who voted for Loveday were L. Meyer, P. Maré, C. Jeppe, L. de Jager and G. de Jager—who, with Loveday, formed the hard core of the Progressives—joined on this occasion by J. Malan and J. P. L. Lombaard.) Loveday, the leader of the 'noble half-dozen' as the Johannesburg *Star* on this occasion called them, refused to withdraw and declared himself ready to submit to the decision of the State Attorney. The latter advised that there was no case against Loveday; but the pro-government faction in the Raad, which had simmered down somewhat but was still righteously indignant, secured the passage of a motion expelling Loveday for one day and threatening to take action against *Land en Volk* for publishing his libellous allegations.[70] Those voting against the motion were, once again, L. Meyer, C. Jeppe, P. Maré, L. de Jager and G. de Jager —five of the 'noble half-dozen' of whom Loveday constituted the sixth—this time swelled by the addition of J. H. de la Rey (who on 29 August had been sworn in for Lichtenburg in the place of

---

[68] This, of course, is also substantially correct. No railway of any size has ever been built without large-scale capital loans, as Schalk Burger himself admitted (see speech at Rietfontein, *Volksstem*, 30 Mar. 1892). Their justification, or condemnation, lies basically in their success or failure. The Netherlands Railway was certainly not a failure.

[69] *Volksstem*, 16 May 1894 (*Notulen*, Eerste Volksraad, 1894, arts. 107–9).

[70] *Land en Volk*, 27 Sept. 1894 (*Notulen*, Eerste Volksraad, 1894, arts. 1775–6).

E. C. Hamman, and who is described, though with somewhat variable justification,[71] by Carl Jeppe as a 'Progressive'), C. Birkenstock and J. du P. de Beer.[72]

This, however, was the solitary firework of the 1894 session as far as railways were concerned. Fear of Rhodes's intrigues had temporarily drawn the parties together;[73] and, apart from a not particularly successful attack by Loveday on the new Railway Commissioner, J. S. (Koos) Smit, there was little political activity on the railway issue. The Railway Report presented to the Volksraad by Smit that year[74] reflected an increasingly sound situation in the Netherlands Railway Company's affairs. Its total assets amounted to £4,175,672. It had paid its interest and other commitments with ease, set aside nearly £60,000 into its reserve fund, and its income averaged £58,827 per month. The *Volkstem* (8 August 1894) commended the Report heartily; and the *Press*, which had now modified its attitude, welcomed the profit of £261,643 (though pointing out that it was the result of high tariffs), praised the Netherlands company highly, and declared that there was no mismanagement or squandering; but, significantly, it voiced a demand for the expropriation of the whole Netherlands Railway Company by the State as soon as the main line was in working order.[75] This was to be the keynote of 'Progressive' demands during the session of the following year.

The Congress of the newly created Volksmacht, described by the *Volksstem* of 9 March 1895 as the 'working Committee of the Progressive movement', set the ball rolling by approving of a resolution calling for 'the taking over of the property of the Netherlands South African Railway Company, if, after thorough investigation, this should appear necessary', a demand immediately approved by *Land en Volk* (14 March 1895). The elections to fill the vacancies caused by biennial retirement of half the First Raad had, according to the *Volksstem*'s rather pessimistic forecast, 'brought new life into the Progressives' camp'. Among the 'all sorts of wonderful things' which they would do, according to the gloomy and somewhat tactless prophecy of that newspaper, they would

---

[71] See below, p. 158, and chart on p. 245.

[72] *Land en Volk*, 27 Sept. 1894.

[73] Below, pp. 233–7.

[74] *Volksstem*, 8 Aug. 1894 (Special Supplement) (*Notulen*, Eerste Volksraad, 1894, art. 1713).

[75] *Press*, 13 July 1894; Van Winter, ii, pp. 254, 267.

'make the Railway national property, clean it of Dutch infection, and have the vacancies filled by streams of talented and worthy Afrikaners, eager to serve the State, and even more eager to live at its cost'.[76]

On 22 August the reconstituted First Raad debated the Progressive demand for expropriation of the Netherlands Railway Company.[77] But, in spite of the *Volksstem*'s pessimistic forecast, the government won the debate by 16 votes to 8. Those who voted for expropriation were[78] R. K. Loveday, L. Meyer, P. Maré, C. Jeppe, G. de Jager, and three new members, J. L. van Wyk (Krugersdorp), W. H. van Niekerk (Lydenburg), and W. J. Steyn (Standerton). L. de Jager, a consistent member of the 'noble half-dozen', expressed no opinion; and among those who voted with the government were such occasional opponents as Schalk Burger (now Chairman of the First Raad), C. Birkenstock, J. H. (Koos) de la Rey and J. du P. de Beer. The *Volksstem* (24 August 1895) rejoiced that 'another still-born child of the so-called Progressives was quietly buried yesterday, accompanied by some eight members of the Volksraad under the leadership of Loveday and Jeppe', while *Land en Volk* (29 August) remarked bitterly that 'the Hollanders could now carry on with their fantastically high freight charges, and with their pocketing of our import duties at the Portuguese border'. The *Press* held the balance by agreeing 'that the time for expropriation will come, but the Volksraad majority are correct in feeling that it has not come yet', and it strongly defended the position of the Netherlands company.[79]

On the 'Drifts Crisis' too, which broke out about this time, and which brought South Africa within measurable distance of an appeal to arms, the Progressive party took an anti-government stand. The crisis had been produced by a rates war between the Cape railways and the Netherlands company.

The pro-government press played the issue down as much as possible, supporting the Netherlands Railway Company's viewpoint and the President's action fully. The *Press* (26 August 1895) described the trebling of the rates on the 40-mile section from the Vaal to Johannesburg, and the closing of the drifts, as 'simply a matter of protection on our part', pledged its full support 'now that the ques-

[76] *Volksstem*, 13 Mar. 1895.
[77] *Notulen*, Eerste Volksraad, 1895, art. 980.
[78] *Volksstem*, 24 Aug. 1895; *Weekly Press*, 24 Aug. 1895, pp. 3–4.
[79] *Weekly Press*, 24 Aug. 1895, p. 4.

tion is being made a political and not a commercial one' (30 September) and laughed off any suggestion that there could be 'any dreadful consequences'.[80] (This in spite of Cape and O.F.S. indignation, and the ordering of British troops to the Cape.) The *Volksstem* (7 September 1895) inveighed against 'Progressive obstructionism' and the 'spirit of blind partisanship' that they had shown, and declared that

'the fact that the Railway is the life-line of our independence means little to this party. As long as Johannesburg, the new Babylon, draws some temporary advantages which enable its already luxury-loving population to make even more profit, these people feel that they have achieved their aim.'

And when *Land en Volk* (5 September 1895) asserted, not without some cause, that

'the closing of the drifts demonstrates clearly how the Netherlands South African Railway Company dictates policy in this Republic. The Hollanders are making enemies of all our best friends, and the Republic will have to pay for it',

the *Volksstem* attacked its whole attitude as 'clearly pro-Cape' and declared itself shocked that 'a paper on this side of the Vaal River' could take up such an unpatriotic tone. The eventual opening of the drifts was similarly played down, the *Volksstem* (surely somewhat dishonestly) describing the intention to reopen them, in a leader of 2 November 1895, as 'a gesture of goodwill to the Cape Colony . . . all the more praiseworthy because it was not yielded under pressure' and advising the government in the coming Railway Conference to 'lay stress on its rights to close the drifts again at any time'. On this note of controversy the year 1895 closed.

We see, to sum up, that, like the other issues which have been considered, disagreement over the government's tender solicitude towards the Netherlands Railway Company formed another nucleus of 'Progressive' discontent. Again, it is the same names which regularly occur in the list of those voting in opposition—R. K. Loveday, L. Meyer, P. Maré, and L. de Jager, swelling to a regular six after the election to the First Raad in 1893 of C. Jeppe and G. de Jager, and after the 1895 elections to an almost equally steady nine or ten with the entry into the Raad of J. L. van Wyk, W. H. van Niekerk,

[80] *Weekly Press*, 12 Oct. 1895, p. 3.

D. J. Joubert and W. J. Steyn. To this number can often be added the name of Schalk Burger, a keen critic of the government's railway policy, until his change of front between 1893 and 1894,[81] and, less frequently, those of such members as C. Birkenstock, J. du P. de Beer, J. J. Spies, C. B. Otto and other political unpredictables. We can therefore safely say that on the Netherlands Railway issue, too, opposition to the government was slowly but steadily mounting in the six years between 1890 and 1895. That this opposition had some justification was suggested in due course by the Report of the Industrial Commission in August 1897, which, while not considering itself competent to go into detail on the matter, laid down as its considered opinion that the Netherlands company's tariffs were far too high,[82] and that a reduction in these tariffs would not only bene-fit the mining industry considerably 'but would carry with it, as a natural consequence, that the neighbouring States and Colonies would have to reduce their tariffs considerably'. They suggested, using the revenue of 1896 as a guide,[83] a reduction in rates of 25 per cent, to be applied chiefly to the traffic in coal, timber, mining machinery and foodstuffs (after negotiations for similar reductions by neighbouring states), and recommended, finally, that the govern-ment 'make such arrangements, as will secure to them in the future, a voice in the fixing of the tariffs of the Netherlands South African Railway Company'. They did not, however, favour expropriation of the company 'provided that by other means terms can be secured from the company so as to obtain the reduction at present urgently required on the basis above set forth'.[84]

The Selati Railway concession, although in every respect as susceptible to criticism as the Netherlands Railway concession, if not a good deal more so, and although certainly infinitely less successful in its practical execution,[85] did not come in for anything like the same

[81] See pp. 225–8.

[82] For details on this point see the evidence of comparative tariffs given to the Industrial Commission by G. Albu, on behalf of the mining interests, on 19 Apr. 1897 (see *Weekly Press*, 24 Apr. 1897, p. 13). See also Van Winter, ii, pp. 300, 303–5.

[83] In 1896 the Netherlands company made a profit of £1,259,108 11*s.* 9*d.* (*Weekly Press*, 7 Aug. 1897).

[84] *Notulen*, Eerste Volksraad, 1897, art. 811, pp. 496–503, Report of the Indus-trial Commission to First Volksraad, 6 Aug. 1897 (*Weekly Press*, 14 Aug. 1897); Van Winter, ii, p. 305.

[85] By 1899 the line had progressed a little more than 70 miles beyond Komati-poort.

amount of hostility from the Progressives—although Fitzpatrick[86] gives it almost as much prominence, in his attack on the Kruger régime, as he does the Netherlands concession. Certainly there was widespread agitation against the 'Spider' and other scandals associated with its inception.[87] But once this had died down, it was allowed to go its way fairly peacefully, apart from an occasional unenthusiastic review of its progress and prospects in the press,[88] until its obvious nearness to collapse in 1894–5 brought upon it the unanimous wrath of government and opposition papers alike.[89] But at no stage, either in the press, or in public meetings, or in the Volksraad, did it have to endure the unending barrage of criticism which the Netherlands concession had to surmount. It can only be guessed to what it owed this relative immunity from attack.[90] In the first place it was a relatively minor affair both politically and economically. It was not fraught with the vital consequences for inter-state relationships,[91] nor subject to the mighty pressures of rival political interests which had attended the Delagoa Bay line since its inception in the time of President Burgers; and it involved the State in lesser liabilities than the concession to the Netherlands company did—for the State guaranteed to the Selati company a dividend of 4 per cent on a share capital of £500,000, and, direct to the holders, debentures of £1,500,000 at an interest of 4 per cent.[92] Then, too, there was the fact that Paul Maré, the First Raad member for Zoutpansberg, was a director of the Selati company at an annual salary of £500,[93] and this doubtless played its part in restraining the otherwise ever-ready anti-concession enthusiasm of his political associates.

The terms of the concession were, certainly, as open to attack as any other that aroused the virtuous ire of the government's opponents. It was originally given to Barend J. Vorster, member of the First Volksraad (and later of the Second) for Zoutpansberg, in the

[86] Fitzpatrick, pp. 56–7, 248–51.

[87] See pp. 17–18.

[88] *Volksstem*, 19 Jan. 1892, 26 Mar. 1892, 22 July 1893; *Press*, 26 Feb. 1892, 13 Sept. 1892.

[89] *Volksstem*, 8 Aug. 1894, 22 Sept. 1894, 3 Nov. 1894, 6 July 1895; *Land en Volk*, 11 Oct. 1894, 17 Oct. 1895.

[90] Van Winter, ii, pp. 117–18, refers to this with some bitterness.

[91] But it was intended by Kruger to enlist the interest and sympathy of French capitalists (Marais, p. 41). See also Van Winter, ii, p. 120.

[92] Marais, p. 44.

[93] *Volksstem*, 22 July 1893.

Volksraad session of 1890, on much the same terms as those set down for the Netherlands company.[94] The concession in its final form empowered its holders to construct and operate a steam railway to the Selati goldfields and to borrow capital of up to £2,000,000, on which the government guaranteed to pay interest at 4 per cent; the line, some 200 miles in extent, was to be built at a maximum cost of £9,600 per mile; the Selati company was granted monopoly powers for twenty years; and provision was made for eventual expropriation by the State. This concession was, in due course, transferred to Baron Eugène Oppenheim, a young French speculator, and after involved financial negotiations[95] the company was duly set up in February 1892. The costs of flotation were charged at over £30,000, the major portion of this sum, according to Baron Oppenheim's own evidence, being 'travelling expenses' and payments 'to different members of the Executive Council and Volksraad of the South African Republic and their relatives and friends as the price for granting the concession'.[96] This left no funds for the actual construction of the railway, and to convince the government of the South African Republic that the share capital had been properly paid up and expended (so as to ensure governmental support for the raising of the debenture capital of £1,500,000) Oppenheim and his group had false entries made in the Selati company's books.[97]

The question of the bribery of members of the Executive Council and Volksraad was never cleared up. Denied by some members, and admitted by others, as we have seen, the allegation never came to proper investigation.[98] Certainly, as an anonymous legislator writing to the *Volksstem* had earlier declared, the concession went through with suspicious speed. Writing in the *Volksstem* of 29 January 1891, under the pseudonym of 'Ook een Raadslid', he attacked attempts to defend the acceptance of presents by members of the Volksraad from the Selati Railway Company, declaring:

'Few will believe that the promises [to vote for the concession] were not made before the decision [to grant the concession]. Four

[94] The detailed terms of the Selati concession are published in *Notulen*, Eerste Volksraad, 1891, art. 918, and also in the *Volksstem* of 8 Aug. 1890.

[95] See Marais, pp. 41–5, for a concise account of these.

[96] Plea of the Selati company during court proceedings in 1898 (*Weekly Press*, 11 June 1898, p. 14; Fitzpatrick, p. 249).

[97] Marais, p. 44.

[98] Fitzpatrick, p. 251.

to five thousand pounds would not be given out by the generous(?) giver for nothing. The morality of the question is clear, in spite of all the fine distinctions drawn . . . between bribery and acceptance of presents.

'In spite of declarations [by previous writers] that the discussions over the Selati Railway concession were long and difficult, the truth is that the discussions did not extend beyond one half of an afternoon sitting and one half of a morning sitting, that only three members spoke against the matter, and that only two voted against it!'

Meanwhile, the original concession was extended by the Volksraad in May 1892[99] and the decision was taken to build the line from Komatipoort;[1] and by August 1893 some 10 miles of rail and 45 miles of earthworks had actually been constructed.[2] By the middle of 1894 less than a third of the line had been completed, and it was obvious that the company was running into the gravest financial difficulties.[3] It asked the government's permission for a further extension of capital. This led to a sharply critical report by J. S. (Koos) Smit, the Railway Commissioner, in which he declared that 'my investigations show that the financial administration of the company leaves much to be desired', and he recommended the government to refuse its support for any further extension of capital without considerable alterations in the conditions of the concession, supervision of contracts, and general financial control.[4] This led *Land en Volk*, justifiably enough, to ask:

'Why was there no word about these irregularities from Dr. Leyds all the time he was Railway Commissioner? Why was there not a word until he resigned and an investigation was made by his successor, Koos Smit?'[5]

Other papers, as has been shown,[6] then joined in the attack upon the company. In September 1895 a Volksraad commission of five

[99] *Notulen*, Eerste Volksraad, 1892, arts. 63–5.

[1] *Volksstem*, 18 Jan. 1893.

[2] *Press*, 30 Aug. 1893.

[3] *Volksstem*, 8 Aug. 1894; *Land en Volk*, 11 Oct. 1894.

[4] *Volksstem*, 8 Aug. 1894 (*Notulen*, Eerste Volksraad, 1894, art. 1713, section II of Report).

[5] *Land en Volk*, 25 Oct. 1894 (Leyds had, in fact, strongly opposed the concession, but Kruger's will had triumphed. See Marais, p. 42.)

[6] Footnote 89, p. 80.

members was appointed to investigate the Selati company's affairs[7] and it reported the grossest negligence and every appearance of the company's having deliberately aimed at harming the State. It recommended the closest expert investigation by the State Attorney, the State Railway Commissioner, and technical and financial experts.[8] This commission in due course proposed the cancellation of the concession and the taking over by the government of all the assets of the Selati Railway Company, so as to avoid further losses to the State. This the company refused to accept. Meanwhile, early in 1895, and not without further sharp practice, the Oppenheim group sold about half their shares in London, and in 1896 a British managing director was appointed. The government, though it went on paying the interest on the debentures, now repudiated its obligation to pay dividends on the Selati company's share capital.[9] In 1898 the company took legal proceedings against the Transvaal Government, and the matter was still *sub judice* when more critical and tragic events overwhelmed the Republic.

This is the brief but unhappy story of the Selati Railway concession. It will be seen that it possesses more than all the elements which caused such stormy opposition to the Netherlands Railway concession. It was a private monopoly, a speculative concession attended by many unsavoury rumours; it involved the State in that the government underwrote the company's major loan; and, finally, as the Netherlands line had threatened to do, but had never actually done, it came to nothing, or at any rate very little. Yet at no stage did it act as a rallying-point for opposition to President Kruger and his government. In the original debate on the granting of the concession there was no opposition worth speaking of.[10] In the debates on the amended concession which took place in May 1892, and in which the President, Schalk Burger and Paul Maré strongly defended the Selati company, only six members[11] voted against the government motion to make the necessary changes in the concession in the Selati company's favour (J. van der Merwe, J. J. Spies, A. A. Stoop, J. de Clercq, L. Meyer and J. Malan) and of these only one, Lukas

[7] *Volksstem*, 11 Sept. 1895; *Land en Volk*, 17 Oct. 1895 (*Notulen*, Eerste Volksraad, 1895, art. 1132).

[8] *Notulen*, Eerste Volksraad, 1895, art. 1552, para. 7.

[9] Marais, p. 44.

[10] *Notulen*, Eerste Volksraad, 1890, arts. 1077–8; *Volksstem*, 28 July 1890. See also letter in *Volksstem*, 29 Jan. 1891, quoted above.

[11] *Volksstem*, 10 May 1892.

Meyer, can be described as a 'Progressive'. Even Loveday, in his Barberton speech of December 1891[12] in which he had attacked nearly everything under the Transvaal governmental sun, had made no mention of the Selati concession. In an equally hostile speech at the same town in February 1892,[13] General Joubert had been extremely critical of the Netherlands Railway Company concession, but had not felt it necessary to say an unkind word against the Selati concession. Neither had Ewald Esselen in a rip-roaringly anti-governmental speech at Potchefstroom in the following month.[14] The Presidential tour at the beginning of 1892 produced innumerable critical questions about the Netherlands company, but, as far as can be ascertained from press reports of his meetings with the burghers,[15] none at all about the Selati concession. Nor does it appear to have been an issue in the 1892–3 election campaign.[16] This immunity from criticism did not escape the notice of the *Volksstem*, which declared on 5 July 1893:

'It is remarkable how quiet the English press is about the Selati Railway Company, which has been given to an English firm of contractors. When the Netherlands South African Railway Company was busy in the Lowveld an ox could not die nor a sack of mealies or cement be unloaded without an unholy row [heidensche lawaai] being raised; and Mr. Loveday was always ready to stand forth as the champion of the people—cheated, oppressed, and sucked dry by the Railway Company!'

In the debates of July 1893[17] the only members to raise their voices against the Selati company were C. Jeppe, J. P. L. Lombaard, J. Malan, A. D. W. Wolmarans, J. J. Spies and J. du P. de Beer—a group ranging from ultra-Progressive to ultra-Conservative. And though the *Volksstem* saw fit to pronounce on 22 September 1894 that 'we have to thank the "Progressives" for the Selati Railway', this was blatantly political propaganda of the same order as *Land en*

[12] *Volksstem*, 31 Dec. 1891.
[13] *Volksstem*, 9 Feb. 1892 and 16 Feb. 1892.
[14] *Press*, 24 Mar. 1892; *Volksstem*, 23 Mar. 1892.
[15] *Volksstem*, 15 Mar. 1892, 16 Mar. 1892, 22 Mar. 1892, 23 Mar. 1892; *Press*, 17 Mar. 1892, 21 Mar. 1892; *Land en Volk*, 23 Feb. 1892, 22 Mar. 1892.
[16] *Volksstem*, 19 Oct. 1892, 22 Oct. 1892, 26 Oct. 1892, 1 Nov. 1892, 5 Nov. 1892; *Land en Volk*, 1 Sept. 1892, 13 Oct. 1892, 27 Oct. 1892, 17 Nov. 1892; *Press*, 26 Oct. 1892, 17 Nov. 1892, 7 Dec. 1892.
[17] *Volksstem*, 25 July 1893 (*Notulen*, Eerste Volksraad, 1893, arts. 846–8).

Volk's occasional attempts to portray President Kruger as an agent of Rhodes,[18] and may be dismissed for what it is worth.

The evidence, then, is largely negative. As a cause of internal political opposition to the régime, or as a rallying point for 'Progressive' opposition, the Selati Railway issue played a negligible role. Nor can we consider support for the Selati company, conversely, to have been an issue uniting the 'Progressives' in the Raad, for Lukas Meyer and C. Jeppe, as we have seen, were among the few to attack the concession; and of the five members of the commission who eventually condemned the Selati company's gross negligence and demanded full investigation of its affairs by the State Attorney (Jan P. Meyer–Chairman, Schalk Burger, R. K. Loveday, C. J. Birkenstock and L. Meyer)[19] Loveday and Lukas Meyer were leading Progressives, and Birkenstock and Burger had frequently voted with them against the government in matters of railway policy.

[18] See p. 67 above, and *Land en Volk*, 19 Jan. 1893.
[19] *Volksstem*, 11 Sept. 1895, 9 Oct. 1895; *Weekly Press*, 12 Oct. 1895, p. 10.

4

The Issues around which Opposition Crystallized
(*continued*)

V. INEFFICIENCY AND CORRUPTION OF THE ADMINISTRATION

THIS issue forms a continual refrain in the allegations of the opponents of the Kruger régime; and could, if one were to go into it in detail, well form the subject of a separate book. That it had some foundation has already been indicated.[1] The brief analyses given of the policy of concessions, more particularly with regard to the dynamite monopoly and Selati Railway concessions, have shown that financial practices were tolerated, and that members of the government, or persons in its good books, were financially benefited by them, to a degree which would have called forth grave condemnation in other states of South Africa and in most countries of Western Europe. Most of the allegations made in the early 1890s by uitlander critics, and by internal critics such as *Land en Volk*, were solidly based. Even such a friendly modern critic as Nathan in his *Paul Kruger, his life and times* (1941) admits the existence of such unsavoury 'pressure-groups' as the so-called 'Third Volksraad' . . . 'with whom seekers of favours negotiated for Concessions, grants of land and appointments to office, [who] intrigued with certain members of the Executive, and with heads of departments', and to which F. C. Eloff and other relatives of the President belonged.[2]

Patronage was widely tolerated. The Joubert Papers, for instance, contain endless examples of letters requesting the General to use his influence to secure positions for their writers. They almost invariably begin with such statements as that the writer 'has heard that the postmastership at Potchefstroom is vacant'[3] or 'has heard that the post of Justice of the Peace at Volksrust is vacant';[4] they go on to express a conviction that 'a noble heart full of sympathy for your

---

[1] See pp. 15–20 above and Marais, pp. 20–2. [2] Nathan, pp. 226, 250.

[3] Joubert Papers, Inkomende Stukke, I A/10–17 (Archives, vol. 5), no. 407 (Hogan to Joubert, Dec. 1892).

[4] Joubert Papers, vol. 5, no. 418 (H. V. Kiezer to Joubert, 19 Aug. 1892).

upright fellow-Afrikaners beats in the General's bosom',[5] or to complain of the appointment of a rival to an important clerical position who 'from his youth upwards was nothing more than a mealie-farmer who possessed not the slightest knowledge or understanding of office work';[6] and all, after copious references to 'my services to the country', 'my heavy sufferings for my native land' or to the fact that the writer was 'a son of the soil', 'a true and upright burgher of this land' or 'capable of doing much for my native land', go on to request the General to use his influence to secure for them 'a post at not less than £250 per annum'[7] or 'a post in the New Republic as landdrost or anything else'[8] or 'any position such as tax-gatherer or Toll-master or any other thing that your Excellency may think fit . . . for it is bitterly painful to be so poor that I cannot help myself'.[9] Many are the letters of thanks for the successful use of influence in the securing of positions;[10] and one, rather pathetically, in appealing to the General to use his good offices to secure a rise in salary for the applicant, reminds him of the story of the lion who was helped by the little mouse, and ends, 'dus stel ik mij in plaats van het kleine muisje. P.S. N.B. Geef mij toch een klein antwoord.'[11] There can be little doubt that the correspondence of other men of eminence in the Republic would yield many similar examples.

That certain papers were government-subsidized or 'bribed' by the preferential placing of advertisements is another complaint which is not without foundation. The government set aside £6,000 a year (later £7,000)[12] for advertisements the great bulk of which quite openly went to papers which largely (though not entirely) supported government policy. President Kruger, in the debate of 20 July 1892 on the matter, defended this practice and was supported by the Volksraad by 15 votes to 8.[13] The papers in question were probably the *Press*, the *Volksstem* and the *Standard & Diggers' News*, all of which were generally pro-government.[14] B. Gluckstein, first editor

[5] Joubert Papers, vol. 5, no. 403 (G. Schonken to Joubert, 15 Mar. 1887).

[6] Joubert Papers, vol. 5, no. 423 (J. Coetzer to Joubert, 4 Nov. 1892).

[7] Joubert Papers, vol. 5, no. 397 (J. R. Joubert to P. J. Joubert, 23 Sept. 1895).

[8] Joubert Papers, vol. 5, no. 405 (J. Zietsman to Joubert, 13 June 1890).

[9] Joubert Papers, vol. 5, no. 409 (P. B. van Kasterop to Joubert, 27 Feb. 1892).

[10] Joubert Papers, vol. 5, nos. 410, 428, 441, etc.

[11] Joubert Papers, vol. 5, no. 429 (C. J. Otto to Joubert, 5 Apr. 1894).

[12] *Weekly Press*, 5 Oct. 1895, p. 16.

[13] *Land en Volk*, 21 July 1892 (*Notulen*, Eerste Volksraad, 1892, arts. 855–6).

[14] See Van Winter, i, p. 238; ii, pp. 11, 132, and preface to this book.

of the *Press*, declared in a letter to *Land en Volk* of 12 January 1893 (after he had been dismissed from his editorship):

'I was asked by the person who calls himself A. Nellmapius to found a paper in the government's interest. . . . The "Press" received a £6,000 per annum subsidy from the government, partly paid via government advertisements, and it was privileged above all other papers in this respect.'

The *Volksstem*, of 5 October 1895, agreed that it received preference in government advertisements over all other Dutch-language newspapers, but denied that this affected its policy, and declared that:

'With the population of a second-rate European city, no paper can exist in South Africa without support of some kind. That the Transvaal Government does what hundreds of others do is not *so* terribly immoral as some of our Pharisees would like to make people believe. To what extent the receipt of Government support via advertisements etc. affects its policy depends on the character and principles of those who control the paper.'

Some doubt, however, is thrown on the complete credibility of the last statement by a secret Executive Council Minute of 5 April 1899 to be found in the Leyds Papers[15] which agrees to advance to E. Mendelssohn of the *Standard & Diggers' News* an amount equivalent to nine payments of 'the usual monthly subsidy . . . of £720 per month' and concludes:

'The Executive Council decided to permit the payment requested, on condition that Mr. Mendelssohn renders as security for this advance his shares in the Standard & Diggers' News as well as his person and his goods, and as a guarantee that he will support in his newspaper the same policy which he has hitherto done to the satisfaction of the Government' ('en als waarborg dat hij dezelfde politiek in zijn courant zal voorstaan die hij tot nu toe heeft gevolgd ten genoege der regeering').

President Kruger himself declared that he had no objection to supporting journals 'which criticised the Government honestly. But for the State to give support to inimical papers would be suicidal. To that he could never agree.'[16]

[15] Leyds Papers, 679, no. 45.   [16] *Weekly Press*, 5 Oct. 1895, p. 16.

It was not, of course, only the government that secured newspaper support in this way. Rhodes, for instance, through his shareholdings in the bitterly anti-government Johannesburg *Star*, dictated much of that paper's policy;[17] and for a period the *Standard & Diggers' News* was subsidized by the 'Corner House' group of mining companies. Lionel Phillips in 1894 writes:

'Lippert was paying at the rate of £1000 per year. He declined to continue. They came to us, and we have agreed to give them £87.6.8. per month so long as they support the true interests of the place [Corner House].'[18]

Fitzpatrick, in similar vein, speaks of 'a good many thousand pounds' being spent in 1894 on press and other political propaganda against the government.[19]

We have already seen that a very great laxity in the keeping of accounts and in the safeguarding of government material was tolerated; that pro-government newspapers such as the *Volksstem* and *Press* (not to speak of opposition journals such as *Land en Volk*) admitted widespread corruption among officials and the constant acceptance of the 'baksheesh' to which J. H. Hofmeyr, in the *Cambridge History of the British Empire*,[20] refers; and that the attitudes of Volksraad members and of the President himself were not as blameless in this respect as they might have been. Allegations that bribery was a common practice abound in other sources than the press. In the plea filed in 1898 by Baron Oppenheim of the Selati Railway Company during court proceedings against the government, we have seen that the allegation was made that many thousands of pounds were expended in cash and shares on payments 'asked by and paid to different members of the Executive Council and Volksraad of the South African Republic and their relatives and friends as the price for granting the Concession',[21] and that Oppenheim's allegations were never subjected to proper investigation. A letter to General Joubert, in 1892, from Julius A. Kiezer, one of his fellow shareholders in the proposed Charlestown–Johannesburg Railway (they included the Vice-President General N. J. Smit, F. C. Eloff,

[17] See the bitter attack on this by F. J. Dormer, editor of the *Star* until he resigned from it on this issue at the beginning of 1895 (F. J. Dormer, *Vengeance as a policy in Afrikanerland*, pp. 24–5).

[18] Leyds Papers, 670 (letter of Lionel Phillips to London H.Q., 8 Dec. 1894).

[19] Fitzpatrick, p. 73.   [20] Vol. viii, p. 555.

[21] *Weekly Press*, 11 June 1898, p. 14; Fitzpatrick, p. 249.

three members of the Wolmarans family and Schalk Burger), suggests 'that the sum of two thousand pounds sterling shall be subtracted from the profits, for two persons who have been helpful to us in the obtaining of this right'.[22]

The letter on dynamite affairs to his government from the French Consul at Pretoria, which, though he denied its authorship,[23] bears every hallmark of authenticity, alleges that Nobel's representatives made widespread use of bribery in their attempts to secure the cancellation of the original dynamite concession.[24] Some years later Max Philipp, Chairman of the amalgamated dynamite company, referring to the need for postponing the erection of an actual dynamite factory, so that maximum profits might be made out of the import of dynamite (rather than its less profitable manufacture), writes to his son Alberto:

'You and Mr. Vorstmann must take care that we have a majority in the Volksraad with us, let it cost what it will so that we may have the further import for years ahead'.[25]

In 1895, after it had become clear that payable reefs existed under the 'bewaarplaatsen'[26] (areas set aside for dumping of crushed residue, conservation of water, etc.), and a number of mining companies had brought to a head a violent struggle to get the underground rights to mine these areas against claimants supported by the President,[27] there were widespread rumours of extensive bribery.[28] These appear to be borne out by a letter from Lionel Phillips to Beit[29] which states:

'The Bewaarplaatsen question will, I think, be settled in our favour, but at a cost of £25,000, and then only because Christiaan Joubert[30] has stuck to us like a leech'.

[22] Joubert Papers, Inkomende Stukke, I A/10–17 (Archives, vol. 7), no. 780 of 22 July 1892.

[23] *Volksstem*, 18 Oct. 1893.

[24] Joubert Papers, Inkomende Stukke, I A/10–17 (Archives, vol. 7), no. 772 of 7 Nov. 1892.

[25] Letter of 17 Apr. 1896, quoted in Etheredge, p. 68.

[26] Marais, pp. 20, 249, 254. Also below, pp. 108–10.

[27] *Volksstem*, 28 Aug. 1895, 21 Sept. 1895; Fitzpatrick, pp. 76–7.

[28] Etheredge, p. 85.   [29] Leyds Papers, 670. Letter of 16 Jan. 1894.

[30] Minister of Mines. (Note that the Volksraad Commission Report of 9 Dec. 1896 declared Joubert 'beyond all suspicion in this matter'. *Weekly Press*, 12 Dec. 1896.)

At least one Second Volksraad member, H. C. W. Vermaas (Lichtenburg), admitted that he had been offered money by Lippert if he voted in favour of the granting of underground mining rights to the mining companies[31]—which he did not do.[32] That these practices possibly extended even to the lowest levels is suggested by the statement of A. H. Dieperink, Progressive member for Johannesburg of the First Raad after 1897, that during the elections 'Five pound notes had been flying round Johannesburg like dust. But honesty had prevailed.'[33] The somewhat unsavoury *Maherry* case of 1897, in which J. S. (Koos) Smit, the Government Railway Commissioner, sued P. J. J. Maherry for a libellous allegation that he, as Railway Commissioner, had used his influence to secure the contract for the building of the Machadodorp–Carolina–Ermelo line for Maherry, produced a number of confessions of somewhat questionable practices. These included an admission by C. J. Tosen, member of the First Raad for Piet Retief, that he had accepted £2,000 and a written promise of £5,000 in shares from Maherry to 'get the matter through', and a suggestion that Gert de Jager (member for Wakkerstroom of the First Raad) and L. de Jager (member for Ermelo of the First Raad) were financially interested in the scheme. Furthermore, although Maherry withdrew the allegation that Koos Smit was involved (and declared his intention of demanding from Tosen half the money and shares, which he had given him on this representation) 'it was not denied', as the defending lawyer, Dieperink, pointed out, 'that Smit had accepted Maherry's tender' after the proper time,[34] thus showing that he had favoured the tender. In the circumstances the presiding magistrate felt that a fine of £20 or one month would meet the case; and on this note the matter ended.[35]

The unsavoury 'Stands Scandal' of 1893, involving high and low officials, and members of the Executive Council, revealed similarly questionable practices.[36]

It is true that these instances—typical ones chosen from many more which could be brought forward—suggest, rather than prove, that an atmosphere more reminiscent of the days of Walpole than

[31] *Weekly Press*, 24 Aug. 1895, p. 3.

[32] *Volksstem*, 28 Aug. 1895.

[33] *Weekly Press*, 20 Feb. 1897.

[34] Koos Smit admitted accepting it at his house, as it 'was too late for handing in at the office'.

[35] *Weekly Press*, 22 May 1897, p. 14; 29 Feb. 1897, pp. 14, 22.

[36] See pp. 99–108.

of those of good Queen Victoria prevailed in the South African Republic. The excuses for this state of affairs, and they were very real ones, have already been indicated. We must make every allowance for what De Kiewiet[37] calls

'the greed of the financial interests that confronted their [the Transvaal's] inexperienced Government, the cynicism of men who could not understand their simple yet deep patriotism, the crookedness and vulgarity that gold had brought into their midst'.

Nevertheless, the existence of a certain degree of corruption in public affairs, admitted by both friends and foes, seems undeniable. On the other hand we must take into account the fact that not inconsiderable attempts to purify the administration were undoubtedly made. We should note, too, that the Volksraad Commission of Inquiry into the allegations of bribery made by Lionel Phillips in his 'Letter Book'[38] failed, after going fully into the matter, to find 'any proof of bribery against any head official or Volksraad member';[39] and that the Report of the Industrial Commission of 1897, though not otherwise at all favourable to the government, was pleased to declare that in the Department of Mines, at any rate, 'there exist at present all the indications of a pure administration'. Further, more than one fair contemporary critic of President Kruger's régime suggests that the allegations of widespread administrative corruption were to some degree exaggerated. Carl Jeppe[40] says, in agreeing that corrupt practices did exist:

'But—and this is greatly to the credit of the South African official as a class—the charge of general widespread corruption can be easily disproved, and in more than one way. The best evidence to the contrary is the fact that since the war the English Government has offered appointments to many, if not most, of the chief officials. It is also a fact that almost all of them—including those who had almost unlimited opportunities for pilfer, had they stooped to it—remained poor men. Finally, the Volksraad passed drastic laws against bribery, which were enforced in more than one instance, prosecutions by the State resulting in conviction and severe sentences.

[37] De Kiewiet (a), p. 132.
[38] Leyds Papers, 670.
[39] *Notulen*, Eerste Volksraad, 1896, art. 2265. But it is difficult to know what degree of credence we should give to the 'fullness' of such an investigation.
[40] Jeppe, pp. 144–5.

'The existence of the so-called 'Third Volksraad', a combination of lobbyists and hangers-on, certainly furnishes some evidence in the contrary direction: but it naturally cannot be ascertained how much of the money they received for the purpose of "distribution" reached those for whom it was intended. Probably very little of it did.'

Francis J. Dormer, one-time editor of the *Star*, who, very accurately, describes himself as 'no friend or upholder of the Transvaal Government', indeed one who has 'waged almost incessant war upon it by voice and pen for seven weary years',[41] has this to say:

'I have laboured long enough in the cause of good government in the Transvaal to warrant my running the risk of being misunderstood when I say that, after all is said and done, the Kruger administration is not quite so black as it is painted. It is not an ideal Government, to be sure; it is far from being up to date; it is not a Republic, as we understand a Republic, in anything but name; it persists in the foolish course of alienating those who should be its best friends; but, with all its faults, it has given the gold-fields the best mining law in the world; it has made railways at a rate never attempted in the Cape Colony . . . its people and its Government have ever betrayed a rare and most wholesome aversion to saddling the country with unnecessary debt.

'When one comes to think of the riot that might have been run if the fields had been located in some parts of the world, we may perceive some set-off even to the misfortune of having such a ruler as Oom Paul. . . . I do venture to believe that he does not want the Republic to lag behind the rest of South Africa in any matter that relates either to material progress or individual liberty; and that, when he once conceives himself free of the danger by which his Government has been openly and covertly menaced for some years past—a danger he has taken most inappropriate means to avert—his milder instincts will get the better of the rude ideas which have been in such painful evidence of late.'[42]

One might say, in summing up, that it would be fairer to compare the South African Republic's emergence into the era of modern industrial economy with the Reconstruction Administration of President Grant in the years that succeeded the Civil War in the

---

[41] Dormer, p. 193 (essay written in December 1895).
[42] Dormer, pp. 152–3 (essay written in September 1898).

United States, than to compare it with the more mature economy of late Victorian England. Like the Transvaal after 1886, the post-war years in the United States saw a revolution in American society and economy and an enormous acceleration of industrial development, mining, manufacturing and banking. Hand in hand with the vast development of natural resources, and the consequent waves of immigration, went an immense expansion of investment and speculation. All these phenomena, on a tinier scale, the Transvaal, too, experienced. One resulting aspect in the United States is graphically described by Nevins and Commager:[43]

'Shortly after [Grant's] access to power, stories of corruption in high places became rife, and they were not without foundation. The Union Pacific, the nation's pride, had been financed by a group of crooked promoters, who hired Congressmen to do their bidding; the Navy Department openly sold business to contractors; the Department of the Interior was a happy hunting ground for land thieves; the Indian Bureau sold post traderships to the highest bidders and neglected the welfare of its wards; the Treasury Department farmed out uncollected taxes to tax gatherers who made a good thing of it; the custom houses of New York and New Orleans were permeated with graft; a "whisky ring" in St. Louis defrauded the government of millions in excise taxes. . . . "It looks", wrote one Republican Senator, "as if the Republican party were going to the dogs. . . . I believe it is today the most corrupt and debauched political party that ever existed."

'This corruption, permeating the entire administration, seeping down into state and local politics, forfeited in time the confidence—though not the affection—of the people of the North. . . . Grant had come to office with greater prestige than any President since Jackson . . . [yet] within four years the party was split, and a Liberal Republican organisation, dedicated to reform and reconciliation, in the field.'

The parallels suggested by this passage are striking. They illustrate, if they do not condone, how a rapid pattern of economic expansion in a pioneer state often tends to produce corruption. Thus, while admitting that two wrongs do not make a right, and making due allowance for the very much smaller opportunities that the minor arena of the Transvaal afforded, one is led to the conclusion that the

[43] Nevins and Commager, pp. 277–8.

South African Republic, in the turbulent teething period of its
emergence as a modern industrial state, was, comparatively speaking,
a model of financial and administrative respectability and restraint.

However, local participants and observers, without the benefit of
the tolerant perspective afforded by history, did not feel anything
like so philosophical; and resentment of corruption and administrative inefficiency played an important, if not a major, part in stimu-
lating the emergence of a movement of opposition among the
burghers, more particularly in the Second Volksraad. We have
already seen the part played by that body in the ever-increasing, and
finally successful, campaign against concessions and monopolies,
and the infection of the First Volksraad with something of their
spirit of opposition; and we have made some reference to the bitter
opposition aroused by the acceptance of 'spiders' and other presents
by Volksraad members. Much of the 1891 session was taken up by
strong recriminations in the press, in the Volksraad, and on public
platforms, on this issue. The *Volksstem*, on 26 January 1891, in a
powerful leading article, attacked such practices, suggested that certain members of the Volksraad should consider resigning, and
admitted that 'great dissatisfaction existed among the burghers'. And
Land en Volk, in attacking President Kruger's exculpation of the
practice,[44] declared in an 'open letter' (12 May 1891) to the President
by 'Afrikanus Junior':

'You know well enough what the opinion of the Volk on the
matter was. Everyone expected you to condemn it as bitterly as the
people of South Africa did. But what was the decision of your
Excellency. "Ik siet daar gen kwaad in ni om persente aan te neem
solank dit ni omkoopery is ni". Dit was slim gese, voorwaar! ("I
see no harm in taking presents, as long as it is not bribery". That
was cunningly said, indeed!) What can we think of you? . . . You
are the man who *could* unite our nation; yet you will not. I know it is
your custom to describe all criticism as coming from enemies of the
Republic and sowers of disunity. This is the method of people like
Jan Lombaard and Stoop[45] too. Only they are the friends of the
Republic, and if anyone mentions the word "Spider", he is the
Republic's enemy. But the dissatisfaction that exists among the great

---

[44] *Volksstem*, 13 Apr. 1891 (speech at Bethal, 31 Mar. 1891).
[45] Both Conservative members of the Volksraad and strong supporters of the
President.

majority of the people does not exist because they are enemies of the Republic. It is your duty to cleanse yourself from such suspicions.'

On 18 July 1891 the *Volksstem* referred again to the growing dissatisfaction among the burghers with the administration of the State, and pressed the electorate to do something more than merely complain.

'What is the good of the public being dissatisfied with the Volksraad', it asked, 'if it keeps on electing them. Look at the storm about corruption etc. What happened to all the determination to clear up the Volksraad. . . . ? At public meetings a few stray questions were asked, the candidates delivered attacks on newspaper editors, and in the end nothing was done. Yet the whole Volk knows that the country's money is being recklessly wasted, that favouritism rules with regard to certain families which have private access to the government, and that the poor people of the country do not enjoy the full attention to which they are entitled.'

With the calling into existence of the Second Volksraad in 1891, concerned as it was chiefly with the interests of the mining and industrial areas of the Republic,[46] a forum was created for the expression of opposition to such undesirable practices, of which certain of its members were not slow to take advantage. Although at first such opposition tended to concentrate on comparatively trivial issues—irregularities in the award of contracts and deficiencies in the carrying out of public works,[47] or the absence of any system of house delivery of letters[48]—it very soon began to coalesce around issues of more importance, such as concessions and their attendant practices and allegations of corruption and maladministration among officials.

During 1892 increasing criticism was being levelled at the administration of various government departments. In an article of 9 January 1892 the *Volksstem* declared administrative reorganization to be essential, and strongly criticized the ridiculous over-centralization which made it necessary for 'every tiny detail to be referred to the President or Executive Council'.

[46] See First Raad debate of 3 July 1893 (*Notulen*, Eerste Volksraad, 1893, arts. 521–3; *Volksstem*, 4 July 1893) for evidence of the growing tendency to regard mining and financial matters as the exclusive sphere of the Second Volksraad.

[47] *Notulen*, Tweede Volksraad, 1891, arts. 461–5; *Volksstem*, 13 June 1891.

[48] *Notulen*, Tweede Volksraad, 1891, art. 169; *Volksstem*, 23 May 1891.

'Yet', it asked, 'how is devolution of authority possible while the majority of heads of Departments are unable to carry responsibility? Over half of them would be doing the country a favour, if they retired into private life, if necessary with a pension. Everyone knows which heads we mean. . . . One Department, it is said, is frankly corrupt;[49] the heads of another couple of Departments are on the brink of insolvency.'

Schalk Burger added his authoritative voice to the cry for reform of the administration.[50] The *Volksstem* on 1 March 1892 repeated its invitation to 'the officials who surround the President to realize that it is essential to put their shoulders to the wheel and extricate the wagon of State from the morass—or else, in heaven's name, make place for better men'.

As time went on it became clearer that the Departments more particularly referred to were those of Prisons, Justice and Mines. The *Press*[51] launched an open attack on Dr. F. E. T. Krause, the State Prosecutor, listing numerous examples of the inefficiency of his department; upon which the editor was duly visited by that official in person and threatened with a horsewhipping.[52] In due course 'memorials' against Krause, complaining of the undoubted inefficiency and maladministration of his Department began to arrive in the Volksraad,[53] and after due investigation, the Volksraad (since the government remained deaf to all complaints against him[54]) dismissed him from his office as 'not only incompetent but negligent', in spite of the President's plea for leniency, by 19 votes to 3.[55] Suspicion began to mount, simultaneously, against the Prisons Department. There was vague talk of corruption and wastefulness running into thousands of pounds, and of poor control of the police;[56] and

[49] 'Wordt—naar gezegd wordt—grofweg geknoeid.'

[50] *Volksstem*, 9 Feb. 1892 (letter). Also speech at Rietfontein, *Volksstem*, 30 Mar. 1892.

[51] *Press*, 11 Feb. 1892, 17 Mar. 1892.

[52] *Volksstem*, 19 Mar. 1892; *Press*, 17 Mar. 1892.

[53] *Notulen*, Eerste Volksraad, 1892, arts. 1286–8; *Volksstem*, 27 Aug. 1892.

[54] *Volksstem*, 7 Apr. 1894.

[55] *Press*, 22 Aug. 1893; *Land en Volk*, 24 Aug. 1893 (*Notulen*, Eerste Volksraad, 1893, arts. 1139–49).

[56] *Volksstem*, 12 July 1892 (*Notulen*, Eerste Volksraad, 1892, arts. 709–10). See also *Volksstem*, 6 Feb. 1890, 17 Apr. 1890. J. J. H. Wolmarans, the official referred to, was at that time Chief Commissioner of Police and Acting Inspector of Prisons.

this, too, ended in May 1894 with the retirement of the official in question, Mr. Josefus Wolmarans, a retirement to which the *Volksstem* (16 May 1894) referred as that of a man who 'though no doubt well intentioned, has been no ornament to his Department and no support to his government'.

At the same time, and very much more explosively, the attention of the Administration's critics was becoming focused increasingly upon the Department of Mines and its head, C. J. Joubert, the Minister of Mines.[57] The first major attack against him was launched in the Second Raad in June 1893 in a series of somewhat violent debates[58] on alleged irregularities in connexion with the issue and staking of mining claims. These were marked by angry exchanges between the President and the Minister of Mines on the one hand, and the by now clearly emerging group of 'Progressives'[59] led by J. F. Celliers (Witwatersrand), E. P. A. Meintjies (Pretoria), B. G. Brecher (Vryheid), J. W. Joubert (Pretoria), F. Watkins (Barberton), W. J. Jooste (Potchefstroom) and D. F. Petersen (Heidelberg), who had been joined by N. S. Malherbe (Potchefstroom) since the beginning of that session. The President admitted the illegality of some of his Minister's actions in this respect, and advanced in defence of these actions the somewhat startling claim that 'where the law is harmful to the land, I must prevent it doing harm'.[60] Subsequently, when the criticism of the Minister of Mines was pressed by N. S. Malherbe, the President stalked out of the Chamber in a rage, declaring, 'Het achtbare lid is kwaad; daarom ga ik maar weg',[61] leaving his Minister (who still persistently refused to answer any detailed questions) to justify himself with the statement that 'he had ruled the Gold Fields for six years without revolution; and that was something extraordinary in the world of Gold Fields'.[62]

[57] The most convenient translation of 'Hoofd van Mijnwezen'; but, like all officials, he was responsible to the President and his Executive, not to the legislature directly. (See *Volksstem*, 7 Mar. 1893, on this point.)

[58] Second Volksraad, 20 June 1893, 22 June 1893 (*Volksstem*, 21 June 1893, 24 June 1893; *Notulen*, Tweede Volksraad, 1893, art. 392–400).

[59] See pp. 230–3.

[60] Second Volksraad, 20 June 1893 (*Volksstem*, 21 June 1893; *Notulen*, Tweede Volksraad, 1893, art. 394).

[61] *Volksstem*, 24 June 1893.

[62] Second Volksraad, 22 June 1893 (*Volksstem*, 24 June 1893; *Notulen*, Tweede Volksraad, 1893, art. 399).

The major clash between the government and the opposition on the issue of C. J. Joubert's maladministration, however, came later in 1893 and in the two succeeding years. This was on the so-called 'Johannesburg Stands Scandal', which produced some rather startling revelations of administrative practice in the Department of Mines, as well as in the matter of the Minister's personal finances. In essence, as the evidence given to the Commission of Enquiry subsequently set up by the Second Volksraad[63] was to show, the matter at issue was the method by which some 300 valuable stands in the Hospital Hill area of Braamfontein, Johannesburg, had been allocated. These stands, the unsold remnant of the erven disposed of by government auction in February 1889,[64] had reverted to the government. In 1892 it transpired[65] that about half of them had been quietly bought up by officials, allegedly without their availability being advertised or their being put up for auction in the legal way, and the other half similarly acquired by speculators, who included[66] Gillingham and Landdrost Schutte (of the omnipresent 'Third Volksraad' referred to by Jeppe) and at least five members of the more constitutional Volksraads—J. du P. de Beer, Jan P. Meyer and Jan P. Lombaard of the First Raad, and Barend J. Vorster and F. Boshoff of the Second Raad.[67] The Minister of Mines himself was alleged to have sold some of these erven privately,[68] and his son, J. S. Joubert, had been among the fortunate recipients.[69] Allegedly transferred to officials as stands 'on which to build houses', the great majority of these stands had been sold within a very short time at many times their purchase price, having been bought at £15 to £20 each and sold, often the next day, at £60 to £135 each.[70] Much of this had occurred with the connivance, and often on the actual instructions, of the Executive Council.[71]

[63] Second Volksraad, Besluit 920 of 1892 (*Volksstem*, 4 Mar. 1893).

[64] *Press*, 16 Mar. 1893, evidence of J. J. C. Leyds, Assistant Registration Clerk to the Johannesburg Mining Commissioner.

[65] Second Volksraad, 28 July 1892 (*Volksstem*, 30 July 1892; *Land en Volk*, 4 Aug. 1892; *Notulen*, Tweede Volksraad, 1892, arts. 922–6).

[66] *Volksstem*, 22 Mar. 1893, evidence of members of this syndicate.

[67] *Land en Volk*, 9 Feb. 1892.

[68] *Land en Volk*, 28 July 1892, gives a full list of these.

[69] *Volksstem*, 12 Apr. 1893, evidence of Minister of Mines.

[70] *Volksstem*, 5 & 8 Apr. 1893, evidence of Gie and Mr. Jan Eloff; 22 Mar. 1893, evidence of F. Strange.

[71] *Volksstem*, 11 Apr. 1893, evidence of Minister of Mines.

Ewald Esselen, at that time the vigorous leader of the Progressive group in the Second Raad, described the whole affair as 'a plot and a swindle'[72] and demanded a full inquiry. The government was strongly opposed to this, desiring instead an investigation by a commission appointed by itself—the usual device when in an embarrassing position. Finally, after a somewhat violent debate, the Progressive motion in the Second Raad for a Volksraad commission of inquiry was rejected, and a government motion for a government commission to go into the allegations and report to the next session of the Raad was adopted by 11 votes to 9. Those voting against the government were E. Esselen, J. F. Celliers, E. P. A. Meintjies, B. G. Brecher, J. W. Joubert, D. F. Petersen, Ferreira, G. de Jager, and W. H. van Niekerk. (F. Watkins and N. S. Malherbe voted with the government on this issue.[73])

The 'Stands Scandal', as it was now popularly known, played its part, together with the other issues we have already considered, in the 1892–3 election campaign. Though General P. J. Joubert himself did not give it undue prominence, contenting himself with saying that he did not know much about it, but that the State had lost at least £20,000 as a result of the Minister of Mines' actions,[74] the President was subjected to frequent questions on the matter during his election tour,[75] from which he tried to extricate himself by saying that 'it was true that Koos Smit, Lombaard, Vorster etc. had secured the best stands—but private people had also got many',[76] or, alternatively, that:

'The sale of stands by public auction had worked against the poorer classes. The government had felt it better to save the costs of advertising in all the local newspapers, which came to more than the stands brought in, by selling the stands by public auction without advertisement'[77]

---

[72] Second Volksraad, 28 July 1892 (*Notulen*, Tweede Volksraad, 1892, art. 924; *Press*, 29 July 1892; *Volksstem*, 30 July 1892).

[73] *Volksstem*, 30 July 1892; *Land en Volk*, 4 Aug. 1892 (*Notulen*, Tweede Volksraad, 1892, art. 926).

[74] *Land en Volk*, 17 Nov. 1892 (speech at Middelburg). See also *Volksstem*, 15 Nov. 1892 (Bronkhorstspruit), 1 Feb. 1893 (Piet Retief).

[75] *Volksstem*, 22 Oct. 1892 (various), 1 Nov. 1892 (Ermelo), 5 Nov. 1892 (Lydenburg), and *Land en Volk*, 17 Nov. 1892 (Ermelo).

[76] *Land en Volk*, 17 Nov. 1892 (Ermelo speech).

[77] *Volksstem*, 1 Nov. 1892 (Ermelo speech).

—a series of falsehoods which produced a rousing reply from the Second Raad member for the Witwatersrand, J. F. Celliers, who declared, in a letter to the *Volksstem* of 9 November 1892, that:

'Everyone who has eyes to see knows that these stands were dealt out to friends and favourites for speculative purposes. Many are now changing hands at three, four or more times the purchase price of two months ago. As for the interests of the poor! Go through the list and see if you can find the name of *one* poor person. But there will be found more than one name of very wealthy persons, Volksraad members, officials and others. To the advantage of the poor! What bitter irony! It is time the government ceased stalling.'

On 17 February 1893 the commission of inquiry appointed by the government began its investigations. Its first session[78] received evidence that the instructions of the Department of Mines had been that eight days' notice must be given of intention to sell stands, and that the highest bid had to be accepted. This had been modified by an instruction from the government that, although all sales were to be by public auction, exceptions might be made in favour of officials. Notice of intention to auction stands had to be displayed (aangeplakt). In May 1892, two Volksraad members, J. du P. de Beer and B. J. Vorster, had been given twelve stands each after due display and in the absence of any higher bids. This was done on Executive Council instructions, and no record of it appeared in the Johannesburg Mine Commissioner's books. On 11 July the government had instructed the Minister of Mines that stands must be sold by public auction and for the highest bid; but had accompanied this by the somewhat unusual proviso that if the 'original applicant' was prepared to pay the same amount as the highest bidder at the auction he should get the preference.

Nevertheless, at subsequent sittings, it became apparent from cross-examination of witnesses (chiefly by J. F. Celliers) that even this rather questionable procedure had not been followed. Two stands for which J. van der Walt had offered £50 had been sold to Gie, a clerk in the Mining Commissioner's Office, for £40 (and sold the next day for £270).[79] Thirteen stands had been granted to a

[78] *Volksstem*, 4 Mar. 1893 (its members were J. F. Celliers, member of the Second Raad, J. M. H. de Kock, member of the Executive Council, and E. H. de Waal, with Mr. Bosch as Secretary).

[79] Mr. Smits, Acting Mine Commissioner, Johannesburg, denied this, and gave £130 as the sale price.

Second Raad Member, F. Boshoff, by the Minister of Mines directly, and without advertisement.[80] Frank Strange, of Pretoria, gave evidence that, 'having heard that the government was prepared to allocate certain stands at Hospital Hill in Johannesburg', he had applied for thirty at £20 each and had been allocated thirty at £15. Asked if he had not thought this unusual, he replied: 'No. I only thought it jolly nice, that's all.'[81] One J. H. E. Bal, agent for the Gillingham–Schutte–Schoeman–P. G. Maré syndicate,[82] testified to having bought between sixty and seventy stands at £20 each, and £25 in Maré's case ('If the books say £15 each, they are wrong'). He agreed that the stands had not been advertised, but said he presumed that everyone knew about them, though of course 'het was niet ieder die aanzoek kon doen' (it was not everyone that could make application). When Celliers asked why Strange's application had been made in the name of C. J. Joubert, the Minister of Mines, and Bal's not in his own name but in those of various officials, no explanation was offered by any of the witnesses except that the names 'must have been altered'.[83] Similarly, J. N. de Jongh gave evidence of successful applications via two Volksraad members, J. P. L. Lombaard (to the Executive Council) and B. J. Vorster (to the Department of Mines), as he 'thought that he himself had not enough influence with the Minister of Mines'.[84]

Meanwhile, during the continuance of these investigations, there appeared before Chief Justice Kotzé, a certain Verstegen, a one-time friend of C. J. Joubert's, on a charge of having stolen, or having received knowing it to have been stolen, a document containing a list of the Minister's debts. His evidence, and the simultaneous arrest on a charge of bribery of one Bension Aaron,[85] were to contribute still further to the decline of the Minister of Mines' rapidly crumbling reputation. Verstegen declared[86] that he had quarrelled with the Minister about certain land deals in areas known as Van Diggelen's Township, Boksburg plantation and Schweizer's Township, and that their friendship had been broken off.

[80] *Volksstem*, 8 Mar. 1893.

[81] *Volksstem*, 22 Mar. 1893 ('echt aardig' were Strange's words); *Press*, 21 Mar. 1893.

[82] Virtually identical with the so-called 'Third Volksraad' (see Nathan, pp. 226–7; Jeppe, pp. 144–5).

[83] *Volksstem*, 22 Mar. 1893; *Press*, 21 Mar. 1893, 24 Mar. 1893.

[84] *Volksstem*, 25 Mar. 1893.

[85] *Volksstem*, 15 Mar. 1893.   [86] *Volksstem*, 12 Apr. 1893.

'However, Isaac van Vooren, responsible clerk to the Minister of Mines . . . promised me that if I kept quiet about Schweizer's Township he would see that I would get 50 to 60 Johannesburg stands at a low price, which would be worth a couple of thousand pounds to me. . . .

'I then met Isaac van Vooren at the North Western Hotel at Johannesburg on Amajuba Day (27 February). He told me that C. J. Joubert was so hard pressed by a certain M. Spence[87] that he did not know what to do any more. The only way to get anything done with the Minister of Mines was to get him thoroughly frightened [om hem vrees aan te jagen]. When I asked how, he handed me certain papers and said, "Look at these!" One of these was a sheet in I. van Vooren's handwriting showing the credits and debits of the Minister of Mines. This, Van Vooren said, is the key to the intimate relationship between the Minister of Mines and Spence, who was C. J. Joubert's guarantor for the debts to his creditors. In return Spence demanded every chance of speculation which cropped up in the Mines Department [alle kansen van speculatien die zich in het Departement van Mynwezen voordeden]. He advised me, if Christiaan Joubert did not give in, to threaten publication in the papers. . . . [But] when Van Vooren next met me he asked for the papers back, saying "They won't help you. Spence will get Schweizer Township. He has got Christiaan Joubert completely under control. . . ." '[88]

Verstegen declared that he had attempted to regain Joubert's friendship by returning the papers given him by Van Vooren, but that Joubert had refused to accept them, saying that he (Verstegen) had stolen the papers. Verstegen was in due course found guilty on the alternative charge of having received property knowing it to have been stolen. The Chief Justice, having commented on 'the low nature of nearly all involved' and having disagreed with the jury's finding, fined Verstegen £50 or 3 months.[89]

To the Stands Enquiry Commission, Spence denied[90] that there was anything 'in Mr. C. J. Joubert's private transactions that would not stand the light of day'. He agreed that the Minister was heavily in debt, and declared that he had taken his affairs in hand 'as a sign of appreciation for all that he had done in the interests of the

[87] An agent of Edward Lippert (*Volksstem*, 21 Mar. 1893).
[88] *Volksstem*, 12 Apr. 1893.
[89] *Volksstem*, 19 Apr. 1893.
[90] *Press*, 20 Mar. 1893.

gold industry'. The Minister had handed over his salary to him for a period of six months,[91] and he had secured certain guarantors of Mr. Joubert's debts. Pressed to name these, he revealed them to be J. B. Robinson, Hermann Eckstein, Edward Lippert, and Messrs. Lewis and Marks[92] (i.e. some of the most powerful mining and financial magnates in the Republic). Mr. Joubert's debts, he declared, were now virtually paid.

A little later, more damaging evidence of conditions in the Mines Department was given by Jan Eloff, Mining Commissioner at Johannesburg from November 1886 to December 1892. In January 1892, he stated, they had planned to hold an auction of stands, but the Stands Syndicate[93] (*sic*) had protested. In April he had heard that the stands had been sold out of hand by officials at Pretoria, of which he was notified. This went on until May when they told him not to accept any more applications as there were already too many. He had 'also allocated himself certain stands in the same way as the public. He had acted according to the instructions of the Minister of Mines.'[94] Shortly before this a number of witnesses had testified that they had applied for stands and had been turned down on the ground that stands could only be sold by public auction. Subsequently, however, they had 'ascertained that these stands were being privately given out'.[95]

When C. J. Joubert himself was called upon to give evidence[96] to the Commission he admitted that a portion of the stands had been given out by the Executive Council and a portion by himself on government instructions, but declared that only about eight people had got stands without making application. Under cross-examination he agreed that the stands of Strange, Boshoff, Klimke (the Government Mining Engineer), Meijer and Cooke had not been displayed. He could not positively say whether those of Van Vooren, J. S. Joubert (his son) or George Meijer were. He 'had not known it was wrong to give officials stands'. He denied that he had given stands to his son, J. S. Joubert. 'Perhaps his registration clerk had made a

---

[91] *Volksstem*, 28 Mar. 1893 (admitted by C. J. Joubert in evidence on 11 Apr. 1893, see *Volksstem*, 12 Apr. 1893).

[92] *Press*, 20 Mar. 1893.

[93] Presumably the Gillingham–Schutte–Schoeman–P. G. Maré group (see above, p. 102).

[94] *Volksstem*, 5 Apr. 1893; *Press*, 13 Apr. 1893.

[95] *Press*, 20 Mar. 1893.

[96] *Volksstem*, 11 Apr. 1893.

mistake.'[97] He admitted that 'he had made no inquiries about the value of the stands, because he had trusted his officials. The Mining Commissioner [Jan Eloff] had recommended their sale. He did not know where they were or what their value was. . . . Many of the stands were granted by the government.'[98] He asseverated that all stands were sold to the highest bidder, but could not explain how it was that many people had got more stands than they had asked for, and blamed the Mining Commissioner for not having informed him of the real value of the stands. However, he denied on oath having ever received any consideration for the sale of stands.[99]

All this evidence, of which only the gist has been presented here, certainly indicated a most unsatisfactory state of affairs in the Mines Department, and this was borne out by further revelations in the prosecution for bribery of Bension Aaron. Chief Justice Kotzé's summing-up showed that Aaron, an influential member of the Jewish community, had applied for a grant of 22 morgen of ground and had been allocated 162 morgen 'in error' by the Minister of Mines. To make matters worse this ground was an area in Braamfontein set aside for a railway station. Messrs. Jan Eloff and Van Vooren were both alleged to have been present when the contract was drawn up, but both denied this on oath. Van Vooren said he had not pointed out the error to the Minister 'because he could not tell his Chief he had made a mistake'. Subsequently Aaron had tried to bribe Smits (the Acting Mining Commissioner for Johannesburg) and P. G. Maré (the Government Commissioner on the Johannesburg Sanitary Board) to hold their tongues about the matter (Maré had been offered £2,000). But both had very correctly refused, and informed the government of the matter. Aaron was found guilty and fined £500 and a month's imprisonment without hard labour.[1]

There could be little doubt in the light of these facts of the negligence, if not of the actual dishonesty, current in the Minister of Mines' Department. Nevertheless, to the indignation of the Progressives, when the Commission's report reflecting all this was duly presented to the Second Volksraad on 31 July,[2] every effort was made

---

[97] *Volksstem*, 11 Apr. 1893.

[98] *Press*, 11 Apr. 1893.

[99] *Volksstem*, 12 Apr. 1893.

[1] For details of the case see *Volksstem*, 15 Mar. 1893, 19 Apr. 1893, 29 Apr. 1893; *Press*, 9 Mar. 1893, 28 Apr. 1893.

[2] Second Volksraad, 31 July 1893, 1 Aug. 1893 (*Volksstem*, 2 Aug. 1893; *Press*, 2 Aug. 1893; *Notulen*, Tweede Volksraad, 1893, art. 702).

by the government to defend the conduct of the officials concerned, President Kruger himself asking 'how the State had in any way been harmed by the sale of these stands?'³ and demanding that those who objected should 'Show me the law that says that all stands must be sold by auction'.⁴

He did not want, he said, to blame officials. They 'suffered from the pressure of work'. In any case the government had the right to decide whether private or public sale was in the best interests of the State. I. J. Meijer (Middelburg) supported him, declaring that 'officials ought not to be blamed for speculation if they saw a chance of profit in it', and other Conservative members expressed similar views.⁵ On the resumption of the debate, the President modified this latter doctrine to a statement 'that an official should not speculate in matters concerning his work, but it was unfair to say that he could not fairly act in his own interests otherwise'.⁶ These views were strongly attacked by the Progressives. N. S. Malherbe said it 'pained him to hear His Excellency repeatedly defending the right of officials to speculate. As he saw it one must choose between being a speculator and an official.' This attitude was supported by Celliers, Meintjies, Petersen and other Progressives. In spite of their eloquence, however, a motion by N. S. Malherbe including the phrase 'that certain officials in Johannesburg had not fully done their duty', asking for a thorough investigation by the government, and requesting the government to sell all future stands by auction, was defeated by 15 votes to 8, and a rival motion by D. Taljaard and J. J. Joubert was accepted by the same number of votes, which declared:

'That there was no fixed rule with regard to the sale of stands; that, after the explanation given by the government, it appears that the government acted according to instructions and in the best interests of the State . . . that the Report of the Committee cannot be accepted; that irregularities have taken place at Johannesburg by officials, and that the government be ordered to instruct the Minister

³ 3 Aug. 1893; *Notulen*, Tweede Volksraad, 1893, art. 728.

⁴ Second Volksraad, 3 Aug. 1893 (*Volksstem*, 5 Aug. 1893; *Notulen*, Tweede Volksraad, 1893, art. 728).

⁵ *Notulen*, Tweede Volksraad, 1893, art. 732.

⁶ Second Volksraad, 5 Aug. 1893 (*Volksstem*, 8 Aug. 1893; *Press*, 7 Aug. 1893). Quoted above, p. 19 (*Notulen*, Tweede Volksraad, 1893, art. 733, p. 357, col. 2).

of Mines to make a strict investigation; that all has been done according to law, and there is nothing to justify the name of "Stands Scandal".'

Thus, by the simple expedient of legislatively declaring black to be white, the 'Stands Scandal' was disposed of and the unsavoury 'irregularities' which have been outlined declared to be 'in the best interests of the State'. The Progressive group refused to accept this piece of whitewashing, and voted solidly in the minority (E. P. A. Meintjies, J. F. Celliers, N. S. Malherbe, B. G. Brecher, F. Watkins, J. W. Joubert, W. J. Jooste, and D. F. Petersen).[7] And, as the Progressives had feared, when the report of the governmental inquiry[8] into the matter was, in due course, presented to the Second Raad, it found that there had been no conspiracy or fraud among officials, that all sales had been properly published on the 'publicatiebord' in the Mining Commissioner's Office, and that the highest bids had been accepted, without exception.[9]

A minor echo of the principles involved in the 'Stands Scandal' occurred in the next year, when a Second Raad commission of inquiry into certain land deals which one of their members, Barend J. Vorster (described by *Land en Volk* of 23 May 1895 as 'een schurk en een schelm'), had negotiated on behalf of Bension Aaron, found that Vorster had defrauded the State of £5,625 and recommended that all sales of land should be by public auction. President Kruger defended Vorster, and accused the Second Volksraad of impugning the honour of the government.

'He did not know whether he ought to continue to sit there! If all sales took place by public auction there would be no opportunity of helping the poor, and only the rich would get the benefit.'[10]

To this J. W. Joubert, a leading Progressive, retorted that the matter had nothing to do with the poor, but only with the loss to the government of a considerable sum. A furious debate took place, the

---

[7] *Volksstem*, 8 Aug. 1893; *Press*, 7 Aug. 1893; *Notulen*, Tweede Volksraad, 1893, art. 734.

[8] Conducted by the Minister of Mines and the Mining Commissioner (*Press*, 1 Sept. 1894).

[9] Second Volksraad, 31 Aug. 1894 (*Volksstem*, 5 Sept. 1894; *Notulen*, Tweede Volksraad, 1894, art. 1086).

[10] *Notulen*, Tweede Volksraad, 1894, art. 1058.

President defending the government's actions (in authorizing such private land deals without recourse to public auction) as in the best interests of the State. But, as we have seen, the public temper against concessions, monopolies, and financial jugglery in general, was steadily rising, and, despite the President's opposition, the commission's report condemning the action as illegal was adopted by 11 votes to 9.[11]

Land en Volk, in a leading article of 30 August 1894, summing up the achievements of the Second Volksraad in the 1894 session, congratulated it on the good work it had done for the country.

'It has refused to consider even one concession, it has instituted a thorough investigation into existing concessions, despite the President's passionate opposition. It has done its best to purify the Administration, which is in a shocking state [treurige toestand]. From all sides, from every district, come continual tales of sharp practice, theft, speculation at the expense of the country by officials, or if not of these, then of neglect of duty, lack of system, chaos and neglect.'

The more loyal *Volksstem* (12 September 1894) spoke gloomily of the need for a new political party which would tackle the questions of administrative reform and financial reorganization.

The next major 'scandal' around which opposition to the government coalesced was the so-called 'Bewaarplaatsen scandal', which has already been referred to briefly. The mining companies, very naturally, desired to have the underground mining rights to the dumping-areas (bewaarplaatsen) whose surface rights they held. In this they were supported by the Progressives,[12] but bitterly opposed by the President and his supporters,[13] who claimed that the underground rights belonged not to the surface-holders but to the State, though there can be little doubt that the immense possibilities of profitable speculation which their denial to the mining companies would ensure, must, as Fitzpatrick alleges (p. 77), have been a considerable factor in determining their attitude. Nevertheless the

[11] Second Volksraad, 28 Aug. 1894 (*Volksstem*, 1 Sept. 1894; *Notulen*, Tweede Volksraad, 1894, art. 1064).

[12] See the division of votes in the First Volksraad debate of 20 Sept. 1895 (*Volksstem*, 25 Sept. 1895).

[13] First Volksraad, 10 Sept. 1895 (*Volksstem*, 21 Sept. 1895; Fitzpatrick, pp. 76–7; *Volksstem*, 28 Aug. 1895, 21 Sept. 1895; *Notulen*, Eerste Volksraad, 1895, arts. 1279–81).

Second Volksraad supported the mining companies against the government, and by 13 votes to 12 awarded the underground mining rights to the holders of the surface rights. Those voting against the government were E. P. A. Meintjies, W. J. Jooste, Geldenhuis, H. P. Steenkamp, I. J. Meijer, B. J. Vorster, W. J. Pretorius, I. J. Breytenbach, P. S. Uys, J. D. R. Opperman, J. J. Burger, F. Boshoff and J. W. Erasmus.[14] (Both J. F. Celliers and J. W. Joubert—a nephew of General P. J. Joubert—had died early in the year, the latter shortly after having been elevated to the First Volksraad. D. F. Petersen had not been re-elected to the Second Raad after 1893.) F. Watkins and G. B. Brecher, two leading Progressives, supported the government.

This was, to say the least, a very mixed bag, for apart from the first three members listed, who were known Progressives, only three of the remainder (H. P. Steenkamp, I. J. Meijer and W. J. Pretorius) had ever voted against the government before on any major issues, and then only rarely.[15]

In the First Raad the President strongly attacked the Second Volksraad's action, asseverating that the underground rights belonged to the State and calling upon the Raad to reverse the decision of the lower Chamber. In this he was vigorously opposed by the Progressives and by Schalk Burger. However, the President, partially at any rate, gained the day, the First Raad, after long debate, voting 14 to 11 for postponement of any action for a year. Those voting against the government were C. Jeppe, R. K. Loveday, L. de Jager, G. de Jager, Schalk Burger, P. Maré, J. du P. de Beer, D. J. Joubert, W. J. Steyn, W. H. van Niekerk and J. Labuschagne.[16] J. H. de la Rey and J. van Wyk, usually regarded as Progressives,[17] supported the government, as did C. Birkenstock.

Meanwhile the Second Raad, as a final flourish before its closure, had passed by 15 votes to 9 a motion condemning the actions of the Minister of Mines and his officials and calling upon the government to punish them, and, if necessary, take the matter to court (13 September 1895).[18] This motion was put forward by two leading Pro-

---

[14] *Volksstem*, 24 Aug. 1895 (*Notulen*, Tweede Volksraad, 1895, art. 1361).

[15] See *Land en Volk*, 23 May 1895, 30 May 1895, on these members.

[16] *Volksstem*, 25 Sept. 1895 (First Volksraad, 20 Sept. 1895); *Notulen*, Eerste Volksraad, 1895, art. 1282.

[17] Jeppe, p. 174.

[18] Second Volksraad, 13 Sept. 1895 (*Volksstem*, 18 Sept. 1895; *Notulen*, Tweede Volksraad, 1895, art. 1629).

gressives, W. J. Jooste and E. P. A. Meintjies, and in a sense reversed the decision of two years before, exculpating the Minister and his officials and refusing to accept their committee's adverse Report on the so-called 'Stands Scandal'.

The *Volksstem's* scathing comment (2 October 1895) on C. J. Joubert's defence of the administration of his department,[19] was that the Minister should be looked upon as being

'like some old historical monument which has fallen into ruin— something respected, but which has to be cleared out of the way. Not one Volksraad session', it continued, 'goes by without further unpleasant allegations against your Department. Your attitude towards some of the Mining Company representatives or their agents is not felt to be the result of their pure admiration of all your actions. All sorts of rumours go around about you. Even if they are not true you owe it to the South African Republic to vacate your position. Our State needs a Minister of Mines who not only *is* honest and clean, but who is *known* to be so.'

We may sum up this section by stressing that the issue of administrative maladministration and corruption played an important part in the steady growth of opposition to the régime. It was never simply a matter of the Progressives campaigning unaided to wipe out these blots on the Transvaal's escutcheon. At no stage, even by the end of 1895, were the Progressives, either in the First or Second Raad, strong enough to have won on their own any of the victories against these abuses which we have traced—the dismissals of Dr. Krause and Josefus Wolmarans (State Prosecutor and Head of the Department of Police and Prisons respectively), the condemnation of Vorster's land deals, the arousing of public opinion on the 'Spider' affair, on the 'Stands Scandal' and on the general maladministration in the Mines Department, and the moral victory in the 'Bewaarplaatsen' question. On all these matters important sections of usually pro-government opinion, both in the two Volksraads and in the press, as we have seen, sided with the Progressive opposition. Nevertheless it was the Progressives who took the lead in raising these issues and in bringing them to public attention, and it was President Kruger and the Conservative 'old guard' who generally fought in defence of the practices complained of. The question of corruption and maladministration can, therefore, be fairly regarded as one of the crucial issues

[19] Letter of 28 Sept. 1895 in *Volksstem*, 2 Oct. 1895.

around which members of the opposition drew together, and which they effectively used in weakening the hold of President Kruger and his supporters upon the country.

VI. EDUCATION AND LANGUAGE POLICY

This was a confused issue, in which the pioneer suspicion of education referred to at the beginning of this book fought with the growing realization of the demands of new times, and growing resentment at seeing the 'zonen des lands' excluded, because of their inferior education, from posts perforce filled by Hollanders, Germans, and Cape Afrikaners;[20] in which dislike and suspicion of the English and their tongue competed with a growing awareness of its commercial importance; and in which sympathy for the desire of the uitlander population to have their children (in their early years, at any rate) educated in a tongue that they understood, often found itself darkly suspected as evidence of a plot to undermine the foundations of the Republic and triumphantly plant the 'roode taal'[21] in the ground from which the 'landstaal' had been extirpated. This fear of English, with its vast prestige and world-wide importance as a language of literature, science and commerce, and of the danger which it presented to the language of the people, though exaggerated, was certainly not unfounded, and must be sympathetically understood, for language and national identity were felt to be inextricably one. But, on the other hand, like all fears when they become neurotic, it sometimes led to actions which even the most loving defender of the 'landstaal' found it difficult not to condemn. On the whole, it cannot be regarded as a major political issue, like those we have already considered, or like the franchise question; but examination of the Volksraad debates, nevertheless, does suggest that opposition to Dr. Mansvelt's education policy[22] served as another issue which tended to draw together those of more progressive and tolerant opinions, those who were more in tune with the new needs of the times and more prepared to adapt the policy of the State to those new needs, and to pit against them those of a more conservative and hide-bound frame of mind. In this sense it may be regarded as an issue of some political significance.

[20] Walker, p. 411.
[21] *Volksstem*, 8 Sept. 1894 (O. J. Coetzee's speech); *Notulen*, Eerste Volksraad, 1894, art. 1615, contains no record of this remark.
[22] See pp. 112 ff., and Ploeger, chs. VII–X.

Before 1877, as Walker points out (pp. 435–6), the Transvaal had been eager to learn English, had given preference to bilingual teachers, and, where these had been unobtainable, to English-speaking ones; but after 1881 S. J. du Toit had made Dutch the sole medium of instruction, though this was not strictly enforced until the arrival of Mansvelt in 1891. Meanwhile, though somewhat slowly, education had expanded. The 116 schools and 2,795 pupils of 1887 had become 225 and 5,475 respectively. The expenditure of £10,500 in 1887 had risen to an estimated £58,000 for 1890, of which £20,000 was for the erection of a high school.[23] This, however, was felt to be lagging behind the times. 'What is the use', the *Volksstem* asked,[24] in referring to the comparative estimate of £325,000 for public works, 'of having fine roads and bridges when the people who use them can hardly read or write?' This was linked with a feeling of resentment that the neglect and apathy of the burghers in educational matters was responsible for the difficulty found by the 'zonen des lands' in competing with 'foreigners and British subjects from the Cape colony'[25] for the vital posts upon which the administration of the State depended; a resentment which went, as late as 1898, to the seemingly ridiculous extent of bringing upon the head of the Inspector of Offices the disapproval of the Chairman of the First Volksraad and the stern rebuke of many of the legislators for 'proposing to take the bread out of the mouths of the sons of the soil . . . and obliging them to make room for strangers', when, in an effort to improve standards, he suggested the institution of Civil Service examinations.[26]

The year 1891 saw the arrival of Dr. N. E. Mansvelt of Stellenbosch as Superintendent of Education, at a salary of £1,200 per annum.[27] The salary, in itself, underlined the need felt for a man of real calibre, for his predecessor, S. J. du Toit, had received two-thirds of that sum.[28] Within a few months of his arrival the new super-

[23] *Volksstem*, 9 June 1890.

[24] The *Press* of 3 Feb. 1893 also declared that 'only a very small proportion of the burghers can read or write'.

[25] *Volksstem*, 20 Feb. 1890; *Land en Volk*, 10 Mar. 1891. (See also Ploeger, pp. 70–1.)

[26] First Volksraad, 17 May 1898 (*Weekly Press*, 21 May 1898, p. 13).

[27] *Volksstem*, 14 July 1891, 15 Oct. 1891; *Land en Volk*, 21 July 1891 (*Notulen*, Eerste Volksraad, 1893, art. 597, Begrooting, ch. XXII).

[28] *Land en Volk*, 21 July 1891; *Notulen*, Eerste Volksraad, 1891, art. 658, Begrooting, ch. XXI.

intendent (a Hollander who had taught for more than seventeen years
in the Cape Colony, and was by now a convinced Afrikaner patriot)[29]
had, by his education law,[30] reimposed the (legal but not actual)
proviso that only Dutch should be used as the medium of instruction
in all higher standards, while allowing the optional use of English
in the lower standards. In doing so, he brought a hornets' nest about
his ears, and convincingly demonstrated the delicate tightrope path
which any Transvaal Superintendent of Education had perforce to
walk. For the first consequence of his action, though it was ostensibly
a mere enforcement of the Volksraad's resolution of the previous
year on the subject,[31] was the peremptory stoppage of grants to a
number of schools in which Dutch was not the medium of instruction. This was done on the instructions of the Executive Council.[32]
It was not, however, the uitlanders alone who were outraged at this
move. The provisions in the law allowing the use of English as a
teaching medium in special circumstances in English-speaking areas,
provided that Dutch was used for a certain time each day (the
period varying with the standards),[33] was regarded as equally out-
rageous by the more conservative sections of Transvaal opinion.[34]
'Klein Joggum', a writer in *Land en Volk* who strove to represent (in
a sort of Afrikaans) the views of the average Transvaaler, added this
to his list of complaints against Kruger's administration, mockingly
putting himself forward as President on the grounds that:

'Ik ben voor Concessies, Monopolies ens.
Ik ben voor Mansvelt's schoolwet—baing Engelsch!
Ik ben voor twee Financiers aanstellen (moet Hollanders wees).
De Volksraad moet tevrede wees met wat ik wil, en moet er niets
van dink als ik dreig om te bedank' . . . etc. etc.

The second 'reason' advanced is typical of much of the platteland
reaction, as later Volksraad debates were to show.

But the main reaction was from those who feared that the law
might lead to a withdrawal of their children from the State's schools

[29] *Land en Volk*, 20 Oct. 1891 (report of welcome to Dr. Mansvelt, and his
reply); Ploeger, pp. 68–9.
[30] *Notulen*, Eerste Volksraad, 1893, art. 974 (see draft in *Land en Volk*,
2 Feb. 1892).
[31] *Press*, 21 Jan. 1892, 29 Feb. 1892.
[32] *Press*, 1 Mar. 1892. (See also Ploeger, pp. 72–5.)
[33] *Press*, 21 Jan. 1892; *Volksstem*, 12 Apr. 1892 (in schools where three-
quarters of the pupils did not speak Dutch).
[34] *Volksstem*, 12 Apr. 1892; *Land en Volk*, 26 Apr. 1892.

by English-speaking parents. Its literal application, the *Press* felt, would lead to the ruin of the educational system and would leave Mansvelt 'in shadowy control of a few dozen dames' schools'.[35]

The insistence on Dutch as a medium, it pointed out, had been allowed, in the interregnum between S. J. du Toit and Mansvelt, to fall into desuetude, first, because of 'the exceedingly awkward fact that, whatever the prevailing legal fiction may happen to be, a majority of the people in the towns speak English and do not speak Dutch', and secondly, because 'inspection in those days was not of a kind which rendered undue insistence on any particular point desirable or even possible'.

It stressed, further, that the country must face the fact that, in Johannesburg, education through Dutch in the lower standards was impracticable, and that if grants were to be stopped 'the only consequence will be that the real educational work which is being done in the country will be withdrawn from the sphere of the official department's control'.

In a later article (29 February 1892) surveying the development of the situation, it admitted that the lax interpretation of the law before Dr. Mansvelt's arrival had not advanced the cause of the Dutch language. As long as a school taught some Dutch it had been eligible for a government grant. One school, for example, had taught Dutch to six pupils (out of more than a hundred) three times a week, and had still been given the full government grant per pupil. But the net result of eliminating from the new measure the optional right to teach through the English medium would be that:

'Schools will carry on privately; and no Dutch will be taught at all. Yet it is impossible to convince opponents of this wise measure of this fact. Already the Dutch papers are filled with correspondence pointing out the Engelschgezindheid of the new law, and the way it will endanger the language, customs, laws and independence of the State.'

At a meeting held in Johannesburg under the auspices of the Teachers' Association there, strong opposition to the law was expressed. Mr. Goch was applauded loudly when he declared:

'It is Mansvelt and not the Government that is the difficulty. He desires in his heart of hearts to eliminate the English language.'[36]

[35] *Press*, 21 Jan. 1892.
[36] *Press*, 2 Apr. 1892. (See Ploeger, p. 74, for confirmation of this.)

Other speakers declared that an honest effort had been made to teach as much Dutch as possible; that the new regulations would force schools in Johannesburg to teach their pupils in a language which they only imperfectly understood; that many parents would object to their children being educated only in the Dutch language, and that those who could afford to would send their children away to the Colony; that the majority of schools would close, thus causing great hardship to poorer parents; that the schools which survived, without the grant, would probably be those in which no Dutch at all was taught; and that, in short, the whole object of the promoters of the law would be defeated.

The *Press* (2 April 1892) reported this with the sad comment that it 'did not envy Dr. Mansvelt's task in sailing between the Scylla of ingrained conservatism and the Charybdis of imported liberalism'.

However, the *Press* was, on this occasion, unnecessarily pessimistic. When, in due course, the Commission set up by the Volksraad to report on the Education Bill (J. du P. de Beer, L. de Jager, Jan Meyer, Lukas Meyer and J. Malan, only one of whom, incidentally—Malan—could be regarded as a thorough Conservative)[37] presented its recommendations to the First Raad, these were found to be, to the delight of that newspaper, 'more liberal than the Bill itself'.[38] The Commission suggested a reduced but fairly generous subsidy (from 20*s.* for a pupil in Standard I to 36*s.* for one in Standard VI)[39] to schools in which Dutch was not the medium, provided that the official language was efficiently taught, that periodical language tests were conducted by government inspectors, and that in all other respects the schools complied with the Education Law. In the ensuing debate, although some hard words were said about education in general and education in English in particular, and although that staunch Conservative, A. D. W. Wolmarans, wished to know what had possessed the Committee to draw up a concept resolution allowing education through a medium other than Dutch, the law was passed, with but little discussion, by 22 votes to 1, P. J. Steenkamp alone voting in the minority.[40] Paul Maré, a leading Progressive, spoke particularly strongly in favour of more education

[37] *Volksstem*, 1 Sept. 1894.
[38] *Press*, 25 May 1892.
[39] First Volksraad, 24 May 1892 (*Volksstem*, 25 May 1892; *Notulen*, Eerste Volksraad, 1892, art. 251).
[40] *Press*, 2 June 1892 (First Volksraad, 1 June 1892, 2 June 1892); *Notulen*, Eerste Volksraad, 1892, art. 344).

in English in all schools.[41]

This did not, however, mean that the First Raad had suddenly turned Anglophile, as Loveday discovered when he attempted, in July, to persuade the Raad to give favourable hearing to a memorial asking that the use of English be allowed in the courts when all parties to the dispute, and the judge as well, were English-speaking— a common enough state of affairs in the towns, for, as Jeppe points out (p. 137), the insistence on translation into Dutch of every word said when judge, jury and witnesses all spoke and understood English perfectly, was often ludicrous. Mr. Justice Morice of the High Court described the procedure, rather more strongly, as 'a solemn farce'.[42] However, the memorial to the Volksraad was rejected as bluntly as a similar request from the Barberton area[43] had been two years earlier, only J. F. Celliers voting in its favour.

There is little in the press reports of the 1892–3 election campaign to suggest that the issue of education played any significant part. Chief Justice Kotzé was the only candidate to make any mention of it, and even that was of the briefest.[44] There is thus every reason to consider the *Press* of 3 February 1893 correct in summing up the average burgher's attitude on the matter as 'he does not want to be troubled about education'.

By 1893 it had become clear that, in spite of his concessions to the wishes of English parents, Mansvelt's schools were running into difficulties. On 7 February the *Press* declared that:

'the sooner it is admitted that the present system of using Dutch as the sole medium of instruction is a dead and hopeless failure in English centres like Johannesburg, the better it will be for the cause of education in this country. The attempts to force Dutch on the Uitlanders have had the opposite effect. They have started their own schools in which no special pains are taken to teach Dutch. . . . There is no hostility to Dutch among the newcomers; but they object to the general education of their offspring being retarded by their being taught in a language that they do not understand. . . . All that is wanted is a compromise.'

[41] *Volksstem*, 31 May 1892; *Press*, 30 May 1892, 31 May 1892, 2 June 1892; *Notulen*, Eerste Volksraad, 1892, art. 288.

[42] *Volksstem*, 14 Apr. 1894 (speech to Pretoria Debating Society).

[43] *Notulen*, Eerste Volksraad, 1890, art. 236.

[44] *Volksstem*, 19 Oct. 1892, 29 Nov. 1892.

It appears, therefore, that in spite of the law of 1892 Dutch was still being enforced as a medium of instruction in Johannesburg schools, or that the grant of 20*s.* to 36*s.* per pupil was inadequate—which is, indeed, suggested by Mansvelt's promise to raise this grant.[45]

On 6 April, the *Press*, in a leader 'The failure of the Education Law', called upon the authorities to emulate the practice of the Orange Free State, and quoted clause 104 of the sister Republic's Education Law, which laid down that:

'In the towns education shall be imparted through the medium of one language, Dutch or English according to the choice of the parents, up to and including Standard II, and thereafter both languages may be used, provided, however, that at least one half of the subjects shall be taught by means of the Dutch tongue',

as a 'tolerant and liberal measure worthy of emulation', and one which had strengthened rather than weakened the Dutch language and the patriotism of the State. It strongly supported what it called 'the enlightened Africander view as opposed to that of the Hollander party' and stressed that the demand for more English was steadily rising among Dutch-speaking parents.

'There is not an appointment worth the taking, nor a business which can be carried on profitably', it declared, 'which can be undertaken by the man who cannot read, write and speak English', and added that the growing frequency with which Dutch parents were removing their children from the State-aided schools on the sole ground that sufficient attention is not paid to the English language 'was a pregnant fact which Professor Mansvelt would be wise not to ignore'.[46]

In a subsequent interview[47] Mansvelt stated that he had been 'grossly misunderstood'. He had, while firmly believing that Dutch must be maintained as the language of the State, endeavoured to meet the wishes of the foreign population as much as possible. Since last June, he declared, the State had allowed the children of foreigners to be taught through the medium of their own language. He had promised a deputation from the Johannesburg Teachers' Association that he would ask the Volksraad to allow the teaching

[45] *Press*, 8 Apr. 1893.
[46] *Press*, 7 Apr. 1893.
[47] *Press*, 8 Apr. 1893.

of English for two hours a week to Dutch children in the second standard, although he himself felt that it was a decided obstacle in the way of their intellectual development for young children to attempt to acquire two languages at the same time—more particularly in view of the fact that few of the burghers' children, as a rule, remained at school for more than two or three years. Children had much knowledge to acquire, in all subjects, and this could only be done in one's own language. Thus he would always oppose the demand that the study of English be begun in the first standard as suicidal to the nation.[48] Not having had a thorough education themselves, and conscious of their inferiority to the foreigners in this respect, the burghers, Mansvelt declared, thought that all that their children needed to place them on an equality with the foreigner was a knowledge of the English language. Nevertheless, he would endeavour to persuade the Volksraad to see that Dutch children received some instruction in English, as a foreign language, while learning all other subjects through their own language, and vice versa with English children. He would request the Volksraad to allow school committees to have separate divisions for the children of foreigners so that they might be instructed in their own language and at the same time be taught Dutch. He denied, in conclusion, any dislike of English. 'I have no objection to English. I love the language myself', he declared. Nevertheless it was his duty to maintain the historical and lawful language of the country.

The *Press* in a later leader (10 April 1893) congratulated Mansvelt on the spirit he had displayed in this interview, and expressed its pleasure that he had 'seen the necessity of trimming his sails to the breeze'.

'So far', it declared, 'the Education Law has been a failure; but it still rests with Professor Mansvelt whether it can be doctored into a success.'

But that this spirit of sweet reasonableness was far from universal was shown by the *Volksstem*'s reaction (8 April 1893), in a leader entitled 'No English in the people's schools!' (Geen Engelsch op Volksschool!) which declared bluntly that English was a foreign language, and that if people came to live in the Transvaal they must use the 'landstaal', and that was all there was to it. That it reflected

[48] There is a certain confusion of thought here, as no pressure was being exerted to teach other subjects in any but the mother tongue.

the popular view more truly than the *Press* was soon to be shown.

Mansvelt's Report on education in April[49] warned the burghers of the alleged dangers of allowing their children to be taught in a foreign language before being trained to think in their own, and deplored the practice of taking children away after two years or so at school. It admitted, significantly, that the number of pupils at school had greatly decreased, one of the causes being the fact that parents were withdrawing their children in order to have them educated in English as well as Dutch. He hoped, however, to recommend certain changes in the law 'by which reasonable wishes in this respect will be partially met' (a somewhat lukewarm statement!) and hoped that the Volksraad would concur.

But Mansvelt's hopes, if they were hopes, were doomed to disappointment, for when in the ensuing Volksraad session his suggestions were put to the Raad that two hours a week be allocated to the teaching of English in Standard II,[50] it was warmly opposed, and rejected by 17 votes to 5 (those voting against the majority[51] being C. Jeppe, Paul Maré, Lukas Meyer, L. de Jager and G. de Jager. Loveday was absent from the Raad on this occasion). Once again, then, it is only the hard core of the Progressives who join in voting for more education in English for the children of the burghers.

By 1894, in consequence, it appears that less than 5 per cent of the children of Johannesburg were attending government-aided schools. Of some 15,000 children of school-going age in the whole Transvaal less than 6,000 attended such schools, and it was estimated that even in Pretoria more children were reached by private enterprise than by Mansvelt's system.[52] *Land en Volk* complained bitterly that, though government supporters backed Mansvelt's ideas verbally, in fact all of them who could afford to do so sent their children to be educated in Cape or Free State schools.[53] The *Volksstem* (25 July 1894), however, dourly supported Mansvelt's policy, declared its contempt for syllabuses in which the battle of Waterloo was regarded as more important than the battle of Amajuba, and reasserted its fullest confidence in Dr. Mansvelt's 'nationale neigingen

[49] *Press*, 22 Apr. 1893.

[50] *Notulen*, Eerste Volksraad, 1893, art. 974, art. 5 of Concept-Wet to change Law 8 of 1892.

[51] *Notulen*, Eerste Volksraad, 1893, arts. 991–3; *Press*, 4 Aug. 1893.

[52] *Press*, 8 May 1894.

[53] *Land en Volk*, 6 Dec. 1894. (See also *Weekly Press*, 6 Aug. 1898, p. 1, for evidence of the increase of this practice four years later.)

en idealen'.

The First Raad debates on education[54] revealed some growth of support for more instruction in English. Commandant J. H. (Koos) de la Rey, member for Lichtenburg since September 1893, sided with the Progressives on this issue, stating that to oppose an extension of the time devoted to English-teaching meant deliberately putting their own children at a disadvantage compared to uitlanders. The most successful people in business and the professions in the Republic, he declared, were the children of Afrikaners who had also learnt English. J. P. L. Labuschagne (Heidelberg) said his children would learn to speak English as well as they spoke Dutch, even if he had to pay for it himself, and they would still remain Afrikaner children. It did not make you a traitor, he asserted, to want to know English. Gert de Jager (Wakkerstroom) declared that the vast majority of the population wanted their children to learn English, and that his children would learn English and still remain 'ware Afrikaanders'. J. du P. de Beer (Waterberg) hailed, somewhat prematurely perhaps,[55] by *Land en Volk* of 27 September 1894 as 'one who has during this session freed himself totally from the influence of the government', spoke in similar vein. But the majority, though significantly decreased by these accessions to more tolerant views, still held the opposite view. A. D. W. Wolmarans (Pretoria) supported by the President,[56] warned that 'if a child learned English at such an early age, he will become poisoned with English ideas' (met Engelsche ideen vergiftigd). C. B. Otto (Zeerust) desired to know why it was necessary to change 'our Dutch language for the red language' (onze Hollandsche taal voor de roode taal) and so 'undermine our nationality'. J. M. Malan (Rustenburg) demanded that 'English be banned from our Christian schools'. J. J. Spies (Utrecht) asked why Afrikaners, in their own land, had to fit themselves to the requirements of foreigners; and J. P. L. Lombaard declared that one heard the same nonsense (gelol) every year—English in the courts! English in the schools! English in the Civil Service offices!—the aim was simply to exterminate the Dutch language.[57] This view prevailed,

---

[54] *Notulen*, Eerste Volksraad, 1894, arts. 1600–28, Debates of 6–7 Sept. 1894; *Volksstem*, 8 Sept. 1894; *Land en Volk*, 20 Sept. 1894; *Press*, 8 Sept. 1894.

[55] See p. 245.

[56] First Volksraad, 6–7 Sept. 1894 (*Volksstem*, 8 Sept. 1894; *Press*, 8 Sept. 1894; *Land en Volk*, 20 Sept. 1894; *Notulen*, Eerste Volksraad, 1894, arts. 1620–8).

[57] *Notulen*, Eerste Volksraad, 1894, arts. 1620–8.

and by 13 votes to 9 it was decided to make no change in the existing arrangements.

The question of education, by 1895, was assuming increasing importance. In a speech at Krugersdorp in April of that year[58] Carl Jeppe placed it second in importance only to the franchise question. He condemned the existing system utterly.

'For fear that the English language might attain an unwarranted influence', he declared, 'we are going to the other extreme and trying to turn our children into Dutch foreigners [Hollandsche vreemdelingen]. Our best boys and girls are being sent out of the country to get a decent education.'

With between one and two million pounds lying idle in the treasury, he continued, there was nevertheless a gross shortage of schools, teachers, and equipment. Whereas in the Free State attendance had risen between 1891 and 1895 from 3,600 to 6,000, in the Transvaal it had declined from 8,200 to less than 6,000.

On the same day (30 April 1894) the *Volksstem* reported a meeting in Johannesburg addressed by such leading exponents of uitlander grievances as J. W. Leonard, Q.C., Lionel Phillips and J. Tudhope, who demanded a total reform in the system of education. Lionel Phillips declared that there was little hope of action by the government. Johannesburg would have to help itself, and the Eckstein group was prepared to contribute £5,000. A committee was then set up. Thus began the organized movement towards a separate system of education which the *Press* had long feared and wisely warned against. Once again that newspaper asserted its view that the aim of the Education Department ought to be 'to deal with the whole population and not with a section of it', and expressed its grave concern about 'the movement at present going forward in Johannesburg for the establishment of an educational council and the erection of independent schools'.[59]

Land en Volk (18 July 1895), ever more passionate, declared bluntly:

'The aim of the Hollander party is to keep our people in ignorance. "No English in our schools!" they shout. "It endangers our independence!" Is there one of them who really believes this? Is there

[58] *Land en Volk*, 2 May 1895 (speech of 30 Apr. 1895).
[59] *Press*, 4 May 1895; Ploeger, pp. 103–5.

one of *them* who does not know English, or, if he does not, does not immediately learn it? For them, the officials, the people who govern us, it is essential. But the poor, stupid people [arme, domme volk] does not need it!'

It ended by offering £10 to the first reader sending a list of ten Hollander officials in important positions who did not know English.

The First Raad debates on education in 1895[60] were signally unproductive. Jeppe delivered a vigorous attack upon the whole system, and declared that many Johannesburg schools were teaching Dutch excellently—he had examined the pupils himself—and yet they got no subsidy. The Superintendent of Education must stop talking about 'liberal grants' for Johannesburg schools as if he were doling out alms. They were not asking for alms but for rights. Mansvelt denied these claims, and alleged that even in the highest classes the standard of Dutch was deplorably deficient. But a number of members expressed dissatisfaction at the shortage of schools and the number of children receiving no education.

The resumption of the debate three months later[61] produced little progress. The most violent argument centred on the necessity or otherwise of teaching English to the children of the burghers. The President asked why it was necessary. What other country, he demanded, spent money on teaching its children foreign languages?

'Every effort to expand English still further', he asserted, 'will work towards the extermination of the language of the country.'[62]

Progressive members, equally vigorously, stressed the vital necessity for the children of the burghers to learn English. It was eventually decided to refer the matter to a Volksraad committee—an action which the *Volksstem* of 10 August 1895, quite correctly, interpreted as 'a victory of the party true to taal and religion over Jeppe and others who are working for English'. The paper was particularly pleased that Jeppe had not even been elected to this committee, and that 'the relatively insignificant member for Utrecht' (J. H. Labuschagne) had been chosen in his stead by a large majority.

[60] First Volksraad, 22 May 1895, 24 May 1895, 25 May 1895, 27 May 1895 (*Press*, 25 May 1895; *Weekly Press*, 29 June 1895, p. 19; *Volksstem*, 22 May 1895, 25 May 1895; *Notulen*, Eerste Volksraad, 1895, arts. 147–88).

[61] First Volksraad, 8 Aug. 1895 (*Volksstem*, 10 Aug. 1895; *Notulen*, Eerste Volksraad, 1895, arts. 865–7).

[62] First Volksraad, 8 Aug. 1895 (*Volksstem*, 10 Aug. 1895; *Notulen*, Eerste Volksraad, 1895, art. 866).

Meanwhile, with the *Volksstem* (19 October 1895) still thundering about the shocking amount of English encountered in the Civil Service, in some departments of which 'English is almost exclusively used', Johannesburg was going ahead on its own, and the newly formed Witwatersrand Council of Education was publishing its plans for the setting up of a system of private schools teaching Dutch and English, on undenominational lines, for the 10,000 or so children of school-going age in that town.[63]

When the Jameson Raid burst upon the Transvaal, among the other promises that President Kruger made to those who would stand by him was one of equal subsidies to Dutch and English schools,[64] and Jeppe, after consultation with the Executive Council, felt able to promise that the question of education would receive the government's closest attention, and that 'a totally different attitude would be found in this matter'.[65]

In due course, in 1896-7, a new Education Law was worked out and brought into operation, which provided for instruction via the home language in the lower standards in State schools to be set up on the goldfields and which was welcomed by Jeppe as conceding all that had been striven for; but progress was slow, and poor teachers, and low standards of qualification for entry into the profession,[66] did not inspire confidence either among the uitlanders or the more ambitious of the burgher population. The Witwatersrand Council of Education began erecting its own schools; and, though there was a significant increase of expenditure on education and in the number of children attending school (£65,656 in 1897 as against £44,548 in 1896; 457 schools and 11,436 scholars as against 395 schools and some 8,000 scholars in 1896)[67] there was difficulty in finding the right people to serve on the new school boards,[68] and complaints that their powers were infinitesimal.[69] Late in 1898 Mansvelt had to

[63] *Weekly Press*, 19 Oct. 1895, pp. 6, 15; 2 Nov. 1895, p. 1. (See also Ploeger, pp. 103–10.)

[64] *Land en Volk*, 30 Dec. 1895 (to a loyal deputation from Johannesburg, led by Jeppe); Marais, p. 102.

[65] *Volksstem*, 31 Dec. 1895.

[66] *Weekly Press*, 12 June 1897, p. 17 (*Notulen*, Eerste Volksraad, 1897, art. 277).

[67] Report of Superintendent for Education, for 1897 (*Weekly Press*, 21 May 1898). Marais, p. 133, points out that in 1898 the government was spending £226,291 on education.

[68] Elected by nationalities (*Weekly Press*, 9 Jan. 1897; Marais, pp. 133–4).

[69] *Weekly Press*, 30 July 1898, p. 19.

admit that there had been little educational progress on the gold-fields (one State school had been set up with 22 pupils)[70] but he claimed that it was not fair to judge a measure that had been in operation for less than two years, and that it was not his fault if the people on the Rand did not send their children to the English schools. By 1899 there were 13 schools, with 1,500 pupils, mostly English-speaking.[71] The position on the Barberton goldfields was equally discouraging. The *Weekly Press* (6 August 1898) pointed out that, although Mansvelt had removed the fantastic chaos which had prevailed six years before, the situation was still such that many patriotic burghers still felt it incumbent upon them to send their children out of the State to receive a proper education.

To sum up, the issue of the education given by the State, centring more particularly upon the question of the use of English as a medium (for the children of uitlanders) and on the importance of the teaching of English as a commercial and social medium (for the children of burghers), was an increasingly important one. An examination of the main debates referred to in this section will show a clear division on the issue. Those who opposed any changes most violently were such members as C. J. Tosen, A. D. W. Wolmarans, F. G. Wolmarans, J. M. Malan, C. B. Otto, P. G. Roos, J. P. L. Lombaard, N. M. S. Prinsloo and J. J. Spies, strongly led, in this matter by President Kruger himself, and all of them (with the exception of J. J. Spies) consistent Conservatives. Those who had their doubts about it included J. H. Labuschagne, Jan P. Meyer, W. J. Steyn and W. H. van Niekerk. And those who spoke firmly for a more flexible and tolerant outlook in education were Lukas Meyer, R. K. Loveday, C. Jeppe, Paul Maré, L. and G. de Jager, L. van Wyk, Commandant J. H. (Koos) de la Rey, Schalk Burger and J. du P. de Beer—the first eight of them acknowledged Progressives, and the last two often associated with them in opposition to the government.[72]

The Volksmacht Congress of 1895,[73] moreover, pressed the government 'to so alter the existing Education Law that two hours a day shall be spent on a living foreign language, and three hours

---

[70] *Weekly Press*, 30 July 1898, p. 19 (*Notulen*, Eerste Volksraad, 1898, art. 887).

[71] Marais, pp. 132–5.

[72] See p. 245 (on Progressive opposition to Mansvelt, see also Ploeger, pp. 111, 115–16).

[73] See pp. 181–2.

per day on the language of the country, while in Standard III both languages should be given equal rights', and *Land en Volk* supported this campaign. Similarly, *Land en Volk*'s special issue of 30 December 1895, devoted to Charles Leonard's manifesto, strongly supported the educational grievances of the uitlanders.[74]

There is reason, therefore, to regard the education and language issue as one of the dividing issues around which the Progressive opposition formed itself.

[74] See also Ploeger, pp. 120–2.

5

The Issues around which Opposition Crystallized
(continued)

VII. HOLLANDER POLICY

ONE of the penalties of the Republic's rise to modern statehood was the need for educated officials who were acquainted with the apparatus of modern government and able to correspond in the leading languages of Europe. After the appointment of Dr. W. J. Leyds as State Attorney in 1884 Kruger turned increasingly to Hollander officials for this purpose, and their influence soon became paramount, more particularly in the public service, education and the railways. Under Leyds's leadership they played a most valuable part in raising beyond all recognition the efficiency, co-ordination and general standards of the Transvaal's government.[1] Kruger, with reason, considered them politically reliable, even though, on the personal level, they were (with some exceptions) never particularly popular with the Boer population; and, by his actions in appointing them to a considerable number of influential positions, showed his agreement with the attitude which the *Volksstem* took up on the dangers of employing Cape Afrikaners.

'We have had enough of the "British subjects" from the Cape Colony. Let us rather use the faithful Hollanders as officials until we have Transvaalers trained in the law', it wrote (on 20 February 1890), at the same time giving a sidelong blow at the burghers 'who have neglected to educate themselves or their children in the necessary knowledge without which the machinery of state cannot be made to work'.[2]

Though their services to the Republic are beyond dispute, the presence of increasing numbers of Hollander officials led to widespread resentment, not only among English-speaking inhabitants

[1] Marais, pp. 14–17, 33.
[2] In this editorial Engelenburg, the Editor of the *Volksstem* and himself a Hollander, was striking a double blow—one in favour of having Dutch officials in the public service, and one on behalf of the increasingly Hollander-dominated education system.

and Cape Afrikaners, but among the Transvaal Boers themselves; and opposition to 'Hollander rule' (as *Land en Volk* regularly called the state of affairs under Leyds) was one of the keynotes of Progressive opposition to Kruger's régime.

General Joubert himself was widely believed to be bitterly anti-Hollander.[3] Leyds's letter to Schmüll of 18 November 1886[4] declares that 'He hates the Hollanders moreover with an inborn hatred' (met een innigen haat), and there can be little doubt that it is to the Hollanders that Joubert was referring when he wrote to C. B. Otto (later member for Marico of the First Raad) on 24 August 1892:[5]

'I shall do what my hand finds to do for our beloved country—not only for independence from England—but also from the foreign unhealthy influence [vreemde onzalige invloet] which is undermining our existence as a people [volksbestaan] and our national character.'

Land en Volk looked forward confidently to Joubert's election as an event which would automatically mark the end of Hollander influence.

'We know well why the Hollanders are so poisonous against General Joubert', it wrote on 29 September 1892, 'for they know well that if he becomes President it will mean an end to their triumphant domination of the Transvaal.'

The same, according to the *Volksstem* of 21 September 1892, was true of Ewald Esselen,[6] the chairman of the Joubert Committee.

'The burghers of the Republic', it declared . . . 'know well that both he and Chief Justice Kotzé nurse a bitter hatred of Hollanders together with their love of Uitlanders.'

Esselen's opponents alleged that this was largely motivated by his envy of Leyds, and his desire to secure Leyds's office;[7] but it should

[3] See *Volksstem*, 2 Mar. 1892, 5 Mar. 1892; *Press*, 22 Oct. 1892 (see also anti-Hollander letter of Joubert in *Volksstem*, 6 Feb. 1888. See also Mouton, pp. 107–8, 122–4).

[4] See above, p. 9, and Van Winter, i, p. 245.

[5] Joubert Papers, Uitgaande Stukke, II A/1–A/3, no. 1997 (Archives, vol. 17), no. 318.

[6] See Walker, p. 436; Marais, p. 16.

[7] See, for example, the statement by F. R. Statham in the *Standard & Diggers' News* reprinted in *Weekly Press*, 27 June 1896, p. 14. Also *Volksstem*, 21 Sept. 1892.

be noted that Esselen himself vigorously denied having worked against Leyds on any occasion.[8] Further, there is little evidence of anti-Hollander sentiment in any of Esselen's public speeches,[9] whatever his private actions may have been.

Most Progressive members, however, were openly against the Hollanders and everything they stood for. They were unanimous, as we have seen, in their attacks upon the Netherlands Railway Company, upon the State loan which had to be raised in 1892 to finance its construction, and in demanding the expropriation of the Netherlands company once the success of the line had become obvious. R. K. Loveday and his supporters in the Raad made no bones about their dislike of Hollanders.[10] They opposed the reappointment of Leyds,[11] and did not conceal their dislike of such Hollander officials as W. E. Bok (Secretary of the Executive Council up to 1892)[12] and Justice Jorissen.[13]

The most untiring and vigorous exponent of anti-Hollander sentiment was the Progressive organ, *Land en Volk*, under the editorship of Eugène Marais. A typical article,[14] for instance, declares:

'President Kruger has made one big mistake, and it is a mistake that can only end with the end of his rule. That mistake is his Hollander-policy. Nowhere is the taint of it absent. It has done the Transvaal more harm than any other thing. President Kruger had a wonderful chance to make the Transvaal a strong Afrikaans state. . . . But instead of that he has directed all his best efforts to the building up and maintenance of a Hollander Party. To it we owe our present financial disasters, and every other mistake that has been made.'

[8] See Esselen's letter of 23 June 1896 in *Weekly Press*, 27 June 1896, p. 14.

[9] See reports of these in *Volksstem*, 30 Sept. 1891; *Land en Volk*, 3 Nov. 1891; *Press*, 24 Mar. 1892; *Volksstem*, 13 Sept. 1892; *Land en Volk*, 15 Nov. 1894.

[10] See, for example, Loveday's speech in the Raad on 30 July 1891, and his speech at Barberton on 10 Dec. 1891 (*Volksstem*, 31 Dec. 1891; *Notulen*, Eerste Volksraad, 1891, art. 1195).

[11] *First Volksraad*, 7 June 1892 (*Notulen*, Eerste Volksraad, 1892, arts. 382–5).

[12] *Press*, 2 June 1892 (First Volksraad, 1 June 1892; *Notulen*, Eerste Volksraad, 1892, arts. 337–9).

[13] First Volksraad, 25 May 1891; *Land en Volk*, 9 Jan. 1893 (*Notulen*, Eerste Volksraad, 1891, arts. 128–9).

[14] *Land en Volk*, 26 Jan. 1892 (see also leader of 8 Dec. 1891).

Again, on 1 March 1892, *Land en Volk* wrote 'the country is ruled by the President, Leyds and Bok. Hollanders are preferred to the sons of the soil', and on 22 March 1892, in a violent attack on Leyds,

'To decide who rules the country it is only necessary to see who fills the government offices. Can the country again entrust its destiny into the hands of a man who has filled all posts of honour with foreign elements?'

The most virulent and persistent single critic of 'Hollander rule' was Afrikanus Junior[15] in *Land en Volk*, some examples of whose outpourings we have already glanced at, or shall glance at.[16] Though his violent attacks are more reminiscent of the hysterical ravings of Goebbels and Streicher than of the usual tone of nineteenth-century newspaper writings, they are well informed, shrewd and hard-hitting, and no doubt played their part in embittering the already widespread feeling of the Boers against the Hollander officials who (according to Afrikanus Junior) occupied the positions which should rightfully have been theirs. Here are some typical extracts.

'We had hardly regained our freedom', he wrote in his first 'Open Letter to His Excellency the President', 'when the men we had chosen to govern us began to import foreigners, flippant drunkards and moderns [ligtsinnige dronkaards en modernen] who infected the country like a dangerous disease. . . . We see the President of a free Republic surrounded by Hollanders and foreign Jews. . . . The whole country is filthy with Hollanders' (*Land en Volk*, 5 May 1891).

In his next article, on 12 May, he told the President that 'to reach you I must penetrate through a commando of Hollanders . . . and if I speak to you Leyds answers me, because he stands for you'.

In an 'Open Letter' to Dr. Leyds (*Land en Volk*, 1 November 1894) —which somewhat contradicts the usual Progressive assertion that Leyds ruled the Transvaal—Afrikanus Junior declared:

'You flatter yourself in thinking that the Volksvereeniging's[17] main aim is to get rid of you. You are too unimportant. You are the inkpot and the pen of Mr. Kruger, and nothing more, with just enough power to move his finger when it suits the interests of your

[15] See p. 196.
[16] See pp. 42, 95–6, 195–6, 244–5.
[17] See pp. 176 ff.

own country, or the interests of your personal friends and compatriots. If the Kruger Government falls you will find that your personal influence among the people is not as substantial as the shadow of a spider's web. You allege that you opposed the Selati Line. But that was no merit. You did not know then of the frauds perpetrated. You opposed *all* branch lines, because they would help the people, and because they threatened the domination of your beloved Netherlands line. Are you merely a low traitor working for the interests of another state and drawing £1500 a year from the South African Republic for doing so?'

That this strong prejudice against Hollanders was not confined to the newspapers is clearly shown by the numerous questions on this issue put to Kruger and Joubert in the course of their electioneering campaigns of 1892 to 1893,[18] and by the sentiments expressed in letters received by General Joubert, whom the burghers regarded as the main bastion of anti-Hollander feeling. Thus, in a fairly typical letter, one J. D. Bosman of Blauwbank, Krugersdorp district, writes:[19]

'In the first place, honoured General, I must remark that much ill-feeling exists among our people against the Government, and particularly against the present President and Messrs. Bok and Leyds. . . .

'It is not necessary to tell you, General, what personal reasons for bitterness I have against the President and the Hollanders. [A position for which Bosman had asked had been given to a Hollander.] God be thanked that you are independent of the President, the Hollanders and the Jews. . . . It is essential that we have a State Secretary who is an Afrikaner . . . and that the positions in State offices now given to Hollanders be given to Afrikaners.'

A letter from one S. J. E. Trichardt of Goede Hoop declares:[20]

'Where is our first birthright? Is it not given to the scum of Holland, and our land sold for concessions and monopolies. Our only hope is to get our General Joubert as president. I am sure he will make right what can still be made right.'

---

[18] See pp. 197–207.

[19] Joubert Papers, Inkomende Stukke, I A/10–17 (Archives, vol. 6), no. 639 of 3 Feb. 1892.

[20] Joubert Papers, no. 652.

Louis Botha, Veld-cornet at Vryheid (and many years later first Prime Minister of the Union of South Africa), writes to Joubert on 22 August 1892:[21]

'Our country certainly needs great changes, and in you we have the man who carries in his heart the independence of our beloved country, and a true friend of the Afrikaners. . . . I hope that the day will speedily dawn when our children will be able to say—away with Kruger's politics, concessions and Hollanders.'

One Van der Poel of Brits, writing on 30 December 1892,[22] sends his best wishes for the election to Joubert, and declares himself 'an enemy of President Kruger, who always gives preference to Hollanders'.

The fact that anti-Hollander sentiment had not in any way declined is demonstrated by the use made of it by Schalk Burger in the 1898 election campaign. His election 'Proclamation',[23] in addition to a strong attack on the dynamite concession, includes such statements as (on railway policy), 'but the President must now fight for his Hollander Company, because otherwise he might get nephew Leyds against him', and,

'Why are our offices filled up with foreigners? Hollanders and Germans draw large salaries while the sons of the soil are treated as outcasts [worden als Bastaards behandeld] unless they belong to this clique',

among many other uncomplimentary references to 'Leyds and his Hollanders'.

What, in actual fact, was the proportion of positions in the State's service occupied by Hollanders and what influence did they wield? The *Volksstem* (3 October 1893), whose editor Engelenburg was in close touch with government circles, estimated the proportion of Hollanders among the officials to be barely 14 per cent as against 70 per cent of colonial origin (and this overwhelming preponderance of colonial Afrikaners existed in spite of the fact, as 'Onze Jan' Hofmeyr pointed out, that most young men from the Cape 'who had passed various examinations . . . could not write Dutch

---

[21] Joubert Papers, Inkomende Stukke, I A/10–17 (Archives, vol. 6), no. 656.
[22] Joubert Papers (Archives, vol. 7), no. 666.
[23] Joubert Papers, Inkomende Stukke, I A/10–17 (Archives, vol. 7), contains a printed copy of this (no. 726).

efficiently').[24]

A statistical analysis some four years later in the *Weekly Press*[25] corresponds closely with this estimate. Tabulated, the figures read as follows:

Born in the Republic	682
Born in the Cape Colony	478
Born in the Orange Free State	105
Born in Natal	42
Born in other parts of South Africa ..	145
Total of South African-born officials..	1,452
Born in Holland	306
Born in England	107
Born in Germany	66
Born in France	6
Born in other European states	17
Born in other parts of the world	4
Total of non-South African-born officials	506
Grand Total	1,958

These figures did not include a large number of officers and men in the State Artillery and Republican Police Force who were 'with few exceptions sons of the soil'. The proportion of Netherlands-born officials, therefore, works out at a little over 15 per cent. The proportion of 'sons of the soil' appears to have risen between 1893 and 1897, but this would not be unexpected, in view of the constant pressure in their favour.

Carl Jeppe,[26] on the question of Hollander influence on State policy, declares that

'With the exception of Dr. Leyds, no Hollander had any important part in shaping Mr. Kruger's views or influencing his course of action. . . . Afrikanders from the Cape would have been the right

[24] J. H. Hofmeyr, *The Life of Jan Hendrik Hofmeyr*, p. 439. (See also Marais, p. 15, on this.)

[25] *Weekly Press*, 10 July 1897, p. 3. (See also Mouton, pp. 171–2.)

[26] Jeppe, pp. 177–80.

people for the expanding Civil Service; but Kruger remembered that many of the Pretorians who had sided with the British in 1880 had been Cape Afrikanders, and he was determined to employ only those whom he could absolutely trust. But Hollanders never had the preference. The first to be selected was always the Boer or Trans-vaaler with some pretensions to education, and often those without it. With the exception of the Education Department all the "Heads" were Afrikanders. Often these were Boers, pure and simple, who, thanks to their natural shrewdness, were able to direct affairs in their department in a general way, while utterly incompetent to write a letter or frame a report, and who had to rely therefore entirely on their clerks to carry out the routine of their office.

'. . . The Hollanders themselves often complained that they were only used as tools, and resented the treatment they received.'

Moreover, as the *Weekly Press* pointed out in 1896,[27] 'with very few exceptions even the Netherlanders have had 15 to 20 years' residence and are fully enfranchised burghers'. Van Boeschoten (Under-Secretary for Foreign Affairs), for example, had been in the Republic for thirty-six years, Van Alphen (Postmaster-General) and Rissik (Surveyor-General) had come as striplings. Bell (Head of the State Printing Office), Kuypers (Orphan Master) and De Waal (Inspector-General of Customs) were in their third decade of residence, and even the much-abused Dr. Mansvelt (Superintendent of Education) had had sixteen years in Cape scholastic institutions and five years in the Republic.

However, though these facts and figures seem to indicate that the importance of Hollander influence, if substantial, was exaggerated, this did not prevent it from being a very strongly-held grievance among opponents of Kruger's régime. The part it played in the opposition to the Netherlands Railway Company, the State loan of 1892, and the National Bank concession, which we have already discussed, was considerable. It also showed itself, *inter alia*, in such issues as the dismissal of W. E. Bok as 'Notulen-houder' (Minutes Secretary) of the Executive Council. *Land en Volk* (10 May 1892), while not denying 'Bok's services to the Republic at a time when there was no hope of reward for them', nevertheless demanded his dismissal mainly on the grounds that

[27] *Weekly Press*, 4 July 1896, p. 4 (this article contains a complete list of important Hollander and Afrikaner officials).

'it is time, in any case, that we had an Afrikaans Council. Is the Afrikaner nation so poor and weak that we must always run to Uitlanders for assistance? The Volksraad must show the world that we can rule ourselves.'

In the Volksraad[28] it was the Progressive members who launched the attack on Bok; and, in spite of a passionate appeal on his behalf by the President, an Afrikaner, J. H. M. de Kock (ex-Landdrost of Potchefstroom), was chosen in his place. There were rumours that the President would resign on this issue.[29] (He had stormed out during the course of the debate, throwing his sash upon Mr. De Beer, and muttering angrily to himself.[30]) But he had finally been pacified by the passing of a Volksraad resolution to pay Bok £42 a month until a suitable position could be found for him.[31]

At about the same time Dr. Leyds felt it politic to resign as Railway Commissioner.[32] His tenure of this office had been violently criticized—again chiefly by the Progressives.[33] An Afrikaner, J. S. (Koos) Smit, succeeded Leyds in this position.

However, the attempt of certain Progressive members, backed by a number of petitions from the burghers, to secure the dismissal of Leyds[34] as State Secretary, achieved not the slightest success, in spite of Leyds's unpopularity;[35] and the First Raad decided to reappoint him by the decisive majority of 20 votes to 3 (R. K. Loveday, Paul Maré and Lukas Meyer voting in the minority).[36]

There is some evidence that opposition to Kruger's Hollander policy was an issue in the 1893 election. Apart from the letters to Joubert already quoted, the newspaper reports of the meetings held during the traditional 'rondreis' (tour of the country districts) of the President and Joubert at the beginning of 1892, and of electoral

---

[28] First Volksraad, 1 June 1892 (*Notulen*, Eerste Volksraad, 1892, arts. 338–9; *Volksstem*, 1 June 1892; *Land en Volk*, 7 June 1892; *Press*, 2 June 1892).

[29] *Volksstem*, 4 June 1892.

[30] *Land en Volk*, 7 June 1892 ('hoog toornig, en iets mombelende dat niet gehoord kon worden').

[31] *Notulen*, Eerste Volksraad, 1892, arts. 405–6; *Volksstem*, 11 June 1892.

[32] *Notulen*, Eerste Volksraad, 1892, arts. 382–5; *Volksstem*, 4 June 1892.

[33] *Notulen*, Eerste Volksraad, 1892, arts. 382–5; *Volksstem*, 31 Dec. 1891, 20 Apr. 1892, 4 June 1892.

[34] The Progressives regarded Leyds as 'the pillar of everything inimical to the Afrikaans cause' (*Land en Volk*, 26 Apr. 1892).

[35] Marais, p. 15.

[36] *Volksstem*, 8 June 1892 (*Notulen*, Eerste Volksraad, 1892, arts. 384–5).

meetings at the end of that year and the beginning of 1893, contain many references to the President's alleged favouritism towards Hollanders, and to the influence of Leyds.

Thus, to take some fairly typical examples, a meeting of the burghers in the Marico area, in early February 1892, demanded 'an Afrikaner as State Secretary, or a trustworthy man'.[37] Kruger, at Amsterdam (in the Piet Retief district) and in Rustenburg, was closely questioned about Hollander influence, and denied that there were unwarranted numbers of Hollanders except in the Telegraphic and State Secretary's office. He stated that this was because of the need for fluency in foreign languages, and added, characteristically, that 'with foreign languages the landdrost of Rustenburg would be a baboon'[38] (a remark which, needless to say, was rapidly twisted by his opponents into an alleged statement that 'all Afrikaners were baboons', until Kruger neatly squashed it by declaring that, in that case, 'he was the biggest baboon of the lot').[39] Similarly, at Bethal, on 11 March 1892, various members of the public asked if it 'was true that Leyds held the reins', declared that it 'grieved them that the government was run by a Hollander' and regretted that the President favoured Hollanders and 'considered that the burghers were baboons'. The President was subjected to an intense barrage of hostile questions on this and other issues, the meeting, which began at 3 p.m., ending only at 8 o'clock that night, with the President still vigorously denying all these allegations.[40] A few days later, at Ermelo, Wakkerstroom and Standerton, Kruger was forced to deny allegations that he 'looked with an unfavourable eye upon Afrikaners, and with a friendly one upon Hollanders', and to declare that nearly all heads of departments were Afrikaners, though he made no bones about defending the employment of Hollander officials and gave adequate reasons why the Republic should be grateful to them and to Holland.[41] At Standerton 'the question of Hollanders took up much time';[42] and the President declared that 87 per cent of head officials were Cape Afrikaners, so that this 'praterij en gebabbel' (rumour-mongering and idle chatter) could well cease.

At Ermelo, towards the end of 1892, a number of cautiously sarcastic questions on the precise role of Dr. Leyds in the State's

[37] *Land en Volk*, 23 Feb. 1892.
[38] *Press*, 17 Mar. 1892.
[39] *Volksstem*, 15 Mar. 1892.
[40] *Volksstem*, 15 Mar. 1892.
[41] *Volksstem*, 16 Mar. 1892, 22 Mar. 1892.
[42] *Volksstem*, 22 Mar. 1892.

affairs forced the President into an interesting constitutional definition. Asked whether the government and the Executive Council were
one and the same body he said:

'Yes and no; the Executive Council consists of the President and
all the other members, whereas the President and State Secretary
form the Government [Regeering]. Big matters, matters of importance, are dealt with by the Executive Council; the others are disposed of [afgemaakt] by myself and Dr. Leyds. I cannot call the
[Executive Council] members out of their offices for every little
matter; I must honestly say that when I call upon the Commandant-
General he always comes.'

Asked by what laws the State Secretary was empowered to put
certain matters before the 'Government' and others before the
Executive Council the President said:

'Look, that shows a lack of trust in our State Secretary!
Mr. T. Smuts: Does that mean that when the Volksraad talks of
the Government, it means the State President and the State
Secretary?
President Kruger: Yes, certainly!
Mr. Smuts: What are the Executive Council members paid for
then, and why do they sit all the time in Pretoria?
President Kruger: Why should they come and sit with us; we don't
need them in these small matters.
Mr. J. Meyer: By whom are officials appointed?
President Kruger: By me. But I usually consult with others first.
Various burghers: Why was Leyds reappointed?
President Kruger: The voice of the Volksraad is sovereign, and
they have decided thus.' (*Land en Volk*, 17 November 1892)

Meanwhile, during the same period, Joubert, at Barberton[43] and
Pietersburg,[44] among other places, was making strong attacks upon
the Netherlands Railway Company and the influence of Hollanders
in the State; and as the election itself drew nearer *Land en Volk* saw
to it that a considerable proportion of the awkward questions which
it thoughtfully provided for Joubert adherents to pose to the President (13 October 1892) dealt with the Hollander issue, e.g.:

[43] *Volksstem*, 9 Feb. 1892, 16 Feb. 1892.
[44] *Volksstem*, 29 Mar. 1892.

'Why was Dr. Leyds reappointed? Why not a competent Afrikaner?

'Why is our country the only one in the world where a foreigner holds the reins?

'Why did the first 75 miles of the Hollander Railway Company cost £20,000 a mile, whereas the Concession lays down £9,500?

'Why were we told that the Delagoa Bay Railway must be built by a Hollander Company to free us from dependence on England, and now we find ourselves dangerously in debt to England?'

This was a useful contribution to what the *Press* of 22 October 1892, somewhat disrespectfully, called 'Pious Piet's anti-Hollander campaign'. Joubert in his electioneering campaign made much use of these issues;[45] and, though he defended Leyds's abilities, declared (presumably of Kruger) that 'it grieved him that an Afrikaner looked down with contempt upon his own nation, and elevated a foreigner to prominence'.[46]

Land en Volk, which, as early as 23 February 1892, had featured the coming election as essentially a struggle as to whether Hollander or Afrikaner should rule, in the words,

'It is Kruger who has built up the Hollander party; and, conversely, the Afrikaans principles of General Joubert are well known; and the choice between these two gentlemen is simply and solely the choice between Afrikaner and Hollander',

continued to add fuel to the flames of anti-Hollander feeling by pointing the contrast between the two chief contestants.

'Kruger has delivered us over to the Hollanders', it wrote on 26 December 'and Joubert has resolutely opposed this', and again, on 29 December, 'Kruger prefers Hollanders and Jews, who encircle him like vultures, to loyal sons of the soil—a policy which Joubert strongly opposes'.

The President, in consequence, found that the barrage of questions on his Hollander policy was as intense during his electoral tour towards the end of 1892 as it had been earlier that year;[47] and while

---

[45] See reports of his speeches at Heidelberg (*Land en Volk*, 20 Oct. 1892), Martinus Wessel Stroom (*Land en Volk*, 3 Nov. 1892), Middelburg (*Land en Volk*, 17 Nov. 1892) and Ermelo (*Land en Volk*, 17 Nov. 1892).

[46] *Land en Volk*, 3 Nov. 1892; and letter from 'Eerlik' in *Land en Volk* of 24 Nov. 1892.

[47] See p. 130 and further reports of rural meetings in *Press*, 7 Dec. 1892, and *Volksstem*, 22 Oct. 1892, 1 Nov. 1892, 9 Nov. 1892.

one cannot prove exactly what part this issue played in his near-defeat, it seems fair to conclude that the prominent role allocated to Kruger's Hollander policy in the pro-Joubert press, in Joubert's own speeches, and in the hostile questioning to which the President was subjected on his tours of the constituencies, indicates that this issue was of considerable importance in securing for Joubert the remarkable number of votes which he did achieve in 1893.

To this extent we may say, therefore, that Kruger's Hollander policy played an important part in the growth of opposition towards the régime. But the related question of the extent of its importance as one of the issues which drew the members of the Progressive party towards one another is a very much harder one to decide upon. It was certainly an element in the hostility of the Progressives towards the government's policy in such matters as the railway question, the setting up of the 'National Bank', the State loan of 1892 and the educational policy of Mansvelt and his increasingly Hollander-dominated schools. But whether the growth of opposition on these issues was largely a result of dislike of Hollanders, or genuinely dictated by concern for the welfare of the Republic, or produced by the universal desire of all opposition parties to seize upon any stick with which they might usefully beat the government, is an almost impossible question to resolve.

The indications are, however, that resentment of Hollander influence was, per se, but a minor factor in these issues. For on matters where such resentment, pure and simple, might reasonably be expected to unite Progressive members in opposition, it failed to do so. Thus, as we have seen, only three Progressive members voted against the reappointment of Leyds; and in the voting on the grant of a pension to Bok after his dismissal as Minutes Secretary of the Executive Committee and his replacement by an Afrikaner, no party divisions are discernible. Those who grudged Bok his pension, on the ground that many old burghers had far greater deserts, included[48] such staunch Conservatives as A. D. W. Wolmarans, J. M. Malan, A. A. Stoop and H. P. Beukes as well as such Progressives as R. K. Loveday, Lukas Meyer, L. de Jager and J. J. Spies.

It seems reasonable to conclude, therefore, that this issue played a considerable part in rallying support around Joubert in the 1893 election; but a comparatively minor, though certainly not negligible,

[48] *Notulen*, Eerste Volksraad, 1892, arts. 383–9, 405–6; *Volksstem*, 11 June 1892.

part in acting as one of the focal points around which the Progressive party crystallized.

VIII. THE FRANCHISE QUESTION

However important any of the preceding issues may be, there can be no doubt that the issue which towered over them all was the question of the relations between the old burgher population and the new immigrants from beyond the borders of the Transvaal. It was natural that this issue should become the fundamental one, for everything that the old conservative Boer population of the Transvaal held most dear was threatened, or seemed to be threatened, with extinction, as the unceasing flood of immigration rose ever higher—their tenuous and hard-won freedom, their stubborn and exclusive racial pride, their language, morals and whole way of life.

As to the exact number of the new immigrants there was much disagreement. Rhodes, in one of his more extravagant moments, declared that 80,000 to 100,000 males were being ruled by 15,000 to 20,000;[49] while, on the other hand, the *Weekly Press* estimated[50] (on the basis of the Johannesburg Sanitary Board Census of July 1896) that there were about 20,000 uitlanders, and (on the basis of statements by the Republican War Office) some 40,000 armed burghers. President Kruger, however, in arguing with Milner at the Bloemfontein Conference against extension of the franchise, estimated the new population at 60,000 to 70,000 and the number of burghers at 30,000,[51] an estimate that is nearer to that of Rhodes than to that of the *Weekly Press*. Yves Guyot, in his bitterly anti-Transvaal book *Boer Politics*, the articles of which originally appeared in *Le Siècle*,[52] gives the total population by 1899 as 300,000 of which 175,000 were males. Burghers between 16 and 60 he gives as 29,447 in number, and uitlanders in the same age group as 81,000[53]—a figure which agrees very closely with that put forward by the President. The *Cambridge History of the British Empire*[54] estimates that by 1895 the uitlanders formed more than half the white population—a figure borne out by

[49] *Weekly Press*, 19 Mar. 1898, p. 2. On another occasion he described the uitlanders as nine-tenths of the population (see Marais, p. 2).

[50] Ibid., p. 2.

[51] C 9404, pp. 19, 25; *Weekly Press*, 24 June, p. 17.

[52] Yves Guyot, *Boer Politics*, Introduction (published 1900).

[53] Guyot, p. 58.

[54] C.H.B.E., vol. viii, p. 554 (based on Parliamentary Papers 1895 LXXI, C 7633).

the estimate of the Pretoria *Press* on 3 and 6 December 1894 that adult burghers at that stage numbered some 20,000 and adult uitlanders about 35,000 (11,000 of them colonial Afrikaners). De Kiewiet's statement[55] that by 1895 there were probably seven uitlanders to every three burghers is not supported by any evidence, and seems extremely unlikely. Marais, in a closely reasoned analysis,[56] concludes that by January 1899 there may even have been more Boers (men, women and children) than uitlanders, but that (because adult males formed a comparatively high proportion of the uitlander population) there may well have been more uitlander than Boer male adults. It must be remembered that, in spite of the virtual agreement on a ratio of seven uitlanders to three burghers by such opposed sources as Rhodes and Guyot on the one hand and Kruger on the other, it was to the interest of both sides (though for totally different reasons) to estimate the ratio as disproportionately high as possible. The inrush of immigrants doubtless seemed to the burgher population all the more menacing just because its relative proportions were unknown.

Before 1882 one year's residence had been all that was necessary to entitle an uitlander to the franchise, but by Law 7 of 1882[57] this had been raised to five years, in an attempt by President Kruger to counteract the possible political consequences of the influx of new immigrants to the Lydenburg goldfields, and a high fee of £25 was required for naturalization. By 1888 Kruger had become increasingly alarmed[58] at the great wave of immigration which had followed the discovery of gold on the Witwatersrand; and two years later the drastic Law 5 of 1890 was passed[59] which divided burghers into two classes, those who were entitled to vote for what was thereafter called the First Volksraad, and those entitled to vote only for the Second Volksraad. The franchise for the lower Raad was now attainable after two years' residence, the payment of only £5 (£2 after 1894),[60] and the taking of an amended oath of allegiance which emphasized the new second-class citizen's renunciation of allegiance to 'all foreign princes, states, sovereignties, and in particular to the prince, government, state or sovereignty of which I am now a subject and citizen'.

But the vote for the First Raad, and for the election of the Presi-

[55] De Kiewiet (*a*), p. 132.   [56] Marais, pp. 2–3.
[57] Eybers, *Select Constitutional Documents*, p. 437.
[58] Marais, p. 53.   [59] Eybers, pp. 488, 495.   [60] Marais, p. 53.

dent and Commandant-General, was now attainable only after fourteen years' residence, with no guarantee that the term might not be further extended. Moreover, the Second Raad had no control over finance, or indeed any funds of its own, and its decisions were subject to the veto of the First Volksraad.[61] Its utter powerlessness was joyfully underlined by the *Volksstem* in a leading article on 28 May 1890, in which it admitted that 'some rights and privileges must be given to these foreign traders and diggers, or whatever they may be', and that, although it had originally opposed the idea of a second Chamber, it felt, on reflection, that no better method could have been devised than the institution of such a Second Volksraad, 'which should bear the character of a "Chamber of Commerce" '.[62]

In a subsequent leading article (9 June 1890), however, it attacked the statement in article 2 of the Bill that the supreme legislative power in the State remained the First Volksraad. Only experience, and not a paper constitution, the *Volksstem* opined (with considerable foresight, as the development in importance of the Second Raad was to prove[63]) would show whether, in practice, 'the First Volksraad, the Second, or the President, would be this'.

The First Volksraad, itself, in debating the proposed introduction of a second Chamber,[64] revealed grave doubts among both those who supported and those who opposed the President's proposals. In answer to the fear expressed by J. F. Celliers[65] (himself later a distinguished member of the Second Volksraad from May 1892 until his death in March 1895) that its introduction would inevitably lead to strife, by the creation of two kinds of voters in opposition to one another, and that the newcomers would never be satisfied by such a second Chamber, Kruger declared that the system 'was working well in the United States and Europe, the only difference [*sic*] being that the same people chose both chambers'; and in answer to the declaration of J. P. L. Lombaard (Standerton) that he could not agree to give *any* rights to people who had insulted the flag of the Republic,[66] Kruger declared that many Englishmen had sprung

[61] *Notulen*, Eerste Volksraad, 1890, art. 431.

[62] 'Die het karakter moet dragen van een "Kamer van Koophandel".'

[63] Marais, p. 53. See above, pp. 42–6, 96–111.

[64] First Volksraad, 16 to 20 June 1890 (*Notulen*, Eerste Volksraad, 1890, arts. 381–448).

[65] *Notulen*, Eerste Volksraad, 1890, art. 381.

[66] A reference to the insulting treatment of the President by some uitlanders on the occasion of his visit to Johannesburg in March 1890 (*Volksstem*, 6 Mar.

to his defence at that time and that 'there were as many loyal people in Johannesburg as elsewhere in the Republic'.[67] There was, he said, a danger of disturbances if the unjust policy of giving the newcomers, already more numerous than the local burghers (*sic*), no rights, was followed; on the other hand the Transvaal would lose its independence if thousands of strangers were to get the franchise. Many of the newcomers meant well by the State, and were prepared to throw in their lot with it. It would be wrong to reject them, and that was why he sought a middle way in this proposed law.

The majority of members supported the President's view, and the principle of a second Chamber was accepted by 28 votes to 8 (J. F. Celliers, Schalk Burger, Paul Maré, B. J. Vorster, G. P. Otto, C. C. van Heerden, E. C. Hamman and P. G. Maré desiring that their votes should be recorded in the minority).[68] There is thus no indication of any division along party lines in this vote, the first three members being, in various degrees, 'Progressive' and the remaining five 'Conservative'. It is noteworthy that such members as J. P. L. Lombaard and F. G. Wolmarans, who had opposed the idea as dangerous to the Republic's independence, voted with the President when it came to a division. It should likewise be noted that the President's insistence that voters for the First Volksraad should also be able to vote for the Second was accepted with acclamation.[69] Most members, at this stage, appeared to share the *Volksstem's* view that the new Chamber would be little more than a sort of chamber of commerce. J. J. Burger (Ermelo), for instance, opined that the proposed Second Volksraad could be regarded as 'nothing more than a Committee whose reports could be accepted or rejected by the First Raad'; and on this comfortable note the matter ended, the legislators deciding, on reflection, to delete 'control of relations between masters and servants' from the powers of the Second Chamber, as the President declared that he

'agreed that members of the First Volksraad had more experience in these matters. He agreed to scrapping it, particularly because in England and the outside world people thought that the natives were

1890; Walker, p. 435; *C.H.B.E.*, vol. viii, p. 556). For Lombaard's speech see *Notulen*, Eerste Volksraad, 1890, art. 381.

[67] *Notulen*, Eerste Volksraad, 1890, art. 395.

[68] *Notulen*, Eerste Volksraad, 1890, art. 430.

[69] First Volksraad, 18 June 1890 (*Volksstem*, 23 June 1890); *Notulen*, Eerste Volksraad, 1890, arts. 396–7.

oppressed and maltreated here. The newcomers very soon realised how wrong this view was.'[70]

('Very soon', as the unwillingness to entrust this vital matter to the representatives of the newcomers showed, apparently meant at least four years.[71])

By February 1891 the new Second Volksraad building, 'in late Renaissance style', was nearing completion, and in May 1891 the new Chamber met for the first time, and chose as its Chairman the same J. J. Burger who had opined that it should be merely a sort of subcommittee of the First Raad—perhaps an index of its humble opinion of its worth, and of its loyal disposition towards the government. Certainly of its twenty-four members nine at the most could be regarded as in any way Progressive[72] (E. Esselen—Potchefstroom, F. Watkins—De Kaap Goldfields, E. P. A. Meintjies—Pretoria, J. W. Joubert—Pretoria, W. H. van Niekerk—Lydenburg, G. de Jager[73]—Wakkerstroom, D. F. Petersen—Heidelberg, B. G. Brecher—Vryheid, and, later, N. S. Malherbe—Potchefstroom). In this, if we may assume progressive views and the degree to which these members represented the newcomers to be synonymous, they were at any rate more representative of the new element than was the First Raad. For in that body, in the same year, only three out of twenty-four[74] can be regarded as falling into the same category (Paul Maré—Zoutpansberg, L. de Jager—Ermelo, and R. K. Loveday) with four others (J. J. Spies—Utrecht, J. P. L. Labuschagne—Heidelberg, J. P. Meyer—Johannesburg and J. du P. de Beer—Waterberg) occasionally wavering in their direction.

But the Second Raad got off to a shaky start, in no way indicative of the importance it was later to assume, and its early sessions were frequently forced to adjourn because there was nothing on the order paper for it to debate.[75] Moreover, Kruger, in the First Raad, on as minor a matter as the regulations for the exploitation of salt-pans,

---

[70] First Volksraad, 19 June 1890 (*Volksstem*, 26 June 1890); *Notulen*, Eerste Volksraad, 1890, art. 418.

[71] Franchise was obtainable after two years, but a seat in the Second Raad only after four years (Walker, p. 436).

[72] See chapter VI.

[73] After 1893 a member of the First Raad.

[74] The First Raad was reduced from 36 to 24 when the Second Raad was instituted (*Notulen*, Eerste Volksraad, 1890, art. 1166).

[75] *Volksstem*, 23 May 1891.

was careful to calm any latent fears among his supporters by emphasizing that 'the First Raad possessed the power to alter or nullify [vernietigen] any resolution of the Second Volksraad', although he was careful to express his appreciation of the smooth co-operation between the two chambers. This co-operation the *Volksstem* (9 June 1891) took leave to doubt, alleging:

'A good deal of tussling and friction has occurred already. Even allowing the position to be satisfactory, the question is for how long or how short a time it will continue. The nature and outlook of the two Chambers is at the moment very similar; but when elections are held in a few years' time the differences between them will increase.'

The actual origin of this first clash had been a request by the Second Raad—Esselen had been the prime mover in this—for information on the concessions and conditions of operation of the salt-pans and wood-forests of the Republic. It had, moreover, had the temerity to ask for the relevant documents for the previous five years.[76] This had been regarded by the Kruger party as an insult to the First Raad.[77] *Land en Volk*, like its rival, the *Volksstem*, regarded this clash as ominous.

'The First Raad', it wrote on 9 June 1891, 'can veto any *decision* of the Second Raad, but not any *motion*. If this is allowed the Second Volksraad means less than nothing. . . . How can a request for information be an insult? Is it perhaps an insult because certain salt-pans were given to Mr. Nellmapius under such favourable conditions?'

Kruger's determination to keep the Second Raad under tight control was shown very much more definitely in July,[78] when Esselen proposed that the First Raad should place a sum at the disposal of the lower Chamber for allocation to the construction of roads and bridges, as it was very difficult, without knowing what money was available, to make the necessary regulations. The President refused firmly to accept this suggestion,

[76] Second Volksraad, 15 May 1891 (*Notulen*, Tweede Volksraad, 1891, art. 122; *Land en Volk*, 2 June 1891, 9 June 1891).
[77] First Volksraad, 3 June 1891 (*Notulen*, Eerste Volksraad, 1891, art. 245; *Volksstem*, 4 June 1891).
[78] Second Volksraad, 21 July 1891 (*Volksstem*, 23 July 1891; *Notulen*, Tweede Volksraad, 1891, art. 888).

'1. Because the finances of the State are the concern solely of the First Volksraad [alleen thuis zijn bij den Eersten Volksraad].

2. Because all resolutions of the Second Raad must be approved by the First Raad.

3. Because, if the First Raad approved, it would allocate the necessary funds.

4. Because the government had to execute the decisions of the First Raad, and must make the necessary financial arrangements.'

Esselen had perforce to withdraw his motion; but the position of the Second Chamber could hardly have been made more clear. It is not surprising, therefore, to find leading members of the 'opposition', at the end of the session, bitterly attacking the complete powerlessness of the Second Raad. In a speech to his constituents at Potchefstroom, in October 1891, Esselen declared that

'he would not say that the Second Volksraad had done nothing; but it was so limited in its power that even its best meant little. As soon as it met it was clear that there were two parties in it. One consisted of the old burghers, many of whom had been members of the First Volksraad,[79] such as Mr. Taljaard. These were entirely under the influence of the government and would like the First Volksraad to control the Second in every particular. The other party consisted of the younger members, to which he belonged, who wished to decide their own rules of procedure [Reglement van Orde]. At the end of the session the division was as great as it had been at the beginning. . . . If matters continued as at present there would be nothing for the Second Volksraad to do in two or three years. The Second Chamber was virtually nothing more than an advisory body to the First Volksraad. . . . He would give an example. A Committee of five members had sat for nearly two months to draw up a revised Gold Law. It had listened to much evidence and had had the help of the Mining Commissioners and the Minister of Mines. The revised law was well drawn up and approved by the Second Raad, and then sent to the First Raad for confirmation [bekrachtiging]. The First Raad was so busy with high politics etc. that it could not consider it, and the result was that the revised law was referred to the Government, with full power to make any regulations that it might think fit! Such an attitude could only serve to make Second

[79] The First Raad had been reduced in numbers from 36 to 24.

Raad members careless of their work.[80] Further, the Second Raad had not the power to dispose of one penny. It could not even buy the paper and ink required for its sessions! (Laughter).'[81]

F. Watkins, speaking in the same vein to his constituents at Kaapsche Hoop, declared bluntly: 'We are just a troop of children. It is a waste of time and money.'[82]

Commenting on Esselen's speech, the *Volksstem*, on 30 October 1891, with less goodwill, but perhaps more historical wisdom, than he, put on record its hope that Esselen's prophecy that the Second Raad would cease to exist within two or three years 'will be verified. But we think he underestimates its importance. Such a body cannot be formed by paper regulations. It forms itself in accordance with the historic flow of circumstances.' But it approved Esselen's forthrightness, and declared that his speech had made a deep impression. On 10 February 1892 it returned to the attack, alleging that 'it is clear that little enthusiasm exists among [members of the Second Raad] for their own College. Its powers are so limited that its influence is negligible. It has not achieved nothing; but its achievements do not justify its continued existence', and it advocated instead a new amalgamated Volksraad, 24 members of which would be chosen by the old burghers and 24 by the old and the new burghers jointly.

However, in the 1892 session the Second Chamber showed interesting signs of its growing determination to be more than a cipher. In June, despite the President's firm opposition, the Second Raad passed a motion requesting the abolition of tolls, and was supported in the First Raad by 11 votes to 10. They had already rejected a number of concessions in spite of the fact that the President had spoken in their favour.[83] On the crucial 'Stands Scandal' affair, opposition pressure for a full inquiry had been narrowly defeated (by 11 votes to 9); and although Esselen in October 1892 repeated to his constituents his view that the Second Raad 'was a waste of time and money',[84] and was echoed in this sentiment by Chief

[80] There was much truth in this. Nevertheless the revised Gold Law was accepted by the Government with some minor modifications (*Volksstem*, 30 July 1891), so that it is not quite accurate to suggest that the work of the Second Raad had been largely in vain.

[81] *Volksstem*, 30 Oct. 1891; *Land en Volk*, 3 Nov. 1891.

[82] *Land en Volk*, 15 Dec. 1891.

[83] See p. 30, pp. 42–6.   [84] *Volksstem*, 18 Oct. 1892.

Justice Kotzé (who declared it in his election address at Lydenburg to be 'als een vyfde wiel aan een wagen'),[85] there are signs that the attitude towards the Second Chamber was changing. It is interesting that the first significant indication of this change in attitude should appear in a source as close to the government as the *Volksstem*. In a leading article of 29 April 1893 it made a plea for the Second Raad's right to control the financial side of its own measures—though 'always under the definite control of the First Raad'—and declared that

'the Second Volksraad enjoys a high moral prestige among members of the public, hardly less than that of the First Volksraad. The Second Volksraad is working well, and should be helped, not hindered.'

It seems as though the respect for the Second Raad, on the part of both opponents and supporters of the government, increased in direct proportion to its obstreperousness; for 1893 saw numerous clashes between that Chamber and the government. The opposition had been strengthened in 1892 by the election of J. F. Celliers (Witwatersrand) and in 1893 by that of W. J. Jooste (Potchefstroom),[86] and the latter year saw a mounting attack upon the defects of the administration.[87] It was marked, moreover, by an increasingly defiant tone on the part of the opposition, and a correspondingly conciliatory tone on the President's part. The opposition's consciousness of rising discontent among the burgher population on the one hand, and the narrowness of Kruger's election victory, on the other, explain this change quite adequately. But what is interesting is the new tone of respect for the lower Chamber to be found in the *Volksstem*, which in a review of the session (19 August 1893) declared:

'The Second Volksraad has now adjourned after a session rich in incidents, but also in useful resolutions. Those who, with us, opposed the institution of the Second Volksraad must admit that the splitting of the popular representation has had good practical results. That is the way with politics. Something that is objectionable in theory often works very well in practice. The birth of the Second Volksraad

[85] *Volksstem*, 19 Oct. 1892.
[86] *Land en Volk*, 20 Apr. 1893; *Press*, 15 Apr. 1893; *Volksstem*, 2 May 1893.
[87] See pp. 43–5.

was not hailed with joy; but the ranks of its opponents are growing steadily thinner.'

This increasing respect was shown not only in the adulatory speeches by members of the First Raad on the occasion of the Second Raad's prorogation;[88] but also by the increasing tendency of the upper Chamber, which we have already noted, to avoid discussion of mining and industrial matters as essentially the sphere of the Second Volksraad.

The year 1894, significantly, saw the Second Raad elect as its Chairman (by 12 votes to 10)[89] the comparatively progressive N. S. Malherbe (Potchefstroom) in place of its previous strongly pro-government chairman, J. J. Burger, and the pattern of the session was just what this would indicate. On 11 August the Second Raad rejected by 15 votes to 5[90] the President's request that they should alter article 21 of the Gold Law so that the government should not be bound by the Committee report on underground rights in the matter of the 'bewaarplaatsen' (which had recommended that the holders of the surface rights—that is the mining companies—should also control the underground rights) but should be able instead to act on the advice of the Executive Council. What this meant, in practice, was that the Executive would possess the power to allocate these potentially extremely lucrative rights as it saw fit. The discussion in the First Volksraad of the Second Raad's refusal to bow to the Presidential[91] will shows clearly the delicate nature of the relationship which had by now grown up between the two legislatures, and is further evidence of the growing unwillingness of the senior Chamber to set aside decisions by the Second Raad on mining and industrial matters—as it was constitutionally entitled to do. Jeppe stressed the extreme unwisdom of 'interfering with the work of the Second Raad in a matter specially allocated to it by law', though he agreed that the First Raad was technically competent to

[88] Second Volksraad, 17 Aug. 1893 (*Notulen*, Tweede Volksraad, 1893, arts. 860–1; *Volksstem*, 19 Aug. 1893).

[89] Second Volksraad, 7 May 1894 (*Notulen*, Tweede Volksraad, 1894, art. 6; *Volksstem*, 8 May 1894).

[90] Second Volksraad, 11 Aug. 1894 (*Notulen*, Tweede Volksraad, 1894, arts. 903–4; *Volksstem*, 15 Aug. 1894).

[91] First Volksraad, 13–14 Aug. 1894 (*Notulen*, Eerste Volksraad, 1894, arts. 1334–7. The official record is very brief. *Volksstem*, 15 Aug. 1894, gives a far fuller account of this debate).

do so. R. K. Loveday, more bluntly, warned the Raad not to negate
the work of the Second Chamber. L. de Jager declared that their
right to reject a decision of the Second Raad must be used very
sparingly if a serious clash was to be avoided. Commandant J. H.
de la Rey asserted that he was 'not prepared to veto a Second Raad
decision'. J. P. L. Labuschagne declared that he 'would feel ashamed
if he rejected the work done by the Second Raad'. And, though the
Chairman, F. G. Wolmarans,[92] alleged that to approve of the Second
Raad's decision 'would put the government into a subordinate
position to a Committee of the Second Raad', and was stoutly
echoed by J. P. L. Lombaard, who asserted that to set aside the
decision 'would not humiliate the Second Raad—it would not be the
first time the First Volksraad had corrected the Second Raad's mistakes, and the latter ought to be glad of it'—the compromise motion
of Loveday and L. de Jager to 'take notice of' (i.e. neither accept nor
reject) the Second Raad's decision, was passed with the contrary
votes of only F. G. Wolmarans, J. P. L. Lombaard, P. G. Roos and
J. M. Malan (the hard core, that is, of the Conservative section).[93]

A few months later[94] F. Watkins put forward a motion 'respect-
fully requesting an extension of the powers of the Second Volksraad,
in view of the tremendous progress of the country, and in the light
of the experience of the last four years'. He pointed out that the
Second Raad represented more burghers than the First, the old
burghers and the new incomers who had acquired the franchise by
naturalization. He thought the franchise regulations at present fair
enough, but he wanted the Second Raad to have considerable funds
at its disposal and far wider powers. He was strongly supported by
J. F. Celliers and G. B. Brecher, who felt that the Second Chamber
had proved its trustworthiness. It ought to be completely independent, and the right of veto ought to be taken away from the First
Raad. E. P. A. Meintjies and W. J. Jooste spoke in a similar strain;
and, though Conservative members such as C. du Plessis (Rustenburg) and E. Boshoff (Waterberg) declared themselves content to
accept the First Raad's veto, Watkins's motion was carried by 15
votes to 8. It came up before the First Raad at the beginning of the
1895 session, and was 'taken notice of'—the *Volksstem* noting
mockingly that the 'progressive' members of the First Volksraad

[92] First Volksraad, 7 May 1894 (*Volksstem*, 8 May 1894).
[93] *Notulen*, Eerste Volksraad, 1894, arts. 1334–7; *Volksstem*, 15 Aug. 1894.
[94] Second Volksraad, 16 Aug. 1894 (*Volksstem*, 18 Aug. 1894).

'kept dead quiet over [the honourable member for Barberton's] lovely extension scheme' and opining that the public was in no mood for any such extension of power.[95]

Four days later came the passing by 14 votes to 9, as we have seen,[96] of the Second Volksraad's celebrated resolution to reject all concessions unconditionally. On 22 August came a further clash with the President over the Second Raad's insistence on investigating a shortage of some £600 in the Johannesburg Mining Commissioner's office, which led to Kruger's jumping up from his seat and leaving the Raad in high dudgeon.[97] A week later, against the President's violent opposition,[98] a motion by J. F. Celliers and W. J. Jooste condemning the land deals of B. J. Vorster and B. Aaron and insisting that all land sales should in future take place by public auction, was carried by 13 votes to 9.

The following year saw no decline in the belligerent mood of the Second Chamber, as its decisive stand on the 'Stands Scandal' and the 'Bewaarplaatsen' question, and its general attack upon the administrative inefficiency of the Minister of Mines, clearly demonstrate.

To sum up these five important years of the Second Volksraad's existence, then, it seems fair to say that, starting under comparatively unfavourable auspices, decried by the press and despised by many of its own members, the Second Chamber had within five years established an important and respected position for itself, and had become an important focus of opposition to the government—very much more so than the First Volksraad. Moreover, as we have seen, the lead given by the Progressives in bringing governmental policy, official maladministration and private corruption under the focus of its searching and always critical gaze, had stimulated significant sections of normally pro-government opinion, in both Chambers and in the press, to support it in demanding a reorganization of public life. In that sense, at any rate, the Second Volksraad had more than justified its existence, and proved itself to be anything but the 'sort of chamber of commerce' that its earlier detractors had either

[95] *Volksstem*, 13 May 1895. (A month later it was finally rejected, only Jeppe and Loveday voting for an extension of the Second Raad's powers. See *Press*, 13 June 1895.)

[96] See p. 45.

[97] *Volksstem*, 25 Aug. 1894.

[98] *Notulen*, Tweede Volksraad, 1894, arts. 1058–64; *Volksstem*, 1 Sept. 1894; *Land en Volk*, 30 Aug. 1894.

wished, or feared, that it would be.

But to say all this, important as it may be in showing that the views of the uitlander community were not entirely without a vehicle of expression, is not to say that it at any time satisfied either them or the more progressive section of burgher opinion; and it is to that side of the matter that we must now turn.

Before analysing to what extent the franchise issue, like those other issues which we have so far dealt with, may be considered a crystallizing issue around which progressive opinion coalesced, let us remind ourselves of its vital importance.

By modifying his intransigent stand on this issue, in time, Kruger might well have secured the very opposite of what he feared, not the destruction of the State, but a loyal rallying to the cause of the Republic of thousands of contented uitlanders, a large mass of whom were Afrikaners from the neighbouring South African states with no very special attachment to the 'Imperial factor', and additional thousands of whom were Germans, Jews, Netherlanders or Frenchmen with even less feeling for the British connexion than the Afrikaners.[99] Marais, in chapter XIII of *The Fall of Kruger's Republic*, adduces ample evidence to suggest that the greatest fear of Chamberlain and Milner was, not that Kruger might continue to withhold the franchise, but that he might admit the uitlanders to the franchise in steadily increasing numbers, a policy that would lead the uitlanders to 'Afrikanderize' and so firmly establish the separate identity and continued existence of the South African Republic outside the sphere of British paramountcy. For all his very real statesmanship, Kruger did not realize this in time. On the issue of reform in general and the franchise in particular, his policy was one of procrastination. As Marais says, 'The procrastination can be explained. But the fact remains that it was fatal.'[1]

It was to this, almost certainly, that Lord Justice De Villiers (Chief Justice of the Cape Colony) was referring when he endeavoured to persuade the President of the urgent necessity of reform, in the interview between them that took place in March 1897 on the High Courts crisis.[2]

'*De Villiers:* Would not the removal of the Uitlanders' grievances have given you a contented population?

Kruger: The discontented people will not be satisfied until they

---

[99] Marais, pp. 1–3.   [1] Marais, p. 331.   [2] Walker, p. 464.

have my country. If I give them the franchise they may ask the Chartered people to rule over them. Their other grievances we are quite ready to redress, if there are any. . . .

. . . Don't be under the delusion that any concessions that I can make will ever satisfy the enemies of my country.

De Villiers: President, you have to satisfy not the enemies but the friends of your country. It is your real friends who would advise you to meet the demands of the new population. Many of them would, perhaps, abuse the franchise; but a majority would be grateful for it and use it for the advantage of the country. . . . If redress is not granted, the danger will always exist that it may be sought elsewhere. I know the main difficulties under which you labour, and I have never wished to add to them by publicly abusing you and the Republic, but if any private advice of mine is of any value, I trust you will accept it in the spirit in which it has been given.

Kruger: I know that you are not one of our enemies. Your mediation shows that you mean it well with us. But I am responsible for the independence of the State, and must take care that it is not lost. You may depend upon my doing what is right and fair to all.'[3]

That this intransigence—the fatal flaw in an otherwise shrewd and flexible statesman—was disastrous there can be no doubt; and, in the light of subsequent events, there can be no doubt, either, about the complete rightness of the Chief Justice's moving words:

'President, you have to satisfy not the enemies but the friends of your country. It is your real friends who would advise you to meet the demands of the new population.'

When one grasps the dogged conviction, not only of the President, but probably of the great mass of the burgher population,[4] that admission of the newcomers to the franchise in any significant numbers would mean the end of their State as they knew it, when one realizes the atmosphere of dislike and suspicion which prevailed on both sides, one's respect for those members of the two Volksraads who had the insight to realize what the situation demanded, and the courage to be prepared for the leap in the dark which extension of the franchise to the uitlander entailed, increases proportionately.

---

[3] *Weekly Press*, 19 Feb. 1898, p. 9, reprinted verbatim from the *Cape Times*, to whom Lord Justice De Villiers had handed his notes of this meeting 'just as they were written down a year ago'.

[4] But on this matter see also pp. 171–4 below.

It is easy for us today to see that such a move was the only feasible solution, and that it might have saved their country from the fate that overtook it; but to see this at a time so clouded with fear and bedevilled by propaganda required insight and generosity of mind. Willingness to admit the uitlander to the franchise, then, can legitimately be regarded as the mark of the true 'progressive'. Subsequent events suggest that, in this matter, the core of the Progressive party were, in the words of De Villiers, the 'true friends of their country'.

Let us first examine the attitude of the President and his conservative supporters on this issue, and then trace the growth of reaction against it towards a more generous point of view.

In the speech which the President made in Johannesburg (at a banquet given in his honour by the Jewish community, when he came to lay the foundation-stone of the synagogue there) he put his views clearly.

'Imagine that a man has given his blood and his substance [zijn goed en bloed] for a farm, and says to someone else—you can come and live on my farm as a squatter [bijwoner] and make a profit from it. But if this bijwoner now starts to declare that he has the same rights to the farm as the owner, then, if this matter were brought before a court, the verdict could never be given in favour of the bijwoner. . . . Now this farm is all that we have left of what our forefathers inherited.

'The stranger comes here to make his profit, and would it be right to hand over to him the voortrekker's rights of ownership?'

But he did go on to say that

'when in the course of time they [the strangers] have shown themselves to be true burghers, then their franchise can be enlarged . . . . 'But first we must know if they are true, if we are to preserve the independence of the country. . . . The old burgher must first know whether the newcomer was to be trusted. He must be sufficiently long in the country for people to say of him, "Look! Here is a man whom you can trust. Here is a man that will not be caught stealing tomorrow!" . . . If the new population showed that they were trustworthy he would give them the right of franchise. But how could he tell that the newcomer was trustworthy? Not till he had been here some considerable time. To the new population he would say—"Be loyal to the laws of the land, have faith in the government, and in time we shall become, in peace and amity, one great people" (Cheers). He did not know whether the newcomer would start stealing or pilfering tomorrow! (Laughter). Let them first know one another. Those were his politics.'[5]

But how, to Conservative eyes, did one become a 'true burgher'? Abjuring one's original nationality and becoming a naturalized Transvaal citizen did not, in the eyes of some at any rate, constitute any guarantee of one's trueness; for as the Chairman of the First Raad, F. G. Wolmarans, had put it a few months earlier:

'Such people had only become naturalized in order to get the vote; and the aim of the [franchise] law was not to take the vote out of the hands of the Voortrekkers.'[6]

Nor was it of much use in the eyes of such old burghers arranging to be born in the South African Republic, as, for instance, the First Raad debates of 1 to 5 June 1894[7] amply demonstrate. A. D. W. Wolmarans declared that he could see no reason why children of non-naturalized fathers, even if born in the South African Republic, should get the franchise, and Kruger supported him, saying:

'It is a foolish argument to say that children of aliens who were born in the State are Transvaalers. Animals, even, retain the nature of their parents, and the children of Englishmen or Frenchmen or Afrikaners, though they were born in the state, retained the nationality of their parents. . . . An Englishman who became naturalised did so simply for the purpose of obtaining the franchise, and remained an Englishman to all intents and purposes.'[8]

R. K. Loveday, Paul Maré and L. de Jager pointed out that article 29 of the Constitution laid down simply that 'All those born in the Republic are burghers', and C. Jeppe asked why it was necessary 'to make enemies even of the children'. But Conservative members opined that to make an exception for children born in the Transvaal would allow 'the children of strangers to side-step the Second Volksraad and get directly into the First Raad'.

[5] *Volksstem*, 24 Sept. 1892; *Press*, 17 Sept. 1892.

[6] First Volksraad, 18 July 1892 (*Volksstem*, 19 July 1892; *Notulen*, Eerste Volksraad, 1892, art. 824).

[7] *Volksstem*, 6 June 1894; *Land en Volk*, 21 June 1894; *Press*, 5 June 1894 (*Notulen*, Eerste Volksraad, 1894, arts. 286–311).

[8] *Press*, 5 June 1894 (*Notulen*, Eerste Volksraad, 1894. arts. 286–90).

A motion, a few minutes later, by Schalk Burger and C. Birken-stock to grant the franchise to ex-Orange Free State burghers who had had the franchise there for fifteen years, on a written declaration of loyalty to the South African Republic was described by J. P. L. Lombaard and J. de Clercq as 'a dangerous extension of the fran-chise',[9] and A. D. W. Wolmarans vehemently denounced the sister Republic, in which the franchise was 'far too lightly treated, and where within three years one was entitled to the full franchise!'[10]

Kruger's views on the uitlander danger were perhaps even more typically expressed in a speech which he had made at Krugersdorp in February of the same year.[11] In this he had likened the inde-pendence and stability of the state to a dam surrounded by waters of questionable cleanliness.

'Inside the dam was clean fresh water; outside was a strange aqueous mixture, containing albeit many drops of good useful water. In order that this might not contaminate the water within, it was subjected to a lengthened process of purification and distilling. . . . But, to drop the metaphor, he would draw up a list of respectable and trustworthy people who could be exempted from the period of probation. . . . It was nothing to him whether a man was an Afri-kaner or not an Afrikaner. He might be an Englishman, a Hollander or a German. If he were a trustworthy man, he would obtain political privileges; if not—he would kick him out. . . . Burghers and brothers! (he continued). Do you love your land? Do you love your Govern-ment? Do you love me? Well then, what is the unreasonable request the strangers urge?—"Give us the whip and reins," they cry. "Our stock, our property, our interests, our homes, are also in the cart!" To that I say, "Yes, that is all very fine. I admit that your belongings are all in the cart; but where are you going to drive me to; and how do I know that you don't purpose upsetting me?" '

A few days later at Potchefstroom, he declared that

'the proportion of newcomers to old burghers was ten thousand to one thousand.[12] He was against extension of the franchise as far as

[9] *Volkstem*, 6 June 1894.
[10] However, Kruger declared that 'he felt an exception might be made for the O.F.S. after close discussion between the two Governments'.
[11] *Press*, 13 Feb. 1894.
[12] It is difficult to credit that the President sincerely believed this.

the First Raad was concerned. The old burghers had suffered and sacrificed much for their country, and were entitled to the direction of affairs.'[13]

A fortnight later, in an address to parents and scholars at Scheerpoort (Rustenburg district) President Kruger declared[14] that only the true burghers had the right to bring about any changes in the state, 'and not any strangers'.

'The chief aim of the strangers is to get the sacred franchise [het heilig stemrecht] into their hands. What would it lead to? The strangers, the new incomers, were many more, yes three and four times more [sic] than the true burghers. And once they had the waggon of the State in their hands, they would easily be able to push it into a strange waggon-house, because they would hold the reins. They have brought much money into this land, and taken much out of it. Nevertheless we say to them, you are welcome in our land . . . we will protect you under our laws, and give you the profits of your labours. Enjoy what our beautiful country offers you; but leave us only our birthright, the direction of our own affairs [maar laat ons slechts ons eigendomsrecht, ons transport, behouden]. Let that remain unharmed [ongeschonken] in the hands of the First Volksraad. We give you the Second Volksraad, to preserve your own interest. But no, they are not satisfied. Unions are set up[15] for the purpose of making plans to rob us of the direction of our own affairs [onze transport].'

There is reason to believe that the President spoke most truly from his heart when he spoke in such simple metaphors to rural audiences. His sentiments were closely echoed by his supporters. In the First Volksraad[16] A. D. W. Wolmarans 'objected to the [franchise] law being tinkered with annually on the representations of people who are not enfranchised' (though he did not explain how they were to become enfranchised without such 'tinkering'), and C. J. Tosen asked:[17] 'Why should we allow the scum of the back streets of the

[13] *Press*, 15 Feb. 1894.

[14] *Volksstem*, 6 Mar. 1894.

[15] A reference to the Volksvereeniging set up by the Progressives, which Kruger attacked in this speech, as a 'daughter of the (Uitlander) Transvaal Union set up in Johannesburg'.

[16] *Press*, 2 June 1894; *Notulen*, Eerste Volksraad, 1894, art. 290.

[17] *Notulen*, Eerste Volksraad, 1894, art. 289.

world, which has been vomited here, to get a say in our affairs?'

J. P. L. Lombaard, 'in a hysterical state of excitement',[18] declared that

'strangers were streaming into this country against the will, against the desires, and against the interests of the burghers, and when they came here they wanted to rule the roost and domineer over those who had shed their blood for the country and stood by it in its darkest hours. . . . Every year they came with their shriek for "A vote! A vote! I am a subject of this or that foreign state, and I want a say in your affairs!" Well, the old burghers had fought for their own—and they meant to keep it (Applause).'

In a similar debate the following year,[19] on the monster petition by the uitlanders for the franchise, F. G. Wolmarans announced that 'no threats would have any effect on him. He regarded the 35,000 signatures (on the petition) as of little worth, since they did not come from burghers.'[20] He was followed by C. B. Otto (Zeerust) who asked:

'Who were these thirty-five thousand people? People who had come to enrich themselves. He feared no threats from these people. If they wanted to fight, let them come—and the sooner the better! (Cries of Order!)',[21]

a sentiment which was echoed by the *Volksstem* in a leading article (17 August 1895) which said:

'All the thousands of immigrants who came flocking here, and were received as welcome guests by the old burghers, knew or should have known before they crossed the Vaal that, whatever equal rights would be allowed them, they would not be given the franchise. And those who have only realized it now, or have been led astray by the agitation of Jeppe and Loveday, are still free to pack their bags and go home if they cannot live without the franchise. We do not believe what certain Progressive members have said, that the uitlanders will seize by force what is not freely given them; but if they wish to, let them understand that force will be met by force.'

[18] *Press*, 2 June 1894.
[19] *Land en Volk*, 22 Aug. 1895; *Volksstem*, 14 Aug. 1895; *Notulen*, Eerste Volksraad, 1895, arts. 908–22.
[20] *Notulen*, Eerste Volksraad, 1895, art. 919.
[21] *Land en Volk*, 22 Aug. 1895; *Notulen*, Eerste Volksraad, 1895, art. 919.

Nor was there any significant change of mind or heart from this obsessional attitude (for that is the only word that can be used to describe the Conservative attitude towards any significant extension of the franchise) by the crisis years of 1898 and 1899.[22] That the Jameson Raid, and the rapid increase in British and uitlander pressure after the arrival of Milner,[23] were additional factors in the situation explains but does not excuse this obduracy. Be that as it may, in June 1898, A. D. W. Wolmarans was still

'warning the Raad that it had acted dangerously in granting the franchise indiscriminately to all those who had stood on the Government's side during the Raid.[24] No one should get it who had not done bona fide military service.'

He was supported by J. H. de la Rey, J. du P. de Beer, and a number of other members, W. J. Steyn (Standerton)[25] adding that those Johannesburgers to whom the franchise had been given possessed quite illegible names, and were 'a lot of meaningless Jews'.[26] The *Weekly Press* of 27 May 1899, in supporting the President's proposal for a nine-year franchise, scathingly attacked the 'mule-like obstinacy to any progress' (*sic*) which characterized the majority of the Volksraad members; and the briefest perusal of the Volksraad debate[27] on the extension of the franchise will show that its remarks were more than justified.

This, then, to the bitter end, was the Conservative attitude on the franchise question. What attitude did 'Progressive' members take on the matter, and to what extent did opposition to the Conservative attitude act as a rallying point for the 'Progressive' group? How progressive were the 'Progressives', in short, upon this most crucial of all issues?

[22] See Marais, pp. 134–5, 201, 251, 280–4, 288–93, 293–301, 328–31.

[23] See Marais. Walker, pp. 454–7, 464–79, 480–6.

[24] It seems to have become increasingly difficult to prove one's 'trustworthiness' to burghers of Mr. Wolmarans's character. (Actually, serious irregularities in the grant of the franchise *had* occurred, but the total of those enfranchised was at its highest just over 3,400 and at its lowest 1,800. Marais, pp. 134–5, footnote 1, p. 135.)

[25] He was elected in 1895 (*Press*, 28 Mar. 1895; *Land en Volk*, 9 May 1895). Steyn often voted against the government.

[26] First Volksraad, 29 June 1898 (*Weekly Press*, 2 July 1898, p. 19). No reference to this exists in the *Notulen*.

[27] First Volksraad, 23 May 1899.

A number of members of the two Volksraads had from an early stage taken a very definite stand on the vital importance of extending the vote for the First Volksraad to the newcomers. Ewald Esselen was one of these. In a speech to his constituents at Potchefstroom in March 1892[28] he stressed that

'during the last eight years the country had changed from an agricultural to an industrial one. New conditions demanded new forms and methods. The President had recognized this two years previously by the creation of a Second Volksraad. But this was not enough. It gave no voice or part to the people who had brought about that change. That people had raised the country's income from one or two hundred thousand pounds to millions, and they had the right to take part in the use of that money; they had capital and experience, and their opinion should count in the financial administration. There was need for an enlarged franchise, so that the new population could help the old. To say that this would endanger our independence was a mere subterfuge. The danger lay in excluding them. The majority of the incomers were attached to the Republican form of government and would not move a finger against our independence. Those who were hostile did not constitute 3 per cent of them. By giving the incomers the franchise we would greatly strengthen the State against those who sought to destroy it.'

Simultaneously, J. F. Celliers (Second Raad member for Johannesburg) was telling the Pretoria Literary and Debating Society[29] that

'the measure to create a Second Volksraad met from the very outset with strong opposition in the Volksraad and was ultimately passed through the sheer force of the President's personality.[30] The experience of the last year had shown quite clearly that the legislative body in the Republic was the First Volksraad. What then was the purpose of the Second Raad? The right way to preserve the independence of the Republic was via a sound administration of finances and a fair recognition of the rights of all inhabitants. The President's fear of the newcomers, though natural, was not justified. He [Celliers] was in constant contact with them. They had many grievances; but these were not directed against the Republican form of government nor

---

[28] *Volksstem*, 23 Mar. 1892; *Press*, 24 Mar. 1892.
[29] *Volksstem*, 30 Mar. 1892; *Press*, 29 Mar. 1892.
[30] Celliers had been a member of the First Raad at the time.

against the independence of the country. He himself favoured an amalgamation of the two Raads.'

In the First Volksraad, at that stage, however, only R. K. Loveday and L. de Jager ventured to defend the rights of the newcomers to a greater say in the affairs of the state.[31] But with the election to the First Raad in 1893 of Carl Jeppe as member for Johannesburg the cause of franchise extension gained an eloquent and indefatigable advocate. In a speech in 1894[32] which even that dour Conservative J. P. L. Lombaard was constrained to describe as 'a masterly plea' (though he added that 'it was just fine words')[33] he adjured the Raad to modify its attitude.

'It was the most important question that the Volksraad had ever discussed. The whole existence of the South African Republic depended on their decision.'

Pleading with members to drop their insistence that, even after fourteen years, the franchise would only be granted if two-thirds of the enfranchised (i.e. old) burghers supported the application, Jeppe stressed that

'the grant of the franchise after fourteen years' residence would now become a favour not a right. Even at elections a two-thirds poll of the burghers did not occur. It made the franchise an impossibility. Immigrants were pouring in not only from overseas, but from the Cape and Orange Free State too. What this motion was saying to all these people was—"Under no circumstances will you ever have the right to a full vote. Perhaps we will give it to you as a favour after fourteen years". There were people among the new population who had lived here since 1876, who used to have the vote, and who had now been deprived of it. There were their brothers from their sister-Republic, from Natal and the Cape Colony—Afrikaners with the same names, of the same descent, as themselves. There were good republicans from America, Switzerland and France. Were they going to reject them all? He did not believe in granting the franchise lightly . . . but there was only one way to preserve the South African Republic—to recruit such loyal elements to their ranks, and so to

[31] First Volksraad, 18 July 1892 (*Volksstem*, 19 July 1892; *Land en Volk*, 21 July 1892; *Notulen*, Eerste Volksraad, 1892, art. 824).

[32] First Volksraad, 4 June 1894 (*Volksstem*, 6 June 1894; *Press*, 5 June 1894; *Notulen*, Eerste Volksraad, 1894, art. 308).

[33] First Volksraad, 4 June 1894 (*Notulen*, Eerste Volksraad, 1894, art. 308).

strengthen themselves and weaken their enemies. . . . But they were making enemies of the Uitlanders, and when the floodgates gave way, would they not all be carried away by the flood?'

In spite of his eloquence, however, a motion by the Conservatives to insist upon a two-thirds vote (in support of applications for the franchise) by all enfranchised burghers in the ward in which the applications were made was carried by 13 votes to 10. Those voting in the progressive minority were[34] R. K. Loveday, C. Jeppe, Lukas Meyer, L. de Jager, G. de Jager, Paul Maré, Schalk Burger, C. Birkenstock, C. B. Otto, and J. du P. de Beer—the last two members making it clear that they were voting as they did on purely technical grounds and not out of sympathy for the newcomers' cause.[35] Schalk Burger joined the opposition on this issue because he felt that the two-thirds stipulation was too high and favoured a simple majority.[36] He had, during the debate, shown little enthusiasm for extension of the franchise. Birkenstock's adherence to the uitlander cause was also lukewarm; and he was to vote against extension of the franchise a year later.[37]

It seems fair to say, therefore, that on this crucial issue the core of progressive opinion consisted essentially of Loveday, Jeppe, L. Meyer, P. Maré and the two De Jagers.

Land en Volk in a powerful article on 21 June 1894 condemned the action of the Volksraad utterly:

'The government party [Regeerings-mannen] know better than the people what the people wants. And what a law! . . . We consider the motion of the member for Vryheid[38] a wise and well-thought-out one. He wanted to give full citizenship to trustworthy persons after five years' residence and on carefully-thought-out conditions. We can well understand that many burghers, at least for the present, do not wish to broaden the franchise, and we respect their opinion. But was it necessary to slap the face of the new population [met den vuist in het gezicht slaan] among whom are some of our best friends, our brothers from the Free State, flesh of our flesh from the Colony?

---

[34] *Press*, 5 June 1894; *Notulen*, Eerste Volksraad, 1894, arts. 310–11.

[35] *Press*, 5 June 1894; *Notulen*, Eerste Volksraad, 1894, arts. 310–11.

[36] First Volksraad, 5 June 1894 (*Notulen*, Eerste Volksraad, 1894, art. 310; *Volksstem*, 6 June 1894).

[37] *Land en Volk*, 22 Aug. 1895 (*Notulen*, Eerste Volksraad, 1895, art. 924).

[38] Lukas Meyer. He had proposed a five-year franchise qualification (see *Volksstem*, 6 June 1894).

Was it fair, or decent, to receive the memorial of 13,000 people in Johannesburg with laughter and contempt? Was it wise to add a stipulation that the Electoral Law could virtually never be altered—a proviso that is really laughable, because what right has this Volksraad to bind future Volksraads?—but a proviso that will lead to the utmost bitterness among the new population. And what must we say of the clause which denies citizenship to children born in the Republic whose parents were not naturalized—in direct contravention of Article 29 of the Constitution which guarantees their citizenship.

'Go on, oh wise Volksraad members with your blessed work for the salvation and welfare of the People. Go on with your continual assault on the sacred rights of the burghers. Go on with your contempt for the wishes of your voters. Go on with your effort to embitter the newcomers to the utmost, to a state of despair. . . .

'But if one day you find the country in ruins, its dearly won independence irreparably lost . . . beat your breast and confess: "That was our work!" '

In spite of its melodrama, and its probable exaggeration about the 'wishes of your voters',[39] the article has, viewed from the perspective of future events, a prophetic tone rarely vouchsafed to newspaper utterances.

The pro-government *Press*, too, on 6 December 1894, stressed the need for some considerable extension of the franchise, in the first place at least to Afrikaners, or, as it defined them, 'Transvaal residents who are South African born', who were all, it declared,

'more South African by training and sympathy than are the English. Ten thousand of them added to the twenty thousand power-holders would give such strength to the State that other Uitlanders desirous of throwing in their lot with the Republic could be welcomed into the fold without raising apprehensions even in the mind of the most conservative Boer. After the Africanders [*sic*], or with them, might come the Hollanders, who are akin to the power-holders, then the Germans and Swedes etc.; lastly the Englishmen born in Great Britain, because they are so numerous and regarded with distrust by

---

[39] The Raad elections of 1895 (see *Land en Volk*, 9 May 1895; *Press*, 28 May 1895) although they increased the Progressive total slightly, did not show anything in the nature of a swing in the Progressive direction. (See below, pp. 238–9.)

the power-holders. Political expediency, not their demerits, must keep them waiting until all the other guests are seated.'

But the most that the *Volksstem* was prepared to advocate, though it conceded that the country was in a bad way,[40] was that there was

'a need for fusion of political parties[41] and the creation of a common political programme which every well-disposed burgher, whatever his origin or church community could support. It must be quite adamant on the question of the country's independence, the country's language and its schools. English must never be looked upon as anything but a foreign language. No preference should be given to those born elsewhere in South Africa over other foreigners from elsewhere.'[42]

A month earlier, on 11 August 1894, the newspaper had published with pride a poem sent in by an anonymous reader, which, if poetry is the true reflection of the soul of a nation, probably mirrors with some accuracy the feelings of the more conservative section of the Boer population. Under the title 'No franchise to the National Union[43] people' (Geen stemrecht aan de Nationale Unie menschen) it read as follows:

> Ze zullen het niet hebben
> Mijn jeugdig Vaderland
> Het blijf' in vreugd en lijden
> Voor de kinderen van het land!
> Ze zullen het niet hebben
> De goden van den tijd
> Niet om hun slaaf te wezen
> Heeft God ons volk bevrijd.
>
> Met al hun schoone woorden
> En al hun stout geschreeuw
> Zij zullen het niet hebben
> De goden dezer eeuw
> De kracht en onze leuze

[40] See leaders on 'Onze Politieke Toestand', I–III (*Volksstem*, 1 Sept., 5 Sept. and 12 Sept. 1894).

[41] Such a fusion (toenadering) movement was at that stage under way; but it split finally on the issue of admitting non-naturalized uitlanders to membership of the movement (see below, pp. 233–7).

[42] *Volksstem*, 12 Sept. 1894.		[43] See pp. 205–6.

Ons schild dat hun bewaakt
Heeft met den Heer den Heeren
Een vast verbond gemaakt.

Zij zullen het niet hebben
Zoo lang Joubert zal staan[44]
Zoo lang als wij Transvalers
De handen ineen blijft slaan
Zoo lang er helden zielsgloed
In ons Transvalers is
Zoo lang de geest van Kruger
Over Transvaal beslis!

(Free Translation)
They shall not take it from us
My youthful Fatherland
It stays, in joy and sorrow,
With the children of the land!
They shall not take it from us
This era's gods; indeed
'Twas not to be the slaves of these
That God our people freed.

For all their words of promise
And all their evil bray
They shall not take it from us
The gods of this our day
Our power and our motto
Our shield of firm renown
Are with the Lord of Heaven
In Covenant firm set down.

They shall not take it from us
So long as Joubert stands
So long as we Transvaalers
Are linked, with hands in hands.
So long as heroes' courage
In us Transvaalers shows
So long as Kruger's spirit
Over the Transvaal glows!

[44] On Joubert's position on the franchise issue see below, pp. 267–70.

The First Volksraad that met in May 1895[45] saw the 'Progressive' opposition somewhat strengthened by the election of J. L. van Wyk (Krugersdorp) and W. H. van Niekerk (Lydenburg), who both regularly voted with them; and of W. J. Steyn (Standerton) and Commandant D. J. Joubert (Carolina), who often did.[46] The new session saw three debates on the franchise issue. The first was a confused debate, which nevertheless showed some softening of attitude, on the comparatively minor question of extending the franchise to those uitlanders who had served on commando in the recent war against the native chief Malaboch. The President pleaded with the Volksraad to 'take the faithful to themselves, not thrust them into the arms of the enemy', and wanted this done by special resolution of the Raad, without in any way changing the existing franchise law.[47] In this he was supported by W. J. Steyn (the newly-elected member for Standerton) who wanted the franchise extended not only to those who had done commando service 'but also to others who had deserved it'. But the Progressives seized the opportunity to demand a fundamental change in the franchise law, after reference to the burghers, since by the present franchise law they had 'got themselves into a position by which no extension of the franchise could be brought about except with the consent of two thirds of the burghers'.[48]

This greatly excited Jan Meyer (Heidelberg) and other Conservative members, and after much argument, the Progressive motion was defeated and a contrary motion passed, referring consideration of the whole matter to a Volksraad Committee of five members, who were to lay their recommendations before the Raad with the proviso that no breach of the existing franchise law must be made. Those voting against this proposal[49] (which was carried by 15 votes to 10) were R. K. Loveday, C. Jeppe, L. Meyer, P. Maré, G. de Jager,

[45] First Volksraad, 6 May 1895 (*Land en Volk*, 9 May 1895; *Press*, 28 May 1895; *Notulen*, Eerste Volksraad, 1895, art. 3).

[46] See table on p. 245.

[47] First Volksraad, 29–31 May 1895 (*Volksstem*, 30 May–1 June 1895; *Press*, 31 May 1895; *Weekly Press*, 27 July 1895, pp. 4–5, 16). 'To change the franchise-law', he said, 'opened the door for great danger [onheil] for the people, and the guilt would be on their heads' (*Volksstem*, 30 May 1895; *Notulen*, Eerste Volksraad, 1895, art. 216).

[48] *Notulen*, Eerste Volksraad, 1895, arts. 215–19.

[49] *Volksstem*, 31 May 1895; *Press*, 31 May 1895; *Notulen*, Eerste Volksraad, 1895, arts. 217–18.

L. de Jager, J. H. de la Rey, J. L. van Wyk, W. J. Steyn and D. Joubert. The Chairman of the Raad, Schalk Burger, and such other occasional Progressives as W. H. van Niekerk and J. H. Labuschagne, voted with the Conservatives.

The next debate on franchise extension took place in July, and was still concerned with the comparatively minor question of granting franchise rights to those who had done commando-duty in the recent Malaboch campaign, a concession which had been recommended by the Committee set up on 31 May. Kruger stressed that this was 'a special resolution to admit only good and faithful men who had proved their trustworthiness', and that it would leave the Franchise Law as such untouched. And though his staunch supporter, J. M. Malan, grumbled that 'the Raad might as well overthrow the whole Franchise Law as pass this special resolution', most of the Conservative members supported the President, and rejected the argument of Lukas Meyer and G. de Jager that thousands of good men would willingly have gone on commando but had not been given the opportunity, preferring to support the optimistic view of F. G. Wolmarans that they should 'strenuously oppose any proposal for the general extension of the franchise . . . for future wars would give others the chance to show their trustworthiness'. The Progressives, however, took up the attitude that the Franchise Law as a whole must be changed. R. K. Loveday declared that the passing of the special resolution advocated by the President was 'a violation of the Franchise Law. The Franchise Law itself must be amended to allow of such grants of the franchise.' W. H. van Niekerk, Lukas Meyer, Paul Maré, J. L. van Wyk, W. J. Steyn and G. de Jager supported this view, pleading, in general, for a more generous extension of the franchise, particularly to Free State and other Afrikaners; and, on the matter being put to the vote, the government won by 14 votes to 10.[50] J. H. de la Rey (who was markedly cautious on the question of franchise extension and who voted against it a few weeks later) and A. D. W. Wolmarans (who declared himself opposed to any extension of franchise rights without a two-thirds majority vote of all the burghers) also asked that their names be recorded in the minority.

The franchise question was resumed in the middle of August.[51] Jeppe prophesied that the Republic would

[50] *Notulen*, Eerste Volksraad, 1895, art. 725.
[51] First Volksraad, 13–20 Aug. 1895 (*Notulen*, Eerste Volksraad, 1895, arts.

'pay bitterly one day [for its refusal to widen the franchise] when the newcomers outnumbered us by twenty to one, and we will not find one friend in the twenty. They will have to be given the franchise one day. And they will say that they wanted to become our friends, but were not allowed to. At the moment, it is true, everything is peaceful and quiet among them. Political life seems dead. They hold no meetings, send no deputations. But, I say, is this a good sign, this hopeless apathetic silence [deze hopelooze, moedelooze stilte]? It makes me think of the calm before the storm.'[52]

This speech was taken to contain an implied threat, and led, as we have seen, to F. G. Wolmarans's declaration that he feared no threats and regarded the 35,000 signatures on the most recent uit-lander petition for the franchise as worthless, 'since they did not come from burghers'; and to C. B. Otto's challenge to the uitlanders —'if they wanted to fight, let them come, and the sooner the better!' Jeppe was strongly supported by Lukas Meyer who, once again, put forward a considered scheme for a five-year franchise, and by R. K. Loveday, Paul Maré and J. L. van Wyk. The President declared that all that uitlanders had to do was become naturalized. Let them, and their sons, blame themselves and not the law. 'The law was fair enough.' Schalk Burger, Chairman of the Raad, agreed with Loveday that it was hard for a newcomer to have to wait until he was 40 before he got the full franchise, but he supported the President in desiring that they should show their good faith by becoming natural-ized. Though, from the discussion, the majority of speakers were against extension of the franchise, he would, he declared, vote for it. On a motion for extension of the franchise being put to the vote, it was defeated by 16 votes to 8. Those voting in the minority were R. K. Loveday, Lukas Meyer, C. Jeppe, Paul Maré, G. de Jager,[53] W. H. van Niekerk, J. L. van Wyk and Schalk Burger.[54] J. H. de la Rey both spoke and voted against any extension of the franchise.

908-9, 919-22, 957-9; *Land en Volk*, 22 Aug. 1895; *Volksstem*, 17 Aug. 1895; *Weekly Press*, 24 Aug. 1895, pp. 2-4).

[52] This was just four months before the Jameson Raid.

[53] L. de Jager appears to have been absent from this and the previous franchise debates. (See *Notulen*, Eerste Volksraad, 1895, arts. 904, 910 and 921.) As his record (see p. 245, below) shows that he never once voted for the government, it seems fair to assume that he would have voted with the Progressive group on this occasion, had he been there.

[54] *Notulen*, Eerste Volksraad, 1895, art. 924; *Land en Volk*, 22 Aug. 1895.

That President Kruger was beginning to realize the consequence of his franchise policy upon the uitlanders, and to modify his attitude—in however minor a fashion—is shown by the changed tone of his pleas to his diehard conservative followers to extend the hand of friendship to those uitlanders who had done commando service, which we have noted; and it was further demonstrated a few months later, when, amid the tensions of the Jameson Raid, he promised a deputation of loyal Johannesburgers, led by Jeppe, that 'all who stood by him, whether it came to fighting or not, would get the full franchise'[55] (a promise which, after some haggling,[56] was fulfilled in the case of some two to three thousand uitlanders[57]).

The subsequent history of the franchise struggle is not the province of this book;[58] but in its essence the struggle inside the Volksraad did not differ in principle from that which we have already traced. The Volksraad debates of 1898 and 1899 show little difference from those of 1894 and 1895, though some of the protagonists have changed; and it is still the Progressives who are vainly trying to conquer the rooted and stubborn Conservative opposition on this most fatal of all issues. The summing-up by Carl Jeppe,[59] who fought most vigorously, and vainly, on this issue in the forefront of his Progressive colleagues, may err on the side of emotionalism, but it is not in essence untrue. After declaring that the majority of the uitlanders, who were British, would never have accepted the franchise once it became clear that it meant the renunciation of British nationality,[60] he points out that all that the refusal of voting rights did was alienate tens of thousands of colonial Afrikaners, Free-Staters, Hollanders, Germans and Americans.

'This tortuous policy proved to be a political blunder of the first magnitude. . . . All these elements, amongst whom our own relations and our best friends, were driven by the blindness of the Volksraad, inspired by Kruger, into the camp of those who wished no good to the Republic. . . . It was an unspeakable blunder, and bore in it the

[55] *Land en Volk*, 30 Dec. 1895 (special 'Jameson Raid' issue). Marais, pp. 102, 134.

[56] *Weekly Press*, 13 Feb. 1897, p. 3; Marais, pp. 134–5.

[57] See Marais, p. 135, footnote 1; Walker, p. 461; Hugo, p. 166.

[58] But see Marais, pp. 134–5, 201, 251, 280–4, 288–91, 293, 299–301, 328–31.

[59] Jeppe, pp. 133–5.

[60] Milner would not have agreed with Jeppe. He believed they *would*. See Marais. Dormer, pp. 150–5, quoted below, supports Jeppe's view.

seeds of the certain destruction of the Republic. Except on the principle of après nous le déluge it is difficult to imagine what the Boer expected to gain by it.'

In short, then, the attitude of Progressive members for the most part on this most important of all issues was one that might well have saved the Transvaal from extinction, for, however determined Chamberlain and Milner might have been on the issue of British 'paramountcy'[61] in South Africa, without the franchise issue to give them their apparent moral justification, they and their supporters would have been hard put to it to carry the country and Parliament with them into war against the Transvaal.

However, it is not our task to deal with what might have been, only with what actually did happen. On the role of the franchise issue in the South African Republic's internal politics, certain facts, to sum up, are clear.

The Second Volksraad was at no time a satisfactory solution of the franchise question either to the uitlanders or to the more progressive burghers. Once it had been brought into existence, however, it was the members of the progressive group—Ewald Esselen, J. F. Celliers, E. P. A. Meintjies, G. B. Brecher, W. J. Jooste, D. F. Petersen, and Frank Watkins—who took the lead, as we have seen, in protesting at its powerlessness, and in making it, by their prolonged and obstinate opposition to the government, very much less of a cipher than it has sometimes been represented as being. There can be little doubt that similarity of outlook on the franchise issue played a considerable part in drawing together the more progressive members of the Second Chamber.

In the First Volksraad expression of opinion on the franchise question seems to have been more inhibited. The feeling of the conservative section, so powerfully led by President Kruger himself, was, on this matter, intense, and logical argument of little value. Nevertheless, though perhaps more reluctantly, the inexorable pressure of events brought about in some First Volksraad members a growing awareness of the need for a painful rethinking of the franchise question; and by 1895 a growing minority had become at least partly persuaded of the need for a fundamental change. In this process the members of the 'Progressive' group at all times played the leading part. The essential core of the group pressing for this

[61] Marais, chapters X–XII.

painful readjustment was made up of such men as R. K. Loveday and L. de Jager at first, rapidly joined by Lukas Meyer, C. Jeppe, Paul Maré and G. de Jager; and subsequently (after the 1895 Volksraad elections) by J. L. van Wyk and W. J. Steyn (though the latter, it has been noted, voted with the Conservatives in opposing the grant of the franchise to all those uitlanders who had stood by the Republic during the Jameson Raid). Of this group Carl Jeppe, for his persistent and powerful eloquence, and Lukas Meyer, because of his very considerable prestige in the eyes of the burghers,[62] were undoubtedly the most impressive figures. W. H. van Niekerk, who generally voted with the Progressives, sided with the Conservatives occasionally on the franchise issue. Commandant J. H. (Koos) de la Rey sided with his Progressive colleagues only once, and voted against extension of the franchise on three occasions (on the question of its extension to the children of non-naturalized uitlanders, of its extension to uitlanders who had shown their loyalty during the Malaboch Campaign, and finally on the general question of any significant extension of the franchise). On this matter, then, he can hardly be classed as a 'Progressive'. Schalk Burger, although progressive-minded on many matters, showed marked hesitation on the franchise issue. We have seen that, though he voted with the Progressives in the debate of June 1894, it was largely on technical grounds; and that during the debate itself he had shown a notable lack of conviction that the franchise should be extended.[63] In the subsequent debate of May 1895, however, he voted on the Conservative side; and in August of the same year he voted, somewhat hesitantly, with the Progressives—but only, as he himself indicated, when it had become obvious that the Progressive resolution was going to be voted down. Clearly he was taking too literally his duty (as Chairman of the Raad) of holding the balance between the opposing sections! As late as 1899 he was one of those members of the Executive Council who was adjuring President Kruger not to yield on the franchise issue.[64]

[62] *Volksstem*, 26 Nov. 1891, 25 Aug. 1894; *Land en Volk*, 24 Nov. 1891.

[63] In July 1893, for instance, Schalk Burger declared: 'According to Republican principles the majority ruled, but supposing the majority consisted of the naturalised burghers? Self-preservation forced them to take proper protective measures' (*Press*, 5 July 1893).

[64] Marais, pp. 282, 292. See also Schalk Burger's extremely cautious statement on extending the franchise during his election campaign in 1897 (*Weekly Press*, 1 Jan. 1898, p. 5).

We are forced to the conclusion, therefore, that on this most testing of all issues, the real core of the Progressive party in the First Volksraad, stripped of all doubters and half-adherents, can be narrowed down to some seven members—C. Jeppe, Lukas Meyer, R. K. Loveday, L. de Jager, G. de Jager, Paul Maré and J. L. van Wyk. At no stage up to the end of 1895, therefore, was there any real doubt that, in opposing any but the most grudging extension of the franchise, the President had with him the overwhelming majority of the First Volksraad, and, in all probability, of the burgher population as well.

On the question of burgher opinion in the matter of the franchise it is difficult, on the evidence, to do more than indicate probabilities. One must not make the error of regarding even the Dutch-language press as synonymous with burgher opinion, for, as the *Press* itself tells us (3 February 1893):

'Not one in a hundred reads the newspapers, an equally small proportion use the post, and only at rare intervals does any one of them travel by rail. . . . Only a very small proportion of the burghers can read or write. . . . The slight knowledge [the burgher] has of politics has been acquired from a casual hearing given to the President or General Joubert on the rare occasions when those eminent personages come near enough to be heard. About the franchise he knows little and cares less . . .';

while the *Volksstem* (9 December 1893), bemoaning the poor attendance at political meetings, declared:

'Our people are immature politically. The excitement at elections is less the result of a general desire to solve the great questions facing the country than of the efforts of certain manipulators in whose interest it is to upset the legal and established order of things. . . . Political programmes do not exist; political organizations exist only among the newcomers; and people vote for persons rather than for policies.'

Yet, on the other hand, the same newspapers that tell us of the total absence of any really significant or formed popular opinion are the first to insist that it is not President Kruger but the burghers and their Volksraad representatives who are the chief stumbling-block in the way of reform.

Thus, the *Press*, for example, in a report of 14 March 1893 of an interview with Kruger on the franchise question, declares:

'The President recognises that the Uitlanders constitute a power which it will be well to conciliate, and we have every reason to believe that he will go as far as he safely can without alienating the burghers. It is to be hoped that the new population will have the sense to recognise the difficulties of the President's position and be patient when patience is the only possible card to play. President Kruger is a typical Boer; he must be coaxed, not driven . . .',

without, apparently, realizing that the last sentence to a very large extent contradicts what the rest of the paragraph alleges. Again, in a leader of 26 September 1893 welcoming the decision of the Johannesburg National Union to launch a campaign of 'political education of the Boer', the *Press* writes:

'It is not the President who bars the way [i.e. to the franchise]. It is the prejudices of the Boers, who do not know to this day that the Uitlanders are anxious to work through and with them—the burghers. . . . It is they who will not allow President Kruger to make concessions . . .';

while the *Volksstem* of 2 December 1893, on much the same lines, declares:

'The present [franchise] law is the expression of the will of the great majority of the burghers of the South African Republic. . . . The "Star" and other Uitlander organs would do better to look to Paul Kruger as the one man who could by his influence persuade the People to make fair concessions to the well-disposed Uitlanders. It is a well-known fact that it is precisely from the great majority of the members of the Volksraad that the most determined opposition has come.'

This view is to some extent borne out by the President's difficulty even in the crisis year of 1899 in convincing the First Volksraad and the Executive Council of the vital need to reduce the time it took for an uitlander to get the franchise, and by that body's reluctant and complicated concessions.[65]

[65] Marais, pp. 295–302; *C.H.B.E.*, p. 594. (See particularly Marais, pp. 300–2, for an explanation of the inevitably complicated nature of the new law.)

There can be no doubt that, by 1899, under unceasing pressure from both his friends and his enemies,[66] Kruger had realized that substantial franchise concessions were essential if the independence, indeed the very existence, of the Transvaal was to be preserved. But the pro-government papers quoted above are, surely, exaggerating the stubborn opposition of the burghers to franchise reform, and, equally, greatly minimizing the part played by Kruger (up to the Jameson Raid at any rate) in staunchly propagating views which could only confirm such stubborn opposition as did exist.[67] It is all very well for the *Weekly Press* (27 May 1899) to allege, in the President's defence, that it 'is utterly wrong to think that he has only to say "Ik heb gezegd" (I have spoken) and the thing is done'. On other matters the Raad and the burghers were capable of opposing the Presidential wishes; but on matters touching the sacred independence of the Transvaal, Kruger was indeed the final oracle to the burghers. That this was so is demonstrated by the ease with which Kruger convinced a huge and excited mass meeting of burghers at Paardekraal (after his return from the Bloemfontein Conference with Milner in June 1899) of the necessity of shortening the franchise period to seven years; an achievement which the *Weekly Press* of 24 June 1899 hailed as clear proof of

'the tremendous confidence that the burghers have in the President. . . . Volksraad members constantly say the "People" will not acquiesce in reforms. Yet when the revolutionary request for approval of a reduction of the franchise requirements from fourteen to seven years is put before 7,000 burghers, the unanimous reply is "Yes, we agree!" '

It was, it declared, convinced that 'if the President had said five years the reply would have been the same'. Had he used his influence in the same direction in earlier years there is little reason to doubt that the First Volksraad's 'mule-like obstinacy' in the face of demands for reform, of which the *Weekly Press* (27 May 1899) so loudly complained, would, by the pressure of popular opinion, have been greatly modified.

This is not to deny that there was profound opposition among many burghers to any major extension of the franchise. What few indications of burgher opinion we have, show clearly that fear of the

---

[66] Marais, pp. 280–4, 288–93, 299–302.

[67] See Kruger's speeches quoted above, pp. 151–2, 153–4, 155–6.

uitlander was of wide extent and deep importance. There is, in the first place, no special reason to presume that the burghers, in election after election, should choose a Volksraad totally unrepresentative of their views on this fundamental issue.

Further, it is noteworthy that though, in the 1893 election campaign, both Kruger and Joubert made vague references to the need for relaxing the strictness of the franchise laws[68] (Joubert going so far as to talk of the desirability of admitting newcomers to the franchise after one year's residence,[69] and Kruger advocating the extension of the full franchise to trustworthy newcomers at any period after four[70]) each side found it politically expedient to attempt to 'smear' the other as favouring a reckless extension of the franchise. Thus General Joubert, at Vryheid,[71] and again at Malanskraal,[72] attacked the President's proposal for a grant of the franchise after a mere four years, warning the burghers of the need to act most carefully, and using almost the identical simile to that which we see Kruger using in the following year[73] of the uitlanders being like a great dam of water, the inflow of which into the lands of the State must be controlled with the utmost care. The election manifesto of the Joubert party, similarly, contains no reference to any easing of the franchise restrictions;[74] nor does the list of awkward questions with which *Land en Volk* of 13 October 1892 provided Joubert supporters, so that they might embarrass the President while he was 'op reis' (on his electioneering campaign), contain any mention of the franchise issue—though that must be virtually the only issue, minor or major, for which that list of questions failed to provide! In the same way, the pro-government press, and Kruger's electioneering agents, found it useful to convey the impression that General Joubert's party and the dissident uitlander National Union were one and the same thing,[75] a campaign which met, apparently, with a sufficient degree of success to render it necessary for Joubert's paper, *Land en Volk*, to declare on 8 December 1892 that it was

---

[68] *Land en Volk*, 24 Nov. 1892; *Press*, 23 Nov. 1892.

[69] *Land en Volk*, 17 Nov. 1892 (speech at Middelburg).

[70] *Press*, 23 Nov. 1892 (in a special interview given to the *Press* by the President, on this question); *Land en Volk*, 24 Nov. 1892.

[71] *Land en Volk*, 26 Jan. 1893. See also *Volksstem*, 15 Nov. 1892.

[72] *Land en Volk*, 2 Feb. 1893.   [73] Above, p. 155.

[74] *Land en Volk*, 30 Aug. 1892; *Press*, 10 Jan. 1893.

[75] *Volksstem*, 21 Sept. 1892, 24 Sept. 1892, 4 Oct. 1892, 18 Oct. 1892, 9 Nov. 1892, 14 Jan. 1893; *Press*, 10 Dec. 1892; *Standard & Diggers' News, passim*.

'typical of the "Volksstem" and the "Press" to wish to smear General Joubert in this way and to continually suggest that if he becomes President he will at once give the vote to every Uitlander, in spite of the fact that General Joubert has never indicated any such intention. Indeed, according to the "Press" it was Kruger who was prepared to grant the franchise to all after four years!'

Joubert himself, similarly, found it necessary to deny, in a statement prominently placed in *Land en Volk* on 12 January 1893 that he had ever had any connexion, direct or indirect, with the Johannesburg National Union.

All this eagerness to deny any desire to extend the franchise to the uitlander, and to saddle the other party with that responsibility, suggests that both parties were united in the opinion that to advocate a significant extension would gravely compromise their election chances, and must be regarded as a pointer to the probable attitude of the majority of the burghers.

Yet the position taken up by both sides is curiously inconsistent. At the same time as the pro-Kruger *Press* violently attacks the National Union for demanding the franchise for the uitlander, declaring (on 15 December 1892) that the uitlanders were disloyal to the Republic, that they desired to destroy its independence, and that 'our sacred birthright, our dearly bought independence, we will keep within our exclusive control'; at the same time as it adjures the burghers to treat with the greatest suspicion the claim that all the uitlanders want to be is 'plain and loyal burghers of the Republic etc.', admonishing them to 'Watch, old burghers. See what fine artifices are being employed to deprive you of your birthright! But watch! Watch for the adder that hides in the grass! As a she-lion defends her cub, and a mother her tender babe in the hour of danger, so should you preserve your precious vote . . .', the *Press* nevertheless attacks General Joubert for failing to give the uitlander any hope. Dealing, in an article of 10 January 1893, with the Joubert party's manifesto, the *Press* declares:

'As far as the Uitlander is concerned General Joubert has defined his position with great lucidity. They are told, in effect, that they can expect nothing of him. If he is elected, therefore, he will refuse all that the National Union asks for. In other words he proposes to sit on the safety valve of a great engine. . . . Although only 300 votes are at stake in Johannesburg it is felt that the General's return as

President would be the last nail in the coffin of the Uitlanders' desires.'

Similarly, at about the same time as Kruger was, in an interview with the *Press* (23 November 1892), advocating extension of the franchise to trustworthy newcomers after four years, he was declaring at Krugersdorp[76] that

'if by granting an indiscriminate franchise to each and all that invaded the country he lost the independence of the country for them, he would call down the curse of Almighty God upon his head. Give these large masses all they ask for and show them an easy road to the poll, and before they knew it the land would be gone from them.'

And, in very much the same way, General Joubert was advocating the franchise after one year,[77] and attacking Kruger for his recklessness in proposing to grant it after four. Would it be unfair to conclude that, if the leaders of the country were in such a confused state of mind on this emotionally-charged issue, the average Boer knew even less than they what to think?

That the conservative element approached the question with especially suspicious caution, however, becomes quite clear when we examine the tortuous negotiations that accompanied the attempt at a fusion of the parties in 1894 to 1895.[78] Towards the end of 1893 Joubert's followers set up a political organization known as the 'Volksvereeniging', to the very title of which the *Volksstem* (9 December 1893) took exception because 'nearly everybody belonged to the Joubert party, and the other side were not invited. It is difficult to see how they can call it a Volksvereeniging in these circumstances.'

The new organization gave as its declared aim[79] the education of the burghers in a more progressive direction, with the clear implication that this would bring about a change in the composition of the Volksraad, and a wider extension of the franchise—though this aim was hinted at rather than clearly stated. Article 1 of the constitution of the Volksvereeniging gave full membership rights in that organization to uitlanders,[80] and numbers of non-naturalized uitlanders,

---

[76] *Press*, 7 Dec. 1892.

[77] *Land en Volk*, 17 Nov. 1892 (quoted above, p. 174).

[78] See also pp. 233–7.

[79] *Land en Volk*, 14 Dec. 1893; *Volksstem*, 23 Jan. 1894.

[80] *Volksstem*, 23 Jan. 1894, 11 Nov. 1894, and *Land en Volk*, 14 Dec. 1893, 22 Nov. 1894.

chiefly Cape and Free State Afrikaners,[81] took an active lead in the organization and sat upon its executive council.

Within a very short time, however, the suspicious welcome given to the new body by the *Volksstem* had turned to open and vigorous hostility. Shortly after the foundation of the Volksvereeniging the pro-government *Volksstem* on 9 December 1893 had declared:

'We do not want to be too hard on the new child. Many of its members are well-intentioned towards our Republic, though we cannot believe this of certain others in the light of their past words and deeds. But we give the new Vereeniging our greeting and will observe its future with a watchful eye.'

But by 23 January of the next year the *Volksstem* was in full attack, declaring the new organization to be nothing more than a branch of the uitlander National Union of Johannesburg—a view that was fully supported by the more conservative burghers at the first rural meetings of the Volksvereeniging. At Kameelfontein on 12 January 1894,[82] for example, one D. S. van der Merwe declared that

'they had made their Union and their vow at Paardekraal. God's will must not be spurned by creating another Union. The aim of the "Volksvereeniging" was to take away their freedom.'

J. J. H. Wolmarans, rather sweepingly, alleged that article 1 of the new Union's constitution 'gave the franchise to all incomers. If that was so the "Volksvereeniging" was a child of the National Union.' He was strongly supported; and one J. B. Wolmarans added that he 'wished to express his pain at the fact that in the days of his old age he must see the independence of the country undermined by Afrikaners from other parts'.

The organizer of the meeting, Abraham Malan (a son-in-law of General Joubert and an executive member of the 'Vereeniging' though not himself an enfranchised burgher),[83] was able to persuade only three people at this meeting to subscribe to the doctrines of the new 'Vereeniging', while one other burgher signed on condition that article 1 should be altered to admit only enfranchised burghers to the organization.[84]

[81] For names see *Land en Volk*, 22 Nov. 1894.
[82] *Volksstem*, 23 Jan. 1894.
[83] *Land en Volk*, 22 Nov. 1894; *Volksstem*, 23 Jan. 1894.
[84] *Volksstem*, 23 Jan. 1894.

That the admission of uitlanders to membership of such a political organization was a situation which the more conservative burghers could not tolerate was shown by the rapid formation of a counter-movement known as the 'Burgermacht'. This determined exclusiveness shines clearly through the well-meaning platitudes of the address given at Heidelberg on 26 April 1894 by H. P. F. Janse van Rensburg, one of its founders:

'It is not our aim', he declared, 'to make the life of the newcomers unbearable, or separate ourselves off from them, or deny them all share in the privileges of the country; it is our duty to work with them and not against them, otherwise we are doomed. Many of their grievances are completely justified.

'But to help them, while at the same time preserving the key to our independence,[85] it is essential to form a union among ourselves as we did at Paardekraal. Then we can see how we can help them. But if we old burghers don't stand together we will lose the key of our independence—the key which has cost us so much—and which I, for myself, am not prepared to see simply handed over to the newcomers.

'But I am prepared to say to our burghers—Come let us with our voice (or vote—"stem") do what we find our hand able to do towards a satisfactory co-existence. Let us treat the new population with justice and love and let us protect their rights and make life pleasant for them. For this purpose I with Sarel Marais and Frederik Bezuidenhout have thought it well to call together such a meeting, with the object of founding an association of enfranchised burghers[86] to be called the "Burgermacht of the South African Republic".'[87]

Pressed to explain why the policy of 'treating the new population with justice and love and protecting their rights and making life pleasant for them' necessitated their exclusion from the Burgermacht (for article III of its constitution excluded from membership not only uitlanders, but even naturalized burghers), Van Rensburg declared:

'We must first heal the breach among the old burghers. If they opened the organisation to newcomers the old burghers would not

---

[85] By this stage an accepted synonym for burgher control of the Volksraad.
[86] This is the crux of the speech.
[87] *Volksstem*, 1 May 1894 (see also *Land en Volk*, 10 May 1894).

join. That was exactly what had kept them out of the Volksvereeniging.'

However, this policy of co-operation by means of exclusion was
felt by the meeting to be not entirely convincing, and after long and
acrimonious discussion of the threat presented by the new population, a cautious compromise resolution empowering the extension of
membership to those who had already become naturalized by 26
April 1894 (i.e. the actual day of the meeting)—but not to uitlanders
—was adopted by general agreement. And in a further meeting at
Kafferspruit (Standerton), in which another branch of the Burgermacht was launched, Van Rensburg excitedly declared his refusal
to share fundamental rights with the uitlanders. 'The new population
cannot yet have any share in my independence, in my inheritance, or
in my franchise!'[88] In a later interview with the *Press* (23 May 1894)
he spoke once again with the two tongues that he had used at
Heidelberg in April, declaring simultaneously that:

'I cannot of course guarantee that the Burgermacht will get the
franchise at once for all the Uitlanders; but the rights due to them
will be well looked after by our people, as we are convinced that they
are doing such a great deal for the present prosperity of the State.
You must own yourself that there would be a grave danger to the
burgher element of this State if the full franchise were granted to
newcomers at once under the present circumstances'; and that 'Our
burghers must be united to take up their own national position
against the enormous influx of foreign nationalities pouring in here
at present . . . seemingly without limit.'

We can see clearly in these utterances a state of mind which, if we
were uncharitable, we might describe as blatant hypocrisy; but which
is probably more clearly grasped if we understand the confusion of
thought brought about when deeply-felt emotions struggle for mastery
with such elements of logical thinking as are present in a man's mind.
It is probable that Van Rensburg's views reflect the state of mind of
considerable numbers of the old burgher population. They loved
their independence deeply; they desperately feared the consequences of admitting the uitlander to the franchise; they desperately
feared the dangerous consequences of *not* admitting him to that
franchise. In such circumstances clear and logical thinking is rarely
found. To accept the 'Progressive' view that admission of the uit-

[88] *Volksstem*, 16 May 1894 (meeting at Kafferspruit on 28 April 1894).

lander to the franchise, paradoxical as it might seem, was the sole guarantee of the State's salvation, was asking the Boer farmers to risk a leap in the dark which only those possessed of the eye of faith might be prepared to take. And there was but little faith in the good intentions of the uitlander among the conservative section of the Transvaal Boers.[89] Wrong as they almost certainly were, they preferred the simpler solution of holding firmly on to what they had, and trusting to the God of their ancestors, somehow, to see them through.

The depth of this fear of opening the door to the uitlander was further demonstrated later in 1894. The clear evidence of mounting crisis and of the need for greater national unity had prompted the appointment by Kruger, in May 1894, of Ewald Esselen, possibly the most active leader among the Progressives,[90] as State Attorney of the Republic. Together with this went a deliberate attempt, under the aegis of Esselen and the chairman of Kruger's election committee,[91] Koos Smit, towards a rapprochement (toenadering) between the Progressive and Conservative parties.[92] It was basically on the question of the admission of uitlanders to membership of the proposed new joint political organization, however, that the negotiations for fusion failed. Delegates of the Burgermacht wanted only burghers and naturalized burghers to be eligible for membership; delegates of the progressive Volksvereeniging, conversely, wanted membership rights of any joint organization to be extended to all who had lived in the Republic for three years and who supported the patriotic aims of the joint political organization which it was hoped to set up.[93] Although the delegates on both sides were unanimous on the main object of the organization to be formed, to wit 'to maintain the independence of the country, to support the Government in all measures which are just and in accordance with the Grondwet [Constitution] and to pass conciliatory laws in regard to the new population',[94] they were forced to postpone discussion on membership qualifications. At a further meeting between some 30 leaders of the Burgermacht and three delegates from the Esselen–

[89] See Marais, pp. 59–60, on this point.

[90] *Land en Volk*, 15 Nov. 1894; Walker, pp. 436, 439; Marais, pp. 57–9.

[91] *Press*, 14 Nov. 1894; Walker, *Lord De Villiers & His Times*, p. 242.

[92] See pp. 236–7.

[93] *Volksstem*, 17 Nov. 1894; *Land en Volk*, 15 Nov. 1894; *Press*, 14 Nov. 1894, 15 Nov. 1894, 19 Nov. 1894.

[94] *Press*, 16 Nov. 1894.

Smit group, general opposition was shown by the overwhelming majority of the Burgermacht to any extension of the vote to the new population; while on the membership question the Burgermacht delegates did not feel that they could accept the far from liberal suggestion put forward by the other side that 'membership of this organisation be open to all burghers and naturalised burghers, but that naturalised burghers should not immediately be eligible as active or committee members' (kunnen niet dadelijk gekozen worden als werkende of bestuursleden).[95]

But tempers ran high and discussions were broken off.[96] It appears that some leading members of the Burgermacht had already broken away to join the Volksvereeniging, which was then renamed the 'Volksmacht';[97] and the thus purified Burgermacht now declared open war on its progressive opponents.[98] Progressive as the Volksmacht was, it too found it expedient at its third Annual Congress in Pretoria in March 1895 to alter its declared aims as follows:

'(a) In the altered circumstances in which the Republic now finds itself, to vigorously support the Government in all its dealings which are right and fair and in accordance with the Grondwet [Constitution].

(b) As far as the new population are concerned, to support the Government and Volksraad in the making and carrying out of such laws as will create a feeling of calm and satisfaction among them, with the proviso that the independence of the South African Republic and the rights of the old burghers are strictly safeguarded and maintained.'[99]

Further the Congress resolved that membership of the Volksmacht should be open only to

'(a) all fully enfranchised burghers of the South African Republic

(b) all naturalised burghers who have taken the oath of allegiance to the South African Republic and are inscribed accordingly on the Field Cornets' lists. (Any present members not yet naturalised to become so by November 1895.)'

[95] *Volksstem*, 28 Jan. 1895; *Press*, 23 Jan. 1895.
[96] *Press*, 23 Jan. 1895.
[97] *Land en Volk*, 22 Nov. 1894.
[98] *Land en Volk*, 31 Jan. 1895 (the *Volksstem*, from this point, refers to the 'Volksmacht' as 'the working committee of the Progressive movement'—ibid., 9 March 1895).
[99] *Land en Volk*, 14 March 1895; *Volksstem*, 9 March 1895.

We can sum up such evidence as we have been able to adduce in the last few pages, then, as follows. The frequently expressed view that not the President but the dour obstinacy of the burghers formed the main obstacle to any extension of the franchise must be regarded with considerable suspicion. There is, on the contrary, much evidence to suggest that, though Kruger certainly did not create anti-uitlander feeling on the franchise issue among his people, he did more than his share in keeping it alive; while the ease with which he convinced a great mass-meeting of the burghers in 1899 of the need for substantial franchise concessions, once he himself had become convinced of its political expedience, suggests that the path to reform might have been a much smoother one if Kruger had, at an earlier stage, used his enormous influence in the direction of such a reform, instead of against it.

On the other hand, the franchise question was, as we have seen, fraught with the deepest emotional consequences for the Boer population. Logic and emotion struggled for mastery, and confusion and contradiction was the consequence. Neither the Conservative party nor the Progressive party as a whole was prepared to either oppose totally or advocate wholeheartedly a significant and generous extension of the franchise.

Finally, that very considerable burgher opposition to such an extension did exist, though it was perhaps more open to change than Kruger's apologists admit, and that it existed in both the Progressive and Conservative camps, is clearly suggested by the outline that has been given of the Volksvereeniging–Burgermacht negotiations, and of the shipwreck—basically on the rock of this crucial issue—of the attempt at a rapprochement between the two parties.

The franchise issue, in short, plays its part in the drawing together in opposition to the government of those of more progressive views. But, though the Progressive group was significantly warmer in its attitude towards the uitlander, even it was not prepared to go the whole way—understandably enough, for, though they saw the issues involved with greater clarity than their Conservative opponents, they were Afrikaner patriots who had no desire to see their country taken over by the uitlander. To them the problem was, if one might put it this way, how to Afrikanerize the newcomers, and thus avoid anglicizing the Republic. The Progressive party's policy was certainly a more likely way of achieving this delicate task, than the blunt opposition of the more extreme Conservatives. However, the

Progressives were not given the opportunity to put that policy into effect; and the Conservative policy of too little and too late was maintained up to the end.

But the dividing line between the parties was, it is clear, much more ill-defined and flexible on the franchise issue, than the clear and vigorous division which existed on the other issues which have hitherto been traced—finance, concessions, dynamite, railways, administrative corruption, and education and language policies. To that extent, therefore, it cannot be regarded as quite the catalyst in the formation of the Progressive party, that these other issues were.

Two main tasks now remain to us—to outline the actual growth of the Progressive party as such between 1890 and 1895, and to estimate the part played by General P. J. Joubert, its alleged leader, during those years.

6

The Growth of the Progressive Party (1890–2)

UP to this point we have examined the main questions at issue between the government and its opponents, and, taking each issue separately, tried to show the divisions which those issues produced among those participating in the political life of the South African Republic. In general the picture that emerges from this piecemeal analysis is a fairly clear one; for, with the exceptions and inevitable confusions which must exist when there is no clear-cut party system, it is always the same group of personalities who stand together in opposition to President Kruger's régime. It now becomes necessary to try to draw together these threads, and by tracing the growing coherence of this opposition group between 1890 and 1895, the increasing support for it both in the press and among the public, and its growing organization outside the Volksraads, to show how something very closely resembling the beginnings of a real party organization (in the usual sense of that phrase) had emerged towards the end of the period under review.

In his chapter on the growth of the Progressive party, Carl Jeppe singles out R. K. Loveday, the member for Barberton, as 'indeed the founder of the party, for it was his able exposition of the dangers of the Kruger policy which first opened the eyes of the Boer'.[1] There is some justice in this claim. Nevertheless, quite apart from Loveday, the years 1890 and 1891 saw a great increase in opposition to the Kruger régime in many quarters. Joubert had bitterly attacked the Netherlands Railway Company. Concessions were coming under increasing fire, and warning of the dangers implicit in the policy had been given by a First Volksraad Commission as early as July 1890.[2] The unsatisfactory financial state of the Republic had come in for much criticism. There had been much bitterness over the acceptance of presents by members of the First Volksraad. The chaos in the

[1] Jeppe, ch. xx.
[2] First Volksraad, 2 July 1890 (*Volksstem*, 3 July 1890; *Notulen*, Eerste Volksraad, 1890, art. 566, Report of Begrootings Commissie, Point 18).

Department of Mines, the general inefficiency of the administration, and the poor state of the educational system, were assailed with increasing vigour, and even the pro-government *Volksstem*, summing up the general state of affairs in a leader of 12 February 1891, agreed that:

'The Government has undoubtedly lost much popularity recently since the end of the last Volksraad session. Then Paul Kruger was the enlightened leader, the father of various new and liberal laws, the mediator between the progressive public and the conservative Chamber of Representatives. But the hour of painful disillusion has come. The financial policy of the government, its inability to raise State loans, its attempts to create a "National Bank", its sudden great need of money, have caused a feeling of sharp disappointment amongst the public. . . . Further the President has not been very successful in his casuistic defence of those representatives of the people who have accepted presents under ambiguous circumstances. The proposed legislative programme of the "Staatscourant", further, gives evidence of a regrettable weakness of legislative talent on the government's part.

'And what of the representatives of the people? The Second Volksraad is a mere question mark; the First a discouraging exclamation mark—the spider question! The Volksraad must decide how it is going to regain the confidence of the public.'

In such circumstances, the article continued, 'the reappearance of General Joubert in our political sky could be rich in happy consequences'; but, the *Volksstem* cautioned,

'The Government must not be weakened, but strengthened and developed in every way. General Joubert and the President must work together for the sake of internal peace guaranteed by firm government.'

It was in these circumstances that Ewald Esselen, in August 1890, tendered his resignation as a judge of the High Court of the Republic to enter political life.[3] He was the son of the Reverend Mr. L. F. Esselen of the Berlin Missionary Society, a most respected and beloved pastor among his coloured congregants at Worcester in the Cape.[4] Ewald Esselen had come to the Transvaal from Scotland,

---

[3] *Land en Volk*, 14 Aug. 1890; *Volksstem*, 8 Nov. 1892.
[4] *Volksstem*, 1 July 1893; *Press*, 30 June 1893.

where he had been studying law, to serve in a medical capacity[5] in the First War of Independence in 1881, and in 1883–4 had accompanied Kruger, S. J. du Toit and General N. J. Smit,[6] as secretary of the deputation to London which secured the modification of the Pretoria Convention of 1881. He had subsequently become a judge of the High Court, and was undoubtedly a man who enjoyed, at this stage, at any rate, the highest respect of both the supporters and opponents of the régime.[7] He was an ardent Afrikaner patriot, and believed by both his friends and enemies to be an equally ardent foe of Hollander influence.[8] He had played a leading role in the formation of the so-called 'Jong Zuid Afrika' League, a newly-formed Transvaal organization of Afrikaner patriots, fearfully believed by its opponents of the Conservative party to be 'another Carbonari',[9] but described by its founders as aiming at 'the spread of pure patriotism, the spread of the South African Dutch language, and the uplifting of the Afrikaner race'.[10] It did not come to very much; but its aims indicate the direction of Esselen's sympathies.

Within a short time, as we have seen, he had launched a vigorous attack upon the financial policy of the government. In 1891 he was elected to the newly-formed Second Volksraad as member for Potchefstroom.

At much the same time as Esselen was delivering his attack upon the government to his constituents at Potchefstroom, the redoubtable Lukas Meyer of New Republic fame,[11] was making his entry into political life, on a strongly anti-government platform of principles. In his acceptance of the requests of many Vryheid burghers to stand for the First Volksraad, Lukas Meyer strongly criticized the political state of the country.[12] The principle of personal liberty, he declared, was being weakened; the policy of concessions and monopolies and

[5] *Land en Volk*, 3 May 1894. (He had originally studied medicine; but had changed to law—*Volksstem*, 29 April 1893.)

[6] *Volksstem*, 13 Sept. 1892. Botha, P. R. H., p. 113.

[7] *Volksstem*, 28 Aug. 1890, 6 Oct. 1890, 8 Nov. 1892; *Press*, 24 Mar. 1892, 27 Jan. 1893, 10 May 1894; *Land en Volk*, 29 Sept. 1892, 13 Oct. 1892, 3 May 1894.

[8] *Land en Volk*, 29 Sept. 1892, 3 May 1894; *Volksstem*, 6 Oct. 1890, 21 Sept. 1892.

[9] *Volksstem*, 28 Aug. 1890.

[10] *Volksstem*, 1 Sept. 1890.

[11] Walker, pp. 402, 404.

[12] *Volksstem*, 26 Nov. 1891; *Land en Volk*, 24 Nov. 1891.

a wrong system of import duties were working against the welfare of the State; the Netherlands Railway concession was a heavy burden upon the Republic, and the three-million pound loan which it had necessitated made that burden even heavier; he could see nothing but danger in the recent Bank and Mint concessions; and he demanded an independent commission of inquiry into the country's financial administration. 'The financial situation is also not particularly rosy', he said, 'and our independence, I consider, will in the future depend very largely on our financial position.'[13]

Asked by the representative of *Land en Volk* (24 November 1891) whether he thought that a more independent party was developing in the First Volksraad, which 'did not just do everything that the Executive Council recommended', Lukas Meyer declared that he was not so optimistic.

'With the Netherlands Railway Concession there had been an eleventh-hour session, at which the Concession could have been destroyed, but, with the President pleading the case in the Raad, the Volksraad, instead of throwing the noose off its neck, had drawn it tighter. Under these circumstances even if the entire Raad consisted of the new party of which you speak, it would still not help us.

Land en Volk Reporter: Well what way out is there? Must there be a change of Government or of the Executive Council?

Meyer: I would rather keep my opinions on that matter to myself.'

Though personal grievances against the Executive and the Volksraad[14] perhaps played a slight part in Lukas Meyer's decision to enter the political struggle, concern for the welfare of the State was with him, as with Esselen, clearly the overriding factor.

Not only *Land en Volk* but the *Volksstem*, too, on 26 November 1891, welcomed this new star on the political horizon.

'We welcome the appearance in the political life of this State', it declared, 'of such a figure—a man who has already done much for this State . . . and whose name is respected everywhere in this Republic and also beyond its borders. . . .

'It has become so much the custom for Volksraad members who belong to the old burgher population of the South African Republic

---

[13] *Land en Volk*, 24 Nov. 1891.
[14] L. Meyer's post as Boundary Commissioner for the South Eastern districts had been declared redundant by the Volksraad (*Volksstem*, 13 Oct. 1891).

to cloud their utterances in secretive vagueness that the manifesto of Mr. Lukas Meyer has come as quite a surprise. For long, any utterance that runs counter to the desires of official circles has led to the branding of the speaker as an enemy of the country, an agitator, or—a candidate for the Presidency! Already such allegations are being muttered. A born Transvaaler—and accused of being an agitator and mischief-maker because he has said things to his fellow-burghers, which, though said a hundred times already, have never been said out loud by anyone wishing to be regarded as belonging to the true Boer party [echte Boeren partij]!

'We welcome the future member for Vryheid as an acquisition to our Volksraad.'

After delivering a strong attack on the failure of the First Volksraad to halt the decline in the country's finances, the article continued:

'Far from placing any stones behind the wheels of the backward-slipping waggon of state, various members of the Volksraad have instead assisted the process of financial decline, by direct or indirect participation in advantageous contracts with the State—the fruits of which we are plucking today. They have not dared to pension off officials unfit for their positions. . . . But men like Mr. Lukas Meyer they have dismissed at the stroke of a pen!

'Our government, which we wish to see replaced by no other, desperately needs able statesmen, who think less of their own pocket than of the general welfare. We consider the government of Paul Kruger indispensable for our Republic, and believe that no one who wishes the land well would like to see him disappear from the head of affairs. But, nevertheless, we look longingly for men without prejudice, with a clean political and social record, and with real love of their fatherland.'

The general malaise which led such a normally staunch supporter of the government as the *Volksstem* to welcome so heartily a man destined to become one of the government's stoutest opponents, is reflected, similarly, in the attempt, a few months previously, to create an organization known as the 'Unie van de Zuid Afrikaansche Republiek' (Union of the South African Republic) to which, at first, both opponents and supporters of the government adhered. Inaugurated late in July 1891, its first meeting at Pretoria[15] was attended by some sixty people, who included Generals Joubert and N. J. Smit, J. M. A. Wolmarans (a member of the Executive Council), C. J. Joubert (Minister of Mines), F. G. H. Wolmarans (Chairman of the First Raad), Landdrost Smit of Pretoria, and various members of the First and Second Volksraads. Its declared aims[16] were:

'to foster co-operation between white residents of all nationalities established in our Republic, with full respect for the laws of the land and determination to uphold the independence of the State.'

Membership was to be open to all white males over the age of sixteen living in the South African Republic; and it advocated, among other things, the development of friendly relations (political, commercial and industrial) with neighbouring South African states and with foreign countries, and the maintenance of the Dutch language (de Hollandsche of landstaal), though 'other languages would not be excluded, and, if requested, the minutes will be translated into another language, and vice versa'.[17]

General Joubert was elected Chairman, by acclamation, and Isaac van Alphen (the Postmaster General) was chosen secretary. Joubert declared that:

'Many people who wished the country well were excluded from any possibility of co-operation. To overcome this difficulty the constitution of the Unie had been drawn up with the most careful consideration. . . . He was glad to report that His Excellency the President, though not agreeing with some of its points, supported the foundation of the Unie'.

General N. J. Smit declared that

'what had led him to participate was the fact that among the Uitlanders there were many well-disposed persons. A place must be found for those who accepted the Republic as their home and fatherland' (*Volksstem*, 28 July 1891).

But it was not many days before the never particularly roseate prospects of the new 'Unie', which, in the somewhat cynical words

[15] *Land en Volk*, 28 July 1891; *Volksstem*, 25 July 1891. 28 July 1891, 30 July 1891.
[16] *Land en Volk*, 23 July 1891.
[17] *Land en Volk*, 23 July 1891.

of *Land en Volk* of 28 July 1891, 'proposes to unite in one organization Boers, Hollander officials, English diggers, German and Jewish speculators . . . in fact all races except the Kaffirs', had foundered on the harsh rocks of reality. Having taken thought for a short period, one conservative member after another, at subsequent meetings,[18] stood up and denounced the new organization at whose birth they had so benevolently assisted. J. P. Meyer (First Volksraad member for Johannesburg) summed up their feelings when he said[19] that 'he had been one of those who had advocated the Unie; but the more he investigated the matter, the more uneasy he became'.

Landdrost Smit and F. G. H. Wolmarans declared such a union to be totally unnecessary, considered it comparable with the detested Afrikaner Bond in the Cape, and affirmed their belief that the oath sworn to one another by the burghers at Paardekraal was the only union that was necessary in the Republic. J. J. Burger (Chairman of the Second Raad) alleged that the creation of such a union might lead to the impression 'that we are no longer capable of defending our position on our own', and, finally, when one J. F. Sellschop (described as 'a small Hollander') ventured to say that 'to describe all uitlanders as monarchists was a lie', general chaos ensued. The *Volksstem* of 30 July 1891 describes the shipwreck of the 'Unie' as follows:

'The violent feeling against the Uitlanders was frightful. Mr. Labuschagne (member of the First Raad) made himself prominent by his shouting and violent abuse of "these uitlanders who come into the country to insult its burghers!" Mr. J. du Plessis de Beer[20] stood with his fist under Mr. Sellschop's nose and threatened to strike him. Others shouted out "We will wait outside for him and settle him there!" . . . General Joubert . . . said he could not associate himself a moment longer with such irregularities and declared the meeting closed.'

The *Volksstem*, in regretting this unfortunate conclusion, attributed the blame for it chiefly to 'the regrettable behaviour of the Volksraad members Labuschagne, De Beer, J. P. Meyer, Stoop, Boshoff and others whose names have escaped us'. It had correctly,

[18] *Volksstem*, 30 July 1891, 4 Aug. 1891; *Land en Volk*, 4 Aug. 1891.
[19] *Volksstem*, 30 July 1891.
[20] First Raad member for Waterberg.

though regretfully, prophesied the 'Union's' failure in a leading article two days before its final collapse (by which time conservative sentiment had become apparent) when it declared, on 28 July 1891:

'It looks as if the refusal to co-operate is coming, not from the uitlanders, but from the burghers. Many feel the idea to be dangerous and against all that they bound themselves to at Paardekraal. This would be correct if it were still 1881 and not 1891. But much has happened in these ten years. Thus it is as sad as it was unexpected that such division arose last night, which has provisionally ended any question of a Union as a matter of practical politics.'

Though the 'Unie' came to nothing, it is in the political unrest of 1890 to 1891, the strivings to find a policy which might offer some hope of a secure future for Boer and uitlander alike, the growing discontent with nearly every aspect of government policy—expressed not only in the First and Second Volksraads, but in the pro-government as well as the opposition press[21]—that we may see the seeds from which the Progressive party sprang. The entry into political life of such prominent men as Esselen and Lukas Meyer, the attempts at the creation of such patriotic organizations (open to Boer and uitlander alike) as the 'Jong Zuid Afrika' league and the 'Unie van de Zuid Afrikaansche Republiek' (though they failed), the mounting criticism of the government with which the major portion of this book deals—are all symptoms of a political unrest from which Progressive opposition to the Kruger régime developed, and from which it drew increasing strength.

Nevertheless, though we see the nucleus of Progressive opposition developing in the two Volksraads, and from time to time winning, on specific issues, the temporary adhesion of normally pro-government members[22] (the government's narrow majority in the First Raad of 13 to 11 on its Netherlands Railway policy[23] being, perhaps, the high-water mark of Progressive achievements in this early stage) we cannot, as yet, talk of a 'Progressive party' in the accepted sense of the word. The *Volksstem*, writing on 9 February 1892, quite correctly declares:

'So-called "Parliamentary" parties supporting or opposing the Government one does not find, and are unnecessary because the

---

[21] See chapters II to V above.
[22] See above, pp. 33–4, 43, 62.   [23] Above, p. 63.

Government is not based on a parliamentary majority but exercises its functions independently of Parliament. There are, it is true, conservative and progressive [vooruitstrewende] individuals, consistent enemies or friends of the government; but these individuals are not eager, apparently, to join together in a permanently united group.'

This agrees well enough with the opinion of another outside observer, Lukas Meyer, already quoted; for opposition to the government, in the tense situation that the presence of increasing numbers of uitlanders gave rise to, was, as the *Volksstem* had pointed out in its article on Lukas Meyer, apt to evoke accusations of lack of patriotism, if not treachery, which incipient 'Progressives' were not anxious to bring down upon their heads. It was for this reason, if for no other, that the acceptance by so indubitable a patriot as General Joubert of the leadership of the Progressive movement,[24] was to prove of such vital importance, and to lead to such sensational results in the 1893 election.

The year 1892 saw a steady rise in opposition to the government. There was, it has been noted, criticism by an increasing number of burghers of the Presidential salary and a move for a reduction in all official salaries. While on tour that year Kruger found widespread dissatisfaction about the effect of import duties on the cost of imported products, and was constrained to promise the removal of some of the more unpopular duties. There was sharp criticism of the government after the failure of the State loan in February 1892, and opposition to the raising of a loan from Rothschild's at 5 per cent. In the First Volksraad, R. K. Loveday, Lukas Meyer, Paul Maré and Schalk Burger emerged as the most resolute critics of the government on the financial issue, though they were occasionally joined by Conservative dissidents.

On the issue of concessions and monopolies, only Loveday and Paul Maré in the First Raad had the courage to vote against *all* concessions, and were defeated by 20 votes to 2. But in the Second Volksraad the steadily rising vehemence against all concessions, which became apparent shortly after its inception, led, in 1892, to the rejection by that body of many concessions, and to the submission by the burghers of a growing number of petitions against all concessions. Anti-governmental feeling on this issue so affected the First Raad that it took, as we have seen, the unprecedented step

[24] Below, pp. 197–204.

of refusing to grant the government its usual 'volmacht' (plenary powers) at the end of the 1892 session—because of burgher allegations that the Executive were making use of this 'volmacht' to grant illegal and undesirable concession and monopoly rights.

In the Second Raad, as in the First, a clear opposition group began to emerge—E. Esselen, E. P. A. Meintjies, G. B. Brecher, F. Watkins, J. F. Celliers, J. W. Joubert, D. F. Petersen, with the occasional adherence of N. S. Malherbe—and to raise their combined voices increasingly against concessions and monopolies of every kind.

The government's dynamite policy, too, was becoming, by 1892, a fertile source of contention. The concession granted to the 'Zuid Afrikaansche Maatschappij voor Ontplofbare Stoffen Beperkt' (the South African Explosives Company Ltd.) was strongly attacked by General Joubert in February of that year, and allegations that the company were importing, rather than manufacturing, dynamite, forced the government to appoint a commission of inquiry. The unfortunate results of that commission led to an acrimonious debate in the First Raad and to the cancellation of the dynamite concession. On the dynamite issue, too, R. K. Loveday, Lukas Meyer, Paul Maré, joined by L. de Jager, emerged as the government's most fiery critics; and they were supported from time to time by Schalk Burger, J. J. Spies, J. de Clercq and Jan P. Meyer.

On the question of railway policy, and in particular on that of governmental support of the Netherlands Railway Company, the Progressive nucleus was even more outspoken, and it gained more adherents, on this issue, than on any other. We have seen that the highlight of its political achievement, by this stage, was its near-defeat of the government in May 1891, when the government won the support of the Volksraad for its railway policy by a mere two votes (13 votes to 11). The prestige of the government suffered further injury when it found itself forced to accept the Rothschild loan of £2½ million engineered by the Cape Government; and there is ample evidence of the very considerable burgher opposition to which this move gave rise, an opposition expressed both in the Volksraad and in the political meetings which preceded the 1893 election.

The issue of corruption and general maladministration played a major role, without any question, in the rapid decline of the government's prestige. A powerful cry for reform was raised in all sections of the press, a cry to which Schalk Burger, in particular, added his authoritative voice. The Second Volksraad made this issue its special concern from 1892 onwards; and the year 1892 saw the beginning of the Progressive group's demand for an investigation into the notorious 'Stands Scandal'—a matter which played an important part in arousing strong burgher opposition to the régime between 1892 and 1893. The function of this issue in drawing the Progressives together in the Second Raad has already been indicated; and the support that they gained, on the issue of corruption and maladministration, from normally conservative members of the two Volksraads, was paralleled, on a country-wide scale, by a great upsurge of support, in 1893, for the party which combined a trusted and conservative-minded leader[25] with a Progressive opposition to these blots on the escutcheon of the State.

The more delicate education and language question played, it has been shown, little or no part in the 1893 election; but here again it was Progressive members, largely, who took the lead in wanting the children of the burghers to be given more opportunity to learn English at school.

On the even more touchy franchise question we have noted that only two members of the Progressive group, R. K. Loveday and Lodewijk de Jager, were prepared, at this stage, to speak up boldly in the First Raad for an extension of the vote to the loyal uitlander. Two vigorous and forthright members of the Second Raad, similarly—Ewald Esselen and Jan. F. Celliers—were not afraid, in March 1892, to tell their fellow-countrymen that their fear of the uitlander was not justified, and that the real danger to the State lay in their continued exclusion from the franchise. But neither party was prepared to make extension of the franchise an election issue; and the pronouncements of both Kruger and Joubert, of their election committees, and of the press-organs committed to their support, are, on this issue, inconsistent, confused, and ultra-cautious.[26]

What degree of organization, if any, had the Progressive group reached by the end of 1892? They already had their candidate for the coming presidential election, for General Joubert, at Barberton, had declared that

'he was sorry that the Presidential election had been mentioned. He had never sought for such a post, and would never give a penny for it or make the least promise in that connection. If they wanted to

[25] See below, chapter IX.   [26] See above, pp. 174–6.

choose him, then he would obey the voice of the people and the voice of God; but he did not seek for such a thing.'[27]

This was an utterance which both the *Press*[28] and *Volksstem*[29] correctly interpreted as a declaration of the General's intention to offer himself for election as President—the former newspaper adding, not without justification, that it hoped that 'Slim Piet', as it called him, 'was not quite so unintelligible as he appears (from the report of Reuter's agent) to have been'.

Early in 1892 *Land en Volk* had begun stepping up its campaign against Kruger. There was nothing novel about its criticism of Kruger. But formerly, even its most bitterly critical writer, 'Afrikanus Junior', had contented himself with adjurations to Kruger for reform, declaring:[30]

'My aim is not, I assure you on my word of honour as an Afrikaner, to increase the people's suspicion of you; nor is it dictated by hate, envy, or a desire to see you dismissed from your high office. I regard you as the best statesman that the people of the South African Republic could ever have chosen as their leader.'

Again, a little later, in *Land en Volk* of 12 May 1891,

'I would like to support you, to stand by you through thick and thin, to give my life for our independence! But how can I do it? To reach you I must penetrate through a Commando of Hollanders. And when I reach you where do I find you? At your right hand stands Nellmapius; at your left Lippert; behind you Ekstein [*sic*], Sammy Marks and a whole gallery [reeks] of Jews. And if I speak to you, Leyds answers me, because he stands for you. Fine company indeed for the President of the South African Republic.

'God forbid that I should judge you by your friends, in spite of the proverb "Soort soek soort" [Like seeks like]. Yet you could have created a strong pure Republic, strong enough to give vigorous opposition to all the threats of English might; you could have made us a name among nations—a name that would earn the respect of even our bitterest enemies; you could have preserved us as a pure

[27] *Volksstem*, 9 Feb. 1892.

[28] *Press*, 8 Feb. 1892.

[29] *Volksstem*, 16 Feb. 1892.

[30] *Land en Volk*, 5 May 1891 ('Open Letter to the President by Afrikanus Junior').

Afrikaans nation, with all our institutions, all our customs and morals, all our traditions—coloured by the purest Afrikaans principles.

'Instead we are ruled by Hollanders. The Cape Afrikaners (with whom I have little sympathy) are correct in that at least. We are ruled by Hollanders! The Hollanders rule us and the Jews rule the Hollanders . . . the Jews who stand in a circle around our once respected President. . . .

'The wish of my heart is that when the time comes,[31] you, your Excellency, may stand on the right side, together with Afrikanus Junior.'[32]

But now, in 1892, *Land en Volk*'s criticisms dropped all pretence of wanting a purified Kruger as President, and began systematically to campaign for General Joubert. It chose the religious issue (Kruger was a 'Dopper' or member of the 'Gereformeerde Kerk' and Joubert of the 'Nederduitsch Hervormde of Gereformeerde Kerk') as a good beginning.

'While the President was spending Christmas with Marks the Concessionaire at Eerste Fabriek',[33] it declared, 'another scene was taking place at Wakkerstroom. A gathering of 4000 people! All of one faith—the Nederduitsch Hervormde of Gereformeerde Kerk— and all of one mind. And their leader was General Joubert. Here is the beginning of a new unity in the State. Wakkerstroom village was Paardekraal in miniature, and the foundation-stone of the bridge which preserves our unity and gives it strength, is, to our way of thinking, the General'. (*Land en Volk*, 12 January 1892)

[31] The time for putting an end, presumably, to this 'scandalous situation'.

[32] The identity of 'Afrikanus Junior' was, incidentally, never revealed. Such facts as can be gathered, are, if his own allegations can be believed, that he was (*a*) an Afrikaner, Transvaal born (*Land en Volk*, 5 May 1891), (*b*) one who had 'rendered great services to his country in war and in the political field' (Editor, *Land en Volk*, 14 Feb. 1895), (*c*) not Jeppe, Loveday or Abraham Malan, nor known to them as being Afrikanus Junior (sworn declaration by Eugène Marais, editor of *Land en Volk*, *Land en Volk*, 21 Feb. 1895), (*d*) some believed him to be General Joubert (Memorials to First Volksraad, 13 June 1895)—but this does not seem likely, for his fervidly nationalistic style and vehement oratory are quite untypical of Joubert, (*e*) he was not Jan F. Celliers, for his extremely well-informed articles continued after Celliers's death in Mar. 1895 (*Land en Volk*, 12 Sept. 1895).

[33] The site of Marks's liquor factory at Hatherley, near Pretoria. (For a full account of the liquor concession see Marais, pp. 25–7.)

In a bitter attack, on 23 February 1892, *Land en Volk* stressed that all the pro-Kruger papers were edited by Hollanders and declared:

'It is Kruger who has built up this Hollander party; and, conversely, the Afrikaans [Afrikaansche] principles of General Joubert are well known. Thus the choice between these two men is simply and only the choice between Afrikaner and Hollander.'

Having turned Kruger into a Hollander, *Land en Volk* was determined to maintain him in this new status, and the ensuing months saw redoubled attacks upon Kruger, State Secretary Leyds and 'Hollander rule' in general. Much of this campaign was directed against Dr. Leyds in particular. But it did not succeed, for he was re-elected State Secretary by the First Raad, by 20 votes to 3 (only R. K. Loveday, Paul Maré and Lukas Meyer voting in the minority)[34] much to the chagrin of *Land en Volk* which declared, somewhat mystically, on 14 June 1892, that

'some members we thought would never vote for him did so. In any event he is re-elected with a majority that shows that he has the confidence of the people. . . . We take our stand with the honourable minority, which we are convinced represents the real will of the people. The Afrikaans spirit is not dead within us!'

June and July saw vigorous attacks on corruption, financial policy, the dynamite question, the presidential salary, the placing of advertisements only in those newspapers which supported official policy, and other weak points in the governmental armour.

In the middle of August 1892, General Joubert, as expected, officially announced his candidature, and Ewald Esselen was listed as the Chairman of the Joubert Committee.[35] Joubert's announcement of his intention to stand for the Presidency had not come, incidentally, without a considerable number of alarmed adjurations from various incipient 'Joubert committees' all over the country. Thus, for example, J. C. Krogh of Marthinus Wessel Stroom begs Joubert, in a letter of 1 August 1892,[36] to *announce* his candidature so that his supporters can form an election committee and 'get into

[34] *Volksstem*, 8 June 1892; *Land en Volk*, 14 June 1892; *Notulen*, Eerste Volksraad, 1892, art. 385.
[35] *Land en Volk*, 11 Aug. 1892, 18 Aug. 1892.
[36] Joubert Papers, Inkomende Stukke, I A/10–17 (Archives, vol. 6), no. 646.

action', and, warning him that the other committees are working hard, asks,

'Why do you sit silent, so that we do not know what to do? . . . Believe me that it will be largely your own fault if you are not chosen.'

A letter from J. S. Joubert of Potchefstroom, of the same date,[37] is couched in virtually identical terms. A similar letter from C. M. Douthwaite of Potchefstroom, dated 4 August,[38] begs General Joubert to announce his candidature and warns of the dangers of delay. After the candidature had at last been announced the understandably admonitory note of these letters is replaced by one of congratulatory joy and of the radiant confidence common to all electioneering agents, amateur or professional, in all times and climes.

Thus, M. König of Klerksdorp, rejoicing at having heard that Joubert will stand for the Presidency, writes that

'with the exception of a few Hervormdes (adherents of the Nederduitsch Hervormde as distinct from the Nederduitsch Hervormde of Gereformeerde Kerk) people here will vote as one man for you'.[39]

S. J. E. Trichardt, of Goede Hoop, declares:

'Where is our birthright is it not given to the scum of hollant is our land not sold for monopolies and concessions the only hope that remains for us is for us to get general Joubert as President i am sure, that he will make right what can still be made right.'[40]

Louis Botha, Veld-cornet of Vryheid (and later first Prime Minister of the Union of South Africa) wrote, on 22 August:[41]

'My dear friend,

You will be very surprised to receive a letter from me; but with politics going the way they are at the moment I feel I must express my gratitude at having heard from my friends Mr. Lucas J. Meyer and Esselen that you will stand in the coming Presidential elections.

---

[37] Joubert Papers, no. 647.

[38] Joubert Papers, no. 648. See also nos. 649, 650, 651.

[39] Joubert Papers, Inkomende Stukke, I A/10–17 (Archives, vol. 6), no. 651 of 9 Aug. 1892.

[40] Joubert Papers, no. 652.

[41] Joubert Papers; Inkomende Stukke, I A/10–17 (Archives, vol. 6), no. 656.

Our country is certainly in need of a great change, and in you we have a man who cherishes the independence of our beloved country in his very heart, and who is a true friend of the Afrikaners. So just take this to show you that you have friends here also who will stand or fall with you. In my ward (wijk) the requisition to you to stand has been signed by every well-disposed Afrikaner, and they will support you to the end. I hope that the day will speedily come when we shall be able to say—away with Kruger's politics, concessions and Hollanders.'

A letter from D. A. de Villiers (place not indicated) dated 22 August 1892[42] assures General Joubert

'that in this district the majority are for your Excellency. . . . The persons who are working for Kruger are not of much importance. They are poor people, and are working for money. . . . As far as I can gather they are paid £3 for each day they work.'[43]

That Joubert, in spite of his refusal to announce a specific electoral programme,[44] was universally regarded as the candidate of the 'Reform' party, is clear not only from a large number of letters to be found in the Joubert papers[45] declaring the General's election as President to be 'the only hope for the whole country', but also from the adjuration to him, from the Kruger party, to withdraw his candidature, which is expressed in an open letter to him from Justice Jorissen[46] dated 17 December 1892.

'It is not as Judge that I speak, nor do I direct myself to the Commandant General. It is Jorissen who speaks to Joubert, in the interests of the people, who regained their independence by our co-operation. . . .

'But there is another Joubert, the chosen one of the Joubert Committee, the candidate of "Land en Volk", the favourite of the "Transvaal Advertiser" and the "Transvaal Times" and other pro-British newspapers. With that Joubert I have nothing to do, nor do I

---

[42] Joubert Papers; no. 657.

[43] Internal evidence shows 'this district' to be Ermelo.

[44] See below, pp. 201–2, 256–61.

[45] See, for example, Joubert Papers, Inkomende Stukke, I A/10–17 (Archives, vol. 6), and I A/10–17 (Archives, vol. 7), nos. 640, 641, 642, 649, 652, 660, 662, 663, 666, 668.

[46] Joubert Papers, Inkomende Stukke, I A/10–17 (Archives, vols. 6 and 7), no. 665. Also in *Volksstem*, 10 Jan. 1893.

direct myself to him. How could I?.... It is clear that they are making use of you, with or without your desire, possibly even against your desire. They need your person for their special purposes. It is a political game well known all over the world. . . .

'I would, (if I were you), say this to Paul Kruger: "My dear friend and brother, I am being impelled by interested friends, now, as it were at the eleventh hour, to [stand] for the Presidency. . . .

'Because there is a very strong opposition towards you, my candidature finds so much more support than previously. Reform is wanted. There is no doubt that Reform is necessary. Because I feel it so strongly, and recognise it so fully, I have carefully questioned myself. I have examined my conscience. I say to you, that if we shake each other by the hand, we can bring about the desired reform, and probably save our Republic from being swallowed by the mighty, and daily increasing, English Power.

'And so I am prepared to stand back this time for you, on one condition, and that is that you bind yourself, by an open proclamation to the people, to put forward the list of reforms which are necessary, and to defend them with all your might, if necessary calling upon the people [for support]. I promise you then my manly support." '

It is clear from all this that the opposition to Kruger, and the widespread demand for reform, which—rightly or wrongly[47]—sought in General Joubert its shield and banner, if not its trumpet, had led to the spontaneous formation all over the Transvaal of innumerable 'Joubert committees' pledged to support the Commandant-General's candidature; and that the motives which led to their formation, though as mixed as all human motives are, were clearly much the same as those which had led to the formation of a consistent 'Progressive' group in the two Volksraads. The allegations that these 'Joubert committees' level against Kruger's régime are indistinguishable from those which have been indicated as forming the issues around which a more or less coherent 'opposition' had formed itself by the end of 1892—railway policy, the dynamite question, concessions, corruption, financial maladministration and pro-Hollander favouritism (though rarely, it is interesting to note, the franchise question or the education and language issue).[48] A

[47] See below, pp. 246–74.
[48] Joubert Papers, Inkomende Stukke I A/10–17 (Archives, vols. 6 and 7). See also the manifesto of the Wakkerstroom 'Joubert Committee' (*Land en*

complete list of the members of the various 'Joubert committees' can be found in the *Volksstem* of 16 November 1892. These committees were responsible for the sending in of many thousands of 'requisitions' to General Joubert to stand for the presidency.[49] (By mid-November 1892 the government offices at Pretoria had received 305 'requisitions' with 7,099 names for Joubert; and 259, with 7,400 names for Kruger.[50] But according to Esselen, the leader of the central Joubert Committee, the number of names for the General was 7,570.[51] By 26 November, according to the *Volksstem* of that date, the total number of 'requisitions' for Kruger had risen to 344, with 7,744 names, and no further 'requisitions' for Joubert had come in. There had been 70 'requisitions' for Chief Justice Kotzé's candidature, with a total of 1,310 names.) Clearly all three 'committees' were working hard. The central Joubert Committee, led by Ewald Esselen, flushed by the great wave of support for its candidate, now proposed to combine the scattered committees into a Joubert Congress at Pretoria, a move which the *Volksstem* (1 November 1892) attacked strongly, asking what the need was for 'the Americanized methods of the Joubert Party', and declaring that the electioneering methods of that party, which it described as 'sowing suspicion everywhere, and using foul personal attacks to blacken the names of its opponents. . . . President Kruger, General Smit, Dr. Leyds, Chief Justice Kotzé, Landdrost Smit, and many others', would not redound to its advantage in the election.

This Joubert Congress met, in the middle of November, at Pretoria,[52] under Esselen's chairmanship; but there is little evidence of the exact nature of its activities.[53] It was attended by virtually every leading member of the 'Joubert Committees' of all areas of the Republic; and it is noteworthy that virtually all the names listed, with insignificant exceptions, are Afrikaans.[54] Some of the leading

Volk, 1 Sept. 1892) and election articles in *Land en Volk*, 26 Dec. 1892, 2 Jan. 1893.

[49] It is interesting to notice that the (pro-Kruger) *Press* of 16 Jan. 1893 considers that 'in general the organization of the Joubert Committee knocks knobs off that of the President'.

[50] *Volksstem*, 19 Nov. 1892.

[51] *Volksstem*, 16 Nov. 1892.

[52] *Volksstem*, 16 Nov. 1892.

[53] *Land en Volk*, *Press*, and *Volksstem* alike contain no information on this point.

[54] *Volksstem*, 16 Nov. 1892.

personalities of this 'Congress', for example, are quoted[55] as being, Ewald Esselen (Chairman), C. F. Ziervogel (Vice-Chairman), Wijnand W. Maré, Eugène Marais (Editor of *Land en Volk*), T. N. de Villiers, H. Marais, A . H. Malan, Paul Maré, E. P. A. Meintjies, G. T. Mynhardt, S. P. Erasmus, Henning Pretorius, W. Hartogh and E. Wilson. Not all of them were enfranchised burghers.[56] A notable absentee from this gathering was Schalk Burger, who had signed the 'requisition' from Lydenburg to General Joubert to stand for the Presidency,[57] had declared himself (even after the election)[58] to be a supporter of Joubert, and was widely regarded as the Commandant-General designate of the Joubert party;[59] but who had opposed the idea of a Joubert Congress from the start, and had never been a member of any 'Joubert Committee'.[60] General Joubert's own contribution to the electoral organization working for him consisted of a statement[61] that he 'thanked the Election Committee for all it had done for him; but he had not created the Committee and he stood outside it. He wished only to do his duty to God and the people', an utterance not very dissimilar, in essence, to his declaration in the *Volksstem* of 30 November 1892, when asked to outline his political programme, that:

'In no single requisition have I been asked to declare my future policy [wordt van mij gevraagd mijne toekomstige politiek bloot te leggen] and this is for me an even stronger proof of your unconditional confidence in me.'

For the General prided himself on the fact that he answered only 'the call of God and the People. To that I subject myself. But to pursue and hunt [te jagen en te haken naar] that position (the Presidency) never!' He would never, he declared, 'ask or beg one single man for his vote or any other favour. If the majority came to him, well and good. But never will I go to them.'[62]

[55] See *Press*, 6 Dec. 1892, 10 Jan. 1893, 16 Mar. 1893; *Volksstem*, 16 Nov. 1892, 21 Mar. 1893, 28 Mar. 1893, 18 Apr. 1893, 26 Apr. 1893, 29 Apr. 1893.

[56] *Volksstem*, 29 Apr. 1893.

[57] *Land en Volk*, 17 Nov. 1892.

[58] *Land en Volk*, 18 May 1893.

[59] *Volksstem*, 20 May 1893.

[60] Statement to *Land en Volk*, 18 May 1893.

[61] *Volksstem*, 12 Nov. 1892 (see also Marais, p. 57).

[62] Joubert Papers, Uitgaande Stukke, II A/1–A/3 (Archives, vol. 17), no. 1997. Letter of 4 Mar. 1892 to Douthwaite, Potchefstroom.

Nevertheless the great feeling of dissatisfaction with the Kruger régime which had arisen by the end of 1892 led, in the months before the 1893 election, to an unprecedented wave of political activity throughout the Transvaal. The formation of the Joubert and Kruger committees, which have been referred to, are clearly more a consequence than a cause of the political awakening of the Transvaal to the dangerous issues which confronted it. The *Volksstem* (9 November 1892) thundered:

'Never have they [the elections] been so important. In previous elections most burghers stayed at home. But not this time! The burghers must wake up! or we shall be overwhelmed by the foreign element. May Providence protect us from such Afrikaners as Esselen who identifies himself fully with those who wish for the end of "the stupid Boer Government",[63] and from General Joubert who has never dissociated himself from Esselen's remarks.'[64]

The *Press* (23 November 1892) denounced Joubert as

'too weak a man, too shilly-shallying a statesman, and altogether too characterless a personality for the Presidency of the South African Republic' and declared that 'his unspoken wish for that political mirage, a United South Africa, which his subtlety cannot foresee must be of great detriment to the Transvaal under present circumstances, is enough to damn his, even otherwise, remote chances of success'.

Land en Volk[65] attacked Kruger as a 'loyal helper of Rhodes'[66] and declared that:

'Joubert must be President—because Kruger has delivered us over to the Hollanders; whereas Joubert has resolutely opposed this;
—because Kruger will not give up his ruinous Concessions policy, and Joubert has declared that he will work against Concessions . . .

---

[63] A reference to a remark allegedly made shortly before this time by a Rev. Mr. Drew, at a meeting of the uitlander 'National Union' in Johannesburg, at which Esselen had been present (*Volksstem*, 13 Sept. 1892; *Land en Volk*, 29 Sept. 1892).

[64] Joubert did so shortly afterwards (*Land en Volk*, 27 Oct. 1892, 8 Dec. 1892; *Volksstem*, 12 Jan. 1893).

[65] *Land en Volk*, 26 Dec. 1892, 29 Dec. 1892, 2 Jan. 1893.

[66] With special reference to Kruger's interdict against the Adendorff Trek to Mashonaland, which Joubert supported (see Walker, p. 423).

—because Kruger prefers Hollanders and Jews, who encircle him like vultures, to loyal sons of the soil—a policy which Joubert strongly opposes. . . .

—because President Kruger in truth desires to act as if he were the sole ruler of this free Republic, bought by our blood. . . .

—because he has used all his influence in the Second Volksraad to get the Stands Scandal referred to the Government for investigation

—because, against the advice of General Joubert, he has negotiated a Bank Concession, by which German, Dutch and English Jews have acquired a great financial power in the land—yet he calls it the "National Bank"!'

7

The Presidential Election of 1893

AMID such mutual recriminations the election campaign of 1893 opened. The 'election-fever' which the *Volksstem* had diagnosed as early as 3 February 1892 was now in full spate. The *Volksstem* of 19 November 1892 remarked on the immense public interest in the elections and the 'requisitions, counter-requisitions, manifestoes and anti-manifestoes' which were everywhere to be seen. No previous election, it declared, had been anything like this; and, a little later (14 January 1893), it pronounced its disapproval of 'the whole attitude and tactics of the Joubert movement'. Meanwhile the rival papers hurled accusations and counter-accusations of bribery, fraud and political gerrymandering at one another.[1] In the words of the *Press* (9 March 1893) it

'could not be denied that the partisans fought with a determination never before shown in the political history of the Transvaal. No effort was spared. The greatest enthusiasm was shown on both sides.'

The uitlander 'National Union' formed in August 1892 added its voice to the hubbub, demanding the franchise for all after two years' residence, and the righting of many grievances, from inadequate control of the liquor trade to insufficient municipal rights for Johannesburg. It was a powerful organization, and influentially backed by mining and commercial interests, as well as by many thousands of uitlanders.[2] By mid-September it had held four public meetings,[3] in all of which it stressed its patriotic and purely internal character, and loudly demanded reform. One of its actions was to send an anti-Kruger manifesto to every farmstead in the Republic.[4]

At its fourth meeting Ewald Esselen, Chairman of Joubert's

[1] *Land en Volk*, 28 Feb. 1893, 2 Mar. 1893, 9 Mar. 1893, 16 Mar. 1893; *Volksstem*, 26 Jan. 1893, 25 Jan. 1893, 11 Feb. 1893; *Press*, 16 Jan. 1893, 21 Feb. 1893.

[2] Marais, pp. 56–7, describes its leaders, and the nature of its support.

[3] *Volksstem*, 13 Sept. 1892.   [4] Marais, p. 57.

election committee, was present on the platform. He declared himself to be 'in full agreement with the aims of the movement. It must keep on agitating, and form branches, until it got its rights.'[5] This was almost certainly a tactical error, although undoubtedly courageous, in view of the tense and delicate nature of Boer-Uitlander feelings. It may well have cost Esselen his seat.[6] Certainly Joubert thought so.

'I am not surprised', he writes,[7] 'that Esselen has also fallen out. He has himself to thank for it. Firstly because he put himself into the hands of Piet Cronjé[8] and his second mistake was his appearance on the platform of the Johannesburg Union.'[9]

It is also possible that it cost Joubert votes, though of this we cannot be certain. The utmost political capital was made out of it by the Kruger party. The *Volksstem*[10] declared:

'The best proof of Joubert's vacillating weakness [wankelmoedigheid] can be seen in the actions of Esselen, who has declared himself in favour of the National Union, and has loudly applauded their plan that every Uitlander should get the vote after two years! General Joubert has said and done nothing to dissociate himself from this. . . '

and the *Standard & Diggers' News* attacked Esselen as 'a friend of Rhodes. A man whose faithfulness begins and ends in his pocket, an out and out supporter of the Cape, a handsome and elegant lady-killer'.

Joubert was forced to deny publicly and frequently any connexion with the National Union,[11] and to place a large and prominent front-page advertisement in *Land en Volk* (12 January 1893) declaring that

[5] *Volksstem*, 13 Sept. 1892.

[6] He was defeated at Potchefstroom where he stood for the First Raad (*Volksstem*, 18 Oct. 1892) by the Conservative candidate Prinsloo (*Press*, 10 Feb. 1893).

[7] Joubert Papers, Uitgaande Stukke, II A/1–A/3 (Archives, vol. 17), no. 1997. Letter of 20 Feb. 1893 to Douthwaite, Potchefstroom (Douthwaite was a veld-cornet there—ibid., no. 361).

[8] I am unable to throw any light on this remark.

[9] Joubert had no love for the National Union, which he described in his Wakkerstroom speech of Oct. 1892 as 'the Jingo Union of Johannesburg' (*Land en Volk*, 27 Oct. 1892).

[10] *Volksstem*, 4 Oct. 1892 (see also *Volksstem*, 18 Oct. 1892).

[11] *Land en Volk*, 8 Dec. 1892, 5 Jan. 1893.

he was not a member of the 'Johannesburg Union' and that he had 'never had any direct or indirect communication with it'. The attacks of his opponents on the alleged connexion of his party with the 'National Union' may also have had something to do with Joubert's action in dissociating himself from his own election committee, headed by Esselen.[12]

Despite the intense excitement which the election campaign of 1892–3 produced, the two leading actors in the drama, Kruger and Joubert, conducted themselves with restraint, and refrained from publicly attacking each other[13]—leaving that to their supporters. The presence of a third participant in the struggle, Chief Justice Kotzé, who based his candidature on what was probably the most clearly thought-out—and therefore the least popular—political platform of the three,[14] was never felt to be a serious threat[15] to the other two candidates, an opinion which the final result of the poll amply bore out.

By late January 'unofficial' results were already being widely featured in all papers, and it was already abundantly clear that the two old rivals were running neck and neck, and that the pattern of the two previous elections of 1882 and 1888 (when Kruger had beaten Joubert by 3,431 votes to 1,171 and 4,483 to 834 respectively)[16] was not, this time, to be repeated. There was no doubt this time that the burghers were voting in large numbers, and that the result was going to be one in which every vote would count. As the (more or less)[17] final results began to be revealed in constituency after constituency the narrowness of the gap between Kruger and Joubert became dramatically obvious. Here are the main constituency results,[18] for whatever regional or other features of interest they may reveal:

Constituency			Kruger	Joubert	Kotzé
Bloemhof	..	..	159	151	0
Ermelo ..	..	..	339	172	8
Heidelberg	..	..	439	550	1

[12] See above, p. 202, and Marais, p. 57.

[13] See *Volksstem, Press, Land en Volk*, Sept. 1892 to Feb. 1893, for fairly full reports of the speeches of Kruger and Joubert.

[14] See letter to Kruger (*Volksstem*, 9 Aug. 1892), speech at Lydenburg (*Volksstem*, 19 Oct. 1892) and outline of policy (*Volksstem*, 29 Nov. 1892).

[15] See *Volksstem*, 10 Aug. 1892; *Land en Volk*, 11 Aug. 1892; *Press*, 3 Feb. 1893.

[16] *Volksstem*, 25 Oct. 1892 (gives the figures for all elections from 1864 to 1888).

[17] They had still to be officially 'scrutinized' by the Executive Council.

[18] From *Volksstem*, 21 Feb. 1893.

Constituency			*Kruger*	*Joubert*	*Kotzé*
Lichtenburg	..	..	409	227	0
Lydenburg	..	..	380	250	4
Marico ..	..	..	380	290	0
Middelburg	..	..	559	535	1
Potchefstroom ..	..	964	1,057	6
Piet Retief	..	..	242	35	0
Pretoria	..	..	1,176	1,201	11
Rustenburg	..	..	1,211	680	30
Standerton	..	..	377	358	0
Utrecht ..	..	..	160	156	5
Vryheid	..	..	213	329	25
Waterberg	..	..	191	214	0
Wakkerstroom..	..	194	370	5
Zoutpansberg ..	..	307	382	8
Barberton	..	..	14	70	3
Johannesburg ..	..	94	120	0
Krugersdorp ..	..	214	131	0

These unofficial results closely correspond to the final results. They reveal, as had been expected,[19] strong local differences in the popularity of the two chief candidates. Thus Vryheid, where local leaders such as Lukas Meyer, Louis Botha and G. B. Brecher (their Second Raad member) were strongly progressive and pro-Joubert, gave the General, proportionately, one of his largest majorities (though it is interesting to note that neither the prediction of *Land en Volk* (11 August 1892) that the constituency 'would vote as one man for Joubert' nor that of the *Volksstem* (20 September) that 'the strong personal influence against the President' would ensure a very small vote for Kruger, was entirely borne out). Similarly Wakkerstroom, Heidelberg, Barberton and Johannesburg showed convincing wins for Joubert. But these Joubert victories were cancelled out by equally impressive majorities for his rival in Rustenburg, Ermelo, Lichtenburg, Lydenburg and Piet Retief. A glance at the figures will show that the differences are largely local, and not in any significant way regional. An addition of the figures for the western Transvaal constituencies (Rustenburg, Bloemhof, Lichtenburg, Marico, Potchefstroom, and Krugersdorp) gives 3,337 votes for Kruger to

[19] See *Land en Volk*, 11 Aug. 1892; *Press*, 16 Jan. 1893, 17 Jan. 1893, 26 Jan. 1893, 1 Feb. 1893, 13–20 Feb. 1893; *Volksstem*, 6 Aug. 1892, 10 Aug. 1892, 20 Sept. 1892.

Joubert's 2,536 and Kotzé's 36, or in terms of percentages 56·4 of the votes to Kruger and 42·9 to Joubert. In the eastern Transvaal constituencies (Barberton, Ermelo, Heidelberg, Lydenburg, Piet Retief, Standerton, Utrecht, Vryheid and Wakkerstroom) Kruger's victory is much narrower (50·3 per cent to Joubert's 48·7); while in the central and northern Transvaal (Pretoria, Johannesburg, Waterberg and Zoutpansberg) Joubert wins every constituency, and has 53·5 per cent of the votes to Kruger's 45·7. Kotzé, in each area, wins less than 1 per cent of the votes cast. The western Transvaal was, of course, Kruger's home country, and traditionally the stronghold of the Gereformeerde or 'Dopper' church; and this may have played its part in the voting. But even here Potchefstroom voted strongly for Joubert, and Bloemhof was won by Kruger with only the narrowest of margins. There is no 'regional' tendency visible in the eastern Transvaal, where Joubert's gains in one constituency are cancelled out by Kruger's in another. In the central and northern Transvaal, where Joubert wins convincingly, the constituencies are highly diverse in nature, the area can only be regarded as a 'region' by courtesy, and Joubert's consistent victories are almost certainly largely the result of local factors in each case.

The announcement of the final result of the election was greeted with stunned amazement by the Joubert party and with modified jubilation by their opponents. The 'final' figures, that is those given by the newspapers before the Executive Committee scrutiny laid down by the Constitution had taken place, gave Kruger 8,114 votes to Joubert's 7,310 and Kotzé's 86[20]—a majority for Kruger over his rival of 804 votes. Even before this date the pattern (for the votes had been anxiously totted up by the various press-organs as the results from each constituency filtered in) had been such as to suggest a narrow victory for the President. On 2 February 1893 *Land en Volk* had published the results up to that date as 'Joubert 4,807; Kruger 5,741; Kotzé 45'. By the 18th the *Volksstem*'s figure showed Kruger's lead to be around 650, with an estimated 15,000 votes cast. And, ten days later, on 28 February, *Land en Volk*, in a bitter leader had conceded Kruger a technical victory; but declared that it

'had no doubt that, had the elections been conducted in an honest and upright way, Joubert would have been President. The votes', it went on, 'must be carefully gone through. General Joubert is vir-

[20] *Volksstem*, 1 Mar. 1893.

tually President of the South African Republic, and if Kruger is sworn in it will always be on his conscience that he holds his position by the falsity and fraud of his friends'.

Already on 22 February Esselen had called upon the Joubert Committee to reassemble in Pretoria,[21] and *Land en Volk*, on 2 March, was talking wildly of opposition or violence (verzettelijkheid of geweld) if a re-count was refused.

'If Paul Kruger's Government desires to maintain peace, it must see to it that an honest and impartial scrutiny takes place.'

On 28 March 1893 the Joubert Committee handed to the government a protest[22] alleging that the conduct of the elections had been grossly irregular, and declaring that, in view of these irregularities, they were not prepared to accept the swearing-in of Kruger as the legally chosen President of the Republic. The most important[23] of the Joubert Committee's detailed allegations are the following:

(1) That the ballot boxes[24] had been opened and the votes counted by landdrosts and mining commissioners in many, if not all, constituencies, instead of being sent straight to the Executive Council.

(2) That innumerable unqualified people had been allowed to vote, including lunatics, children under 16, persons resident in other constituencies, persons whose names had been removed from the voting lists, and persons who had not even been to the polls. (Full details of these allegations were given.)

(3) That qualified voters had been refused permission to cast their votes.

A protest on more general lines had been made personally in a letter by General Joubert to President Kruger a week earlier.[25] It contains, in essence, the same allegations of what Joubert terms

'gross negligence and illegality on the part of officials—with the result that many qualified voters were hindered in, or totally pre-

[21] *Volksstem*, 22 Feb. 1893; *Press*, 16 Mar. 1893.

[22] *Volksstem*, 28 Mar. 1893; *Land en Volk*, 20 Apr. 1893.

[23] It is pointless to go into these allegations, in detail, because, as will be shown, it is impossible, at this stage, to establish the truth either way.

[24] For a detailed examination of how the burghers voted see Hugo, *Die Stemregvraagstuk in die Suid Afrikaanse Republiek*, Archives Year Book for S.A. History, 1947.

[25] *Land en Volk*, 11 May 1893 (letter of Joubert to Kruger, dated 21 Mar. 1893).

vented from, casting their votes; and, conversely, many other unqualified voters were given the opportunity, or allowed, to cast votes which were totally illegal and invalid'.

That the General himself felt very hardly done by is clearly shown, not only by this protest, but by a number of letters in the 'Joubert Papers'. In a letter to his friend Douthwaite, a veld-cornet at Potchefstroom, General Joubert writes:

'A hard-fought election has now come to its end, and I presume that the result will be well known to you; although not so gloriously(?) as "Press" and "Volksstem" had prophesied, yet His Excellency has been chosen—I shall for the meantime not say why or in what manner.'[26]

In a similar letter (unheaded and undated)[27] he writes bitterly of the approach made to him by President Kruger:

'Yesterday Simon du Tooi [*sic*] of Luipaardsvlei came here. I was to go with him to see the President. When we got there he had something to say. It was that I and the President together should sign a circular and send it out to warn the people that they must be satisfied and not rebellious. His Excellency at once said yes. But I said that the people that had voted for me would all be satisfied even if His Excellency had received only one legal vote more than me, and so that as far as I was concerned(?) such a circular was unnecessary etc. etc. But it looks as if considerable doubt exists that if all the votes were(?) legal, then His Excellency would have a minority instead of a majority. That is why they want me to acknowledge [or sign—it is not clear if the word is "erkennen" or "tekenen"] right away that I am in the minority. Well, my dear friend, even if our Excellency [onze Hoog Edele] had a legal majority of only one vote, let us nevertheless [tog] recognize it and be satisfied, knowing that the all-wise and good God knows what he desires for us. Let us keep our ways pure and clean. . . .'

A letter to B. J. Vorster senior(?) which follows upon this one[28] includes the statement, in a passage on the result of the election, that

---

[26] Joubert Papers, Uitgaande Stukke, II A/1–A/3, no. 1997 (Archives, vol. 17), no. 361 of 20 Feb. 1893.

[27] Joubert Papers, no. 365 (parts of this letter are illegible).

[28] Joubert Papers, no. 367 (undated).

'I may not express myself too freely on this matter. If one observed what was going on in the country and what took place [wat er in dat land gaande was en wat er omging] then every understanding person could have foreseen clearly what was coming, and thus I am in no way surprised at what has happened.'

Another letter, to Engelbrecht of Piet Retief, while apparently including an acknowledgement of Kruger's majority, declares:[29]

'Well, dear friend, our President has come in again, by a small majority. I am glad that I did not obtain a majority in such a manner. I would ten times rather be in the minority than obtain a majority in such a manner [op zoo een wijze].'

In none of these passages does the pious resignation that is expressed, though no doubt sincerely meant, fully conceal General Joubert's undoubted bitterness.

The actual polling had ceased on 20 February; and, by law, another month had to elapse to allow for the sending in of the voting papers from the most distant districts. The official announcement of the final result of the scrutiny of the electoral officers' returns could, therefore, not be expected until about the middle of April.

Meanwhile Esselen's 'Joubert Committee', which included delegates from all parts of the country, met in Pretoria[30] and on 16 March[31] waited on the Executive Council with a request that four members from each 'Committee' should be allowed to assist at the scrutiny of votes. The President pointed out that the law did not provide for such an arrangement, but promised that the Executive Council would give the request its most serious consideration. The 'Kruger Committee', however, apparently used its influence to see that nothing came of this request.[32]

On 21 March the official scrutiny began. In the words of the *Press* of 22 March:

'All the members of the Executive Council, including the President and General Joubert, were engaged most of yesterday opening the sealed papers which have been sent in by the Landdrosts and returning officers in connection with the Presidential election. The whole time was occupied in arranging the lines, according to constitutional usage, on which the scrutiny shall proceed.'

[29] Joubert Papers, no. 370 of 23 Feb. 1892.   [30] *Press*, 16 Mar. 1893.
[31] *Press*, 17 Mar. 1893.   [32] *Volksstem*, 21 Mar. 1893.

A week later the *Press* reported that good progress was being made with the checking of the votes, and that General Joubert was in constant attendance. He had, it was admitted,[33] written a letter threatening to withdraw a few days before this 'unless the scrutiny proceeded along certain lines'; but the government had been 'at one with him' on this matter and the General had withdrawn his letter. The *Volksstem*, like the *Press*, was at great pains to insist on the constant attendance of Joubert at the scrutiny, and the falsity of the prevalent rumours that he had refused to have anything to do with it.[34]

The Executive Council's scrutiny was completed on 5 April, and the *Volksstem* of that date announced that, as soon as an answer had been received about doubtful votes from certain districts, the final result would be made known. The *Press* (6 April) added that, although the official result would take some days, 'we understand that President Kruger is left with a large majority'. On 12 April a letter was sent from the Joubert Committee to the Kruger Central Committee declaring that the election was not legal; that both the returning officers and the majority of the Executive Council had acted illegally; and demanding an impartial re-count.[35]

Three days later, brushing this further protest aside, the government announced the official result of the scrutiny as 7,881 votes for Kruger, 7,009 for Joubert and 81 for Chief Justice Kotzé,[36] a majority for Kruger of 872 votes. Joubert had been notified of the same figures in a letter from Leyds on the previous day.[37] According to the official notification in the *Volksstem* (15 April 1893), the voting had shown 7,528 votes for Kruger and 6,768 for Joubert. To these had been added 352 votes [*sic*] for Kruger, and 241 for Joubert, 'of persons voting outside their district, or who, though on the Veld-cornet's lists, had not been published in the "Staatscourant" . . . bringing the total for Kruger to 7,881 and for Joubert to 7,009'.

Accompanying this announcement was a letter to the *Volksstem* by President Kruger, refusing to believe that the degree of division was as great as the *Volksstem* articles had suggested, and announcing

---

[33] *Press*, 28 Mar. 1893.
[34] *Volksstem*, 29 Mar. 1893; *Press*, 28 Mar. 1893, 13 Apr. 1893, 14 Apr. 1893.
[35] *Volksstem*, 18 Apr. 1893.   [36] *Volksstem*, 15 Apr. 1893.
[37] Joubert Papers, Inkomende Stukke, I A/10–17 (Archives, vol. 7), no. 673 of 14 Apr. 1893.

that the final result of the scrutiny, together with the protest of the Joubert Election Committee, would be laid before the Executive Council. The first part of this letter doubtless refers to a leading article in the *Volksstem* of 5 April 1893 which included the words:

'Some people have talked as if the country is about to burst into civil war. There must be no more talk of armed revolt against the result of the election.'[38]

But it was hardly a fair criticism, as this very article concluded with the statement that 'fortunately the rest of the country is not in the same hysterical mood as Pretoria', a point that was underlined again, in a later article, which contrasted 'the excited state of some people in Pretoria' with the 'deep calm which reigned in the country districts'.[39]

Meanwhile the Joubert Committee had decided to call a full 'Congress' of the party.

'A serious step', as *Land en Volk* (20 April 1893) put it, 'but the views of the whole party are needed, for matters have now reached a crisis. . . . The party Committee has protested strongly to the Executive Council against any taking of oaths of office by members or officials, on the ground that the election was, for various reasons, illegal. Yet the senders of this protest have been treated with less courtesy than if they were Hottentots or dogs. Leyds did not even acknowledge it, and the President says he will put it before the Volksraad, and adds in his usual oily manner (in zijn gewone olie-achtige manier) that he is ready to submit himself to their decision. Submit himself to the decision of a Volksraad packed with Kruger-men, such honest and upright people as Lombaard and De Beer!

'The people demand a thorough and impartial scrutiny.'

A characteristically equivocal open letter of General Joubert's, dated 13 April, and published in the *Volksstem* of 22 April,[40] appealed for calm and patriotic restraint and denied that there was any danger of civil disturbance; but declared that there was 'a great measure of dissatisfaction among the burghers at the manner in which the election had been conducted'.

[38] This, again, probably refers to *Land en Volk's* threats of 'opposition and violence', on 2 Mar. 1893, quoted above (p. 210).

[39] *Volksstem*, 3 May 1893.

[40] Also in *Land en Volk*, 20 Apr. 1893, and *Press*, 21 Apr. 1893.

At the 'Congress' of the Joubert party the General, now apparently more prepared to be associated with his party—perhaps because of the massive popular support for him which the elections had revealed—was, according to *Land en Volk* of 20 April, 'received with deafening applause' and listened to 'in utter silence', as he made his, by now familiar, declaration that 'he knew that the delegates were acting not for him, but in the interests of the people'.

Matters continued in this tense and unhappy state until the start of the 1893 Volksraad session. As the legality or otherwise of the Presidential election was to depend upon the attitude of the First Volksraad, half the members of which had, in accordance with constitutional practice, retired at the end of the previous session (though they were eligible for re-election),[41] we must turn, briefly, to that body. Were there any signs that the wave of opposition to the Kruger régime had materially altered the composition of the senior chamber? *Land en Volk*, well before the result of the Presidential election became known, had emphasized the crucial nature of the simultaneous Volksraad elections:

'The Presidential election', it wrote on 19 January 1893, 'has temporarily blinded people to the importance of the Volksraad elections, which are virtually just as vital. This is the first time in the South African Republic that two parties are working so hard, not only for two presidential candidates, but also for different representatives in the Volksraad.'

It cordially recommended to the electorate the names of Esselen, Lukas Meyer, Ockert Coetzee (for Lydenburg), Danie Erasmus (for Pretoria), and, without specifying them,

'other similar great-hearted Afrikaners, in whose souls the Afrikaner flame burns inextinguishably, (and in whom) we see the hope of the future for the Afrikaner Volk in this Republic and throughout South Africa'.

These adjurations, however, had little effect. The outcome of the elections for the First Raad gives no evidence of anything even remotely resembling a significant swing towards the Progressives. Of some seventeen constituencies in which First Raad elections were

---

[41] Marais, p. 11. (See *Notulen*, Eerste Volksraad, 1890, art. 1166 for the complicated regulations by which this matter was decided.)

held,[42] only six returned Progressive candidates—Lydenburg (Schalk Burger), Vryheid (Lukas Meyer), Lichtenburg (Commandant J. H. de la Rey), Zoutpansberg (Paul Maré), Wakkerstroom (G. J. W. de Jager) and Johannesburg (Carl Jeppe). Of these, only two, Gert de Jager and Koos de la Rey were new choices; and Schalk Burger was soon to become suspect to the Progressives.[43] The remaining eleven members, ten of them re-elected, were all in varying degrees acknowledged supporters of the government.[44] A. D. W. Wolmarans (Pretoria) and F. G. H. Wolmarans (Rustenburg) were Kruger men to the hilt. J. M. Malan (Rustenburg) and C. J. Tosen (Piet Retief) were strong Conservatives.[45] J. du P. de Beer (Waterberg), although described as the *enfant terrible* of the Volksraad, could be relied upon to vote with the government in any emergency.[46] C. J. A. Birkenstock (Vryheid), though moderately independent, is correctly described as 'a moderate government member'.[47] P. J. Schutte (the newly-elected member for one of the two Potchefstroom seats) was 'a supporter of the government through thick and thin'.[48] N. M. S. Prinsloo (the victor over Esselen in the other Potchefstroom seat) was 'usually to be found among the ranks of the old leaders [voormannen] at voting times and can be regarded as one of the old school'.[49] J. de Clercq (Middelburg), though occasionally to be found voting with the opposition, is described[50] as one who 'will never agree to measures that go too far, and will support the government in every reasonable way'.

Of C. B. Otto (Zeerust) the *Volksstem* of 1 September 1894 says:

'When he was elected, it was regarded as a victory for the opposition party. Time has shown how wrong this was. . . . All good measures proposed by the government earn his support, though none would dare call him a government member.'

[42] For election results see *Land en Volk*, 20 Apr. 1893; *Press*, 15 Apr. 1893; *Volksstem*, 2 May 1893 and 6 May 1893.

[43] See below, pp. 225–8.

[44] See *Volksstem*, 15 Aug. 1894, 22 Aug. 1894, 25 Aug. 1894, and 1 Sept. 1894, for shrewd and interesting character sketches of all the First Raad Members. (Articles headed 'Onze Raadsleden'.)

[45] *Volksstem*, 15 Aug. 1894, 22 Aug. 1894, 25 Aug. 1894, 1 Sept. 1894.

[46] *Volksstem*, 15 Aug. 1894.

[47] *Volksstem*, 25 Aug. 1894.

[48] *Volksstem*, 1 Sept. 1894.

[49] *Volksstem*, 1 Sept. 1894.

[50] *Volksstem*, 1 Sept. 1894.

In practice this meant[51] that he voted against the government on such issues as the dynamite monopoly, and the extension of the Natal line, but for them on virtually every other major issue.

Lastly, of the eleven members in question, we have J. C. Fourie (Lydenburg) whom the *Volksstem* (1 September 1894) sums up as one who 'takes little part in debates; but who, when he speaks, shows real judgement, and who always votes on the right side'.

The 1893 elections to the vacant seats in the Second Raad showed very similar results. In the twelve constituencies in which voting took place only four Progressive members—F. Watkins (Barberton), E. P. A. Meintjies (Pretoria), B. G. Brecher (Vryheid) and W. J. Jooste (Potchefstroom)—were returned; and if H. P. Steenkamp (Lydenburg) is counted as half-progressive, for he occasionally voted against the government,[52] four-and-a-half out of twelve.

In the light of all this we can say categorically that the Volksraad elections of 1893 showed no significant evidence of a swing towards the Progressive party; and this in its turn raises the interesting, but probably insoluble, question of the extent to which the mass of support for General Joubert can be regarded as support for 'Progressive' views. This may become a little clearer when we examine the 'progressiveness' of Joubert himself.[53]

The two Volksraads met, for the new session, on 1 May 1893, and as if to confirm the unsensational result of the Raad elections, chose as their respective chairmen two strong conservatives, F. G. H. Wolmarans for the First Raad (by 15 votes to Schalk Burger's 5 and Lukas Meyer's 1) and J. J. Burger for the Second Raad by an equally overwhelming majority.[54] Similarly General N. J. Smit and J. M. A. Wolmarans were re-elected by the First Raad to the two vacant places in the Executive Council, Smit receiving 17 votes and Wolmarans 15, as against Schalk Burger's 5 and Lukas Meyer's 2.[55] This, again, hardly looks like a Progressive renaissance.

The first few days were spent on the usual haggling over the legality or otherwise of the election of various individual candidates,[56] an

---

[51] See below, p. 245.   [52] See below, p. 245.

[53] See below, pp. 246–74.

[54] *Notulen*, Eerste Volksraad, 1893, art. 10; *Notulen*, Tweede Volksraad, 1893, art. 5; *Volksstem*, 2 May 1893; *Land en Volk*, 4 May 1893.

[55] *Notulen*, Eerste Volksraad, 1893, art. 35; *Press*, 2 May 1893; *Volksstem*, 6 May 1893.

[56] *Notulen*, Eerste Volksraad, 1893, arts. 26–30, 41–2; *Volksstem*, 3 May 1893; *Land en Volk*, 4 May 1893.

all-too-familiar process which led the *Volksstem* (6 May 1893) to admit that 'defects do exist in our electoral system' and to refer with pained resignation to 'the wholesale accusations against Landdrosts, Veld-cornets, candidates etc.' On 4 May, however, the First Raad was at last able to turn its attention to the burning question of the legality of President Kruger's re-election. Dr. Leyds reported that, in the scrutiny, 233 votes in favour of Kruger had been disqualified, and 265 in favour of Joubert, leaving the final result at 7,884 votes [*sic*] for Kruger, 7,009 for Joubert and 81 for Kotzé.[57] On 5 May the official protest from the Joubert Committee, supported by a personal letter of protest from Joubert, and a further letter of protest by Esselen, were taken note of by the First Raad.[58] Joubert, in his letter,[59] declared that he could not accept the decision of the Executive Council and fully supported his Committee's protest. Esselen's letter alleged numerous irregularities, and requested an inquiry by a commission to be formed of equal numbers from both parties, not members of the Raads or of the Executive, and with the right to choose an arbitrator, or, if they disagreed on this, to have an arbitrator chosen by the full High Court. The protest itself, the gist of which has already been given, consisted of a detailed series of some ten allegations of electoral illegalities,[60] declared the refusal of the Joubert party to recognize Kruger as duly elected, and made the same demands as Esselen's letter for a bipartisan commission of inquiry and High Court arbitration. Kruger himself favoured the idea of a commission of inquiry, declaring that he had no desire to hold supreme office in the State while any doubt existed of the legality of his election.

'I hope', he declared,[61] 'that the Committee will show no favour or bias towards myself, and that right and justice will sway them in their decisions. You will please institute a thorough and searching investigation upon each point in the matter. . . . I ask for a fair field and no favour.'

[57] *Notulen*, Eerste Volksraad, 1893, art. 45; *Press*, 5 May 1893; *Volksstem*, 6 May 1893.

[58] *Notulen*, Eerste Volksraad, 1893, art. 45, no. 52; *Press*, 6 May 1893; *Volksstem*, 6 May 1893.

[59] *Notulen*, Eerste Volksraad, 1893, art. 53.

[60] *Press*, 24 Apr. 1893, gives the Joubert Committee protest in full. (See also *Volksstem*, 28 Mar. 1893; *Land en Volk*, 20 Apr. 1893; and *Notulen*, Eerste Volksraad, 1893, art. 53.)

[61] *Press*, 6 May 1893; *Notulen*, Eerste Volksraad, 1893, art. 52.

He then left the Raad,[62] which, after a very short debate, rejected the Joubert Committee's proposal to choose a commission of inquiry from outside the Raad, turned down a motion by Schalk Burger and J. du P. de Beer 'to investigate all documents in connexion with the Presidential election', and adopted instead, by the narrow majority of 13 votes to 11, a motion of J. J. Spies and J. C. Fourie 'to investigate all submitted documents'.[63] Thus the foundation was laid for the extremely rapid, and inevitably somewhat shallow, inquiry into the election. The Raad then proceeded to choose a commission of inquiry, and elected—I quote from the *Press* of 6 May 1893—

'A. D. Wolmarans (Krugerite) 23, F. G. Wolmarans (Krugerite) 23, J. A. Lombaard (Krugerite) 18, Lucas Meyer (Jouberite) 23, L. de Jager (Jouberite) 23, S. W. Burger (Jouberite) 23'.

This was the Commission which, in the phrase of the *Press* of 18 March 1893, was to 'rescrutinise the scrutinised scrutiny'; but its examination, alas, was nowhere near as thorough as that phrase might suggest. Nor, in the light of the narrowly passed Volksraad resolution to investigate 'all submitted documents' rather than 'all documents', could it be.

It is clear that the Commission regarded speed as the essence of its task. One of its first actions was to reject a request of the Joubert Committee for a prolongation of the time for the handing in of evidence.[64] Within three days of its appointment[65] the Commission's report on this highly intricate matter was ready for presentation to the Volksraad. No doubt this haste was due to a strong desire to end the suspense in which the country was held, and to what the *Volksstem* of 9 May 1893 called 'the critical nature of the last few days'; but it was certainly not conducive to thorough investigation.

The report on the election,[66] carried, after Schalk Burger's defection to the Kruger side, by 4 votes to 2,[67] was submitted to the First

[62] *Volksstem*, 6 May 1893.

[63] *Notulen*, Eerste Volksraad, 1893, art. 55 (*Press*, 6 May 1893; *Volksstem* 6 May 1893).

[64] *Land en Volk*, 25 May 1893 (letter of 6 May 1893 from Commission of Enquiry into the 1893 election, to the Joubert Committee).

[65] The Report is dated 8 May 1893 (*Land en Volk*, 18 May 1893).

[66] The report is given in full in *Land en Volk*, 18 May 1893, and also in *Notulen* Eerste Volksraad, 1893, art. 69.

[67] See below, pp. 225–8.

Raad on 9 May. It declared the election of Kruger to be legal; 27 further votes for Kruger had been discarded, leaving the totals as, Kruger 7,854,[68] Joubert 7,009 and Kotzé 81.

'All irregularities had been carefully gone into', the Commission declared, 'but the Commission had decided that the decision must be given in favour of Mr. Kruger, with a majority of 745 votes.'

The report then proceeded to a rapid examination of the alleged irregularities. The gist of its findings was as follows:

(*a*) Points 1, 2 and 3 of the Joubert Committee's protest had alleged that the votes had been counted by landdrosts and mining commissioners in a number of areas, instead of being sent direct to Pretoria.

The Commission found that all the officials involved had received special instructions from the Executive Council to count the votes, and that this was therefore not in conflict with the law, in that article 10 of Law 13 of 1891 empowered the Executive to instruct landdrosts to act in this way, and in that 'mining commissioners have always acted as returning officers in the districts, and fulfil, in these cases, the functions of the landdrost'.

(*b*) Point 4 of the Joubert Committee's protest had alleged that hundreds of illegal votes had been accepted by polling officers.

The Commission found that all votes in this category (with the exception of 16 whose names had been wrongly included on the voting lists, but had not been objected to, and who were therefore entitled to vote) had been adjudged illegal by the Executive Council.

(*c*) Point 5 of the Joubert protest had referred to defective electoral lists.

The Commission declared that 'no evidence had been furnished in support of the protests in this connexion'.

(*d*) Point 6 had alleged voting by lunatics and disfranchised criminals.

The Commission found that all these votes had been adjudged illegal by the Executive Council 'in so far as they were aware of them'.

(*e*) Points 7 and 8 alleged that votes had been cast by children under 16; and that votes had been collected at the houses of certain

---

[68] This does not tally completely with the figure of 7,884 given by Leyds, to the Raad (see above, p. 218) but it does with the figure of 7,881 officially announced on 14–15 Apr. (see above, p. 213).

people who had not appeared at the polling station.

The Commission found the first allegation to involve three persons, of whom it had 'no relevant information'; and the second to involve seven persons, of whom six had been prevented by illness from polling in person, while 'the allegation against the seventh was strongly denied'.

(*f*) Point 9 of the Joubert Protest had alleged that several veld-cornets' lists had been made up only after the election.

The Commission found that 'the possibility exists that lists were amended by the veld-cornets of various districts after the election', but that such lists had not been accepted by the landdrost of the district concerned as valid. This finding was based upon an affidavit submitted by the official in question.

(*g*) Point 10 made detailed allegations of various instances in which illegal votes had been allowed, and legal votes refused.

(i) Thirty-six burghers were alleged to have voted at Johannesburg and again at Florida.

The Commission found the number involved to have been thirty-eight, and the votes which they had registered at Florida to have been adjudged illegal.

(ii) It was alleged that numbers of voters had voted in wards other than those in which they resided.

The Commission quoted the opinion of the State Attorney (Dr. Krause) that this was not contrary to law.

(iii) Twelve votes by enfranchised burghers on the veld-cornet's list at Gatsrand had, it was declared, been disallowed by the Landdrost of Potchefstroom.

The Commission declared that 'no evidence of this had been laid before the Commission'.

(iv) The Landdrost of Potchefstroom was alleged to have allowed votes by burghers whose names were not on the veld-cornets' lists, and to have inserted these names subsequently.

The landdrost in question, in a telegram, declared that he had received such lists from veld-cornets; but that he had not allowed them as valid.

(v) 180 votes of ex-burghers who had left for Damaraland in 1875, and only returned many years after, were alleged to have been wrongly allowed.

The Commission declared that 'no proofs of this had been submitted'.

(vi) 400 votes of ex-burghers who had had their names removed from the veld-cornets' lists for the purpose of going to Mossamedes were alleged to have been wrongly allowed.

The Commission declared that 'no proofs of this had been submitted'.

(vii) Finally, the Joubert Committee's protest alleged that a number of polling officers had not signed, or taken, the required oath.

The Commission's finding on this point was that 'it appears to your Commission that all returning officers were properly sworn in according to law'.

It is difficult not to feel some sympathy for Carl Jeppe's remark in the subsequent debate on this report[69] that he found it difficult to understand how matters of such complexity and magnitude 'could have been completed in a couple of hours'.[70] Even if we agree that Jeppe was possibly exaggerating (and he may, in fact, not have been), the report of the Commission of Enquiry gives every evidence of the utmost haste. A court of law would not have decided a dispute about the possession of a stray donkey—let alone the legality of the most crucial presidential election in the history of the Transvaal—in this cavalier fashion.

It will be seen that on no less than six points, (*c*), (*d*), (*e*), (*g*)(iii), (*g*)(v), and (*g*)(vi), involving between them many hundreds of votes, the Commission was prepared to vouch for the legality of such actions as had been complained of, on largely unsupported evidence, or to reject important allegations because 'no evidence of this had been laid before the Commission'. On two further points, (*f*) and (*g*)(iv), they were content to accept denials of alleged malpractices by affidavit or telegram, without cross-examination or further questioning. No witnesses of any kind were called at any stage. Such blatant omissions must lead us to regard the Report as evidence, chiefly, of the desire of the majority of the Commission's members to settle the question of the election with all speed, rather than as evidence of the legality or otherwise of the election of President Kruger. As a letter to *Land en Volk* of 20 April 1893, by an anonymous correspondent called 'Opmerker', very rightly stressed—and

---

[69] *Notulen*, Eerste Volksraad, 1893, arts. 71–5 (*Land en Volk*, 18 May 1893; *Press*, 10 May 1893).
[70] *Notulen*, Eerste Volksraad, 1893, art. 73.

though his remarks apply to the scrutiny by the Executive Council, they are just as true of the Commission of Enquiry—

'It is impossible for the Executive Council to examine the allegations with any real thoroughness. To take one small example, the allegations of voting by those under sixteen years of age. Who is to know that hundreds of them did not vote? How can these be checked by the Executive Council? The only real check would be a series of local committees in districts and wards which will go into matters in thorough detail.'

It is not surprising, therefore, that the two Progressive members of the Volksraad Commission, Lukas Meyer and Lodewyk de Jager, refused to accept the majority finding, and insisted on submitting minority reports. These demanded 'a thorough investigation into every allegation in detail'; declared their opinion that the election ought to have taken place under Law 4 of 1871 (which insisted that the list of votes cast be sent by landdrost or other electoral officers direct to the Executive Council) and not under Law 13 of 1891 (which empowered the landdrosts to check the votes cast); and ended by asserting that the election was illegal, and that a fresh election should be held, 'by which all parties can be satisfied'.[71]

On 9 May the Commission's report was laid before the First Raad[72] by its Chairman, Schalk Burger. Lukas Meyer and Lodewyk de Jager stressed, in debate, their contention that it had been impossible for the Commission to pronounce on the legality of the election in the absence of a thorough investigation. The main clash in the Raad centred on the question of whether the election should have been conducted in accordance with Law 4 of 1871 or Law 13 of 1891. Kruger strongly defended the latter thesis, and stressed that the last article of Law 13 of 1891 'specifically repealed all laws and regulations in conflict with it'. Carl Jeppe, however, supported Lukas Meyer in asserting 'that a special law could not be altered by a general law'.[73] Schalk Burger took his stand on the somewhat more questionable proposition that even Law 4 of 1871 laid down that elections took place 'through the landdrosts authorized thereto by

[71] Appendices I and II to the Report.

[72] *Notulen*, Eerste Volksraad, 1893, art. 69 (*Land en Volk*, 11 May 1893; *Press*, 10 May 1893).

[73] A view strongly supported by Advocate Wessels, a leading (Progressive) lawyer, in a closely reasoned article on the election in *Land en Volk* of 20 July 1893.

the Executive Council' (na kennisgeving aan de Landdrosten, door den Uitvoerende Raad daartoe belast). 'If elections took place, as it were, through the landdrosts,' he asked, 'why should not the results also be forwarded through them?' This is not a very strong argument, as the fact that the landdrosts were authorized to declare a state of election can hardly be regarded as automatically qualifying them to check and count the votes. More impressively, he pointed out that Law 13 of 1891 had been passed for the specific purpose of clarifying the laws regulating elections, because of the unsatisfactory nature of Law 4 of 1871. He declared 'his profound conviction that the election had occurred according to law'. Lukas Meyer reiterated his regret that the Commission had been precluded from calling in judicial opinion. 'The election was', he emphatically asserted, 'illegal.' Jeppe's insistence that judicial opinion should have been called in was strongly attacked by the Chairman, F. G. Wolmarans, who declared that

'he saw it coming! Such members as Johannesburg's representative [i.e. Jeppe] were seeking to drive in the thin end of the wedge by which the Volksraad would be made subservient to the High Court.'

Debate raged backwards and forwards over these points, and on 10 May the Raad adopted the Commission's report by 18 votes to 3 (Lukas Meyer, Lodewyk de Jager and Gert de Jager voting in the minority. Jeppe was temporarily absent);[74] and, immediately after this, passed a motion, by 18 votes to 6, declaring Kruger to be the legally elected President of the Republic.[75] One cannot help feeling that Advocate Wessels's pronouncement on the legality of this decision (*Land en Volk*, 20 July 1893) that 'the Volksraad can only decide who was chosen if it constitutes itself as a court; otherwise the Volksraad might as well choose the President directly itself', is not entirely inapposite.

Nothing that I have said up to this point must be construed as suggesting that Kruger did not, in fact, get the majority of the votes in 1893. All that can be said is that the Commission of Enquiry set up by the Volksraad provided the last opportunity for finding out the full truth. That it failed to take this opportunity is obvious. But

[74] *Notulen*, Eerste Volksraad, 1893, arts. 74–5.

[75] *Notulen*, Eerste Volksraad, 1893, art. 75 (Lukas Meyer, R. K. Loveday, Paul Maré and Jeppe asked for their minority vote to be recorded).

we cannot, because the Volksraad clearly wished the Commission to avoid a full inquiry, jump to the conclusion that a thorough and detailed inquiry such as the Joubert party desired would inevitably have shown Joubert to have had a majority of the votes. The answer is that we shall probably never know.

On the whole, it is hard to disagree with the opinion of the *Volksstem* (22 April 1893) on the Progressive demand for a new election and on the whole question of the Transvaal's clumsy electoral machinery.

'What guarantee is there', it asked, 'that it [another election] would be any better? We have already indicated that our electoral system is wholly unsatisfactory. In many places the registration of enfranchised burghers was defective or inaccurate [gebrekkig of onjuist]; in others the officials have shown themselves incompetent to carry out the provisions of the law; in yet other instances the law itself is so ambiguous that one could ride around in it with cart and horses.

'In short the existing organization was not designed to cater for such a sharp election struggle as that which has just been thrust upon it by the Kruger and Joubert parties.

'Is there any point in forcing our creaking and sighing electoral machinery into action once again? ... Moreover, we doubt whether any large number of the burghers is desirous of another election. Mistakes [*sic*] may have been made by both factions; but one is convinced that they were not so weighty and numerous as to have tipped the election scale in the wrong direction.

'That [irregularities] occurred is possible, when one takes into account the slapdash manner in which the matter was sometimes dealt with [de slordige manier waarop soms te werk is gegaan]. But it is difficult to accept that only the Joubert party suffered. There is no one who dares swear that the Joubert people were invariably honest and legal, and the Kruger people on the other hand shockingly dishonest and illegal.'

This is a devastating condemnation of the Republic's electoral arrangements; but it is probably as fair a summing up of the essential position as we are likely to find.

One point remains for us to consider—the question of Schalk Burger's defection to the Kruger side. Before embarking upon this, it must be pointed out that it is a matter of purely academic interest.

It has already been shown that the 1893 Volksraad elections give no evidence of a swing towards the Progressives. In the final event it would have been the First Volksraad which would have decided on the legality of Kruger's election; and the overwhelming majorities for the old president (18 votes to 3 on the Report, and 18 votes to 6 for his swearing in) leave no doubt what their decision would have been. But it is interesting to speculate on what the motives for Schalk Burger's defection—for defection it certainly was—might have been.

There can be no doubt that the Joubert party had accepted the idea of a six-member Volksraad Commission on the understanding that they would have three members. General Joubert himself makes this clear in a letter of 8 May 1893 (*Land en Volk*, 18 May 1893) to Esselen.

'I was approached', he writes, 'by Mr. J. M. A. Wolmarans, Member of the Executive Council, who spoke to me with great earnestness about the position. I must do what I could to avoid a clash which might lead to great disaster [onheil] for land and people. On his request I agreed to meet Wolmarans and Vice-President Smit [together] to see if we could find a way to avoid such disaster. They asked me if I would agree to a Committee of the Volksraad consisting of three of the Joubert and three of the Kruger party. They assured me that such a Committee would be instructed to investigate the matter root and branch [om de zaak van den wortel tot den tak te onderzoeken]. I asked if it could call in jurists. N. Smit answered, "Yes, one jurist for each side". Wolmarans agreed, and talked of two jurists on each side. As for my attitude to the result; I must abide by what the Volksraad decides. I will not oppose such a decision in the slightest, or do anything unconstitutional.'

Further, there can be little doubt that the Joubert party looked upon Schalk Burger as one of themselves, which is hardly surprising in the light of the fact that, even after his defection, he claimed to be a Joubert supporter.

'He had been, and he still was of the opinion', he declared in an interview after the swearing-in of President Kruger, 'that General Joubert would be a better president than Mr. Kruger. . . . He had suffered personally in defending the General. The great majority of his family were on the side of Mr. Kruger, and it was easy to understand that unpleasantnesses had arisen in these circumstances. Notwithstanding this he remained true to his opinion.'

He went on to declare, however, that

'he had never said the election was illegal, or ever denied the legal majority of Mr. Kruger'. Reminded by the reporter of *Land en Volk* that 'the public had been under the impression that he identified himself wholly with the protest and would stand fast with the other Joubert members in demanding a thorough investigation; and that when he had placed himself on the side of the Kruger members the public had reason to believe that he had altered his opinions— honestly or dishonestly as the case may be', Mr. Burger answered 'that the public had been under a false impression then. He had come there as a member of the Raad to do his duty, not to defend protests, and had never contested the legality of the election. As they knew he had never been concerned with any Committee or Congress, and had opposed that body from the start' (*Land en Volk*, 18 May 1893).

This is a very admirable stand, and might even have been a defensible one, had the other five members of the Commission been equally noble in their sentiments. But, since the whole idea of the Commission had been that it would consist of equal numbers from each party, Schalk Burger's attitude becomes more questionable. As *Land en Volk* put it (in the same issue):

'We have weighed [Mr. Burger's] statement carefully, and find it completely unacceptable. . . . The Joubert party accepted the plan suggested by the Executive Council because they were under the firm impression that they would have three members on the Commission. This Mr. Burger must have been aware of.'

Can there have been any connexion between Burger's change of front and the appearance of a, perhaps inspired, article in the *Volksstem* of 6 May which prophesied that:

'Mr. Burger, who got five votes in the Volksraad (in the elections to the Executive Council), will probably soon enjoy a well-deserved share in the government of the country, perhaps at the next vacancy, perhaps by the enlargement of the number of Executive Council members?'

There was much to be said, in a divided Volksraad in which there was no caucus system[76] and in which the Executive Council could include members of the 'opposition' such as Joubert himself, for making a bid for influence by the 'balance of power' tactics that Schalk Burger used. His election to the chairmanship of the Volksraad in 1895, and his subsequent elevation to the Executive Council in 1896 after the death of General Smit, show that, in the words of the *Volksstem* (25 August 1894) he

'did not have cause to regret [the fact that] despite his false friends, he gave his vote to the winning party [when] during the recent election struggle he had to decide as Commission member on the appointment of President Kruger'.

Such an interpretation, unproved though it is, perhaps partly explains Schalk Burger's swing to the Kruger side; but it does not necessarily confirm *Land en Volk*'s nasty suspicion when it declared (18 May 1893):

'the main circumstance to consider is that Mr. Burger was chosen as Chairman of the Commission. . . . The question arises; would the three Kruger members have voted for him in the first place if they had not known previously that they could rely on him?'

---

[76] The detailed statements of the fluctuating votes of the various members of both Volksraads which have been given in this book, make it clear that neither government nor Progressives worked on the caucus system, and that when Jeppe was referred to as the Progressive 'whip' (*Volksstem*, 27 May 1895; below, p. 239) this was a mere courtesy title. See remarks on pp. 230-1 and diagrams on pp. 232 and 239.

8

The Growth of the Progressive Party after 1893

KRUGER was duly sworn in as President on 10 May 1893. But the enormous vote for Joubert was clear evidence of the waning popularity of the President, and a great encouragement to the Progressive party. 'Now our real work begins!' declared *Land en Volk* (11 May 1893). F. J. Dormer, one-time editor of the *Cape Argus* and the Johannesburg *Star*, declares:[1]

'the Progressive party, both within the pale of the Constitution and without, became a great and growing force. It was never so strong as in the years immediately succeeding the fraudulent re-election of Mr. Kruger in 1892 [*sic*].'

It is this period that we must briefly sum up, as we have already done with the three and a half years that preceded it.

We have seen, in chapter II, the issues around which opposition to the government gathered. As the Republic's prosperity boomed, opposition to the government's financial policy became less and less emphatic. But on concessions and monopolies the opposite was true, and the government was forced to moderate its stance considerably. And here the credit must go to the Progressive group, under Esselen's leadership, in the Second Raad. The same pattern was shown in the steady growth of opposition to the dynamite monopoly and the government's railway policy.

The temporary drawing together of the parties, in 1894, in the face of Rhodes's intrigues, was of short duration, and the keynote of the newly formed 'Volksmacht' (the 'working committee of the Progressive movement' according to the *Volksstem*) became the demand for the expropriation of the Netherlands South African Railway Company's property.

In the Second Raad the issue of governmental corruption and maladministration played an increasingly important part after 1893; and the unsavoury state of affairs revealed by the 'Stands Scandal',

[1] Dormer, p. 10.

229

and the persistent efforts of the President and his supporters to whitewash the Department of Mines and to defend the right of officials to speculate, led to increasing support for the Progressives by what we should today call the 'floating vote', culminating in the motion condemning the Minister of Mines by 15 votes to 9. On this issue the Progressives did the State a signal service in rallying opposition not only inside the Volksraads, but in the press and among the public, and, by so doing, did much to achieve the cleaner and better administration to which the Industrial Commission's Report of 1897 refers.

The education and language issue was another in which the Progressives took the lead in asking, both for the sake of the uitlanders and that of the burghers' own children, for a more understanding and flexible approach, and they did much to achieve an eventual First Raad majority in favour of a more tolerant policy.

On the franchise question emotions were more inflamed, and it was harder (though correspondingly more necessary) for a Transvaal patriot to take a truly imaginative and liberal line. Yet, even here, we have seen the Progressive vote swell from a mere two in 1893 to ten in 1895.

From the detailed tracing in the preceding chapters of the issues around which opposition to President Kruger's policies crystallized, and from the attempt to draw together the threads and show how various personalities gradually came to form a group in common opposition to the government's policy on these issues between 1890 and 1895—to form what both its supporters and opponents referred to as the Progressive party—a fairly clear picture should have emerged of who these people were and what they stood for.

It is clear that they were a small group at first, in both Volksraads. In the First Raad they grew from a group of some 5 or 6 between 1890 and 1892 to between 10 and 11 in 1895.

From 1890 to 1892 the main Progressive group in the First Volksraad may be regarded as consisting of R. K. Loveday, Lukas Meyer (after 1891), Lodewijk de Jager, Paul Maré, Schalk Burger and J. J. Spies, with the occasional support of C. Birkenstock and J. du P. de Beer.

By 1893 their ranks were swelled by the election to the First Raad of Gert de Jager, Carl Jeppe and J. H. (Koos) de la Rey—giving the Progressives nine members out of 24. In addition they had the occasional support of Birkenstock, De Beer, C. B. Otto and J. de

Clercq. There was, immediately after the election results became known, some tendency to overestimate the strength of the Progressives, for no one could ever be sure how a particular member would vote on any issue. Thus the *Press*, for example, in a leader of 14 March 1893 on 'The Coming Volksraad session', writes:

'President Kruger will find a strong and able opposition in the new Volksraad, who will urge their claims without the least diffidence, and without much regard for the feelings of the Transvaal's Grand Old Man. He will no longer be supreme in the Raad and able to override all opposition with impunity, with placidity, and even with amusement. . . . Whether the opposition will succeed in putting enough starch into General Joubert to make him stand stiffly to the programme issued by his supporters during the election remains to be seen.'

This was a shrewd and discerning article, but it erred (for a pro-government newspaper) on the pessimistic side, just as *Land en Volk*, writing from the opposite point of view, exaggerated when it declared on 13 September, in a review of the 1893 session, that:

'Our hope was that Kruger, knowing that he had lost the people's trust, that he was unjustly in his position and that the whole election was dishonest, would act with caution.

'But he has behaved in a more gross and scandalous [grove en schandelijke] way than before, and has lorded it [baasgespeeld] over the Volksraad representatives more than ever. But thank God we have some honest and upright Afrikaners who will withstand Kruger and his Jews—such men as Lukas Meyer, Gert and Lodewyk de Jager, Commandant de la Rey, Otto, Loveday and Jeppe.'

The truth was between these extremes. Esselen, in a speech at Krugersdorp towards the end of 1893, was closer to reality when he spoke of 'the President and his majority of 13 in the Volksraad'.[2] For, taking into account what we have called the 'floating vote', the government, on any issue of confidence, could rely on a minimum of 13 votes, whereas the opposition was able to rely on a reasonably hard core of 8 with a possible further 3. Diagrammatically, the position of the parties in the 1893 First Volksraad could be shown

[2] *Land en Volk*, 14 Dec. 1893.

as follows, the arrows indicating the direction in which the member concerned was likely to go at a pinch.[3]

Government	Floating Vote		Progressives
A. D. W. Wolmarans	← J. de Clercq		R. K. Loveday
F. G. H. Wolmarans	← J. du P. de Beer		L. Meyer
P. G. Roos	← C. B. Otto		G. de Jager
J. M. Malan	S. W. Burger	→	L. de Jager
J. P. L. Lombaard	J. H. Labuschagne	→	P. Maré
C. J. Tosen	C. J. A. Birkenstock	→	C. Jeppe
J. C. Fourie			J. H. de la Rey*
P. J. Schutte			J. J. Spies
N. M. S. Prinsloo			
P. de la Rey			*Replaced E. C. Hamman on 29 Aug. 1893.

Total: 10   ← 3   3 →   8   =24

Clearly, in the light of these figures, it was hardly possible for Kruger, in the words of *Land en Volk*, to 'lord it over the Volksraad representatives'. It was necessary for him to proceed with caution, and considerable evidence has been adduced to show that he did indeed find himself compelled to do so—particularly in the debates on concessions and monopolies, dynamite policy and railway matters.

Nor, to take a more minor point, is it possible to agree with *Land en Volk* in including C. B. Otto among the 'honest and upright Afrikaners who will withstand Kruger', as a glance at his voting record will show.[4]

Nevertheless, though Kruger was obliged to move with some caution, the review of the 1893 session by *Land en Volk* quoted above is basically correct in its suggestion that, in spite of the near-defeat of the régime at the beginning of the year, 1893 saw little in the way of really important liberal reforms. All that the *Press*, in a review of the 1893 session on 30 August, could find to say in the government's defence was that 'although [its policies] had been

---

[3] Based upon the information on the way members voted, to be found in the *Volksstem*, *Press*, and *Land en Volk* reports of the debates of the 1893 session; and on the very shrewd analysis of the proclivities of each member contained in the character sketches of each by the *Volksstem* of 15 Aug., 18 Aug., 25 Aug. and 1 Sept. 1894. See also the chart of opposition votes, p. 245, below.

[4] Below, p. 245. See also the *Volksstem's* remarks quoted on p. 216 above.

referred to by some as more retrogressive than ever [they] have been most progressive with reference to railways. . . . With these . . . the Volksraad may well rest content for some time to come . . .'; while the *Volksstem*, in reviewing on 12 September 1893 what it called 'one of the longest legislative sessions in our history'[5] and one which 'clearly marked the entry of the Republic into a new epoch of its development', declared:

'A healthy critical spirit was, in general, shown. . . . A number of vital matters have been accomplished, among others the approval of railway extensions, the new regulations for the dynamite monopoly and the changes in the education law. . . . Members of the Raad are not perfect, but they have shown a strong sense of duty throughout.'

While agreeing with *Land en Volk* on the paucity of the Raad's accomplishments in this session—for railway policy marked the only significant advance, and the modifications of dynamite and educational policies went a very small way indeed towards meeting Progressive objections—I think it is fair to support the *Volksstem*'s remarks on the 'healthy critical spirit' shown by the Raad. In this respect the improvement in the whole tone of the Raad's approach towards the problems of the day was remarkable in comparison with that which had prevailed in 1890–1; and for this improvement the Progressive opposition must take a good deal—though not all— of the credit. Not all, because some of it at least must go to the pro-government press, which as we have seen in the earlier sections of this book, was often intensely critical of the defects of the government and Volksraad, and made no attempt to evade publication of scandals and corruption which would reflect badly on both.

The year 1894 saw little change in the tone of affairs, for the election of half the members of the Volksraad occurred only every two years. Thus the membership of the Raad did not alter. If there was any change it showed itself, perhaps, in a slight drift towards the right by J. J. Spies, whose name now rarely occurs in the list of those voting on the Progressive side, and in a similar tendency by Schalk Burger.[6] Nevertheless, as in 1893, the Progressive side continued to rally between 10 and 11 votes on most important motions.

Outside the Raad, however, 1894 was remarkable for an intense but short-lived attempt at a rapprochement (toenadering) between

[5] A fraction over four months.
[6] Below, p. 245.

the Progressive and Conservative groups. As early as September 1893 the *Press*, markedly more sympathetic to the Progressives after Kruger had been safely ensconced in the presidential seat than it had been before that time, had noted with approval[7] the new policy of the uitlander 'National Union' to do active political work among the Boer population by 'appointing agents in every part of the State and influencing every election to the best of its ability', though it warned the 'National Union' against any attempt at representing President Kruger as the enemy of progress.

'The Boers, whether contents or non-contents [*sic*], would', it declared, 'almost unanimously resent any interference on the part of the Uitlanders with the Government of the country.

'They would sympathise with a grievance well put, but would certainly refuse to ally themselves with the newcomers in any attempt to "clip the wings" of President Kruger, even though they might privately consider such clipping desirable' (*Press*, 26 October 1893).

On the Boer political front this increased uitlander pressure, the growing sympathy of views between the Progressive Boers and the uitlander 'National Union',[8] and, above all, Rhodes's 'increasing power and arrogance',[9] provided the impetus for an interesting attempt by Kruger to steal, or at any rate, quieten, some of the thunder of the opposition by appointing Ewald Esselen, the chief organizer of the 1893 election campaign against him, as State Attorney.[10] Although a fiery critic of the government, and one whose defeat at Potchefstroom had been hailed by the Vice-President, General N. J. Smit, as 'a distinct blessing on the land',[11] his qualities as an Afrikaner patriot had not gone unrecognized.[12] The *Press*, though it gave little for his election chances at Potchefstroom, had summed Esselen up (on 27 January 1893) as:

'One of the few who is both intimately acquainted with the feelings, prejudices, aspirations and peculiarities of the burghers, yet in the

[7] *Press*, 26 Sept. 1893, 26 Oct. 1893.
[8] Marais, p. 58.   [9] Marais, p. 58.
[10] Marais, pp. 57–9; *Volksstem*, 1 May 1894; *Land en Volk*, 3 May 1894. See also *Press*, 14 Nov. 1894, for a description by Esselen of how his appointment came about.
[11] *Press*, 10 Feb. 1893.
[12] See *Volksstem*, 13 Sept. 1892, 8 Nov. 1892; *Press*, 27 Jan. 1893.

fullest touch with the aspirations of the Uitlanders . . . one of the few who enjoys the confidence of both the new and the old population, can speak eloquently in both Dutch and English, and can mix on confidential terms with the leaders of the two great races who are destined sooner or later to rule this country together in harmony.'

It was a wise choice, and a move that was clearly designed to help bridge the growing gulf between the Boer parties. Later, when it had obviously failed to do this, the *Volksstem* wrote (17 October 1894):

'His [Esselen's] appointment was regarded as doubly satisfying because (*a*) it brought a competent person to the head of a department which had been pitifully neglected, and (*b*) because it would work towards a bringing together [toenadering] of the burghers.

'But it has been a double disappointment. The organs which supported Esselen maintain their hostile attitude towards the President, the State Secretary and the Executive Committee. Louder than ever they cry, "away with Dr. Leyds! Away with the Volksraad!" . . . Esselen has the right to desire to be State Secretary or even State President one day. But the burghers have the right to demand this of him—that he be a good State Attorney. The work of the State Attorney's department is still anything but exemplary. The Constitution is about to be revised. New penal laws are called for. Let him concentrate on these, and not give the impression that he is using his office merely as a stepping-stone to higher things.'

Leaving aside the not particularly justified[13] criticism of Esselen's ability as State Attorney (which the *Volksstem* on 15 May 1895 itself contradicted by calling on the government to 'clearly show its confidence in one of its most able officials') this provides interesting evidence of the motives which had led to this appointment.

However, the honeymoon was not destined to last. The refusal to confirm the appointment of Andrew Trimble (chosen by Esselen to command the special force of detectives, financed jointly by the government and Chamber of Mines, which had been set up in 1894 to check gold and gold-amalgam thefts from the mines[14]) was regarded by Esselen as an issue of confidence[15]—as indeed it was meant to be by the extreme Conservative group, who had never

[13] See *Press*, 10 May 1894, 10 Oct. 1894; *Volksstem*, 16 Nov. 1895.
[14] Marais, pp. 58–9.
[15] *Weekly Press*, 2 Nov. 1895, p. 7; Fitzpatrick, pp. 78–9.

fully approved of Esselen's appointment. Of this affair the *Volksstem* wrote (on 16 November 1895):

'A certain clique, alas, has been opposed to him from the start. They have not been able to forgive him his full-blooded progressive views—though his readiness to put his talents at the government's disposal should have shown them his inclination to co-operation. By doing so they have neutralised his influence. And soon enough a stick was found to beat him with—in the Trimble case. . . . Esselen hoped to do great things in the Detective Department with Trimble, and as it were stood or fell by him. Every influence was brought to bear to prejudice Trimble in the government's eyes by Esselen's enemies, and in a moment of weakness the President gave these people his word not to appoint this non-naturalized Englishman. This is a crisis which should never have occurred. . . . To err is human, and the government should admit its error.'

1894 also saw, simultaneously with Esselen's appointment, the attempted rapprochement between the Progressive 'Volksvereeniging', formed late in 1893,[16] and the Conservative 'Burgermacht', formed in April 1894[17] in opposition to it. The opposed aims of these two organizations, and the failure of their attempt at finding a *modus vivendi*, have been described in some detail; but this failure demonstrated the deepening division between the parties.

The failure, however, was not for want of trying. Both sides realized the critical nature of the situation in which they were involved. As Esselen put it to a congress of delegates from both parties held in Pretoria in November 1894 in a final attempt to find common ground: 'The parties should come together and make the Volk a strong and safe one';[18] and the *Press* in a leader of 15 November 1894 referred to the congress of the two parties as:

'the outcome of the increasing strength and influence of the Uitlanders, and the increasing division among the Boers. Consciousness of weakness has prevented many progressive Boers from advocating concessions to the Uitlanders which they feel should justly be made, and also the suspicion that the Uitlander would join first the one party to crush the other, and then desert that party and crush it also.

[16] *Press*, 8 Dec. 1893; *Land en Volk*, 14 Dec. 1893; *Volksstem*, 9 Dec. 1893.
[17] *Volksstem*, 5 May 1894; *Land en Volk*, 10 May 1894.
[18] *Press*, 14 Nov. 1894. See also the circular issued by Esselen and Koos Smit in October 1894 (*Press*, 25 Oct. 1894).

Mr. Esselen, however, saw the danger of shutting out the Uitlander indefinitely, and presumably decided that the sooner the Boers were induced to unite, the sooner would justice be done to the alien.'

But although the delegates agreed on the vital necessity of Boer unity in the face of the dangers with which they were confronted, and got as far as electing a committee consisting of equal numbers of members of the Progressive 'Volksvereeniging' and the Conservative 'Burgermacht', the two sides were unable to come to any agreement, as we have seen, on the fundamental question of the role which the well-disposed uitlander was to be allowed to play both in the proposed new organization itself and in the State; for, whereas the 'Volksvereeniging' members felt that 'the whole aim was the fusion of the good elements of the new population with the old',[19] the Burgermacht delegates 'insisted on excluding all non-burghers'.[20]

The contribution of General Joubert to the occasion was, incidentally, a brief appearance at the Volksvereeniging Congress late in the afternoon, where he declared:

' "that he did not exactly know the object and work of this organisation; but he did not fear any combination of persons or any meeting, and therefore did not object to appear here. The question put to him (whether he would stand again as Commandant-General) was most important; but contrary to the law of the country. . . . The laws of the land did not require from him to answer yes or no. He begged not to be asked today what his wishes and desires were. He would place himself under the direct guidance and influence of God and do His will". Mr. Neethling expressed the thanks of the assembly to the General for what he had said (*sic*) and hoped he would accept the Commandant-Generalship if re-elected (Cheers).'[21]

On this note of failure the political developments of 1894 ended. One can agree with the *Volksstem* of 14 November 1894 that by this stage, if not before it, 'Party lines are at last becoming clearly visible; so that, in the forthcoming elections for half the First Raad, the burghers would, by this point, know, roughly at least, what line

[19] *Volksstem*, 17 Nov. 1894 (report of the 'Fusion' congress).

[20] Ibid. (This definition of non-burghers, incidentally, was specifically explained by Burgermacht delegates as including naturalized burghers. See the *Volksstem* and *Press* reports of delegates' speeches in *Volksstem*, 17 Nov. 1894, and *Press*, 16 Nov. 1894.)

[21] *Press*, 16 Nov. 1894. (*Volksstem*, 21 Nov. 1894, is virtually identical.)

of policy they were committing themselves to when they elected a candidate of acknowledged Progressive inclinations'.

Certainly every effort had been made, to use Fitzpatrick's words, 'to educate Boer opinion to better things, and to bring such influence to bear on the electorate as would result in the return of a better class of men to the Volksraad. Newspapers conducted with this end in view were circulated throughout the country, and when the elections for the Volksraad took place, especially qualified agents were sent to ascertain the feeling of the districts, and to work up an opposition to the existing methods of Government. In every case endeavours were made to select a popular resident within a district of more enlightened views and higher character than his fellows. A good many thousand pounds were contributed and expended for this purpose.'[22]

At first, when the results of the elections became known, it looked as if the Progressive group had at last attained a majority in the First Raad.[23] The defeat of F. G. H. Wolmarans by Schalk Burger (who got 13 votes to Wolmarans's 10) in the Raad's election of its Chairman,[24] a change which 'was greeted with loud jubilation by the Progressive members',[25] seemed to be a further indication that the tide had turned, as did the Raad's decision, by 15 votes to 7, to accept J. L. van Wyk (Progressive) as the legally elected member for Krugersdorp. (Those voting in the minority[26] were the hard core of the Conservative party—A. D. W. Wolmarans, F. G. H. Wolmarans, J. M. Malan, C. J. Tosen, P. J. Schutte, N. M. S. Prinsloo and P. de la Rey.[27])

But it did not take very long before the pattern of the voting demonstrated that startling political changes came neither easily nor rapidly to the South African Republic; and before a month was out the *Volksstem* had summed up the situation in very different terms:

'How many parties are there?' it asked on 27 May 1895. 'To judge from the discussions,[28] at least six or more, or even as many opinions

---

[22] Fitzpatrick, p. 73. See also Marais, p. 59, on this point.

[23] *Volksstem*, 9 Mar. 1895, 13 Mar. 1895.

[24] First Volksraad, 6 May 1895 (*Notulen*, Eerste Volksraad, 1895, art. 7; *Volksstem*, 6 May 1895).

[25] *Land en Volk*, 9 May 1895.   [26] *Land en Volk*, 16 May 1895.

[27] See diagram on p. 232, above (P. G. Roos, J. P. L. Lombaard and J. C. Fourie were not re-elected in 1895—see *Land en Volk*, 4 May 1895).

[28] i.e. in the Volksraad.

as there are members [zooveel hoofden, zooveel zinnen]. The old national party appears best off in this respect, and shows, in most cases, that it knows what it wants.

'One thing is certain, that in spite of the loud hosannahs of the so-called Progressives, that party is not in the least organized, and much water will flow through the Vaal River before the majority of the Raad will follow the leading-strings of Jeppe and Loveday. If Mr. Meyer is, allegedly, the leader of the Progressives, then Jeppe is certainly their whip. But he has the greatest difficulty in keeping them to his path.'

That this estimate was reasonably near the mark is clearly shown by the pattern of votes.[29] The Progressive party had lost its (fairly frequent) supporter J. J. Spies, who was not re-elected after 1894, and had gained J. L. van Wyk, W. H. van Niekerk, and the somewhat doubtful adherence of W. J. Steyn and Commandant D. Joubert. There was, it seems, in spite of the *Volksstem*'s reference to Carl Jeppe as the Progressive party's 'whip', nothing approaching a caucus system; and the tendency of so-called Progressive members to vote on the side of authority when faced with what Fitzpatrick calls[30] 'the President and his party in battle array', appears in the 1895 session to have become stronger rather than weaker. Diagrammatically, the position of the parties after the 1895 election might be shown as follows, the arrows, once again, indicating the direction in which the member concerned was likely to go on some strongly patriotic issue, such as the franchise.

Government	Floating Vote	Progressives
A. D. W. Wolmarans	← J. de Clercq	R. K. Loveday
F. G. H. Wolmarans	← J. du P. de Beer	L. Meyer
J. M. Malan	← C. B. Otto	G. de Jager
C. J. Tosen	← J. H. Labuschagne	L. de Jager
P. J. Schutte	← C. J. A. Birkenstock	P. Maré
N. M. S. Prinsloo	S. W. Burger →	C. Jeppe
P. de la Rey		J. L. van Wyk
J. P. Meyer		W. H. van Niekerk
L. F. Erasmus*		← J. H. de la Rey
(after end of 1895)		← W. J. Steyn
		← D. Joubert

*Defeated the Progressive candidate J. J. Fourie in the vacancy caused by the sudden death of J. W. Joubert (Pretoria).

Total: 9   ← 5   1 → ← 3   8   = 26

[29] See chart on p. 245.   [30] Fitzpatrick, p. 73.

Thus the Progressive party, though somewhat increased in size, was not in a position during 1895 to win a debate on any major issue of confidence, nor did it do so.[31] Nevertheless, it was clearly a growing force; and things had come far, indeed, from the days of 1890 and 1891, when opposition to the government had demanded real stoutness of heart. The government's awareness of the growing tenuousness of its position in the First Raad is suggested by the tone of the *Volksstem*'s references to the importance of the election, in December 1895, to fill the vacancy caused by the death of J. W. Joubert (the newly elected Progressive member for Pretoria,[32] who had died suddenly a few days after his election, in May 1895). Whereas the *Weekly Press* more moderately opined (23 November 1895) that 'the result of the election is looked forward to with great interest, as it is felt that it will practically turn the scales in the Volksraad either in favour of the Conservatives or the opposite party', the *Volksstem* declared (9 November 1895) that this was

'no time for the party of independence to sleep. Many are working in a direction which will bring about our total downfall, who would like to sell our dearly-bought franchise rights to the stranger for a mess of pottage. . . . It is vital that the balance be restored in favour of the Government in the First Volksraad. The Opposition is putting up Josef Fourie, a leader of the hated Volksmacht. It is essential for our party to pick a strong candidate.'

As it turned out, Fourie was defeated by the Conservative candidate, L. F. Erasmus, by 504 votes to 386.[33] However, the fact that so much concern could be felt about the result of one by-election is a measure of the distance that things had come in the course of the six years that we have been surveying; and a justification of the views of such friends of Progressive Afrikanerdom as Francis Dormer, who wrote in an essay of December 1895:[34]

'There are Boers and Boers, and it must not for a moment be supposed that the misgovernment of the rude oligarchs who are grouped around President Kruger at Pretoria commands the undivided support and approval of the burghers on their farms. . . . Changes in the composition of the Volksraad are gradual, and the

---

[31] See chart on p. 245.
[32] He had defeated P. G. Roos in the 1895 election (*Volksstem*, 9 Mar. 1895).
[33] *Volksstem*, 21 Dec. 1895.   [34] Dormer, pp, 193–5.

delay in giving effect to public opinion is almost as great, though not quite, as the law's delays in our own incomparable island. At the present moment the Administration is representative of nothing more than a minority of a minority, and the day cannot be long distant when Boer opinion of the better sort will be able to assert itself in the form of legislative amelioration and administrative change.

'All those who believe with me that this happy issue out of all the Uitlanders' afflictions is near at hand must view with unfeigned alarm and regret every suggestion, however veiled, that a policy of interference, whether direct or through the instrumentality of the Cape or any other agency, should be adopted and avowed by Her Majesty's Government. . . . It would detach from the cause of political equality some of its most ardent champions, while strengthening, on the other hand, President Kruger and his adherents in the foolish determination to persevere in their reactionary policy to the very end.'

But the description of a visit which Dormer—in spite of his breach with Rhodes[35]—paid to him late in 1894 or early in 1895[36] indicates why what Dormer hoped for in the first paragraph was not to be.

' "There is a strong Progressive party in the Raad" , Dormer said to Rhodes, "and if we go the right way about the business, some man of liberal tendencies will become President at the next election. Then we shall get all that is necessary in the way of reforms."

' "But I don't want your reforms, or rather your reformed Republic", was his quick response. "The ideal system is that of a British colony. . . . I also do not like the idea of British subjects becoming burghers, and that is why I prefer that burghers should become British subjects". . . . "Believe me, my dear Rhodes, it would be better to leave Boer Tories and Boer Progressives to fight it out among themselves". . . .

'Rhodes, however, who seems to think far more of giving Kruger a fall than of dealing with these difficulties in the manner of a prudent statesman, will listen to none of this, and he seems to be under

---

[35] Dormer, p. 25. (The breach had occurred, on the question of interference in Transvaal affairs, at the beginning of 1895; but Dormer went to see Rhodes, when in Cape Town, because, as he says, 'long years of association had their force'.)

[36] See essay 'Preparing for the Plunge' (July 1895) in Dormer's book (p. 203 ff.) and 'The parting of the ways' (written in Jan. 1895, pp. 217–20).

the impression that there is an urgency in the matter which I am quite unable to comprehend. . . . Whether he thinks his own time is short, or has had it conveyed to him that a South African Confederation would be an acceptable addition to the glories of the present reign, I must confess myself unable to divine; but the ostensible reason for his great show of interest and activity is that Krugerism is a growing force that cannot be dealt with internally and must be crushed by external agencies, or it will become dangerous to ourselves.

'I, on the other hand, regard it as a declining force that nothing can revivify, or at any rate an ephemeral phenomenon, that nothing can make permanent except interference from without.'

Thus, up to the Jameson Raid, the Progressive party can be looked upon as a small party, but one that was steadily (if slowly, by uitlander standards) growing in numbers and influence. What heights it might have achieved had the Raid not occurred, it is, of course, impossible for us to say. There is no doubt that the Raid greatly strengthened Kruger's hold on his own people,[37] and increased Boer suspicion of any party that supported the rights of the uitlanders.

Nevertheless, the Progressive party did not fade away, or even suffer any notable diminution of its members in the Raad. The first Volksraad elections after the Raid returned 5 Progressive members out of a total of 13 to the First Raad[38] (A. A. J. Dieperink for Johannesburg; J. du P. de Beer and D. Joubert, both listed by the *Weekly Press* as Progressive, for Waterberg and Carolina respectively; Lukas Meyer and Louis Botha for Vryheid, the latter beating C. J. A. Birkenstock by a considerable majority). On the other hand only one Progressive was returned in eleven electoral contests for seats in the Second Volksraad (B. G. Brecher for Vryheid). The 1898 presidential elections, it is true, showed a sweeping victory for Kruger[39]—12,858 votes for him, as against 3,753 for Schalk Burger and a mere 2,001 for General Joubert. But this need not be construed as showing that Progressive sentiment had died among the Boers. The times were too troublesome for an untried man to be placed at the helm of the State; and Joubert's prestige had, in any case, declined sharply after 1893.[40]

[37] Marais, p. 96.   [38] *Weekly Press*, 20 Mar. 1897, p. 19.
[39] *Weekly Press*, 12 Feb. 1898, p. 12.   [40] See below, pp. 246–74.

The Volksraad elections give a better indication; and they show that the Progressive party by 1899 still retained some 10 adherents out of a total of 27 members of the First Raad.[41]

It seems fair to say, therefore, that though the Progressive party did not continue to increase its representation after the Raid as it might otherwise have done, it did not suffer any disastrous decline.

The words of Carl Jeppe[42] may well serve as the party's epitaph:

'Still they were gaining ground, and would probably have prevailed before long, when events intervened which made a peaceful solution of the problem impossible.

'Two consolations, however, are with the Progressive Party. They did all that in them lay to save their country. And when all endeavours proved futile, when their worst fears were realised, and they found the Republic pitted against irresistible strength, the great majority of those who led the Commandos in victory and defeat, and of the burghers who fought for independence until the bitter end, were members of the Progressive party.'

[41] *Weekly Press*, 6 May 1899, p. 9.
[42] Jeppe, p. 176.

SOURCES OF INFORMATION ON MEMBERS' VOTES

Chart

No.	Date of Debate	
1.	6 May 1891.	*Land en Volk*, 12 May 1891.
		Volksstem, 6 May 1891.
2.	28 June 1892.	*Land en Volk*, 30 June 1892.
		Volksstem, 29 June 1892.
3.	1 July 1892.	*Volksstem*, 2 July 1892.
4.		Article (not debate) in *Land en Volk*, 21 July 1892.
5.	29 Aug. 1892.	*Land en Volk*, 1 Sept. 1892.
		Volksstem, 31 Aug. 1892.
6.	30 Aug. 1892.	*Land en Volk*, 1 Sept. 1892.
		Volksstem, 31 Aug. 1892.
7.	3 May 1893.	*Volksstem*, 3 May 1893.
8.	12 Aug. 1893.	*Volksstem*, 15 Aug. 1893.
9.	24 Aug. 1893.	*Land en Volk*, 31 Aug. 1893.
		Volksstem, 26 Aug. 1893.

10.	31 Aug. 1893.	*Volksstem*, 2 Sept. 1893.
11.	5 June 1894.	*Press*, 6 June 1894.
12.	7 June 1894.	*Volksstem*, 9 June 1894.
13.	30 Aug. 1894.	*Volksstem*, 1 Sept. 1894.
14.	6 Sept. 1894.	*Volksstem*, 8 Sept. 1894.
15.	11 Sept. 1894.	*Land en Volk*, 13 Sept. 1894.
		Volksstem, 15 Sept. 1894.
16.	18 Sept. 1894.	*Land en Volk*, 27 Sept. 1894.
17.	15 May 1895.	*Press*, 16 May 1895.
		Land en Volk, 16 May 1895.
18.	30 May 1895.	*Press*, 31 May 1895.
		Volksstem, 31 May 1895.
19.	14 Aug. 1895.	*Land en Volk*, 22 Aug. 1895.
20.	20 Aug. 1895.	*Volksstem*, 24 Aug. 1895.
21.	20 Sept. 1895.	*Volksstem*, 25 Sept. 1895
22.	15 June 1896.	*Weekly Press*, 20 June 1896.

KEY TO CHART ON NEXT PAGE

'Won' and 'lost' = Won or lost by the Progressives.

× = Voted against government.

v = Voted for government.

? = No information available. The newspapers (the only regular source of information, since the way individual members voted was not invariably recorded in the *Notulen* of the Volksraads during this period) often give only those who voted against, or for, a specific motion.

— = Not yet a member of the Volksraad, or had ceased to be a member of the Volksraad.

VR = Volksraad debate dated................................

N.Z.A.S.M. = Netherlands South African Railway Company.

Chart showing votes against the govt. on typical issues during the period under review. See previous page for key and footnotes.

Column key (in order, left to right):

1. Move to investigate N.Z.A.S.M. VR 6/5/91, Lost 13-11.
2. Condemnation of State Loan of £3m. VR 28/6/92, Lost 15-7.
3. Move to reduce Salaries. VR 1/7/92, Lost 13-8.
4. Condemnation of Govt. Press Advertisements. VR Aug. 92, Lost.
5. Refusing Volmacht to Govt. VR 29/8/92, Won 10-9.
6. Volmacht as issue of confidence. VR 30/8/92, Lost.
7. Protest re Jhb. & Waterberg Elections. VR 3/5/93, Lost 12-10.
8. Dynamite Concession. VR 12/8/93. Lost 13-11.
9. Prog. Motion re Natal Line. VR 24/8/93, Lost 12-11.
10. Import Duty on Dynamite. VR 31/8/93, Lost 13-10.
11. Move for more Liberal Franchise. VR 5/6/94, Lost 13-10.
12. Reduction of Import Duty to 5 per cent. VR 7/6/94, Lost 16-8.
13. Move to expel Loveday and Jeppe. VR 30/8/94, Won 11-10.
14. Move to expand Volksraad. VR 6/9/94, Lost 11-10.
15. Final Rejection of Jam Concession. VR 11/6/94, Won 12-10.
16. Expulsion of Loveday for one day. VR 18/9/94, Lost 13-8.
17. Election of Van Wyk for Krugersdorp. VR 15/5/95, Won 14-11.
18. Extension of Franchise. VR 30/5/95, Lost 15-10.
19. Extension of Franchise. VR 14/8/95, Lost 13-8.
20. Expropriation of N.Z.A.S.M. VR 20/8/95, Lost 16-8.
21. Postponing Second Raad Decision on Bewaarplaatsen. VR 20/9/95, Lost 14-11.
22. Introduction of Secret Ballot. VR 15/6/96, Won 13-11.

Member	1	2	3	4	5	6	7	8	9	10	11	12	13	14	15	16	17	18	19	20	21	22
R. K. Loveday	×	×	×	×	×	×	×	×	×	×	×	×	×	×	×	|	×	×	×	×	×	×
P. Maré	×	×	×	×	×	?	×	×	×	×	×	?	×	×	×	×	×	×	×	×	×	×
L. Meyer	×	×	×	×	×	×	×	×	×	×	×	×	×	×	×	×	×	×	×	×	abs.	×
L. de Jager	|	?	|	|	|	×	×	×	×	×	×	×	?	×	×	×	×	×	?	?	×	×
G. de Jager	|	|	|	|	|	|	×	×	×	×	×	×	×	×	×	×	×	×	×	×	×	×
C. Jeppe	|	|	|	|	|	|	|	×	×	×	×	×	×	×	×	×	×	×	×	×	×	×
J. H. de la Rey	|	|	|	|	|	|	|	|	|	|	|	|	|	✓	|	×	×	✓	✓	✓	✓	×
J. L. van Wyk	×	|	|	|	|	|	|	|	|	|	|	|	|	|	|	|	|	×	✓	✓	✓	×
W. H. van Niekerk	|	|	|	|	|	|	|	|	|	|	|	|	|	|	|	|	×	✓	|	|	|	×
S. W. Burger	|	×	×	?	×	✓	×	×	×	?	×	?	?	abs.	abs.	abs.	×	✓	✓	✓	×	✓
J. J. Spies	|	?	?	×	?	?	×	×	×	×	×	×	?	?	✓	?	|	|	|	|	✓	|
W. J. Steyn	|	|	|	|	|	|	×	|	|	|	|	|	|	|	|	|	|	×	✓	✓	|	×
D. J. Joubert	×	|	|	|	|	|	×	×	×	|	×	|	|	|	|	|	×	×	✓	×	✓	×
C. B. Otto	×	|	|	|	|	|	×	×	×	?	×	?	?	?	✓	?	×	✓	✓	✓	✓	✓
C. J. A. Birkenstock	×	×	×	×	×	?	abs.	?	×	×	×	×	×?	?	×	×	×	✓	✓	✓	×	|
J. du P. de Beer	×	✓	×	✓	×	✓	?	×	×	×	×	×	?	×	×	×	×	✓	✓	✓	×	✓
J. H. Labuschagne	✓	?	?	✓	?	?	?	?	?	✓	✓	?	?	×	×	✓	×	✓	✓	✓	×	×
J. de Clercq	✓	×	?	×	✓	✓	×	✓	✓	?	?	✓	✓	?	×	✓	?	✓	✓	✓	✓	×

9

The Role of Commandant-General P. J. Joubert in the Progressive Party

IT remains for us to estimate the part played by General P. J. Joubert himself in the rise of the Progressive Party. There have been many indications already in this book[1] which suggest that, though the Commandant-General's 'leadership' of the Progressive group gave it a most welcome aura of patriotism and respectability, and to this extent greatly facilitated its rise to importance and its continued existence after the Jameson Raid, that 'leadership' was more nominal than real. It becomes necessary therefore, to try to assess more exactly the depth of Joubert's 'progressiveness', the nature of his relations with the government (of which, as a member of the Executive Council, he was himself a member) and the extent to which, if our suspicions are correct, Joubert—like the Duke of Plaza Toro—'led his regiment from behind', or, perhaps more accurately, was pushed forward from behind as a rather unwilling, if impressively patriarchal, figure-head by the more resolute and radical members of the Progressive group.

In background and upbringing Joubert was a typical Boer, deeply pious,[2] almost mystically patriotic,[3] shrewd and kindly,[4] yet comparatively poorly educated[5] and sometimes inclined to be vindictive towards his opponents.[6] Orphaned at an early age, he had made his own way in life, as a farmer, trader, general agent and speculator.[7] As a man of affairs he had attained considerable success by the time with which this study deals. He owned farms in every corner of the Republic—in the Piet Retief, Wakkerstroom, Lydenburg, Stander-

[1] See, for example, above, pp. 176, 194, 197–8, 202, 214–15, 237.

[2] See Letters nos. 2299 and 2309, for example, in Joubert Papers, Uitgaande Stukke, II A/4 (Archives, vol. 23).

[3] Mouton, J. A., ch. XXV.

[4] See Mouton, and Nathan, p. 228.

[5] See Joubert's speech on his own poor education in his welcome to Dr. Mansvelt (*Land en Volk*, 20 Oct. 1891).

[6] Mouton, p. 273.

[7] Mouton, ch. II, XX.

ton, Potchefstroom and Middelburg areas in particular[8]—to a total number of 29.[9] Besides this he rented a large number of houses and stands to a variety of tenants, from which he must have derived a comfortable income.[10] He was, further, the director of, or a large shareholder in, a considerable number of gold-mining companies, of which the most important were the 'Zoutpansbergsche Exploratie Maatschappij (Beperkt)', the 'Leeuwpoort Goudmyn Maatschappij (Beperkt)', the 'Ariston Gold Mining Company (Ltd)', the 'Rietkuil Main Reef Goudmyn Maatschappij (Beperkt)' and the 'Paarl–Pretoria Gold Mining and Exploration Company'; and he had similar interests in a number of financial companies such as the 'Pretoria Board of Executors and Trust Company', the 'Durban Investment Syndicate' and the 'Zoutpansberg–Palmietfontein Company'.[11] His dealings in these matters were not small in scale. In September 1895, for example, he sold his Palmietfontein shares to Messrs. Lewis and Marks, for £12,500 in cash plus 17,500 fully paid up shares in a company to be floated by that firm; and the same firm offered to buy back the shares, a year later, for £17,500 in cash.[12] One of his numerous houses was bought by the government for £8,550.[13] The list of his shareholdings in various gold-mining and speculative companies runs into nearly three-quarters of a page of fine print.[14] His financial needs were on an equal scale, and his letter-books give many examples of his requests (couched sometimes in despairing language) for loans of sums varying from £3,000 to £8,000.[15] He was, in spite of his party's strong opposition to concessions, himself involved in a number of applications for such concessions—a difficult matter for a man with such widely ramified financial interests to avoid—though he claimed that, unlike other concession-holders, he was inspired not by a spirit of speculation but by a desire for the welfare of the country.[16] The concessions in which Joubert was interested varied from such large-scale affairs

[8] Joubert Papers, Uitgaande Stukke, II A/4–B/3 (Archives, vol. 24, Business Letter Book), and Inkomende Stukke, I A/10–17 (Archives, vols. 5 and 6).

[9] Mouton, p. 201.

[10] Joubert Papers, Uitgaande Stukke, II A/4–B/3 (Archives, vol. 24), pp. 87, 139, 153, 238–45.

[11] Joubert Papers, vol. 24.   [12] Mouton, p. 207.

[13] *Volksstem*, 18 Nov. 1893.   [14] Mouton, p. 207.

[15] Joubert Papers, Uitgaande Stukke, II A/1–A/3 (Archives, vol. 16), nos. 782–8. See also Mouton, pp. 204–5.

[16] *Volksstem*, 1 Feb. 1893 (report of speech at Piet Retief).

as his application (with the Vice-President, General N. J. Smit, F. G. Wolmarans, F. C. Eloff, J. J. H. Wolmarans, Schalk Burger and others) for the right to build a railway from Charlestown on the Natal border to Johannesburg,[17] and his attempt to found a Netherlands–South African Steamship Company,[18] to such comparatively minor affairs as the Swazi railway concession which his son and others sold to the government for £12,500[19] and his own personal concession—never exercised—giving him the sole right to erect sawmills in the Zoutpansberg area.[20]

All these intricate financial affairs, in addition to his official duties, kept Joubert hard at work, and involved him in extensive correspondence with interested parties in the United States, Europe and all parts of South Africa. His letter-books contain many hundreds of letters in his own hand on these matters. In spite of his occasional moments of financial stress, his affairs, on the whole, prospered. He was one of the richest men in the Republic, and at his death he left an estate of nearly £230,000.[21]

These multifarious activities, of which only a small number have been outlined here,[22] are mentioned to explain something of the esteem in which Joubert was held by large sections of his own and of the uitlander community, and to refute the allegations made by his opponents, particularly in connexion with the Netherlands Railway Company's affairs, that Joubert was a simpleton who knew nothing of financial matters.[23] There were few members of the Boer community, it may safely be said, who had a tithe of Joubert's detailed and practical knowledge of business affairs.

What did Joubert's contemporaries think of him? Carl Jeppe, who knew him well, writes:[24]

---

[17] Joubert Papers, Inkomende Stukke, I A/10–17 (Archives, vol. 7), nos. 776–80.

[18] Joubert Papers, II A/4–B/3 (Archives, vol. 23), nos. 2225–31 and Mouton, ch. XIX, pp. 198–200.

[19] *Press*, 31 Jan. 1893, 2 Feb. 1893; *Volksstem*, 1 Feb. 1893. Joubert Papers, Uitgaande Stukke, II A/1–A/3 (Archives, vol. 17), p. 611 (letter of 6 Jan. 1894 to Viljoen, Heidelberg).

[20] Joubert Papers, Inkomende Stukke (B), Privaat 1543–1704 (Archives, vol. 12), no. 1702.

[21] Mouton, p. 209 (Will No. 17175, Palace of Justice, Pretoria).

[22] Mouton, ch. XIX and XX, deals very fully with this subject.

[23] See p. 82.

[24] Jeppe, pp. 172–3.

'Joubert was, next to Kruger, undoubtedly the keenest intellect among the Boers. Much better educated than his opponent, a still more eloquent speaker, more enlightened and broad-minded, and possessing a nimbleness of mind which almost amounted to cunning, he was yet no match for the President, since he lacked moral courage. He could never be got to face Kruger in debate, and in all the long struggle between them, it was always Joubert's heart that failed at the crucial moment.'

Frederick Rompel, in his *Heroes of the Boer War*, says:

'. . . It must be admitted that in time of peace Slim Piet's appearance was not sympathetic. His high piping voice, his small, beady eyes, the sly smile that played about his mouth, gave him an air of falseness which made an unpleasant impression, and, rightly or wrongly, prejudiced many persons against him. Besides, his character was not open and square like that, for instance, of Koos de la Rey. He was essentially a trimmer, liked to remain on good terms with friend and foe, and ended by estranging both' (page 95),[25] and

'As a politician Joubert was neither so eminent nor so capable as he showed himself as a commander. He never clearly saw his political line before him. He always hesitated . . .' (page 103).

The *Press* (23 November 1892), which supported Kruger in the 1893 election, condemned Joubert utterly as 'too weak a man, too shilly-shallying a statesman, and altogether too characterless a personality to be President of the South African Republic'.

Both the uitlander *Star*[26] and the pro-Kruger *Volksstem*, divided as they were on almost every other issue, were united in considering Joubert as a much weaker man, if more broadly liberal in his sympathies, than the redoubtable Kruger. The *Star* opined that he had 'a thicker veneer, but was not to be mentioned in the same breath with his rugged Cromwell-like opponent', and the *Volksstem*, commenting sarcastically on his ability to say nothing in a great many words, strongly echoed this sentiment,[27] and attacked his candidature as a device by his supporters 'to get rid of Paul Kruger, that strong giant, and to acquire a weaker President in his stead with whom they can do what they desire'.[28]

[25] Rompel, as one of the senior reporters on the *Volksstem*, probably knew Joubert fairly well.
[26] Quoted in *Volksstem*, 16 Feb. 1892.
[27] *Volksstem*, 16 Feb. 1892.   [28] *Volksstem*, 15 Nov. 1892.

Land en Volk, on the other hand, eulogized Joubert as a great and tolerant Afrikaner patriot, a beloved leader, a brave fighter, and a foe of all that was corrupt and reactionary in the Republic;[29] and the large proportion of the vote which the Commandant-General received in the 1893 election showed that many burghers shared this view. Even Joubert's political opponent, the Vice-President, General N. J. Smit, described him as 'a bosom-friend of mine, and a good, brave and clever general',[30] while his military opponent, Lord Roberts, in a letter of condolence after Joubert's death,[31] expressed his

'feeling of deep regret at the sudden and untimely end of so distinguished a soldier whose personal gallantry was only surpassed by his humane conduct and chivalrous bearing under all circumstances'.

What are we to make of this mixed evidence? Personal kindliness, a high military reputation, and deep patriotism, all who knew him are convinced of. But friends and opponents alike offer evidence of an inner weakness and lack of self-confidence which appears to have been one of Joubert's most marked features; of an almost ingrained inability to say things simply and forthrightly; and of a sensitivity to criticism which became at times almost paranoid in its intensity.

Of these defects of his character his speeches and letters give ample evidence. Let us take Joubert's lack of self-confidence first. Writing to his friend Douthwaite, Veld-cornet at Potchefstroom, in March 1892, when the presidential election campaign was just about to start, Joubert says:[32]

'That the state of affairs is reprehensible [treurig] and that a change is highly desirable, indeed essential, [I fully agree]. . . . But now the question arises to me of how should, and how must, such a change take place, and of how it should be brought about. On this point many will reply to me—"another President". Well, I will keep silence on that matter. But will the majority say this? Will not the great majority still choose the present President? To me it seems certain that the President with his influential Press and his many supporters will know how to manage matters so that he will once

[29] See, for example, *Land en Volk*, 11 Aug. 1892, 26 Dec. 1892, 29 Dec. 1892, 2 Jan. 1893.

[30] *Press*, 3 Aug. 1892.

[31] Joubert Papers, Inkomende Stukke (B), Privaat 1888–1994. (Archives, vol. 14).

[32] Joubert Papers, Uitgaande Stukke, II A/1–A/3. No. 1997 (Archives, vol. 17), p. 224. Letter to Douthwaite of 4 Mar. 1892.

again get the majority—and I can therefore reckon upon it that by putting myself forward I will achieve not only the [illegible] but also the ingrained hatred and contempt [de innige haat en veragting] of His Honour Kruger [van H. E. Kruger]. . . . After I was sworn in as General I found that the President had persuaded the Volksraad not to restore me to full honour and thus to give to his supporter Mr. C. J. Joubert the office of Vice-President . . . an affront and an insult . . . and a degradation to me. Well, I have borne it all for the sake of peace and quietness. But if it is the voice of God and the people that calls me, I must subject myself to it.'

This is a quite typical letter, and confirms Jeppe's statement of Joubert's unwillingness to face Kruger in open contest. It is very similar, in essence, to his answer to the requests to him to stand for the presidency in 1887, to which he replied:[33]

'No, and once again no! I have said it and I will not go back on it, God helping me. . . . Yet if you get your wish and I am unexpectedly chosen, I will always look to the people of this land, relying upon their trust and support . . . and give myself unconditionally to do what God and the people desire of me.'

Yet on both these occasions, as in 1882 and again in 1898, Joubert did stand for the Presidency. This show of unwillingness was not, in my opinion, an elaborate and hypocritical display of conventional coyness. It sprang from a real fear and dislike of, as well as respect for, Kruger and his party, and a considerable lack of confidence in himself on Joubert's part. Dr. Leyds, it is true, in his notorious letter of 18 November 1886 to Schmüll declares that:

'the key to Piet Joubert's behaviour must be sought in his jealousy of the President. His candidature for the presidential seat was meant very seriously at the time. Every time that he has to say "President" to another man, it hurts him.'[34]

Personal ambition, and jealousy of Kruger, were undoubtedly an important part of Joubert's political make-up; but they are not the whole explanation. There is evidence of a very real unwillingness to oppose the President. Even after allowing his candidature to be announced, Joubert, as we have seen,[35] had to be virtually dragooned

[33] *Volksstem*, 12 Apr. 1892, quotes this in full.
[34] Joubert Papers, Inkomende Stukke, I A/18–26 (Archives vol. 10), no. 1302.
[35] See p. 197–8.

by his supporters into doing something in support of his own cause; and after his return from his electoral campaign he declared that he

'thanked the election Committee for all it had done for him; but he had not created the Committee, and he stood outside it. He wished only to do his duty to God and the people.'[36]

And in a letter to C. B. Otto, a friend and supporter, Joubert's proudest boast about the 1893 election was that:

'not one single person can be found who dares to say—General Joubert advised me or asked me to vote for him, still less to work for him; and not one single person who dares to say that General Joubert promised him or allowed him to expect that if he or they voted for him or worked for him, he or they could expect or receive the slightest personal advantage or reward.'[37]

Joubert's proud and stubborn refusal to lift a finger in his own cause, and his continual falling back upon a pietistic belief that, if he was fated to become President, 'God and the people' would, in some mystical way, see to it that this came about, display not only a considerable lack of recognition of the country-wide labours of his Election Committee, but also the profound insecurity from which Joubert always suffered. To thrust himself forward, to advocate his own cause, to even appear to be supporting his supporters, invited rebuff and insult. Better by far to leave it to a higher hand.

'Twice before', he wrote to Commandant Viljoen in Utrecht,[38] 'there was an election for the Presidency, and many times did His Excellency the President strongly advise me, indeed he insisted upon it, that I should stand for election, against my own inclination . . . but if it is not by God's will and the people's free choice that I should be chosen, then I neither wish to be, nor shall ever be, President. But if the people desire it, and God so wills it, what will all the clamour of the newspapers matter?'

In a very typical letter to his son[39] he writes that he has no intention of answering the attacks upon him by the papers, for people will only say:

[36] *Volksstem*, 12 Nov. 1892 (quoted on p. 202 above).

[37] Joubert Papers, Uitgaande Stukke, II A/1–A/3, no. 1997, p. 609 (Archives, vol. 17), letter of 25 Jan. 1894 to C. B. Otto.

[38] Joubert Papers, Uitgaande Stukke, II A/1–A/3 (Archives, vol. 17), no. 1997, p. 228 (letter of 4 Mar. 1892).

[39] Joubert Papers, no. 1997 (vol. 17).

'See how greatly Piet Joubert desires to be President. Therefore let them write what they will . . . let the people make their noise, for in vain do the captains [vorsten] rage. . . . God the Lord reigns!'

Yet this mystic resignation did not, in fact, prevent Joubert from complaining strongly to the papers of their attacks upon him, or from writing in bitterness and grief to his children:[40]

'I do not know what some members of the honourable Volksraad have against me. Hardly any one of them comes to see me, and if in any way they can hurt me, they do so; more particularly A. Stoop and J. Lombaard. I see also no possibility of working together with the Government the way matters are going at the moment. I have *a letter* [*sic*] ready to send in, but am waiting for the right moment.'

This feeling of grievance became very much more intense after Joubert's near-success in the 1893 election, and the Commandant-General's dislike of the victorious Kruger party, and his fears of its vengeance, are clearly shown. To his friend Douthwaite he writes that he is sure that Kruger is working to elevate Piet Cronjé (Joubert's successor as Superintendent of Native Affairs),

'and even wants to make him General in my place . . . [I would rather resign and perhaps] serve the country as a Raad member or unofficial member of the Executive Council, but never, never again as a subordinate official of President Kruger's imperial administration [nooit of nimmer meer als een ondergeschikte ambtenaar in President Krugers Rijks bestuur]. No—not for any money in the world.'[41]

To his son J. S. Joubert he writes, shortly after,[42]

'To remain here in Pretoria will be *im*possible. I think, therefore, that I shall come back to Rustfontein as soon as I am dismissed. . . .'

To another son, P. J. Joubert, a month later,[43]

[40] See, for example, his letter of Mar. 1892 to the *Volksstem* (Joubert Papers, Uitgaande Stukke, II A/1–A/3 (Archives, vol. 17), no. 1997, p. 233), and p. 305 (letter of 27 July 1892).
[41] Joubert Papers, Uitgaande Stukke, II A/1–A/3, no. 1997, p. 361 (Archives, vol. 17), letter of 20 Feb. 1893.
[42] Joubert Papers, vol. 17, p. 372 (letter of 5 Mar. 1893).
[43] Joubert Papers, vol. 17, p. 411 (letter of 19 Apr. 1893).

'I do not know where I shall stay, because once His Excellency the President is sworn in, then my employment is finished, and without income I cannot remain living in Pretoria. I do not know yet where I shall go.'

To his old associate Schmüll (of the proposed Netherlands–South Africa Steamship Company) he writes:[44]

'The tension of the recently concluded election has not made the relationships between [myself and President Kruger] any better. . . . I have given up all hope of a Steamship Company; nor do I feel inclined to run like a beggar after the government again.'

In two letters to J. P. Trigaardt, Native Commissioner at Middelburg,[45] Joubert refers with deep bitterness to the determination of the 'Kruger Volksraad clique and party' to revenge themselves on their opponents, and in particular of their intention to use allegations of the inefficient administration of the Artillery Camp at Pretoria as a method of 'blackening my name'; and in a letter of September (3rd or 9th—illegible) 1893 to one Viljoen, Mining Commissioner at Heidelberg, Joubert says that the Kruger party's attitude is quite simply:

'We have the overwhelming majority in the Volksraad, and, over and above this, power over everybody, and need pay no attention to the Joubert party. They [the Joubert party] must bow their heads or out with them. [And as for Joubert himself, with the Artillery Camp and other matters] we will work his dismissal [zoo zullen wij zijn ontslacht bewerken] in such a manner that he will be harmless to us.'[46]

And, on 6 January 1894:

'Joubert, and all who were for him, are doomed to the uttermost [is tot de eynde gedoemt] and there are still many more who must and shall see what it means and what it brings upon you to have dared to desire to have another President. Trigaardt is already out, and the others will be dealt with.'[47]

[44] Joubert Papers, Uitgaande Stukke II A/1–A/3, no. 1997 (Archives, vol. 17), no. 425 of 27 May 1893.
[45] Joubert Papers, vol. 17, pp. 439 and 443–4 (letters of 19 Aug. 1893 and 23 Aug. 1893).
[46] Joubert Papers, Uitgaande Stukke II A/1–A/3, no. 1997 (Archives, vol. 17), p. 453.
[47] Joubert Papers, vol. 17, p. 611.

Nevertheless, as subsequent events showed, much of this self-pity was unnecessary. In spite of frequent references to the intolerable nature of his position, Joubert did not, in fact, resign as Commandant-General; and the disappearance from office of one native commissioner,[48] within a period of almost a year after Kruger's re-election, can hardly be regarded as evidence of a whole-sale persecution of Joubert's adherents. His defence of his own action in requesting the government to make arrangements for the election of a new commandant-general (28 January 1893) display, as Mouton points out,[49] his usual bitterness and 'a pitiable lack of self-confidence'. He did not want to resign, he stated, because people would say the Volksraad had dismissed him, and that he had left his office in disorder, and that the people did not trust him;[50] and there can be little doubt that he believed what he said. Yet there was no doubt at all in actual fact that the people did trust him. On 20 September 1894 the First Raad decided to ask the government to call for an election to the position of commandant-general in the following year, since Joubert's period of office expired in June 1895, but to reduce the period of office from ten to five years. 'Requisitions' to Joubert to stand poured in in great numbers, and he was in due course re-elected to the Commandant-Generalship by an over-whelming majority (9,031 votes to the 205 of his nearest rival, Schalk Burger, while the man whom he had feared that Kruger was setting up as his rival, Piet Cronjé, attained a mere 22 votes).[51] In the following year, after the death of General N. J. Smit, Joubert was duly elected Vice-President by 13 votes to 11.[52]

Enough has been written to illustrate Joubert's extreme lack of self-confidence, and to indicate that it was logically (if not psychologically) largely unjustified. But that Joubert's conviction that a campaign was being waged against him by his enemies had at least some basis in fact was revealed in the bitter attacks on him by some members of the Kruger party which accompanied the decision to end his dual position as Superintendent of Native Affairs and Commandant-General. The separation of these two offices, and the appointment of Piet Cronjé as Superintendent of Native Affairs,

[48] J. P. Trigaardt was Native Commissioner at Middelburg.
[49] Mouton, pp. 134–6.
[50] First Volksraad, 30 Aug. 1893 (*Notulen*, Eerste Volksraad, 1893, art. 50).
[51] Mouton, pp. 137–8.
[52] First Volksraad, 13 May 1896 (*Notulen*, Eerste Volksraad, 1896, art. 59).

was described by Joubert as 'a slap in the face . . . a humiliation and insult . . .' and the result of a long 'campaign of unfounded condemnation and relentless undermining by my implacable enemies'.[53] There is reason to believe that Joubert's loudly expressed bitterness[54] was partially justified, if not as dignified as it might have been.

We have mentioned, among the weaknesses of Joubert's character upon which friend and foe alike agree, his inability to say briefly and clearly, if at all, what he meant. This is often a characteristic of 'eloquent orators'; but in Joubert's case it was probably intensified by his innate cautiousness and hesitancy. From the many examples available let us choose two quite typical ones. In November 1894 he appeared in person—though, in the light of his speech, it is difficult to know exactly how or why—at the Congress of the Volksvereeniging then in progress at Pretoria,[55] and after being greeted enthusiastically by the assembled delegates with the singing of a verse of the national anthem, declared:

'Gentlemen of the Congress here present, I understand that you are holding a Congress here. What the object and work of this organisation is, I do not exactly know. It is being said that I fear a combination of persons; but, as Luther said when he stood under the tiles and roofs of Worms, I am not afraid of anyone, and therefore do not object to appear here. . . . Now you have put a question to me [whether he would agree to stand for the Commandant-Generalship in 1895] which is not included among the laws of the land. Indeed, it is contrary to the law. You ask me—'What will you do?' The laws of the land do not require from me that I answer yes or no. In short, I do not know. I am not omniscient. I shall do on that day what God wills. When He calls me to an action or to any deed in the interest of the country . . . I shall answer. You must not ask me what I shall do. I trust in God under whose direct control [directe bestuur] and under whose direct influence I wish to continue, so long as I live.'[56]

As a statement of personal intentions to a group of people working in his interests, and generally referred to as the 'Joubert party' (and

---

[53] *Weekly Press*, 12 Sept. 1896, pp. 1–5.

[54] First Volksraad, 4 Sept. 1896 (*Notulen*, Eerste Volksraad, 1896, art. 62).

[55] See p. 237.

[56] *Land en Volk*, 22 Nov. 1894 (Appendix); *Press*, 16 Nov. 1894; *Volksstem*, 21 Nov. 1894; another (very similar) version of some of this speech was quoted on p. 237 above.

certainly the nearest approach to a 'party congress', in the usual sense of that term, that the Republic had yet achieved) this utterance of Joubert's would be hard to equal for imprecision and verbosity. The practised student of Joubert's utterances, nevertheless, would have no difficulty in recognizing this as a declaration of the General's intention to stand, once again, for the Commandant-Generalship.

Joubert's election speeches demonstrate the same lack of precision. Speaking at Wakkerstroom in October 1892 Joubert stated[57] that:

'it was not his intention to attack the government, and he did not think anyone expected it from him. He would, however, answer all questions. Asked whether he had voted for the loans to the Netherlands Railway Company he said he had been in Europe at the time that the £600,000 loan was voted. When the £100,000 loan was voted he had been at Barberton.[58] He had been consulted neither before nor after.

'The desire for a change in the government did not come from him, but from the Volk. It was not his desire to attack the government. He would make no promises. All that he would say was that he would do everything that his hand found to do for the happiness and welfare of the land, with God's help and support.

'Asked about the grant of franchise rights to the newcomers, the General said that this was a difficult question. Even the Chief Justice had not been able to answer a similar question satisfactorily. He thought it might be best to go back to the original law passed shortly after the war.[59] The matter was, however, in the hands of the old burghers. They had the right to give or to refuse.'

It is difficult, in the light of such utterances, not to agree with the *Volksstem*'s opinion of Joubert (16 February 1892) as one 'who certainly used many words, without giving expression to much in the way of ideas . . .', while the *Press* of 8 February 1892, reporting on Joubert's speech at Barberton in which he declared that 'he was sorry that the Presidential election had been mentioned. He had never sought after that position, and he would not give a penny for it or make the smallest promise in that connection; if they wanted to choose him he would obey the voice of God and the people, but

---

[57] *Land en Volk*, 27 Oct. 1892.

[58] There is some evidence that the government had, indeed, contrived Joubert's absence on similar occasions. See p. 66.

[59] Law 7 of 1882 Eybers, *Select Constitutional Documents*, p. 437.

he did not seek for it',[60] poked some mild fun at the speech in the following words:

'[The General declared that] he would tell them his whole mind candidly. At this point Reuter's agent becomes a little vague. As far as can be ascertained the speaker seems to have informed his audience that if he could become President without paying a penny or making any promises, he would be disposed to regard a majority at the election as the voice of "God and the people"; but in certain other events, the character of which was not apparent, he was prepared "never to see the sun shine again on the Transvaal".'

It went on to express the hope that the General 'was not quite so unintelligible as he appears to have been'.[61] The sarcasm was not uncalled for.

Some of the main facets of Joubert's personality have been outlined in the previous pages—his dislike of the Kruger 'party' or 'clique', yet his unwillingness to oppose Kruger manfully and openly; his curious mystic pietism and defeatism, which did not, however, prevent a thoroughly human bitterness and resentment against his opponents; his remarkable ability to use words to cloak rather than to convey his meaning.

To what did these add up when Joubert took upon himself, or more probably had thrust upon him, the role of political leader of the growing number of Boers who were becoming discontented with Kruger and his policies?

Certainly Joubert cannot be regarded as a vigorous campaigner in his own cause. We have seen that, in his election tour of 1892–3 he denied at Wakkerstroom that he desired any change in government.[62] He had made precisely the same declaration at Heidelberg a few days previously, when he had stated that the 'desire for a change did not stem from him, but . . . from the burghers who had asked him to stand' (*Land en Volk*, 20 October, 1892). Such an attitude (even making allowance for the fact that the Transvaal burghers knew Joubert well and did not necessarily take his statements at their face value) can hardly be regarded as vigorous campaigning. The really vigorous campaigning that did come from *Land en Volk* and from his 'Election Committee', Joubert persistently declined to associate himself with. He categorically disowned his

---

[60] *Volksstem*, 9 Feb. 1892.   [61] *Press*, 8 Feb. 1892.
[62] See p. 257 (*Land en Volk*, 27 Oct. 1892—Wakkerstroom speech).

Election Committee,[63] and as firmly held himself aloof from the more extreme actions of the 'Joubert Congress' of 1893, an attitude which earned him the warm praise of the pro-government *Volksstem*.[64] In 1894, though present, amid emotional scenes, at a congress of his supporters, the 'Volksvereeniging', he affected to have come there as it were by accident (one might almost say to have stumbled upon this great meeting of his party by a delightfully lucky chance) but to know nothing whatever of their nature, their work or their aims.[65] Although this was partly due to a feeling that a political 'party' was something slightly disreputable,[66] that the 'government' and the 'State' were in some way one, and that to attack the former was to imperil the latter[67]—a view skilfully traded upon in Jorissen's 'Open Letter' to P. J. Joubert of 17 December 1892, appealing to him not to oppose Kruger, which we have already quoted[68]—it was also due, as we have suggested, to the defects of Joubert's own personality, to his innate fear of compromising himself, and to his conviction (if we may modify Paul Kruger's oft-quoted words) that the tortoise may avoid having its head cut off if it refrains from poking it out. Whatever its causes, this loathness to attack must certainly have detracted considerably from Joubert's forcefulness as a political leader, and to that extent it must have prejudiced his chances and those of the Progressive party. It is not surprising, therefore, to find occasional criticism of him from his own party, as well as the inevitable sneers of his opponents. Thus his strong supporter, Carl Jeppe, as we have seen, criticized Joubert's lack of 'moral courage'; and, writing of his attitude towards the 1893 election result, declared:[69]

'On this occasion, too, he had only himself to thank for his defeat. To this day his party maintains that he won at the poll, but was beaten at the counting of the votes. This was the time he could have asserted himself, but "counsels of prudence" prevailed and he withdrew, on the plea that persistence would cause a quarrel which

[63] *Volksstem*, 12 Nov. 1892 (quoted above, p. 252).

[64] *Volksstem*, 9 May 1893.

[65] See pp. 256–7.

[66] A feeling shared by the great William Pitt, Earl of Chatham. (See Churchill's *History of the English-speaking peoples*, vol. III, p. 143.)

[67] See J. Albert Coetzee, for evidence that this notion is by no means extinct in South African politics.

[68] See pp. 199–200.   [69] Jeppe, p. 173.

might endanger the Republic. Today it seems reasonable to believe that persistence would possibly have been the means of saving it.'

On the same matter a Potchefstroom Joubert organ[70] wrote that

'the attitude taken up by General Joubert during the last few weeks has awakened a feeling of distrust even amongst his most faithful supporters. . . . It is now an open question whether the General has not shown the white feather and betrayed his party.'

The adjurations of his own supporters to Joubert to announce his candidature and act more vigorously in his own interest have already been mentioned.[71] The *Press*, generally sympathetic to the Progressive party, in spite of its support of Kruger personally, criticized Joubert's failure to make any clear statement of his policy, and considered that his failure, or refusal, to commit himself to any definite line of conduct

'recalls the magnificent reply of Mr. Disraeli—a politician with whom General Joubert has some points in common—when at a mass meeting on the eve of the general election in 1868 he was asked to outline a definite policy. "I have no policy," he said, "I repose my trust in the sublime instincts of an ancient people" ' (*Press*, 8 February 1892).

It did not, however, think that General Joubert would be any more successful than Disraeli had been in that year; Joubert appeared content to declare to his supporters that

'in no single requisition am I asked to reveal my future policy, and this is, to me, an even stronger proof of the unconditional trust which you put in me'.[72]

Indeed, the nearest that Joubert got to committing himself on even such a fundamental issue as whether it was desirable for a change to be made in the government of the Republic—surely the central issue of the 1893 election—was a statement that

'it was a difficult question to answer; but since our wise Chief Justice Kotzé, whose ability we all admire, and who is a bosom

[70] Unnamed, but quoted in *Volksstem*, 20 May 1893. (In all probability the *Vierkleur*, a Potchefstroom paper which was violently opposed to Kruger—see *Volksstem*, 3 Feb. 1894.)

[71] See pp. 197–8.

[72] Letter of Joubert to his supporters, 14 Nov. 1892 (*Volksstem*, 30 Nov. 1892).

friend of our respected President, declares it is essential, we can hardly doubt it'.[73]

The *Volksstem* was therefore not unjustified in declaring, on 5 September 1894, in a retrospective survey of the 1893 election, that

'the chief cause of the political poverty of the country seems to us the entire absence of any clear and understandable political pro-gramme in any party. Thus the continual use of personalities rather than principles. The last Presidential election was a good example. Not one of the candidates except Chief Justice Kotzé could offer the public any definite programme of principles which, if elected, he pledged himself to carry out. No one knows to this day in what points of *politics* Piet Joubert differs from his fellow-candidates. We still remember how one earnest supporter of our Commandant-General, pressed to define the motives of his choice, could give no other answer than "Well, we must also give Piet Joubert a chance for once!" '

In the light of the criticism of his contemporaries it appears a rash task to try to answer the question—what could the Boers, and the uitlander population, reasonably have expected in the way of policy, if Joubert had indeed been elected to office? Yet it is a ques-tion that we must, however unsatisfactorily, at least essay to answer. Let us approach it by taking, briefly, the major issues around which, as we have tried to show, opposition to the régime crystallized, and asking what evidence we have of Joubert's own attitudes on each.

Would the Transvaal under Joubert, for instance, have been free of the stain of the concessions and monopolies about which Joubert's supporters so loudly complained? Of the attitude of his party there can, as we have seen, be no doubt; and certainly their violent cam-paign against concessions and monopolies would have held any personal inclination of Joubert's towards the policy of granting concessions in check—as indeed it did with Kruger himself. But in point of fact Joubert was personally involved in numerous con-cessions. The unsuccessful 'Netherlands–South African Steamship Company', which he played a large part in attempting to found,[74] was to have been based upon a concession very similar in its nature

[73] *Land en Volk*, 26 Jan. 1893 (report of Vryheid speech).
[74] Joubert Papers, Uitgaande Stukke, II A/4–B/3 (Archives, vol. 23), gives full details of this. (See also Mouton, ch. XIX, pp. 198–200.)

to that granted to the Netherlands South African Railway Company.[75] A year later Joubert, with G. R. von Wielligh and I. van Alphen (the Surveyor-General and Postmaster-General respectively) applied, unsuccessfully, for a concession from the government to build and exploit a railway from Coldstream (on the O.F.S. border) to Pretoria.[76] Four years before this time Joubert, Von Wielligh and General N. J. Smit (the Vice-President) had, in spite of Joubert's loudly-expressed opposition to the concession which the government proposed to grant to the Netherlands Railway Company, applied for a concession to build a railway line from the Portuguese border to Pretoria on terms virtually identical with those asked for by the Netherlands company.[77] Together with General N. J. Smit, F. C. Eloff, Schalk Burger and others, he had played a leading part in attempting to secure from the government a concession to build and exploit a railway line from Charlestown to Johannesburg[78] (generally referred to as the 'Natal line'). Nor, in spite of his vehement denials,[79] can there be any doubt that he was, at any rate, heavily involved, via his son, J. A. Joubert, in the doings of a syndicate led by one Julius Kieser, which obtained from the Swazi king a concession for the building of a railway through Swaziland, which was subsequently offered to the Volksraad for the sum of £10,500.[80] He had had no objection to acting as director of the 'Pretoria Waterworks Company', which operated under a monopolistic concession, and he had been a director of the 'Cigar and Tobacco Factory' even though he 'in no way supported the grant of a concession to them'.[81] He admitted, to a meeting at Piet Retief, that he had also applied for a concession to develop certain dry lands in the north by the construction of a canal.[82]

[75] Joubert Papers, Uitgaande Stukke, II A/4–B/3 (Archives, vol. 23), no. 2231, gives the terms in full.

[76] Joubert Papers, Inkomende Stukke, I A/10–17 (Archives, vol. 7), no. 789. Dr. Leyds to Joubert, Von Wielligh and Van Alphen (14 Apr. 1890).

[77] See Mouton, pp. 189–90.

[78] Joubert Papers, Inkomende Stukke, I A/10–17 (Archives, vol. 7), nos. 775, 776, 777, 779, 780. (See also *Volksstem*, 1 Feb. 1893 — Joubert's speech at Piet Retief.)

[79] Joubert Papers, Uitgaande Stukke, II A/1–A/3 (Archives, vol. 17), pp. 662–5, dated 30 Apr. 1894.

[80] *Press*, 31 Jan. 1893; *Volksstem*, 1 Feb. 1893 (Joubert's speech at Piet Retief) and 4 Feb. 1893.

[81] *Land en Volk*, 24 Nov. 1892 (Joubert's speech at Ermelo).

[82] *Volksstem*, 1 Feb. 1893.

These are hardly the actions of a man to whom the whole policy of concessions and monopolies was utterly repugnant in principle; Joubert could not, nor did he, pretend, in the light of all this, to oppose concessions unconditionally. On the other hand, since the attack on the concessions policy was one of his party's main planks in the 1893 election campaign, Joubert was forced to take up a somewhat equivocal position. Thus he could declare at one stage that 'Concessions were a curse on the land',[83] at another that he 'disliked a general Concessions policy but was not prepared to condemn every concession',[84] and at yet another: 'You must not think that I condemn all concessions equally. If you suffer from this illusion, do not choose me.'[85]

He resolved the internal contradictions of his own position, to his own satisfaction at any rate, by stating that he opposed concessions in general but that 'certain concessions were good, and he did not oppose them unless they were injurious to the country's interests . . . and as long as they were not motivated by a spirit of speculation'.[86]

There is not, really, much to choose between this philosophy and Kruger's statement to the Second Volksraad[87] that he was 'against concessions, but if something could be made here that would compete with an imported article, a monopoly could work well'.

Both statements amount, in essence, to a declaration that one opposes concessions in general but is prepared to allow any that one personally favours.

It was, in short, popular opposition that led to the virtual death of the concessions policy; and there is no reason to believe that the election of Joubert in 1893 would, in itself, have speeded up the process at all.

On the question of railway policy, another great issue drawing the Progressives together, Joubert's position is certainly less equivocal—though even here it was not entirely free from some confusions of thought. Joubert personally, as we have seen, played an important part in acting as a focus of the opposition to the Netherlands Railway Company. His main objections were to Hollander control of the Republic's railway, to the very advantageous conditions which

---

[83] *Land en Volk*, 17 Nov. 1892 (speech at Middelburg).
[84] *Land en Volk*, 24 Nov. 1892 (speech at Ermelo).
[85] *Land en Volk*, 26 Jan. 1893 (speech at Vryheid).
[86] *Volksstem*, 1 Feb. 1893 (speech at Piet Retief).
[87] Quoted on p. 44, above.

had been granted to the railway concessionaires, and to the inhibiting effect which the Netherlands company's monopolistic powers would have upon the development of other lines in the Transvaal. He made much, however, of the defects of the company's administration, and of the expensive nature of its constructional work, stating, during his election campaign of 1892, that 'half the money spent on the Delagoa Bay line had been wasted'. He declared, quite correctly, as we have seen, that the concession had been arranged not by the Executive Council, but at a private meeting, from which his absence had been deliberately contrived. His followers were even more blunt and violent in their attacks upon the Netherlands Railway Company, and by 1895 the Progressive demand for expropriation had reached significant proportions, though it never achieved success.

There was certainly much to criticize. The construction costs of the Delagoa Bay line were unnecessarily high, and the terms of the concession most solicitously favourable to the Netherlands company. Van den Wallbake himself implicitly admits this, as does the company's historian, Van Winter.[88] Even that doughty defender of the Netherlands company, Dr. Leyds, referring to the Volksraad's acceptance of the Rothschild loan, agreed that 'The Company has certainly come out of it very well. Sooner or later it must come to expropriation . . . and the Company has itself chiefly to blame for this'.[89]

There can be no doubt that the expenses of construction, as Marais clearly underlines,[90] were materially increased by the company's patriotic policy of buying equipment in Holland or Germany rather than in the cheapest market, by its recruitment of personnel largely from the Netherlands, and by its desire to earn excess profits both in the interests of its own shareholders and of the Transvaal Government (which took 85 per cent of such excess profits—that is of the amount left once running costs and the interest payments on shares and debenture capital had been subtracted from the company's earnings[91]).

Nevertheless Kruger's insistence on the completion of the Delagoa Bay line, dictated by his desire to make the Republic less dependent

[88] See chapter III.
[89] Letter of 6 May 1893 to Beelaerts, quoted in Van Winter, ii, p. 147.
[90] Marais, pp. 40–1.
[91] Marais, p. 34; Van Winter, i, pp. 68, 81–2, 261–3.

on the British ports of Natal and the Cape Colony, is not difficult to understand. Nor is his belief in the political reliability of a Netherlands company, and his unwillingness to add the burdens of the construction and management of a large and expensive railway system to the already vast problems of his struggling civil service. It is doubtful whether Joubert's Progressive followers would have been doing the Republic any real service if they had, in fact, achieved their object of an early expropriation of the Netherlands Railway Company's lines.

Once the teething troubles of the Netherlands Railway were over, the truth of the old adage that 'nothing succeeds like success' was amply demonstrated and from 1894 Progressive opposition concentrated, therefore, on the demand for expropriation. There is no evidence that General Joubert ever publicly supported them in this demand. Indeed once Kruger had, after August 1892, wisely yielded to the pressure to admit the Natal (as well as the Cape) line into the Republic (in spite of the Netherlands company's opposition),[92] there is little evidence of anything in the way of pronouncements on railway policy on Joubert's part. Nor did he join his party in agitation against the *real* price which had to be paid for the Republic's support of the Netherlands Railway Company—the high import duties ($5-7\frac{1}{2}$ per cent *ad valorem*, and even more on certain special items) under which the Transvaalers suffered and which did so much to embitter the industrial and commercial section of the population, who were largely uitlanders. These had to be paid in addition to the duties levied at the coastal ports. But even here the position had improved by 1898, as the competition between the lines gradually forced the Cape and Natal ports to bring their import duties down to the Delagoa Bay level of 3 per cent.

There is thus no special reason for believing that the replacement of Kruger as President by Joubert, had it occurred in 1893, would have led, in fact, to any very marked changes in the railway policy of the Republic. As early as February 1892 Joubert was already declaring[93] that

'he was sorry that he had been much misunderstood about the Delagoa Bay Railway, and that he was regarded as an opponent of the Netherlands Company. That was totally incorrect. From the

---

[92] Marais, p. 36.
[93] *Volksstem*, 16 Feb. 1892 (report of Barberton speech).

first he had favoured the line to Delagoa Bay because he regarded it as the natural harbour of the Transvaal (Applause)'.[94]

He did, however, go on to declare that he still opposed the terms and conditions which had been granted to the Netherlands company.

The two conceivable changes in railway policy that such a change of presidents might have led to were, the extension of greater control by the state over the Netherlands company, and a more liberal outlook towards a customs union with the Cape and Orange Free State. But even this latter possibility is doubtful in the light of the lengths to which Joubert went, in this same speech, to make clear his indignation at the fact that

'when he and other Volksraad members had gone into the question of what could be done to get another line if they *could* not get this [Delagoa Bay] line they had been misunderstood and represented as disloyal towards the State, and as working for the interests of the Cape Colony and Natal instead of building up this country'.[95]

On the other hand Joubert did work hard for a railway from Natal to the Transvaal, and this in spite of his eagerness to dissociate himself from the charge of 'working for the interests of the Cape Colony and Natal', does imply a greater degree of readiness on Joubert's part than there was on Kruger's to co-operate with the British colonies in South Africa. But once again, although Joubert's statements in London, in 1890,[96] were full of goodwill about the necessity for co-operation between Afrikaner and Englishman in South Africa, and although he declared that he regarded the eventual fusion of the races not only in the Transvaal but in the whole of South Africa as 'only a question of time', he was not prepared to recommend the Republic's entry into a general customs union, declaring that it 'would affect Natal very badly'. He contented himself with a vague statement that 'he looked hopefully towards an eventual federation of all South Africa, and believed that every step taken must have this aim in view'.

Thus, although his fundamental ideal—a united South Africa

[94] It must be remembered that this speech was made in Barberton, which had a strong geographical interest in the Delagoa Bay line.

[95] *Volksstem*, 16 Feb. 1892 (Barberton speech).

[96] *Land en Volk*, 13 Jan. 1891 (speech of 8 Dec. 1890 at a dinner given by London merchants 'connected with the South African trade'); *Volksstem*, 15 Sept. 1890 (statement in an interview with the London *Times*).

under its own flag[97]—was a broader and more tolerant one than Kruger's, it is difficult to be sure whether Joubert, had he attained power, would have acted, in practice, very differently from the way in which Kruger acted on the railway and customs union question.

What of Joubert's attitude to the delicate and crucial franchise question? The ambivalent and wary attitude of some members of the Progressive party on this issue has already been indicated. A reputation for readiness to extend the franchise to the newcomers was an electoral incubus with which neither party had any particular desire to be saddled, as the mutual accusations of Kruger and Joubert in 1892–3 demonstrated, and as the subsequent tortuous negotiations between the Volksvereeniging and the Burgermacht emphasized.[98]

Joubert, ever ultra-sensitive to the least threat of burgher criticism, went to considerable lengths to make his lack of any connexion with the uitlander 'National Union' clear; and he was resolutely ambiguous about his own attitude towards extension of the franchise on the rare occasions when a direct question forced him to make some sort of pronouncement on the matter. (There was, as we have seen, no reference to extension of the franchise in his party's election manifesto.)

The few occasions on which Joubert was forced to answer such direct questions on his franchise policy demonstrate his refusal to commit himself. Thus at Wakkerstroom[99] we have found him declaring that

'it was a difficult question. Even the Chief Justice had not been able to answer a similar question satisfactorily. He thought it might be best to go back to the original law passed shortly after the war.[1]

The matter was, however, in the hands of the old burghers. They had the right to give or to refuse.'

In this speech, too, he referred in uncomplimentary terms to 'the Jingo (National) Union of Johannesburg'.

Shortly afterwards, at Marthinus Wessel Stroom, he fobbed off a question asking him to 'explain his political feelings' by saying[2] that

---

[97] See Mouton, ch. xii; and Joubert's speech at Paarl early in 1891, condemning the British loyalties of the Cape 'Afrikaner Bond' (*Volksstem*, 12 Feb. 1891).

[98] See chapter III(viii).   [99] *Land en Volk*, 27 Oct. 1892.

[1] Law 7 of 1882 (Eybers, *Select Constitutional Documents*, p. 437).

[2] *Land en Volk*, 3 Nov. 1892.

'he had not come to praise himself via his political feelings as the President-to-be. The people knew him. He had no need to say who he was, and also he did not wish to promise that he would do this or that.'

Some weeks later, at Middelburg,[3] he was more reckless.

'He would gladly see the franchise laws made more lenient. He thought that after a year's residence in the State a man with fixed property could take the oath of allegiance to the Government and then get the franchise. If one had no fixed property the term could be two or three years. This had not been done, and the result was that thousands were now simultaneously demanding the franchise.

'A change in the electoral laws was essential, and in this one must obey the sovereign will of the people. They must decide this point and make the necessary provisions.'

On a subsequent occasion he was markedly more cautious. In answer to a questioner at Ermelo, he stated[4] that the matter of franchise extension

'was a difficult question, and one that affected the very roots of our independence. He wanted [the franchise law] altered so that the franchise was accessible to the well-disposed and inaccessible to a scoundrel' (voor een schurk).

But his somewhat careless pronouncement at Middelburg had begun to rebound upon him, and, by the time he had reached Vryheid, General Joubert was strongly attacking Kruger's alleged willingness to grant the franchise to the uitlander within a period of four years.

'[This plan] is wrong to my mind', he declared.[5] 'We must act carefully. It is like a dam full of water. Slowly must this [new] population be added to us, when we are sure that we have need of them. I would like to hold a Congress which would set up Committees all over the Republic which would decide which people were suitable to share in our rights.'

And, once again, he was at great pains to deny any connexion with the National Union, and to share his responsibility for Esselen

---

[3] *Land en Volk*, 17 Nov. 1892. [4] *Land en Volk*, 24 Nov. 1892.
[5] *Land en Volk*, 26 Jan. 1893.

(who had appeared upon the National Union's platform) with Kruger.

'I know nothing about this Union. To those who allege that Esselen is associated with them I say—do you know who Esselen is? He is a man born in Cape Town, educated in Edinburgh, who came specially over to help us in our War of Independence, but arrived just as the struggle was over. He has travelled through the whole of Europe with Kruger, and was his guide and counsellor. It was Kruger who brought him to the Transvaal; and now that he is on my side he is suddenly everything that is bad.'[6]

Finally, at Malanskraal, questioned again on his attitude towards extension of the franchise, he declared that it was

'a difficult question. He was against [Kruger's] plan to give the franchise after four years to those recommended by the old burghers. It would not work. He [Joubert] had come to a plan in his own mind which he thought was better. Let one or two be chosen from every two hundred burghers to form a Commission to go into the Constitution and to reform it and lay down new qualifications for the franchise.'[7]

What are we to make of all this, apart from the fact that the matter of extending the franchise to the uitlander was 'a difficult question', and that Joubert was determined to give no lead on it? He proposes admission after one year (at Middelburg) and attacks Kruger a short while later (at Vryheid) for being prepared to consider a four-year period. His only concrete proposal is the somewhat vague one for the formation of some kind of national convention in the shape of a series of 'committees all over the Republic' or a commission composed of 'one or two . . . chosen from every two hundred burghers' who would 'go into the Constitution and . . . reform it and lay down new qualifications for the franchise'. In the light of the complete inability of meetings of representative burghers to agree upon even the smallest concession to the uitlander which the Volksvereeniging and Burgermacht negotiations demonstrate, it is not, I think, unfair to Joubert to reject this proposal as entirely unpractical. Its sole purpose was to evade responsibility for personal decision—and if ever there was a matter on which the unhappy

---

[6] *Land en Volk*, 26 Jan. 1893.
[7] *Land en Volk*, 2 Feb. 1893.

burghers needed statesmanlike guidance from their leaders, it was this one.

They got it neither from Kruger[8] nor from Joubert. There is no special reason to believe that Joubert as President would have been more courageous than Joubert as election candidate. It is probable, from his pronouncements, that Joubert's own personal views lay closer to the hesitant opinions of Schalk Burger, J. H. de la Rey and W. H. van Niekerk than they did to the more liberal and courageous views of such of his followers as Esselen, J. F. Celliers, L. and G. de Jager, Lukas Meyer, Paul Maré and Carl Jeppe.

To have taken what was probably, in its own way, an even greater 'leap in the dark' than Disraeli took in 1867, would have required a very considerable degree of moral courage. It is understandable, but regrettable, that the 'leader' of the Progressive party did not possess it.

The dynamite concession was one of the few major political questions upon which General Joubert, from the start, took up and maintained a fairly unequivocal attitude.

Speaking on this matter at Barberton, in February 1892, he affected ignorance of the details of what was happening, but declared that he was not prepared to say that the concession must be cancelled. The matter demanded careful investigation.[9]

In the course of the 1892 election campaign he was still treading cautiously.

'The Dynamite Concession', he declared at Wakkerstroom,[10] 'was not wholly bad, but the concessionaires had not kept to the terms of their concession. The Concession had now been cancelled, and there was a court-case pending.'

But a month later he was much more forthright:

'He had at first thought', he stated at Middelburg,[11] 'that [the Dynamite Concession] was advantageous. But he had not been present when the Concession had been signed and had always thought that the dynamite was being manufactured here, until he later became aware that it was being imported ready-made [kant en klaar] from Europe. Concessions were a curse on the land.'

[8] See Marais, ch. xiii.
[9] The relevant portion of his speech is quoted on p. 48, above.
[10] *Land en Volk*, 27 Oct. 1892.   [11] *Land en Volk*, 17 Nov. 1892.

In October 1893, just before the new contract appointing Vorstman as the government's agent was signed, Joubert sent a letter to
Kruger and the Executive Council in which he recorded his protest
against the terms of the 'new' contract about to be signed. Emphasizing the considerable opposition to the government's proposals
that existed in many quarters, he declared:[12]

'As far as the delivery of bullets and ammunition of war is concerned I must declare once again that I cannot and dare not identify
myself with the honourable Volksraad's resolution or instruction;[13]
and I fear that any contract or monopoly granted in accordance
with that by the government to any Agent or other person will in
one way or another prove injurious [to the country] as we have found
with the previous contracts, now fortunately cancelled.'

The dynamite concession ceased for a while after 1894 to be a
major political issue between the parties, though the mining industry,
'now in the grip of a monopoly far stronger than the original one'[14]
never ceased to agitate against it; but the Report of the Industrial
Commission of 1897 once more brought it into the foreground.
Joubert, in common (for once) with the rest of the Progressive
party, seized the opportunity in the Volksraad to attack the government's policy. He emphasized that he had protested by letter to the
Executive Council from the very start, and went on to declare that:

'the whole country had been brought to the verge of rebellion over
the matter. The State had no proper control over the sources of its
own ammunition. If a man with a special rifle of a different pattern
wanted to get any ammunition, why, he must go to Mr. Vorstman.
Even he, as Commandant-General, had to get a permit from Mr.
Vorstman. The argument adduced when the monopoly was granted
to the Company was the need of the breaking of the Nobel ring. And
what did they find? Why, the Nobel's Trust was as much concerned
in the monopoly as anyone, and that they were drawing more in
profits than if there had been open trade and competition in the
article. . . . They should do everything in their power to help the

---

[12] Joubert Papers, Uitgaande Stukke, II A/1–A/3 (Archives, vol. 17), no. 1997,
p. 525. Letter of 12 Oct. 1893.
[13] Passed by a narrow majority of the Raad on 12 Aug. 1893, the Progressives
voting solidly in the minority (see p. 51, above.)
[14] Marais, p. 30 (see above, pp. 54–5, for details of the merger between the
Nobel and French trusts).

mines. He hoped that the monopoly would no longer be allowed to injure the unity of the nation; but that instead they should guard the great industry of the country—the Mining Industry. They would thus bring about peace and unity in the land.'[15]

And a few days later the Commandant-General declared, even more forcibly, that:

'He had opposed the Dynamite Concession from the start, and, since there were no minutes of Executive Council meetings, had written to the President to make this clear in anticipation of evils to follow. He took exception to Mr. [A. D. W.] Wolmarans's remark that the opposition to the Dynamite Concession was proof of its value to the country. This contract still contained the disastrous germs of the old one; it was merely a transference from one agent to another, from Lippert to Vorstman. Mr. Lippert did not move a little finger, but by some means or other £30,000 managed to travel to his pocket year after year. And if the Raad deemed the old contract deserving of a stroke of the pen, then, under similar circumstances, he could not see why the present contract should not be cancelled as well. . . .

'As regards the idea of some members that the independence of the Republic was dependent on the monopoly, he was of the opinion that just as little as the tobacco monopoly of France had to do with the independence of that Republic, so little has this dynamite monopoly to do with the independence of the South African Republic. . . . The State must be instructed by the Raad to take the monopoly into its own hands, and appoint State officials to conduct it.'[16]

On this issue, therefore, Joubert clearly gave vigorous and definite personal support to his party's bitter struggle against the dynamite monopoly. Whether his leading motive was sympathy for the woes of the mining industry, or personal bitterness that he, as Commandant-General, did not control the sources of the country's ammunition, or whether (as his opponents implied)[17] he saw in the country-wide dislike of the monopoly a useful electioneering weapon, or whether he was genuinely indignant at the monopolists'

[15] *Weekly Press*, 30 Oct. 1897, p. 23.

[16] *Weekly Press*, 6 Nov. 1897, p. 21.

[17] See the remark of A. D. W. Wolmarans, reported in the *Weekly Press* of 6 Nov. 1897, p. 22, that he regarded Joubert's 'whole attitude as an electioneering dodge'.

undoubted abuse of their favoured and protected position, it is impossible to determine. Motives in politics are rarely pure and never simple, and Joubert was quite as complex as most political leaders.

While we can conclude, therefore, from the statements by Joubert that we have quoted, that the Commandant-General genuinely favoured expropriation by the State of the dynamite monopoly, we may be permitted to doubt whether he would, if he had become President, have found himself, in fact, able to take any such step. Kruger had cogent reasons, as Marais points out,[18] for desiring the maintenance of the dynamite monopoly. Would Joubert, with perhaps half the burgher vote behind him, have been prepared to risk the international unpleasantness which an appeal to law would have led to? Louis Botha, who had attacked the monopoly much more bitterly than Joubert,[19] found himself forced, in August 1899, to support its continuance, as there was 'no other course open to him after he had examined the matter carefully and had seen how the government had allied the Transvaal to the concessionaires with that concession and other concomitant agreements. There was definitely no way out.'[20]

The strong probability is that Joubert would have found himself in very much the same position.

Let us sum up, briefly, what has been said about Joubert in the preceding pages. Broader-minded in many respects, more liberal in his political approach, Joubert was politically, nevertheless, a lesser man than Kruger, and, what is more, felt himself to be so. In many ways Joubert impresses one as being one of nature's born 'seconds-in-command'; jealous of his superior, but instinctively respecting him; grumbling, but obeying; subtly suggesting without ever actually stating it, that he could do the job better, but, inside himself, shrinking from the responsibilities of political command; happier to criticize major decisions of policy than to make them himself in the dangerous and troubled times in which the South African Republic found itself.

His lack of self-confidence and his sensitivity to criticism reinforce this impression. His failure to come out with any clear statement of principles, his unwillingness to associate himself with his own

---

[18] Marais, p. 32.
[19] *Weekly Press*, 30 Oct. 1897, pp. 15, 17, 22.
[20] Quoted in Marais, p. 33.

election committee, his lack of energy in advocating his own cause, all compel the conviction that stronger personalities than he (and Esselen in particular) were the real driving force behind the Progressive party. It is fair, I think, to conclude that the Progressive party chose him as the shield and banner behind which to advance, rather than that Joubert chose the Progressive party because they represented the principles for which he stood.

Of course, he sympathized very largely with those principles; but the analysis that has been made of his stand on some of the major issues which separated the two parties, suggests that the election of Joubert in Kruger's place would not, in itself, necessarily have led to a wave of progressive reforms. Joubert was himself too closely associated with much of what his party condemned for this to have been likely. His election might, of course, have created an atmosphere in which such changes could have come more easily. But they would have come from the Progressive party rather than from Joubert.

10

Conclusion

By 1895, then—the end of the period with which this study deals— the Progressive party had emerged and taken a rough but recognizable shape as a clearly acknowledged opposition to Kruger's régime. The years between 1890 and 1892 saw a great increase, among the Transvaal Boer population, of opposition to the government. Financial policy, railway policy, the concessions policy in general and the dynamite monopoly in particular, and the widespread suspicion of official corruption and maladministration, all played their part in arousing this discontent. Among the more forward-looking burghers, too, the increasing unhappiness of many of the uitlander population on the franchise, language and education questions, and the difficult and fundamental problems that these questions posed, played their part in leading them to inquire whether the conservative attitude of their own people to the newcomers offered any permanent hope for the State's future.

Starting with a small group of critics of the régime, the most consistent of whom was the member for Barberton, R. K. Loveday, Kruger's opponents had been greatly strengthened by the entry into political life of men of the calibre of Lukas Meyer and Ewald Esselen, both of whom became, in the First and Second Volksraads respectively, rallying points of the opposition. Lukas Meyer and R. K. Loveday in the First Raad were rapidly joined by such men as Schalk Burger, Paul Maré and Lodewyk de Jager, and, after 1893 by Gert de Jager, Carl Jeppe, and, sometimes, Koos de la Rey and J. J. Spies. In the Second Raad Esselen gathered around him an able and vigorous group of opposition members, of whom E. P. A. Meintjies, G. B. Brecher, F. Watkins, J. F. Celliers, J. W. Joubert, D. F. Petersen and N. S. Malherbe were the nucleus. From time to time, as we have seen, they were joined by occasional members of what we may call the 'centre party' or floating vote.

The subsequent growth of the opposition in both Volksraads, and the emergence of the Progressive party to a position where a change

275

in one or two seats might well have faced Kruger with a Progressive majority in the First Raad, has been traced in detail in the preceding pages, as have the issues which drew them together. The main points which emerge from that examination are these.

First, though the great growth in opposition to Kruger's régime among the burghers occurred simultaneously with the rise of agitation among the uitlanders, and was undoubtedly influenced by it, the Progressive party was essentially an Afrikaner opposition[1] whose members were fervently determined to keep the South African Republic an Afrikaner state. Apart from R. K. Loveday and F. Watkins (who were of English origin)[2] and Carl Jeppe (whose family was German),[3] all the leading members of the party in both Volksraads, and the great majority of their supporters and active committee workers, were Afrikaners (even though many of the latter group were not Transvaal Afrikaners) by background and tradition. Uitlander and Afrikaner opposition to the Kruger régime proceeded along separate, if often parallel, tracks; and most of the leading Progressives (apart from Esselen) were careful to avoid being tarred with the 'National Union' brush.

The only move towards uniting themselves with any other group that the Progressives made was the attempt at the formation of a combined burgher front; and when that failed it was not succeeded by any attempt at a rapprochement with the uitlander. The Jameson Raid helped to make such a move even more unlikely after 1895.

Secondly, it is clear that, although there was never anything like a party caucus, a clearly defined leadership, a definite political programme, or an efficient party organization, as we should understand any of these terms today, nevertheless the Progressive party was undoubtedly beginning to emerge by 1895 as an important political group, with markedly different opinions on most of the important issues of the day from those of the conservative group who looked to Kruger as their leader. The steadily rising number of their adherents in the First Volksraad, even after the Jameson Raid, suggests that, if events had been allowed to run their normal course, the Progressive party would sooner or later have attained a majority in the upper chamber, and applied their more liberal and tolerant spirit to the solution of the Republic's many problems.

[1] Above, pp. 201–2.
[2] *Press*, 12 Mar. 1892; *Volksstem*, 27 Aug. 1892.
[3] *Weekly Press*, 23 July 1898, p. 9, gives the family background.

That their leading personalities were intelligent and able men there can be no doubt. Esselen's abilities were acknowledged by his most resolute opponents. The briefest perusal of any of the major speeches of such men as Lukas Meyer, Carl Jeppe, R. K. Loveday, J. F. Celliers, Schalk Burger, and such later recruits to the party[4] as A. A. J. Dieperink and Louis Botha, to name but a few, will convince the sceptic of the ability of these men to think clearly and constructively on involved and emotionally clouded issues.

Nevertheless, although the Progressives spent the whole of their brief political lives in opposition, their efforts were certainly not without result. They introduced a more broad-minded and liberal spirit into the often narrow and patriarchal atmosphere of the First Volksraad. They forced their fellow-legislators to take cognizance of the new forces that were working in the nineteenth-century world, and though they did not usually win the day, they were too able and eloquent to be ignored. Their relentless attack on much that stained the honour of the Republic—corruption in high places, official maladministration, an unimaginative and backward educational system, and the spirit of narrow bigotry which too often prevailed—as well as on aspects of the government's policy with which they profoundly disagreed—the concessions policy, railway policy, financial policy, and the dynamite monopoly—did not go unheeded. The combined pressure of the Progressives, the public and the press (including, with surprising frequency, the pro-government press) had, as we have seen, an undeniable effect in every one of these fields. By as early a date as 1893, Kruger could no longer 'lord it over the Volksraad representatives',[5] and found himself forced to proceed with considerable caution on all these issues. The whole tone of the State gave evidence of a far healthier and more critical spirit than that which had prevailed in 1890 and 1891.

Particular credit must go to the group of Progressives, led at first by Esselen, who did so much to make the Second Volksraad anything but the uninfluential 'Chamber of Commerce' which its opponents had hopefully prophesied that it would be. Indeed, considering the fundamental limitations on its power, it is remarkable what influence the Second Raad came to exercise. The decisive stand that the Progressive group in the second chamber took, particularly on the questions of official corruption, administrative inefficiency, the policy of concessions and monopolies, the notorious 'Stands

[4] After 1895. [5] *Land en Volk*, 13 Sept. 1893.

Scandal' and the 'Bewaarplaatsen' affair, have all been dealt with in some detail. The Progressive attack forced the President on to the defensive and won for the Second Raad a considerable degree of respect.

There is one important point which arises from all this. True as it certainly is that Kruger fought a resolute rearguard action in defence of concessions, dynamite and monopolies, and some very questionable official practices, the fact that he was so patently on the defensive (sometimes almost pathetically so), and that he modified his policies to meet some, if not all, of the criticism levelled against his administration, and the partial degree of reform which had been achieved by 1895, are all powerful arguments against the view of Kruger—iron-hard, ruthless, immovable—which is sometimes put forward. It was only because Kruger and his government were sensitive to the pressure of public opinion, both at home and abroad, and, however reluctantly at times, ready to respond to it, that the Progressives were able to make the impact that they did. Against a tough, cynical, arrogant and racketeering government they would have achieved nothing at all.

Some evidence, to lead on from this, has been submitted in this study to suggest that Kruger was very much more flexible and open-minded than he is often represented as having been—by his enemies and his admirers alike. His decision to create a Second Volksraad, his defence of 'well-disposed' uitlanders against the attacks of the more extreme members of the First Raad, his advocacy of such liberal (and bitterly opposed) moves as civil marriage for natives and partial exemption of educated natives from the provisions of the pass laws, his tolerance towards Jews and Catholics, the legislation for the administration of the goldfields, and, in general, the degree of adaptability that he showed towards the enormous changes which had swept down upon his state—all indicate, as we have suggested, the need for some modification of the still current picture of Kruger as a granite Cromwellian patriarch entirely unmoved by the fierce blasts of change assailing his state.[6]

Nor should we make the converse mistake of thinking of his Progressive opponents as an entirely enlightened, strongly modern and liberal group, even in the Victorian senses of those words. In general they were, as the whole tenor of this book has tried to show, very much more enlightened, liberal, and in tune with the needs of their

[6] See p. 21.

times than Kruger's conservatives. But the Progressives shared with the most extreme conservative a determination to rigorously exclude any coloured person from any say in the affairs of church or State, and some of the strongest opposition to Kruger's suggestions for a more liberal treatment of educated natives came from such 'progressive' members as R. K. Loveday, Schalk Burger, A. A. J. Dieperink, J. du P. de Beer and Louis Botha; while the most powerful insistence on the segregation of 'coolies and coloureds' came in the speeches of Carl Jeppe and R. K. Loveday. Schalk Burger, for a long time one of the leading lights of the Progressive party, similarly, displayed a narrow dislike of colonial Afrikaners and an even deeper distrust of Roman Catholics.[7] On the other hand, the Progressives were, it must be granted, rarely guilty of the obscurantist views which distinguished the utterances of some of the profound conservatives—though, even in this field, we find Paul Maré and Schalk Burger pleading for the closing down of mines on the Sabbath.[8] Nor must the strongly anti-Hollander tone of the Progressive party and press be forgotten, or the violently anti-Jewish tone of *Land en Volk*.[9] The avowedly pro-Afrikaner Progressive party, though a mixed group and without a definite policy, was not without some touches of the xenophobia which most incipient nationalist movements share. Kruger's day-to-day pragmatism was in some respects more kindly, tolerant and urbane than the violent, and sometimes hysterical, views propagated by *Land en Volk*, the acknowledged organ of the Progressive party.

We should also underline, once again, in this summing-up, the fact that the printed expression of opposition to defects of the régime was by no means confined to the opposition press. We have had many occasions to note the strong and frequent criticism of aspects of governmental policy by such undoubtedly pro-government newspapers as the *Volksstem* and *Press*; and this, together with the free expression of opinion in the two Volksraads, shows that the South African Republic was anything but an authoritarian state, even at the stage when the pressing problems with which it was trying to cope would, no doubt, have made the absence of such free criticism from among its own people welcome to the government.

We should note, too, that all those forces working towards a more liberal solution of the Republic's problems, whether the Pro-

---

[7] See ch. I for evidence on all these points.
[8] See p. 15. [9] See pp. 42, 66, 137.

gressive party, the press, or the President himself, were up against a formidable obstacle in the shape of a strongly conservative, ill-educated, rural community of burghers, who, by and large, moved forward with excessive slowness. All efforts towards rapprochement between the various political movements among the burghers, with the ultimate aim of a more generally acceptable solution of the franchise problem, broke down in consequence of the obdurate determination of the majority of the burghers to retain their identity and their privileges exclusively for themselves.[10] Nevertheless, the large vote for Joubert in 1893, and the fact that by 1895 over a third of the seats of each Volksraad were filled by Progressive members, and that this tendency continued even after the Jameson Raid, are indications that the tide might possibly have turned.

Conversely, however, the fact that Joubert obtained nearly half the votes cast in the 1893 presidential election, when considered together with the fact that the results of the 1892–3 elections for the vacant seats in the two Volksraads showed no significant evidence of a swing towards the Progressive party,[11] does pose the awkward question—to what extent can a vote for Joubert be regarded as a vote for Progressive principles?

The probable answer is that many of the votes for Joubert were cast for Joubert as a person, because of the general dissatisfaction with the state of affairs in the Republic, and because, like Kruger and unlike Chief Justice Kotzé, he was known and trusted by the burghers. The large vote for Joubert cannot automatically be construed as a vote for Progressive ideas. This is particularly likely in view of the facts that those principles were never very clearly defined, and that Joubert never fully identified himself with either Progressive principles or even the Progressive party.

The last section of this book suggests that Joubert's role as leader of the Progressive party was more nominal than real. A kindly, intelligent and capable man, a devout Christian, a brave soldier, and an ardent patriot, he was not the stuff of which really great political leaders are made. In the years of crisis which succeeded the Jameson Raid the burghers of the Republic showed that they felt this quite clearly by the overwhelming majority which they gave to Kruger in 1898.

This study has attempted to show the rise of opposition to the Kruger régime. To some extent uitlander pressure must have been

[10] See pp. 176–83, 189–91.   [11] See pp. 215–17.

an important cause of the rising tide of criticism by which, between 1890 and 1895, Kruger found himself surrounded. That this was so does not in any way diminish the achievements of the Progressive group. An understanding and sympathetic response to a changed situation is the essence of political realism, and all the more commendable because of its comparative rarity in our human story. In any case, the word 'uitlander', particularly to the ultra-conservatives among the Boers, was extremely wide in its connotations, and included Afrikaners from the Cape, Orange Free State and Natal. This latter group, and the Progressives among the Transvaal Boers, prided themselves on being Afrikaner patriots, and looked forward to a great and prosperous future for the Transvaal. It was in the light of this ambition that they attacked what they felt was corrupt, dishonest, inefficient or dangerously narrow and bigoted in the administration of the State. Esselen, Lukas Meyer, Paul Maré, Gert and Lodewyk de Jager and the other stalwarts of the Progressive party—not to speak of their titular leader, Piet Joubert—wanted a Transvaal under the British flag, or under the domination of British ideas, as little as Kruger or his most die-hard conservative follower. But they sensed, in the cruel dilemma which the wave of uitlander immigration into their state imposed upon them, that the way of salvation was not that of suspicion and exclusiveness; that their only hope lay in winning the newcomers to their side, in making Transvaal patriots of them. Kruger and the more intelligent of his conservative supporters in the Volksraad sensed this too; but they were less generous and less positive in their approach than were most of the Progressives. That such a policy of winning the uitlanders over to the Transvaal side, had it been more generously and more rapidly applied, might well have succeeded, is suggested by the fact that fear of this very possibility was at the root of the policy of Chamberlain and Milner after 1895.[12]

Of course, this does raise the possibility that a Progressive victory in 1893 might have made Chamberlain and Milner all the more determined to deal ruthlessly with the South African Republic. They feared above all else the threat to British supremacy in South Africa which the admission of uitlanders to the franchise in gradually increasing numbers, and the strong possibility that they would subsequently 'Afrikanderize', would entail.[13] And it is just this that a

[12] Marais, ch. xiii, section III.
[13] Marais, pp. 330–1.

Progressive government in the Republic might well have brought about. But it would have made an excuse for 'a military solution of the Transvaal problem'[14] very much harder to find, and stripped such a solution of any shreds of apparent morality or justice that it might have contained.

[14] Marais, p. 285.

Bibliography

A. PRIMARY SOURCES

I. UNPUBLISHED MANUSCRIPTS

(a) The collected papers of Commandant-General P. J. Joubert (Transvaal Archives). Referred to according to classification, Archives volume number, and number and/or date of document.

e.g. Joubert Papers, Inkomende Stukke, I A/10–17 (Archives, vol. 6), no. 639 of 3 Feb. 1892.

(b) The Leyds Papers (Transvaal Archives). Referred to according to Archives classification number, details and date.

e.g. Leyds Papers, 627, Leyds to Acting State Secretary, 5 Jan. 1894.

II. PUBLISHED PRIMARY SOURCES

(a) *Official Publications*

1. *Notulen der Verrichtingen van den Hoog Edel Achtbaren Volksraad, 1890.*
2. *Notulen der Verrichtingen van den Hoog Edel Achtbaren Eersten Volksraad, 1891–1899.*
3. *Notulen der Verrichtingen van den Hoog Edel Achtbaren Tweede Volksraad, 1891–1899.*

   All the above are referred to by name, date and article number as follows:
   e.g. *Notulen*, Eerste (or Tweede) Volksraad, 1893, art. 95.
4. Imperial Blue Books and South African Republic Green Books. Referred to by number, year and page.
   e.g. C 7911 of 1895, p. 10.

(b) *Contemporary Newspapers*

1. *Land en Volk*, 1890–1895.
2. *Press*, 1890–1895.
3. *Weekly Press*, 1895–1899.
4. *Volksstem*, 1890–1895.

(c) *Collected historical records*

Eybers, G. W. (ed.), *Select Constitutional Documents Illustrating South African History, 1795–1910* (1918).

(d) *Memoirs, contemporary histories, etc.*

Dormer, F. J., *Vengeance as a Policy in Afrikanerland; a plea for a new departure* (1901).

Fitzpatrick, J. P., *The Transvaal from within* (1899). (All references to Fitzpatrick in this book are to Heinemann's popular edition, 9th impression, March 1900.)
Jeppe, C., *The Kaleidoscopic Transvaal* (1906).
Leyds, W. J., *Onze Eerste Jaren in Zuid Afrika* (1939).
Phillips, Mrs. Lionel, *Some South African Recollections* (1900).
Statham, F. R., *Paul Kruger and His Times* (1898).
Taylor, J. B., *A Pioneer Looks Back* (1939).

B. SECONDARY SOURCES

I. PUBLISHED SOURCES

Botha, P. R., *Die Staatkundige Ontwikkeling van die Suid-Afrikaanse Republiek onder Kruger en Leyds* (1926).
Bredell, H. C. en Grobler, P., *Gedenkschriften van Paul Kruger* (1902).
Cambridge History of the British Empire, vol. VIII (abbreviated to *C.H.B.E.*, vol. viii).
Coetzee, D. J., *Spoorwegontwikkeling in die Suid-Afrikaanse Republiek* (1940).
Coetzee, J. Albert, *Politieke Groepering in die Wording van die Afrikanernasie* (1941).
De Kiewiet, C. W., (a) *A History of South Africa, Social and Economic* (1941).
De Kiewiet, C. W., (b) *The Imperial Factor in South Africa* (1937).
Du Plessis, J. S., *Die Ontstaan en Ontwikkeling van die Amp van Staatspresident in die Suid-Afrikaanse Republiek* (Archives Year Book for South African History, 1955, vol. i).
Guyot, Y., *Boer Politics* (1900).
Hofmeyr, J. H., *The Life of Jan Hendrik Hofmeyr (Onze Jan)* (1913).
Hugo, M., *Die Stemregvraagstuk in die Zuid-Afrikaansche Republiek* (Archives Year Book for South African History, 1947).
Jorissen, E. J. P., *Transvaalsche Herinneringen, 1876–1896* (1897).
Kotzé, J. G., *Memoirs and Reminiscences*, 2 vols. (1934–41).
Lombaard, J. P. la G., *Paul Kruger die Volksman* (1925).
Malherbe, E. G., *Education in South Africa, 1652–1922* (1925).
Marais, J. S., *The Fall of Kruger's Republic* (1961).
Mouton, J. A., *Generaal Piet Joubert in die Transvaalse Geskiedenis* (Archives Year Book for South African History, 1957, vol. i).
Nathan, M., *Paul Kruger, His Life and Times* (1941).
Ploeger, J., *Onderwys en Onderwysbeleid in die Suid-Afrikaanse Republiek onder Ds. S. J. du Toit en Dr. N. Mansvelt* (Archives Year Book for South African History, 1952, vol. i).
Rompel, F., *Heroes of the Boer War* (1903).
Scoble, J. and Abercrombie, H. R., *The Rise and Fall of Krugerism* (1900).
Smit, F. P., *Die Staatsopvattinge van Paul Kruger* (1951).
Struben, H. W., *Recollections of Adventures—Pioneering and development in S. Africa, 1850–1911* (1920).
Van der Poel, J., *Railway and Customs Policies in South Africa, 1885–1910* (1933).
Van Hoek, K., *Kruger Days. Reminiscences of Dr. Leyds* (1939).
Van Oordt, J. F., *Paul Kruger en de Opkomst der Zuid-Afrikaansche Republiek* (1898).

Van Winter, P. J., *Onder Kruger's Hollanders*, 2 vols. (1937–8).

Walker, E. A., (*a*) *History of Southern Africa*, 3rd ed. (1957).

Walker, E. A., (*b*) *Lord de Villiers and His Times* (1925).

II. UNPUBLISHED SOURCES

Etheredge, D. A., The Early History of the Chamber of Mines 1887–1897. (Unpublished post-graduate thesis, University of the Witwatersrand.)

Index

Aaron, Bension, 102, 105–6, 107, 150; *see also* 'Stands Scandal', Vorster, B. J.
Adendorff Trek, 203n.
Africans, *see* Natives
Afrikaans, examples of, 95, 113
Afrikaner Bond, 28n., 190, 267n.
Afrikaner patriotism, growth of, in S.A. Republic, xi, xvii, 9–10, 21, 28n., 74–5, 77, 111, 120, 127–8, 129, 131, 134 and n., 135, 137, 177, 182, 186, 188, 195–6, 197, 199, 201–2, 215, 234–5, 276, 279, 281
Afrikaners, from O.F.S. and British colonies, 10, 111, 112, 126–7, 131–3, 135, 140, 151, 160, 161–3, 166, 168–9, 177, 196, 279, 280
'Afrikanus Junior', 42, 42n., 95–6, 129–30, 195–6, 196n.
Albu, G., 2n., 16, 79n.
Amajuba, battle of, 119
America, United States of, 16, 93–4, 141, 160
apprenticeship system, 6–7; *see also* Natives
Asiatics, *see* Indians

Beit, A., 90
Beukes, H. P., 64, 138
'Bewaarplaatsen question', 90, 108–11, 148, 150, 243–5
Birkenstock, C. J. A., 31, 34, 45, 52, 63, 72, 76, 77, 78, 85, 109, 155, 161, 216, 230, 242
Boers, 1–7, 7–8, 9–11, 11–13, 13–15, 15–20, 111–25 passim, 126, 133, 139–40, 152–8, 162, 163–5, 171, 173, 176–83, 191, 280
Bok, W. E., 31, 129, 130, 133–4, 138
Boshoff, E., 149, 190
Botha, L. (Louis), 4, 131, 198–9, 208, 242, 273, 277, 279
Brecher, B. G., 41, 42, 43, 98, 100, 107, 109, 143, 149, 169, 193, 208, 217, 242, 276
Breytenbach, I. J., 109
Britain, 5n., 48, 51, 78, 111, 127, 137, 142, 151, 158, 169, 200, 241, 265, 266, 281
Burger, J. J., 109, 142, 143, 149, 190, 217

Burger, Schalk W., xii, 2, 9–10, 11, 15, 18, 19, 31, 33, 34, 38, 50, 51, 57, 61–2, 63, 67, 72, 73, 75n., 77, 79, 83, 85, 90, 97, 109, 124, 142, 155, 161, 167, 170, 170n., 192, 193, 202, 216, 217, 219, 219n., 223, 225–8, 230, 233, 238, 242, 248, 255, 262, 270, 276, 277, 279
Burgermacht, 178–80, 182, 236–7, 269; *see also* Conservative party

Cape Colony, 6, 62, 65, 67, 70, 77, 78, 93, 119, 132, 151, 190, 193, 241, 265, 266
Catholics, xiv, xvii, 10–11, 24, 278, 279
Celliers, Jan F., x, xiv, 10, 22, 39n., 40, 41, 42, 43, 44, 54, 98, 100, 101, 102, 106, 107, 141, 142, 147, 149, 150, 159, 169, 193, 194, 270, 276, 277
Chamberlain, Joseph, 151, 169, 281
Coetzee, O. J. (Ockert), 2n., 8, 13, 62, 215
colour policy, in S.A. Republic, 1–7, 2n., 279; in Natal and the Cape, 2–3; *see also* Natives, Indians, coloured people
coloured people (Cape), Boer attitude to, in S.A. Republic, 2, 3, 4, 25, 279
concessions policy, in S.A. Republic, xv, 35–46, 108, 131, 143, 144, 150, 184, 186, 192, 203, 243–5, 247–8, 261–3; *see also* 'Bewaarplaatsen question', corruption and maladministration, dynamite monopoly, Netherlands Railway Company, railway policy, Selati Railway Company
Conservative party ('National party'), xv, 52, 72, 75, 95n., 106, 108, 110, 111, 115, 120, 122, 124, 138, 142, 144, 149, 154, 158, 161, 165, 166, 168, 169, 182–3, 216, 234, 235–6, 238, 239, 241, 251, 253, 254, 255, 258, 276, 281; *see also* Burgermacht
corruption and maladministration, in S.A. Republic, 15–20, 40n., 80ff., 86–111, 184–5, 193–4, 229; *see also* concessions policy
Cronjé, General P. (Piet), 3, 206, 253, 255

286